OLD MAN LOGAN
END OF THE WORLD

WRITER **ED BRISSON**

NORTHERN FLIGHT (#46-47)
ARTIST **DAMIAN COUCEIRO**
COLOR ARTIST **CARLOS LOPEZ**

KING OF NOTHING (#48-50)
IBRAIM ROBERSON WITH
ARTISTS **NEIL EDWARDS** (#50)
COLOR ARTIST **CARLOS LOPEZ**

PRIDE & PUNISHMENT (ANNUAL #1)
ARTIST **SIMONE DI MEO**
COLOR ARTIST **DONO SÁNCHEZ-ALMARA**

LETTERER **VC'S CORY PETIT**

COVER ART **ANDREA SORRENTINO** (#46-49);
ANDREA SORRENTINO & GIADA MARCHISIO (#50); AND
SHANE DAVIS, MICHELLE DELECKI & VAL STAPLES (ANNUAL #1)

ASSISTANT EDITOR **CHRIS ROBINSON**

EDITORS **CHRISTINA HARRINGTON & JORDAN D. WHITE**

COLLECTION EDITOR **MARK D. BEAZLEY**
ASSISTANT EDITOR **CAITLIN O'CONNELL**
ASSOCIATE MANAGING EDITOR **KATERI WOODY**
SENIOR EDITOR, SPECIAL PROJECTS **JENNIFER GRÜNWALD**
VP PRODUCTION & SPECIAL PROJECTS **JEFF YOUNGQUIST**
SVP PRINT, SALES & MARKETING **DAVID GABRIEL**

BOOK DESIGNER **ADAM DEL RE**

EDITOR IN CHIEF **C.B. CEBULSKI**
CHIEF CREATIVE OFFICER **JOE QUESADA**
PRESIDENT **DAN BUCKLEY**
EXECUTIVE PRODUCER **ALAN FINE**

WOLVERINE: OLD MAN LOGAN VOL. 10 — END OF THE WORLD. Contains material originally published in magazine form as OLD MAN LOGAN #46-50 and ANNUAL #1. First printing 2018. ISBN 978-1-302-91342-7. Published by MARVEL WORLDWIDE, INC., a subsidiary of MARVEL ENTERTAINMENT, LLC. OFFICE OF PUBLICATION: 135 West 50th Street, New York, NY 10020. Copyright © 2018 MARVEL No similarity between any of the names, characters, persons, and/or institutions in this magazine with those of any living or dead person or institution is intended, and any such similarity which may exist is purely coincidental. **Printed in the U.S.A.** DAN BUCKLEY, President, Marvel Entertainment; JOHN NEE, Publisher; JOE QUESADA, Chief Creative Officer; TOM BREVOORT, SVP of Publishing; DAVID BOGART, SVP of Business Affairs & Operations, Publishing & Partnership; DAVID GABRIEL, SVP of Sales & Marketing, Publishing; JEFF YOUNGQUIST, VP of Production & Special Projects; DAN CARR, Executive Director of Publishing Technology; ALEX MORALES, Director of Publishing Operations; DAN EDINGTON, Managing Editor; SUSAN CRESPI, Production Manager; STAN LEE, Chairman Emeritus. For information regarding advertising in Marvel Comics or on Marvel.com, please contact Vit DeBellis, Custom Solutions & Integrated Advertising Manager, at vdebellis@marvel.com. For Marvel subscription inquiries, please call 888-511-5480. **Manufactured between 11/9/2018 and 12/11/2018 by LSC COMMUNICATIONS INC., KENDALLVILLE, IN, USA.**

10 9 8 7 6 5 4 3 2 1

Surviving a future known as the Wastelands, where everything good in the world, including his family, was destroyed, Old Man Logan awoke in the present determined to prevent this catastrophic reality from ever coming to pass. Now, Logan tries to find his place in a world not quite his own.

Logan's healing factor is mysteriously weakening. Injuries that normally would have healed rapidly, aren't. Without the help of a dangerous pharmaceutical called Regenix to boost his healing, Logan is more vulnerable than ever.

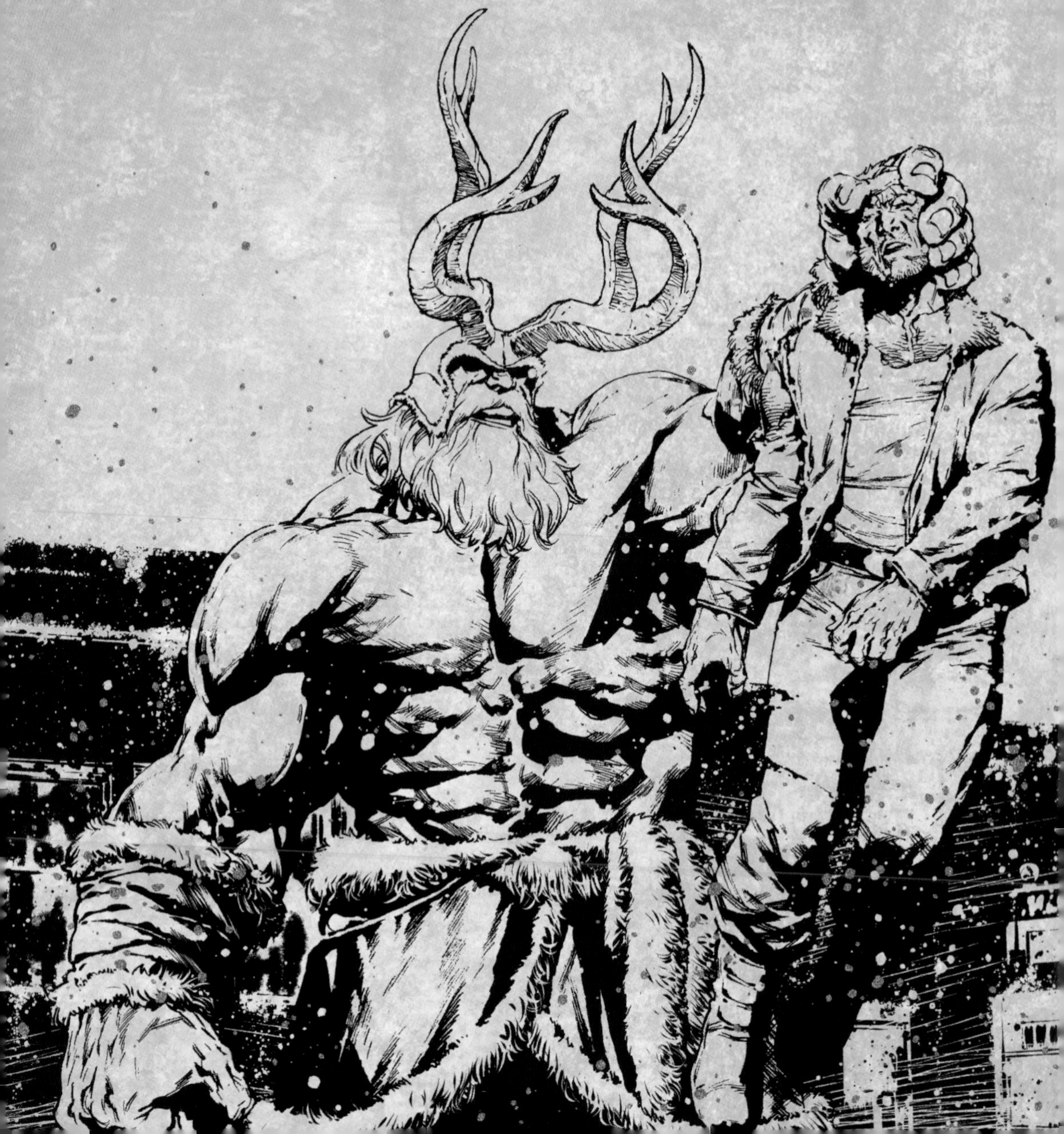

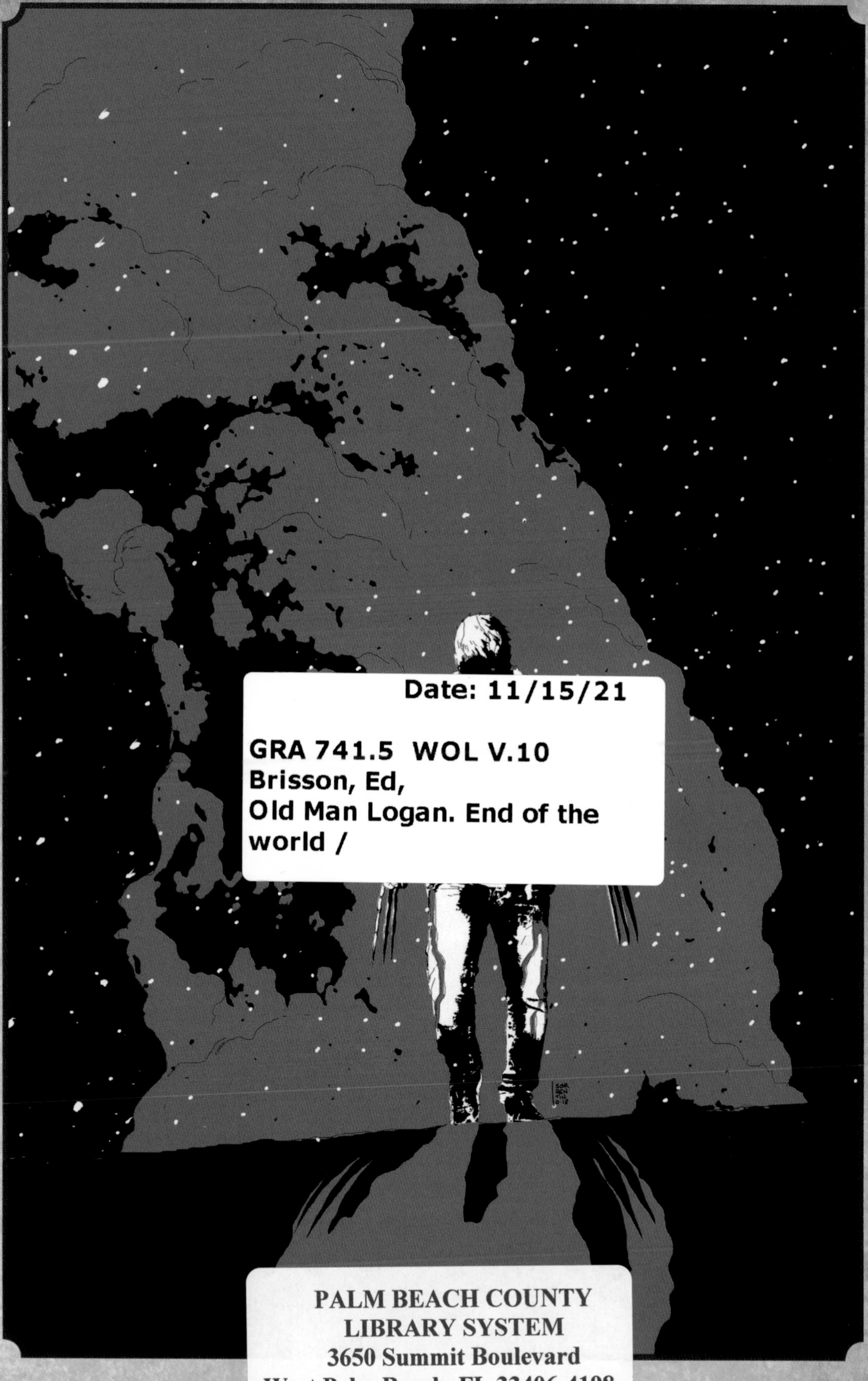

46

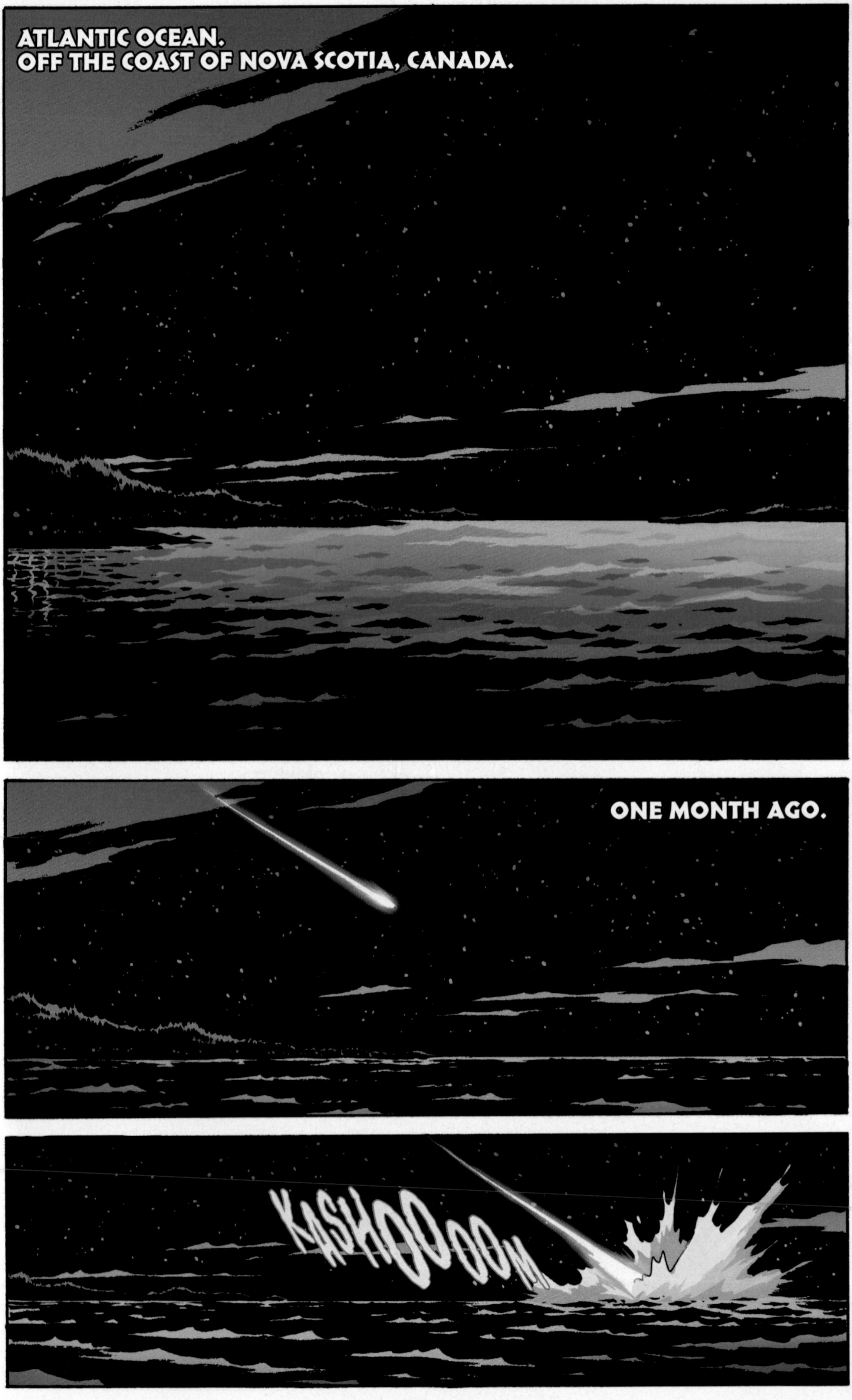
ATLANTIC OCEAN.
OFF THE COAST OF NOVA SCOTIA, CANADA.
ONE MONTH AGO.
KASHOOOOM

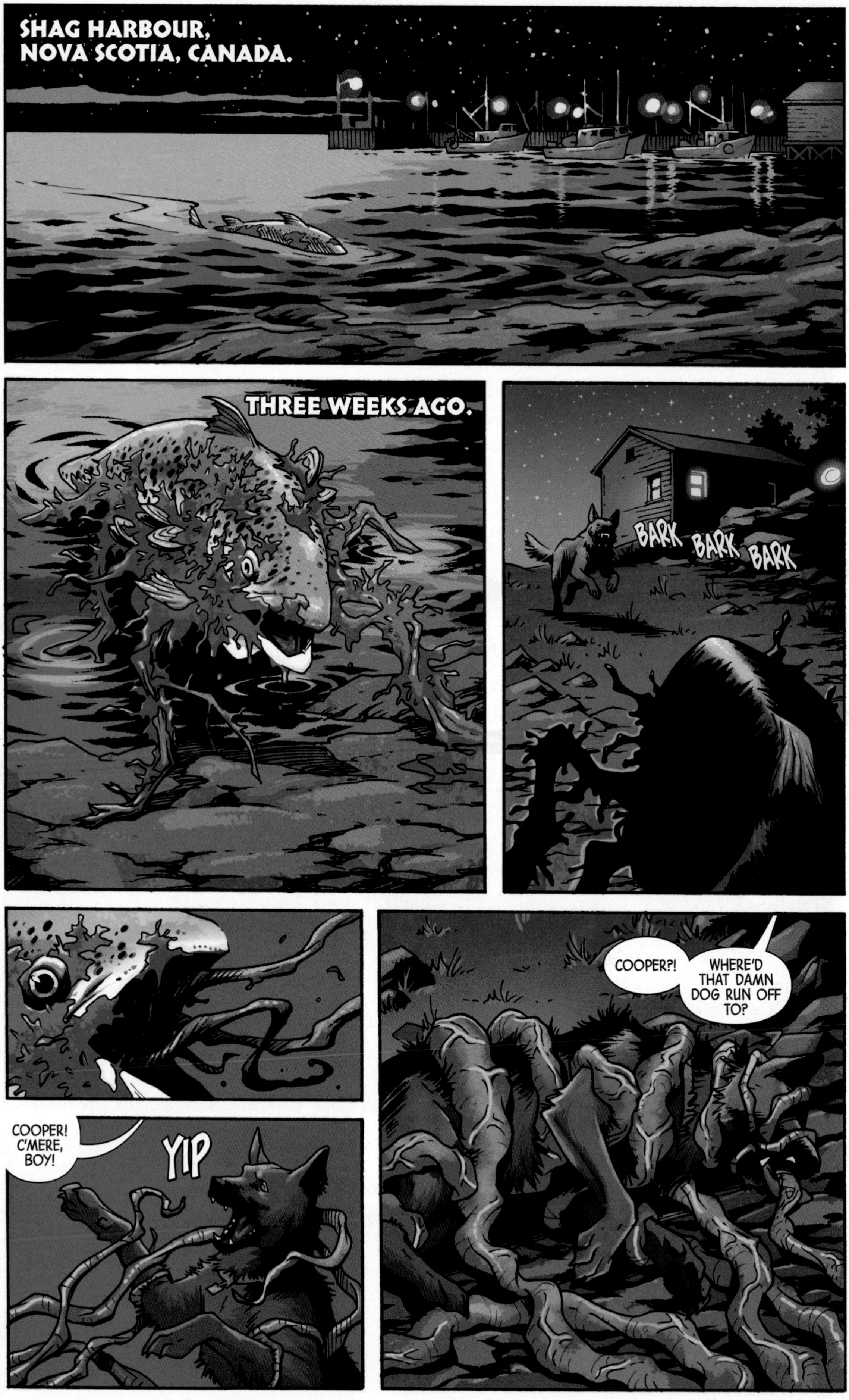
SHAG HARBOUR,
NOVA SCOTIA, CANADA.
THREE WEEKS AGO.
BARK BARK BARK
COOPER! C'MERE, BOY!
YIP
COOPER?!
WHERE'D THAT DAMN DOG RUN OFF TO?

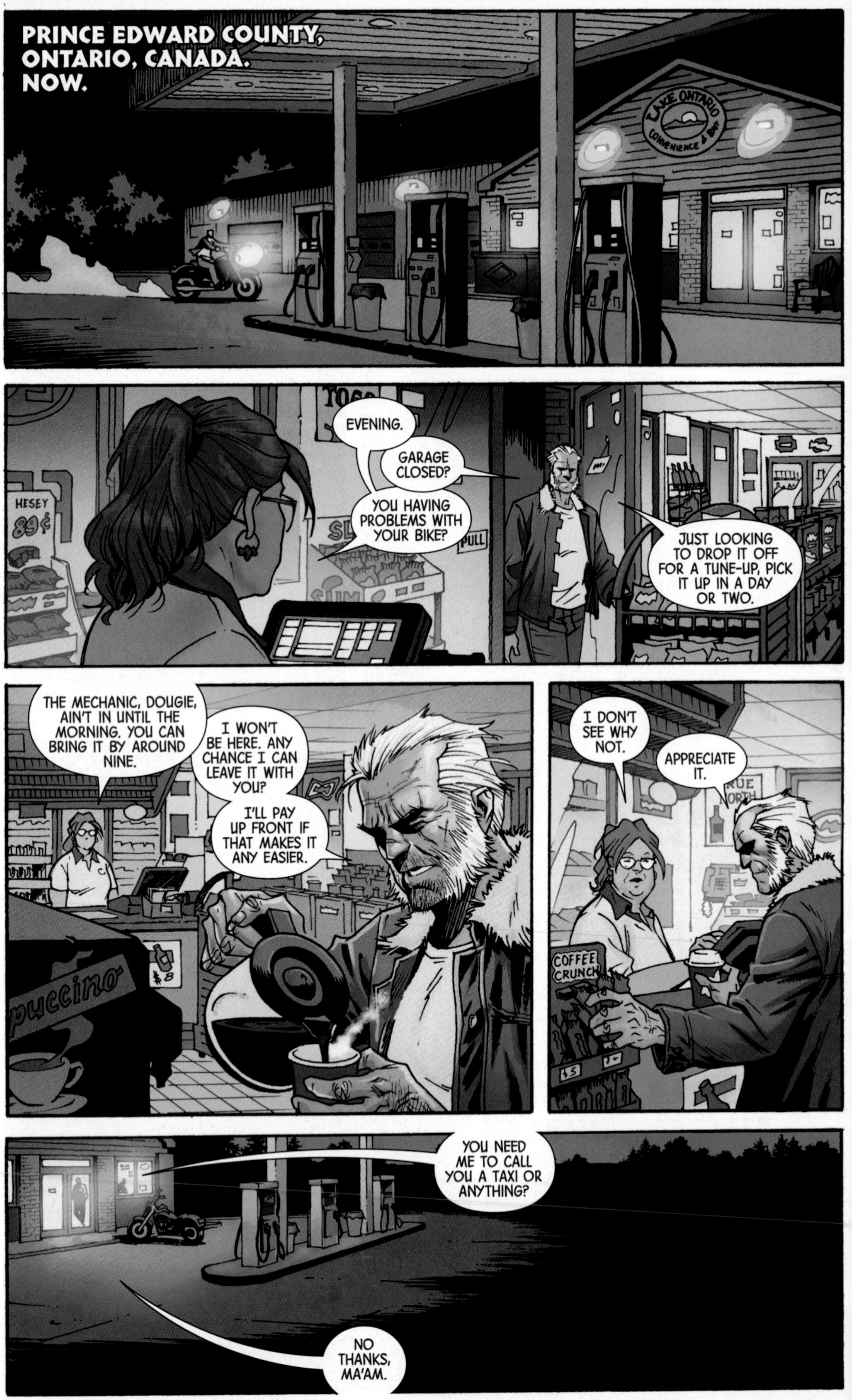
PRINCE EDWARD COUNTY, ONTARIO, CANADA. NOW.
LAKE ONTARIO CONVENIENCE & BAIT
EVENING.
GARAGE CLOSED?
YOU HAVING PROBLEMS WITH YOUR BIKE?
JUST LOOKING TO DROP IT OFF FOR A TUNE-UP, PICK IT UP IN A DAY OR TWO.
THE MECHANIC, DOUGIE, AIN'T IN UNTIL THE MORNING. YOU CAN BRING IT BY AROUND NINE.
I WON'T BE HERE. ANY CHANCE I CAN LEAVE IT WITH YOU?
I'LL PAY UP FRONT IF THAT MAKES IT ANY EASIER.
I DON'T SEE WHY NOT.
APPRECIATE IT.
COFFEE CRUNCH
YOU NEED ME TO CALL YOU A TAXI OR ANYTHING?
NO THANKS, MA'AM.

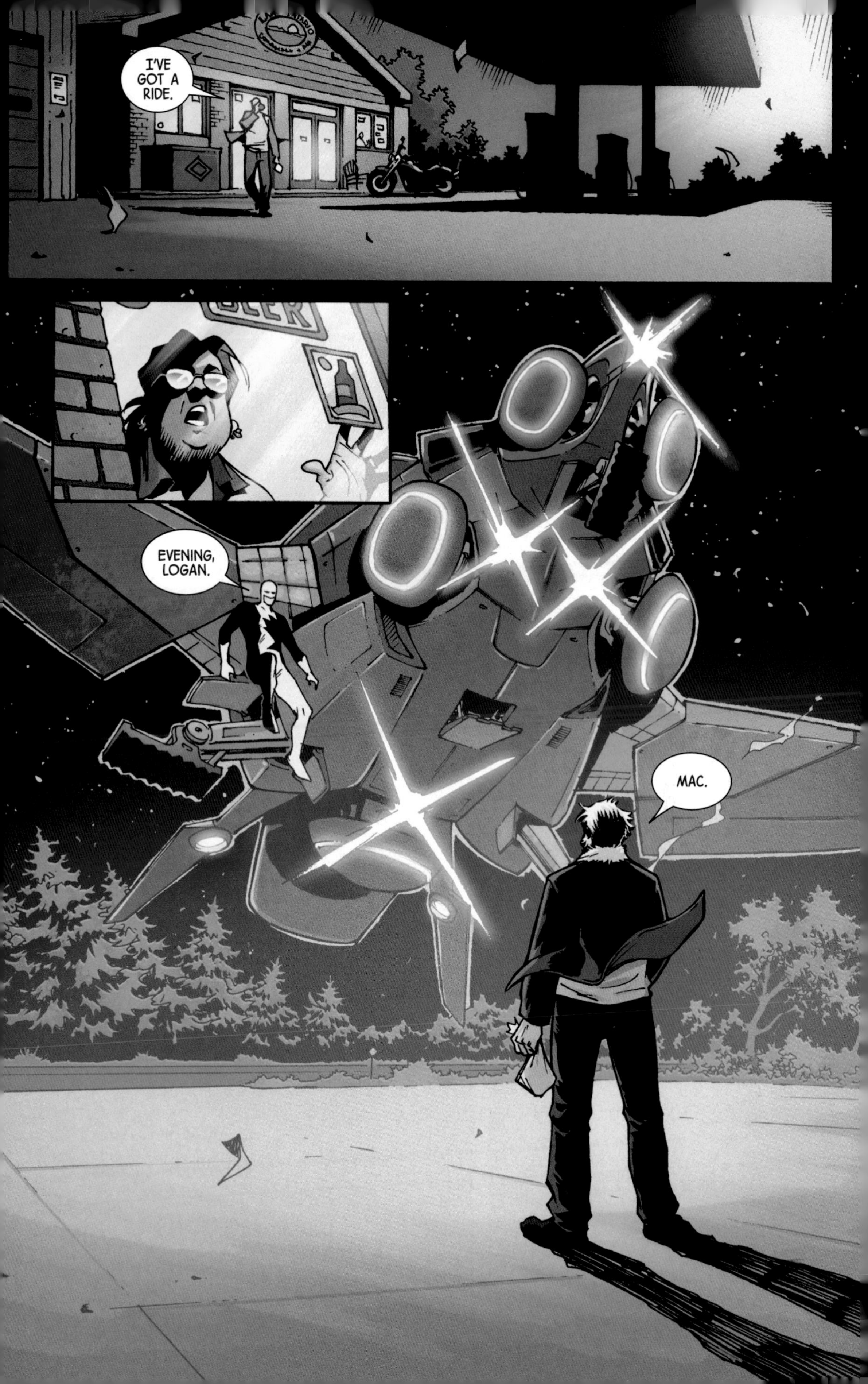
I'VE GOT A RIDE.
EVENING, LOGAN.
MAC.

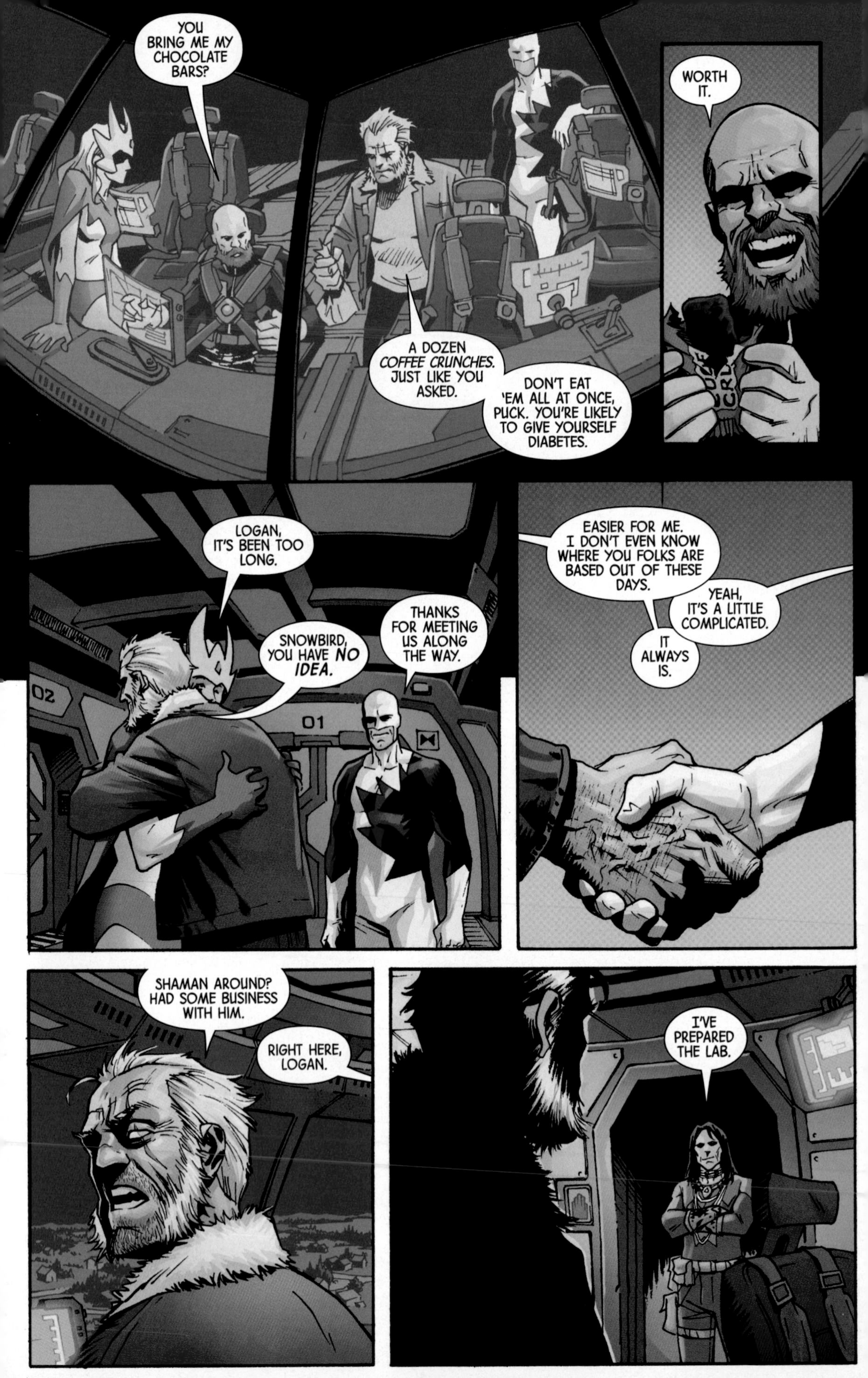
YOU BRING ME MY CHOCOLATE BARS?
A DOZEN COFFEE CRUNCHES. JUST LIKE YOU ASKED.
DON'T EAT 'EM ALL AT ONCE, PUCK. YOU'RE LIKELY TO GIVE YOURSELF DIABETES.
WORTH IT.
LOGAN, IT'S BEEN TOO LONG.
SNOWBIRD, YOU HAVE NO IDEA.
THANKS FOR MEETING US ALONG THE WAY.
EASIER FOR ME. I DON'T EVEN KNOW WHERE YOU FOLKS ARE BASED OUT OF THESE DAYS.
YEAH, IT'S A LITTLE COMPLICATED.
IT ALWAYS IS.
SHAMAN AROUND? HAD SOME BUSINESS WITH HIM.
RIGHT HERE, LOGAN.
I'VE PREPARED THE LAB.

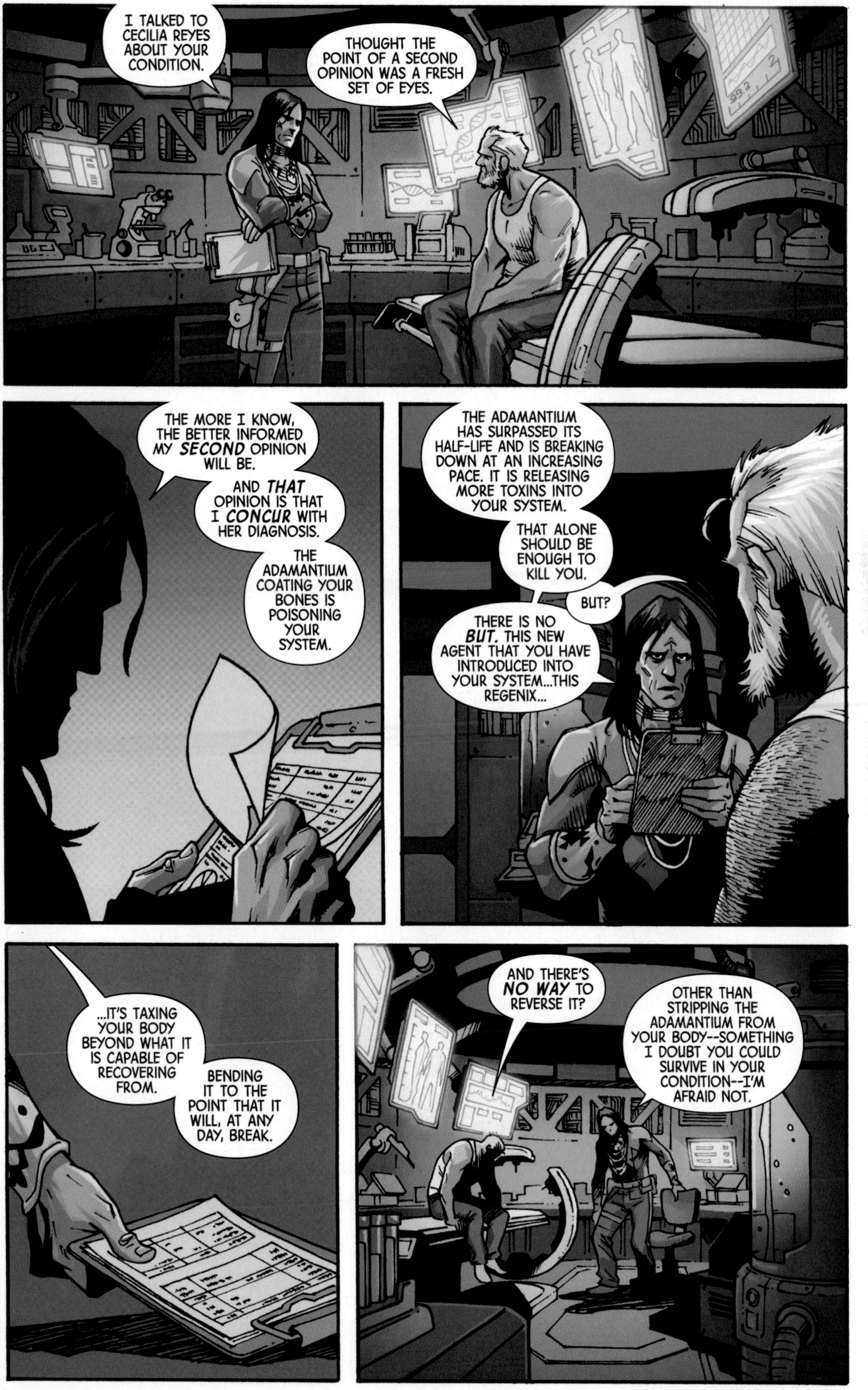

I TALKED TO CECILIA REYES ABOUT YOUR CONDITION.
THOUGHT THE POINT OF A SECOND OPINION WAS A FRESH SET OF EYES.
THE MORE I KNOW, THE BETTER INFORMED MY SECOND OPINION WILL BE.
AND THAT OPINION IS THAT I CONCUR WITH HER DIAGNOSIS.
THE ADAMANTIUM COATING YOUR BONES IS POISONING YOUR SYSTEM.
THE ADAMANTIUM HAS SURPASSED ITS HALF-LIFE AND IS BREAKING DOWN AT AN INCREASING PACE. IT IS RELEASING MORE TOXINS INTO YOUR SYSTEM.
THAT ALONE SHOULD BE ENOUGH TO KILL YOU.
BUT?
THERE IS NO BUT. THIS NEW AGENT THAT YOU HAVE INTRODUCED INTO YOUR SYSTEM...THIS REGENIX...
...IT'S TAXING YOUR BODY BEYOND WHAT IT IS CAPABLE OF RECOVERING FROM.
BENDING IT TO THE POINT THAT IT WILL, AT ANY DAY, BREAK.
AND THERE'S NO WAY TO REVERSE IT?
OTHER THAN STRIPPING THE ADAMANTIUM FROM YOUR BODY--SOMETHING I DOUBT YOU COULD SURVIVE IN YOUR CONDITION--I'M AFRAID NOT.

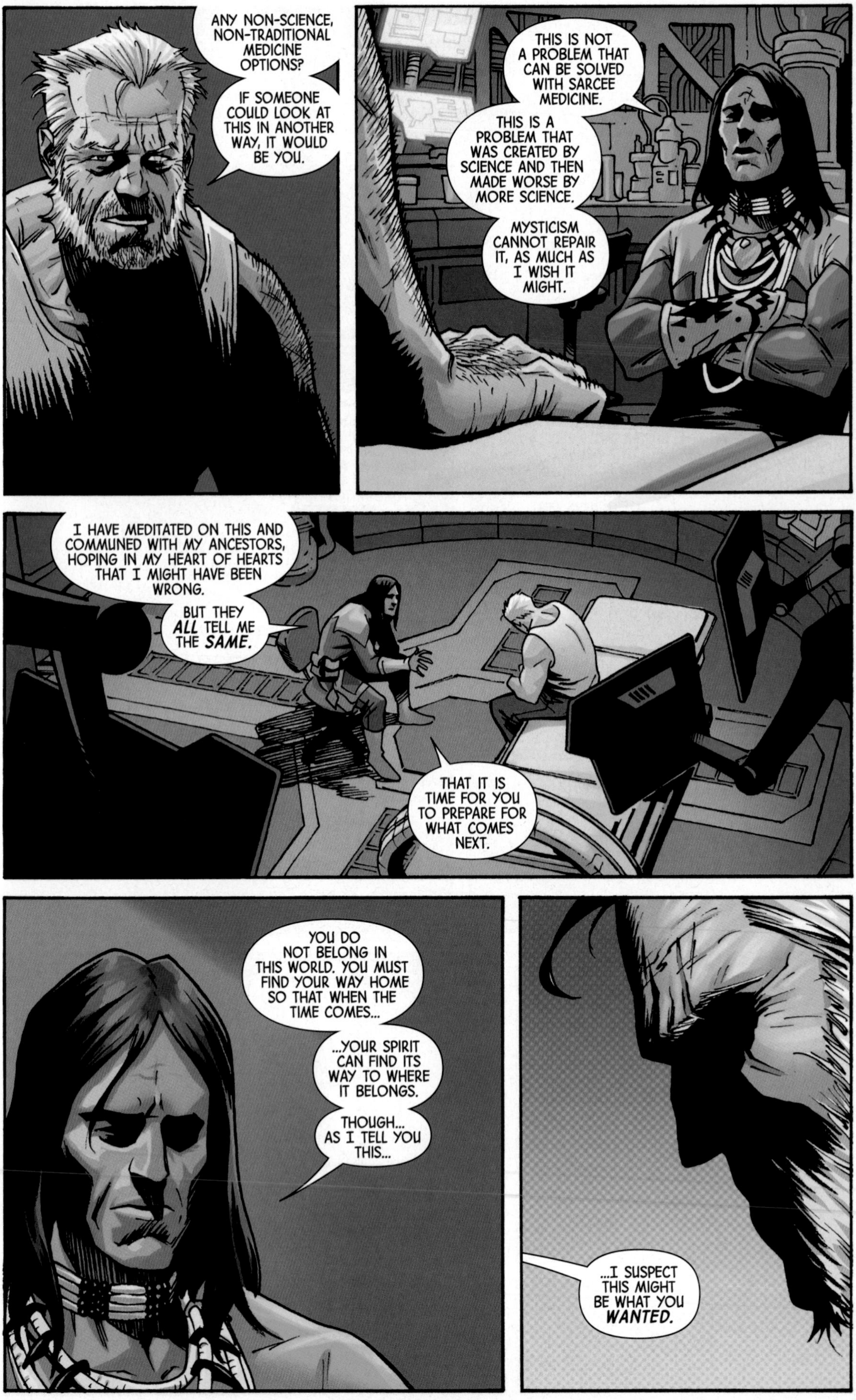
ANY NON-SCIENCE, NON-TRADITIONAL MEDICINE OPTIONS?
IF SOMEONE COULD LOOK AT THIS IN ANOTHER WAY, IT WOULD BE YOU.
THIS IS NOT A PROBLEM THAT CAN BE SOLVED WITH SARCEE MEDICINE.
THIS IS A PROBLEM THAT WAS CREATED BY SCIENCE AND THEN MADE WORSE BY MORE SCIENCE.
MYSTICISM CANNOT REPAIR IT, AS MUCH AS I WISH IT MIGHT.
I HAVE MEDITATED ON THIS AND COMMUNED WITH MY ANCESTORS, HOPING IN MY HEART OF HEARTS THAT I MIGHT HAVE BEEN WRONG.
BUT THEY *ALL* TELL ME THE *SAME.*
THAT IT IS TIME FOR YOU TO PREPARE FOR WHAT COMES NEXT.
YOU DO NOT BELONG IN THIS WORLD. YOU MUST FIND YOUR WAY HOME SO THAT WHEN THE TIME COMES...
...YOUR SPIRIT CAN FIND ITS WAY TO WHERE IT BELONGS.
THOUGH... AS I TELL YOU THIS...
...I SUSPECT THIS MIGHT BE WHAT YOU *WANTED.*

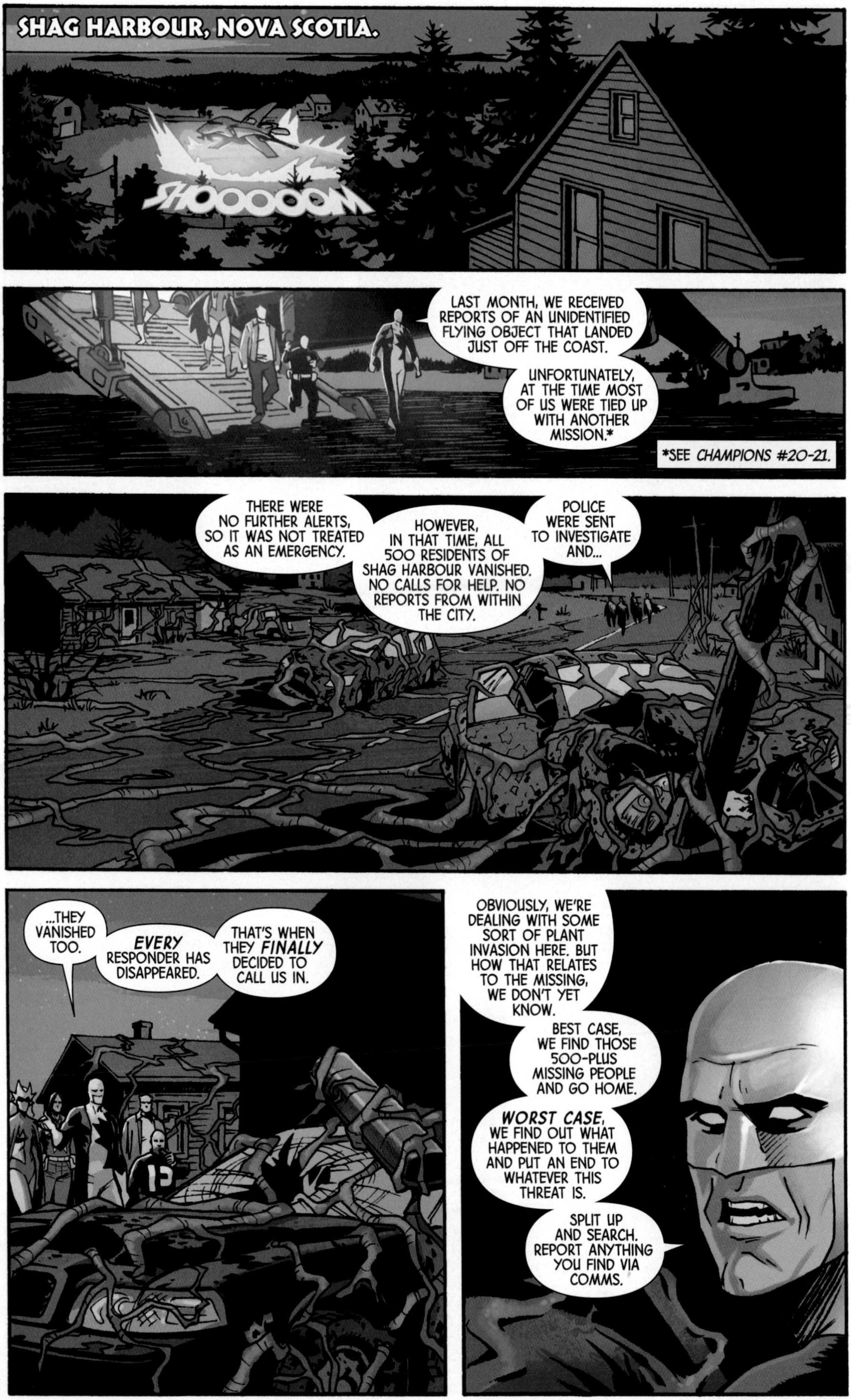
SHAG HARBOUR, NOVA SCOTIA.
SHOOOOOM
LAST MONTH, WE RECEIVED REPORTS OF AN UNIDENTIFIED FLYING OBJECT THAT LANDED JUST OFF THE COAST.
UNFORTUNATELY, AT THE TIME MOST OF US WERE TIED UP WITH ANOTHER MISSION.*
*SEE CHAMPIONS #20-21.
THERE WERE NO FURTHER ALERTS, SO IT WAS NOT TREATED AS AN EMERGENCY.
HOWEVER, IN THAT TIME, ALL 500 RESIDENTS OF SHAG HARBOUR VANISHED. NO CALLS FOR HELP. NO REPORTS FROM WITHIN THE CITY.
POLICE WERE SENT TO INVESTIGATE AND...
...THEY VANISHED TOO.
EVERY RESPONDER HAS DISAPPEARED.
THAT'S WHEN THEY FINALLY DECIDED TO CALL US IN.
OBVIOUSLY, WE'RE DEALING WITH SOME SORT OF PLANT INVASION HERE. BUT HOW THAT RELATES TO THE MISSING, WE DON'T YET KNOW.
BEST CASE, WE FIND THOSE 500-PLUS MISSING PEOPLE AND GO HOME.
WORST CASE, WE FIND OUT WHAT HAPPENED TO THEM AND PUT AN END TO WHATEVER THIS THREAT IS.
SPLIT UP AND SEARCH. REPORT ANYTHING YOU FIND VIA COMMS.

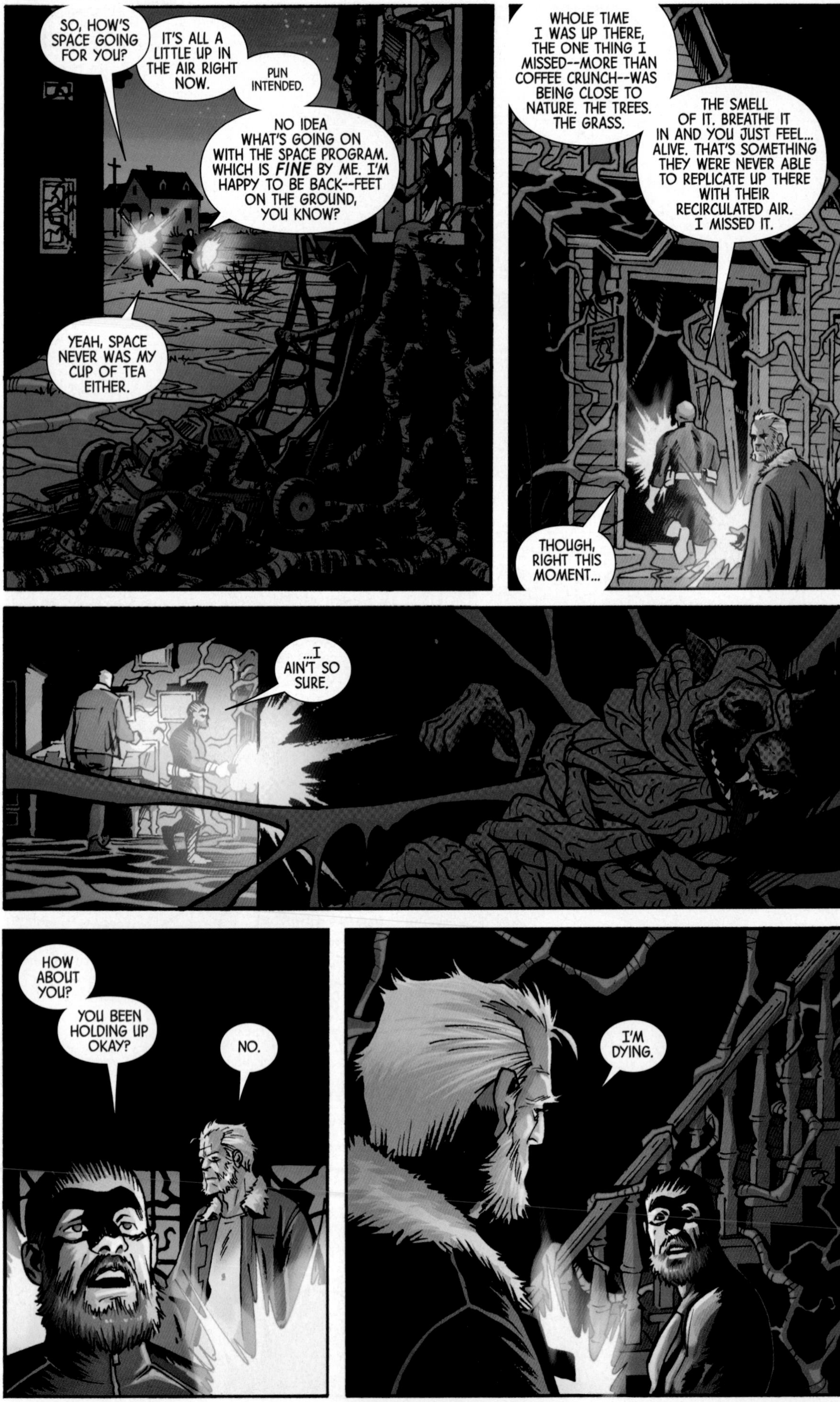
SO, HOW'S SPACE GOING FOR YOU?
IT'S ALL A LITTLE UP IN THE AIR RIGHT NOW.
PUN INTENDED.
NO IDEA WHAT'S GOING ON WITH THE SPACE PROGRAM. WHICH IS *FINE* BY ME. I'M HAPPY TO BE BACK--FEET ON THE GROUND, YOU KNOW?
YEAH, SPACE NEVER WAS MY CUP OF TEA EITHER.
WHOLE TIME I WAS UP THERE, THE ONE THING I MISSED--MORE THAN COFFEE CRUNCH--WAS BEING CLOSE TO NATURE. THE TREES. THE GRASS.
THE SMELL OF IT. BREATHE IT IN AND YOU JUST FEEL... ALIVE. THAT'S SOMETHING THEY WERE NEVER ABLE TO REPLICATE UP THERE WITH THEIR RECIRCULATED AIR. I MISSED IT.
THOUGH, RIGHT THIS MOMENT...
...I AIN'T SO SURE.
HOW ABOUT YOU?
YOU BEEN HOLDING UP OKAY?
NO.
I'M DYING.

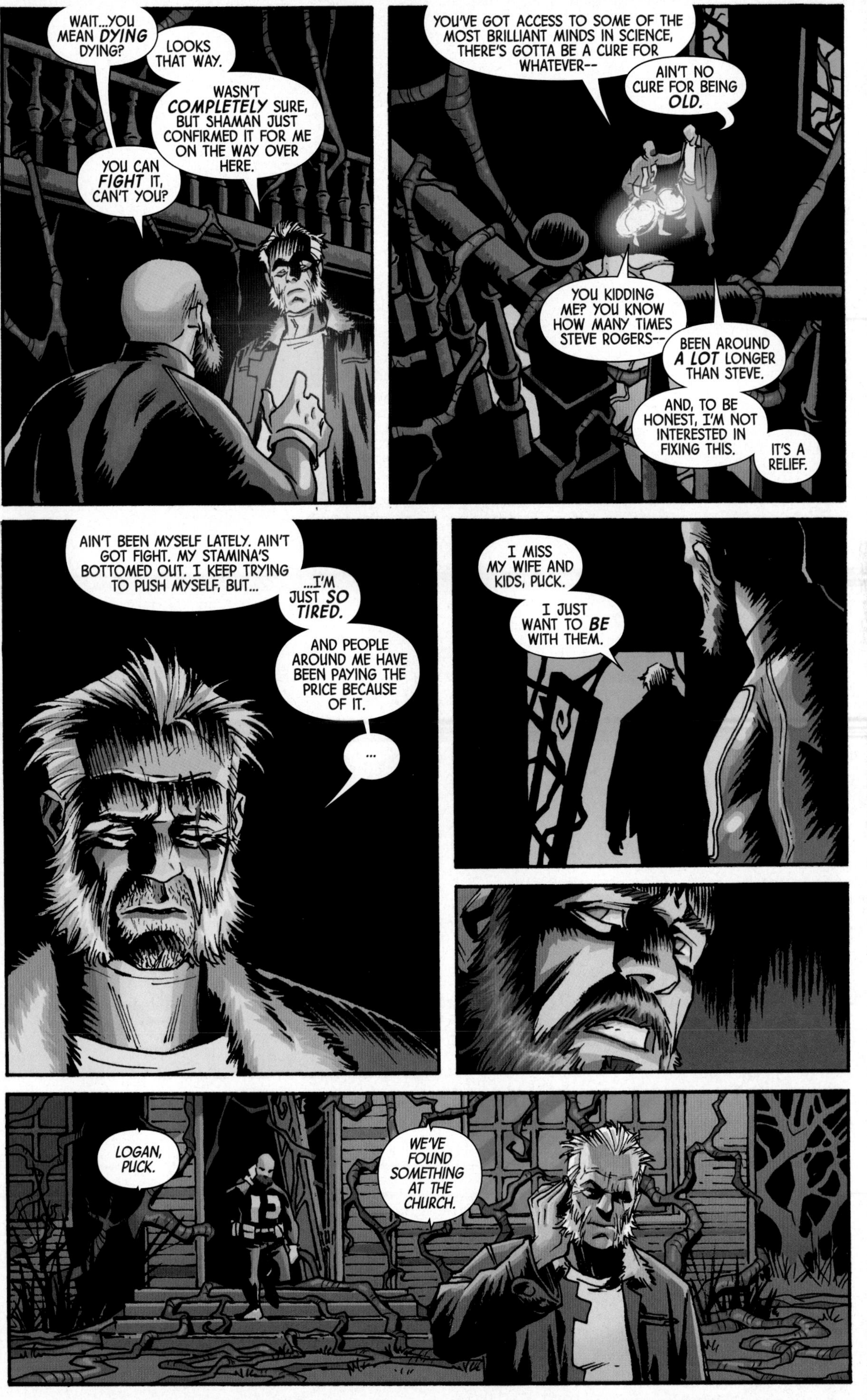
WAIT...YOU MEAN DYING DYING?
LOOKS THAT WAY.
WASN'T COMPLETELY SURE, BUT SHAMAN JUST CONFIRMED IT FOR ME ON THE WAY OVER HERE.
YOU CAN FIGHT IT, CAN'T YOU?
YOU'VE GOT ACCESS TO SOME OF THE MOST BRILLIANT MINDS IN SCIENCE, THERE'S GOTTA BE A CURE FOR WHATEVER--
AIN'T NO CURE FOR BEING OLD.
YOU KIDDING ME? YOU KNOW HOW MANY TIMES STEVE ROGERS--
BEEN AROUND A LOT LONGER THAN STEVE.
AND, TO BE HONEST, I'M NOT INTERESTED IN FIXING THIS.
IT'S A RELIEF.
AIN'T BEEN MYSELF LATELY. AIN'T GOT FIGHT. MY STAMINA'S BOTTOMED OUT. I KEEP TRYING TO PUSH MYSELF, BUT...
...I'M JUST SO TIRED.
AND PEOPLE AROUND ME HAVE BEEN PAYING THE PRICE BECAUSE OF IT.
...
I MISS MY WIFE AND KIDS, PUCK.
I JUST WANT TO BE WITH THEM.
LOGAN, PUCK.
WE'VE FOUND SOMETHING AT THE CHURCH.

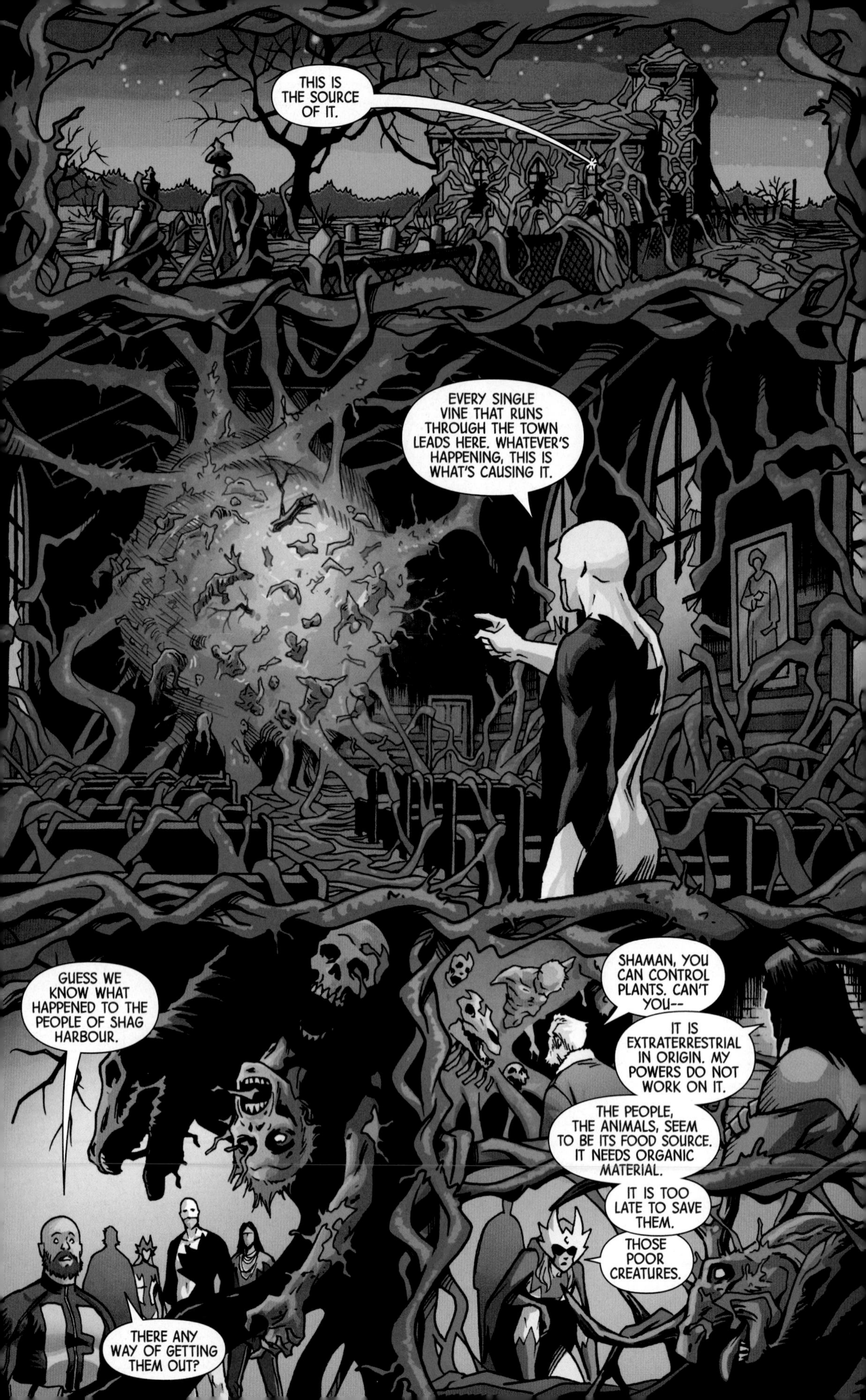
THIS IS THE SOURCE OF IT.
EVERY SINGLE VINE THAT RUNS THROUGH THE TOWN LEADS HERE. WHATEVER'S HAPPENING, THIS IS WHAT'S CAUSING IT.
GUESS WE KNOW WHAT HAPPENED TO THE PEOPLE OF SHAG HARBOUR.
THERE ANY WAY OF GETTING THEM OUT?
SHAMAN, YOU CAN CONTROL PLANTS. CAN'T YOU--
IT IS EXTRATERRESTRIAL IN ORIGIN. MY POWERS DO NOT WORK ON IT.
THE PEOPLE, THE ANIMALS, SEEM TO BE ITS FOOD SOURCE. IT NEEDS ORGANIC MATERIAL.
IT IS TOO LATE TO SAVE THEM.
THOSE POOR CREATURES.

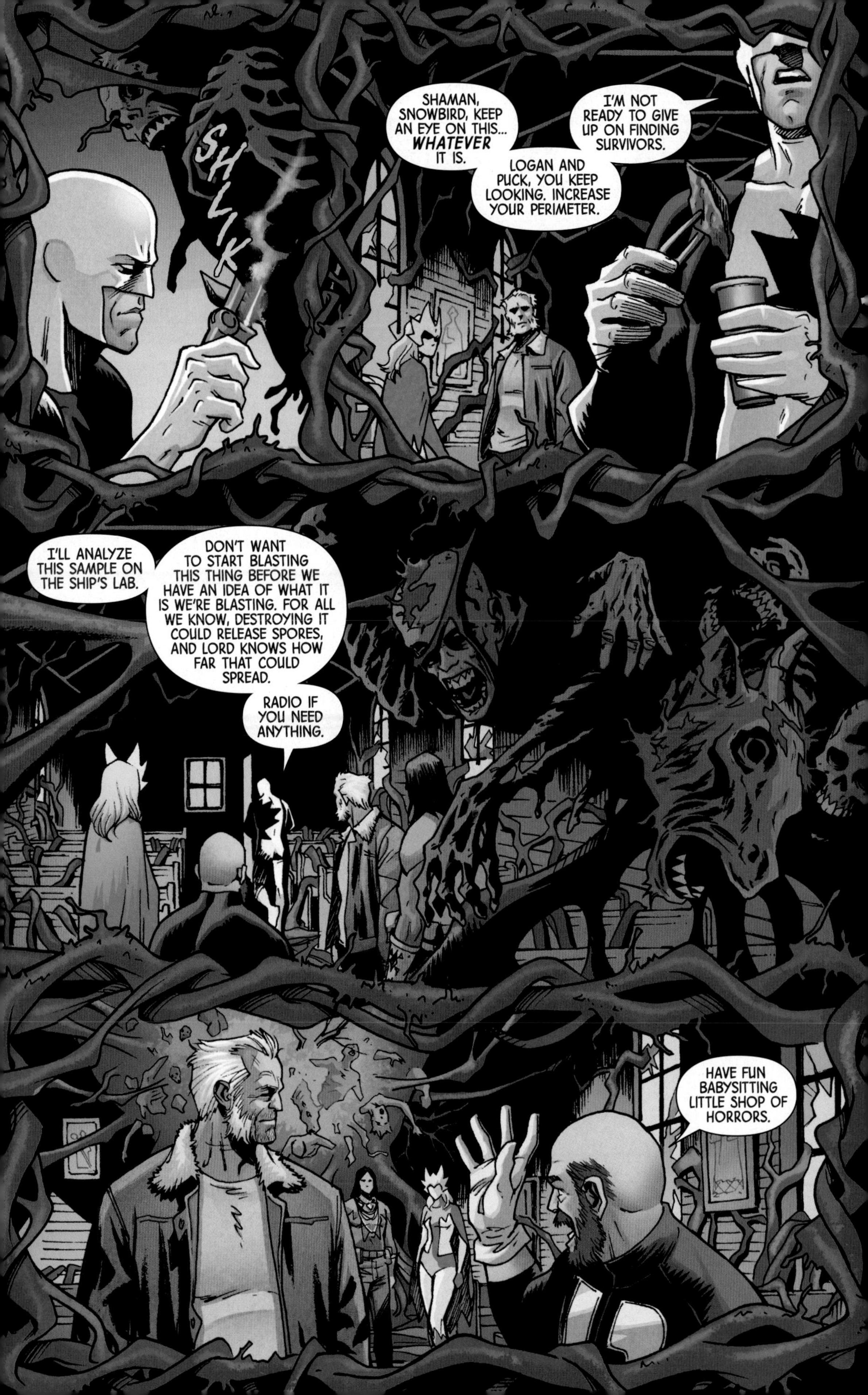
SHLIK
SHAMAN, SNOWBIRD, KEEP AN EYE ON THIS... *WHATEVER* IT IS.
I'M NOT READY TO GIVE UP ON FINDING SURVIVORS.
LOGAN AND PUCK, YOU KEEP LOOKING. INCREASE YOUR PERIMETER.
I'LL ANALYZE THIS SAMPLE ON THE SHIP'S LAB.
DON'T WANT TO START BLASTING THIS THING BEFORE WE HAVE AN IDEA OF WHAT IT IS WE'RE BLASTING. FOR ALL WE KNOW, DESTROYING IT COULD RELEASE SPORES, AND LORD KNOWS HOW FAR THAT COULD SPREAD.
RADIO IF YOU NEED ANYTHING.
HAVE FUN BABYSITTING LITTLE SHOP OF HORRORS.

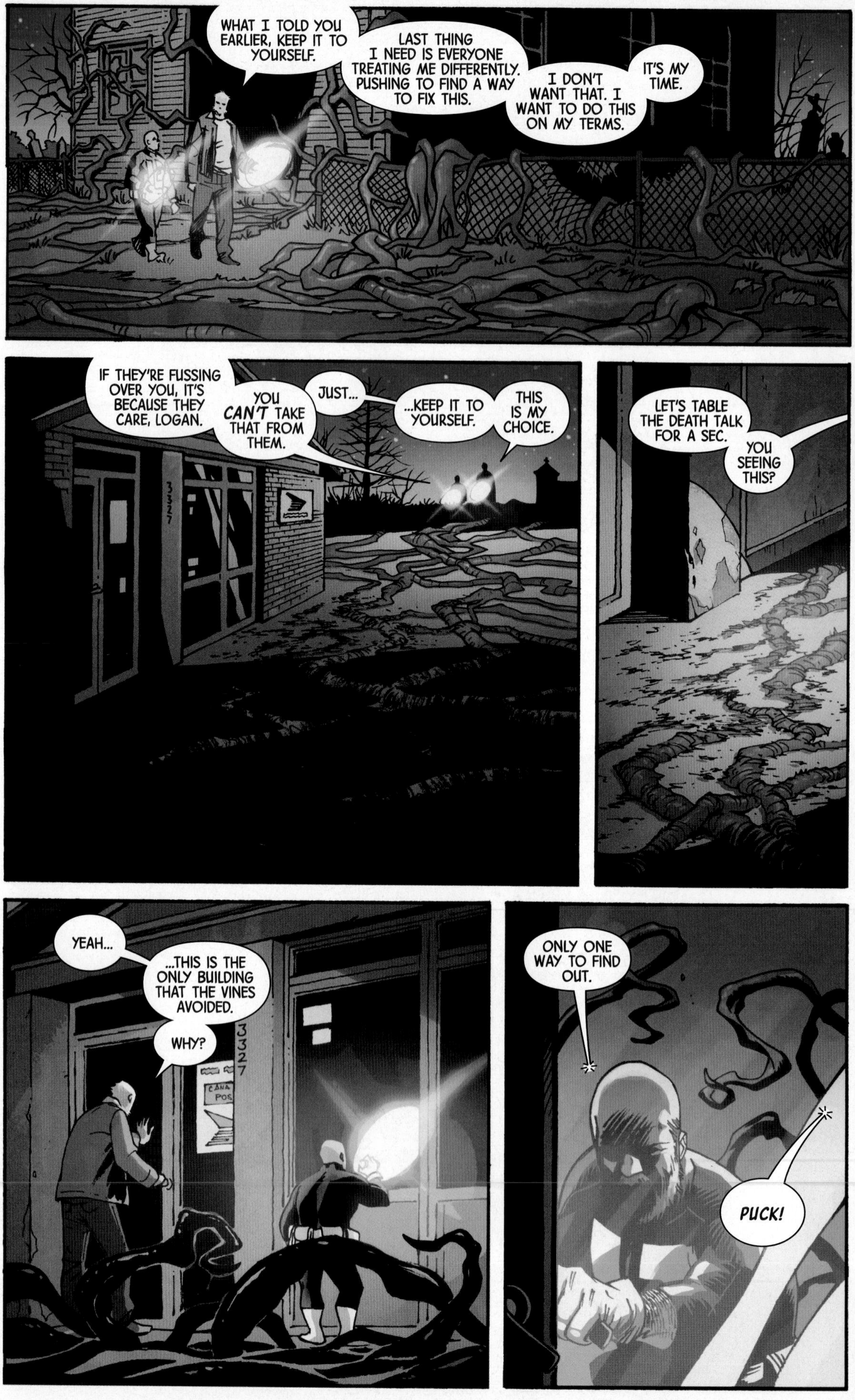
WHAT I TOLD YOU EARLIER, KEEP IT TO YOURSELF.
LAST THING I NEED IS EVERYONE TREATING ME DIFFERENTLY. PUSHING TO FIND A WAY TO FIX THIS.
I DON'T WANT THAT. I WANT TO DO THIS ON MY TERMS.
IT'S MY TIME.
IF THEY'RE FUSSING OVER YOU, IT'S BECAUSE THEY CARE, LOGAN.
YOU *CAN'T* TAKE THAT FROM THEM.
JUST...
...KEEP IT TO YOURSELF.
THIS IS MY CHOICE.
3327
LET'S TABLE THE DEATH TALK FOR A SEC.
YOU SEEING THIS?
YEAH...
...THIS IS THE ONLY BUILDING THAT THE VINES AVOIDED.
WHY?
3327
ONLY ONE WAY TO FIND OUT.
PUCK!

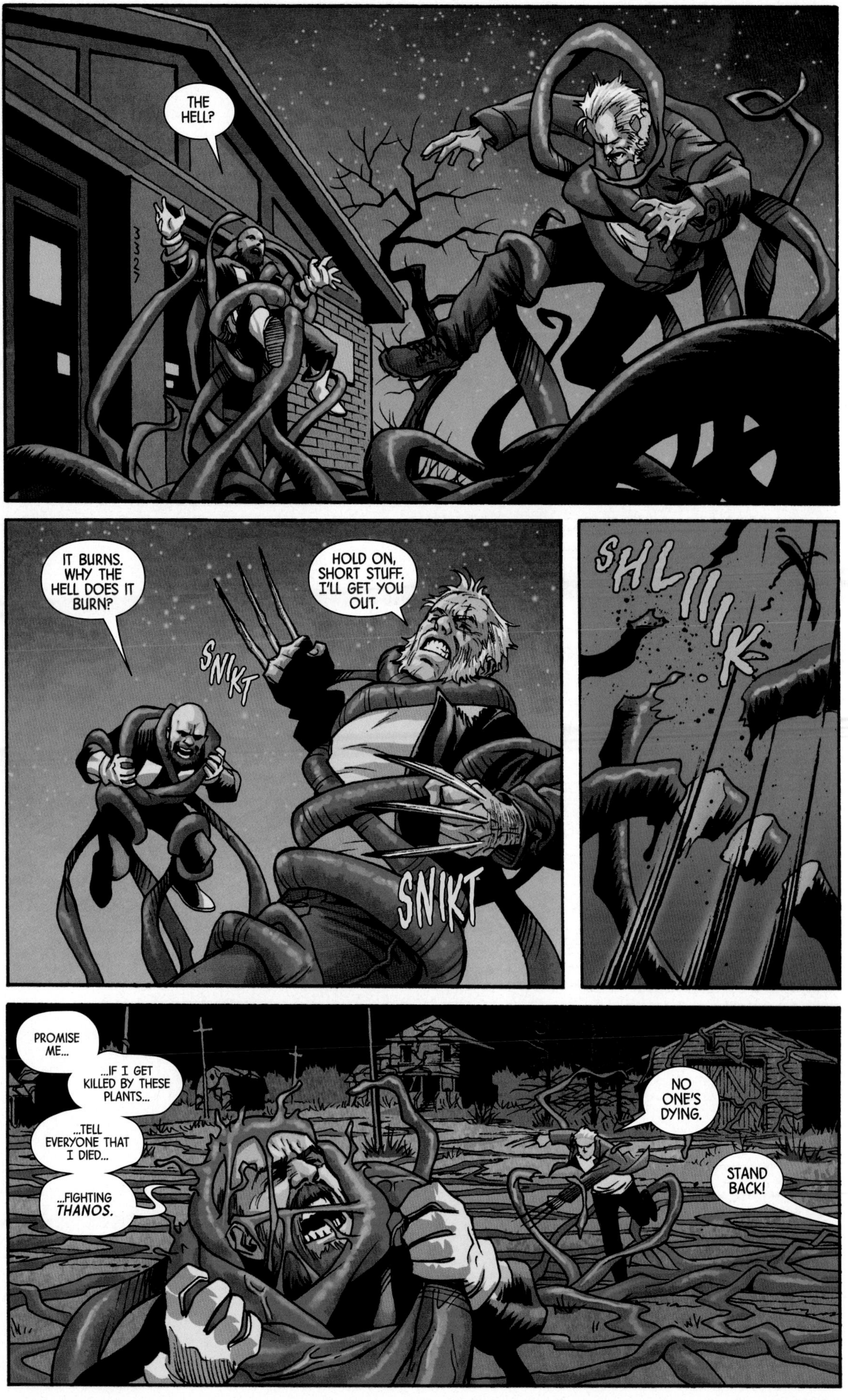
THE HELL?
3327
IT BURNS. WHY THE HELL DOES IT BURN?
HOLD ON, SHORT STUFF. I'LL GET YOU OUT.
SNIKT
SNIKT
SHLIIIK
PROMISE ME...
...IF I GET KILLED BY THESE PLANTS...
...TELL EVERYONE THAT I DIED...
...FIGHTING *THANOS.*
NO ONE'S DYING.
STAND BACK!

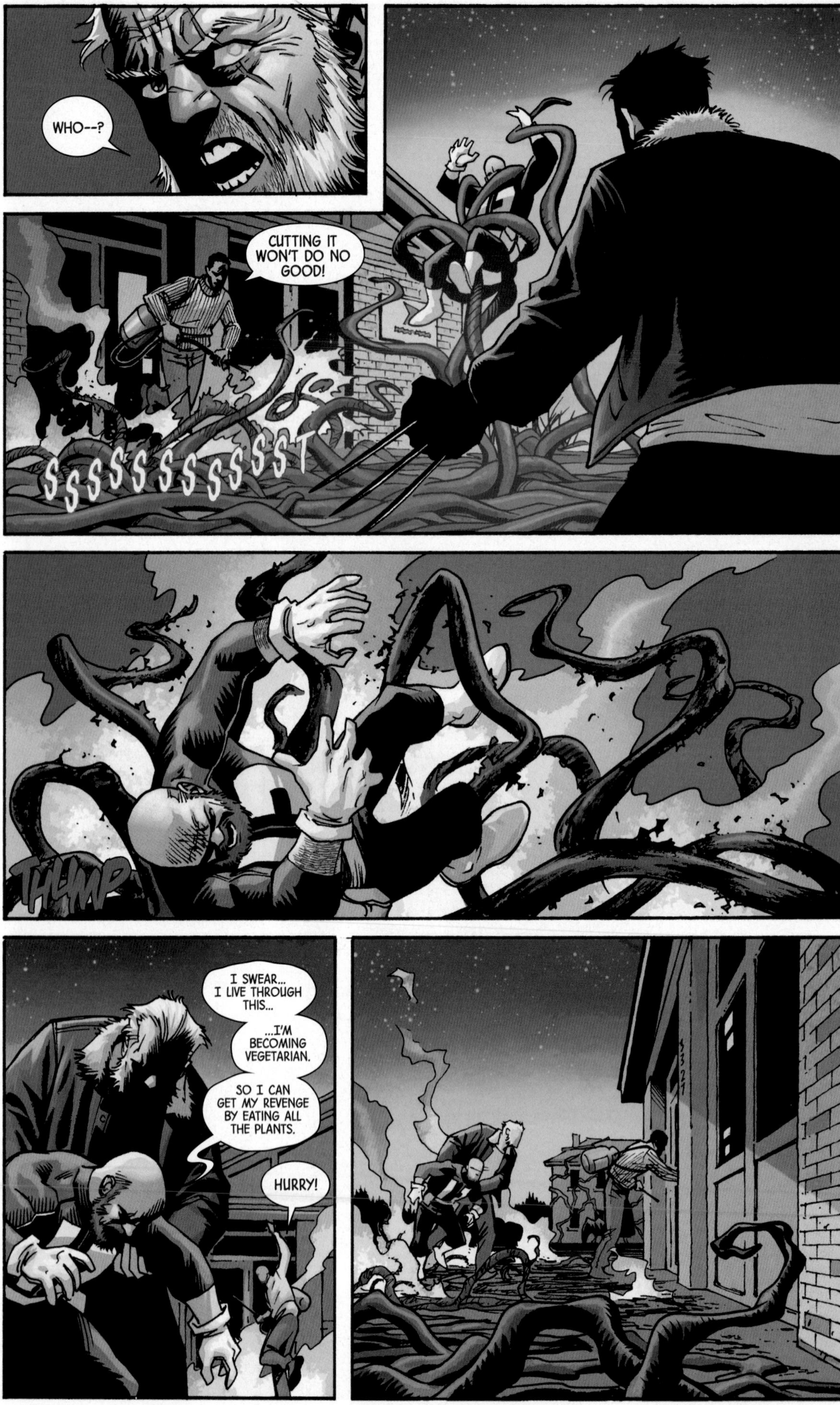
WHO--?
CUTTING IT WON'T DO NO GOOD!
SSSSSSSSSSSST
THUMP
I SWEAR... I LIVE THROUGH THIS...
...I'M BECOMING VEGETARIAN.
SO I CAN GET MY REVENGE BY EATING ALL THE PLANTS.
HURRY!

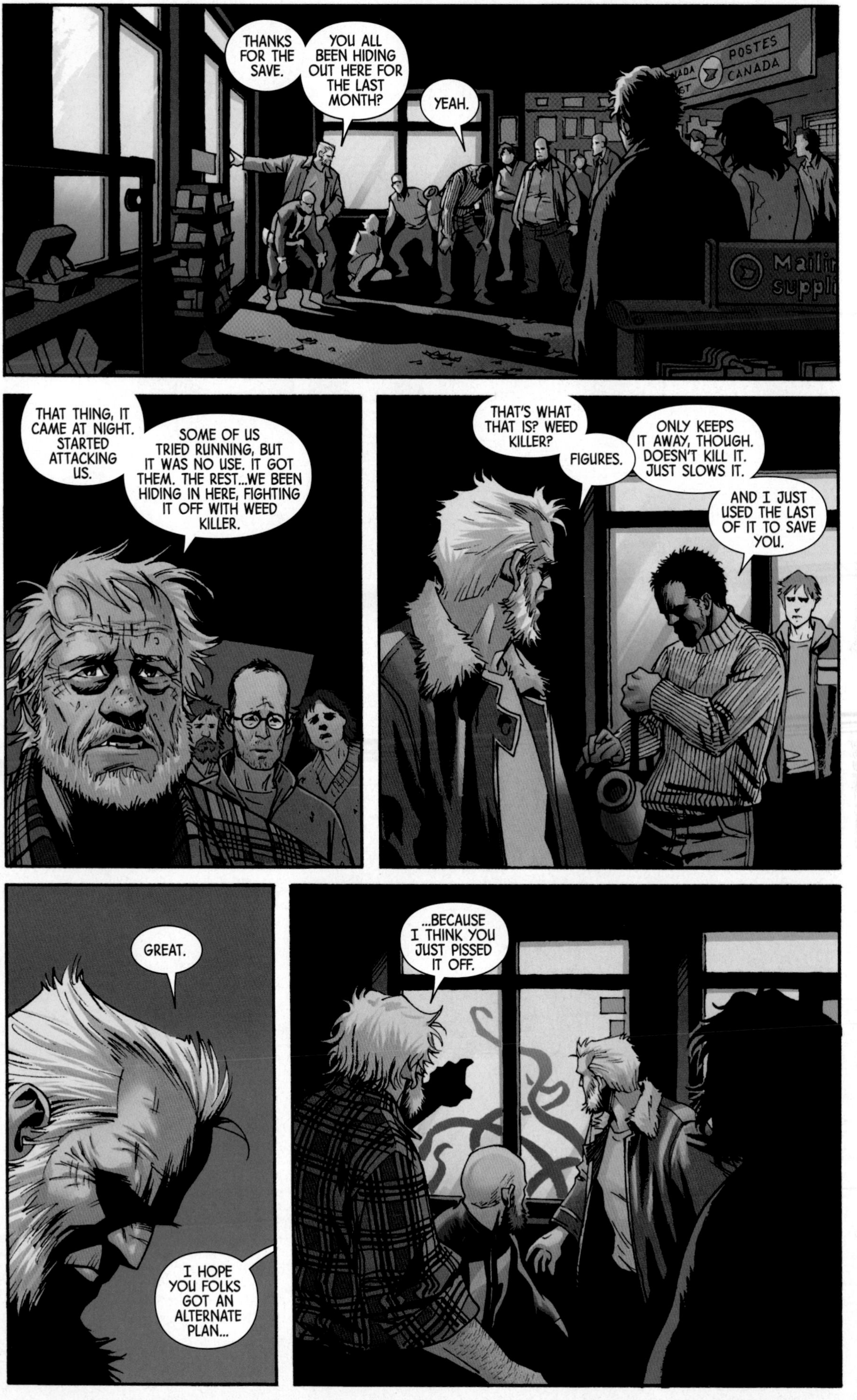
THANKS FOR THE SAVE.
YOU ALL BEEN HIDING OUT HERE FOR THE LAST MONTH?
YEAH.
POSTES CANADA
THAT THING, IT CAME AT NIGHT. STARTED ATTACKING US.
SOME OF US TRIED RUNNING, BUT IT WAS NO USE. IT GOT THEM. THE REST...WE BEEN HIDING IN HERE, FIGHTING IT OFF WITH WEED KILLER.
THAT'S WHAT THAT IS? WEED KILLER?
FIGURES.
ONLY KEEPS IT AWAY, THOUGH. DOESN'T KILL IT. JUST SLOWS IT.
AND I JUST USED THE LAST OF IT TO SAVE YOU.
GREAT.
I HOPE YOU FOLKS GOT AN ALTERNATE PLAN...
...BECAUSE I THINK YOU JUST PISSED IT OFF.

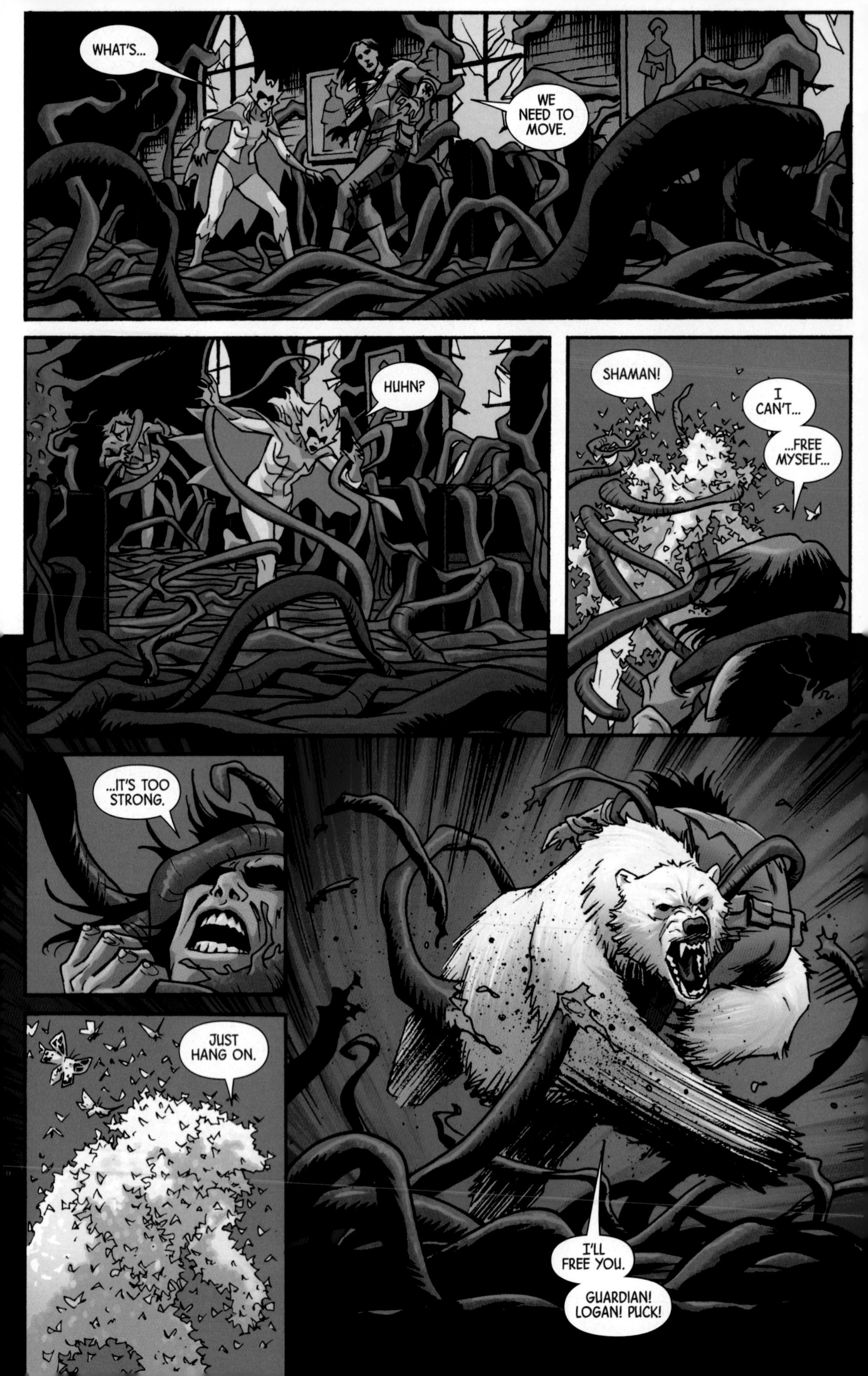
WHAT'S...
WE NEED TO MOVE.
HUHN?
SHAMAN!
I CAN'T...
...FREE MYSELF...
...IT'S TOO STRONG.
JUST HANG ON.
I'LL FREE YOU.
GUARDIAN! LOGAN! PUCK!

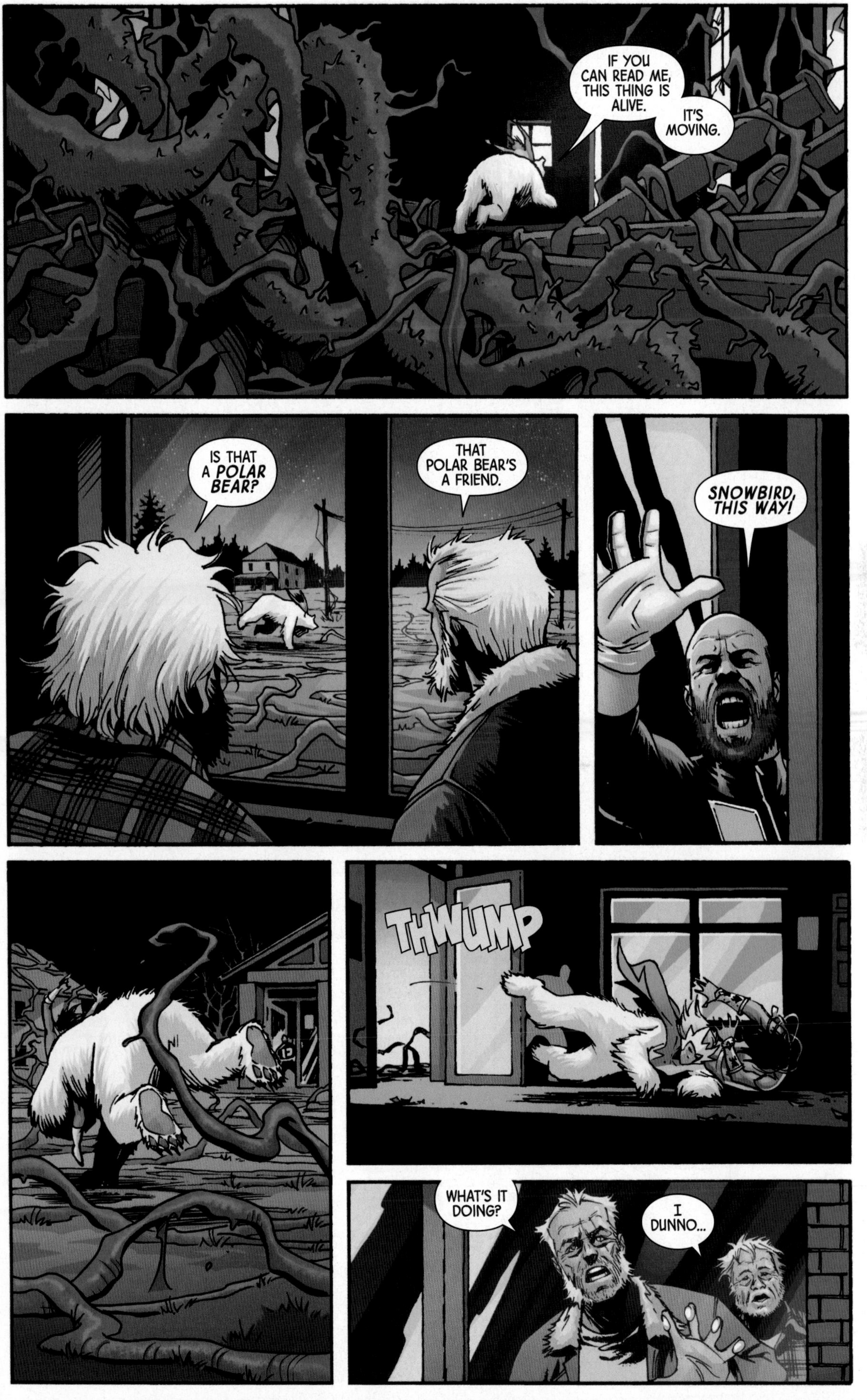
IF YOU CAN READ ME, THIS THING IS ALIVE.
IT'S MOVING.
IS THAT A POLAR BEAR?
THAT POLAR BEAR'S A FRIEND.
SNOWBIRD, THIS WAY!
THWUMP
WHAT'S IT DOING?
I DUNNO...

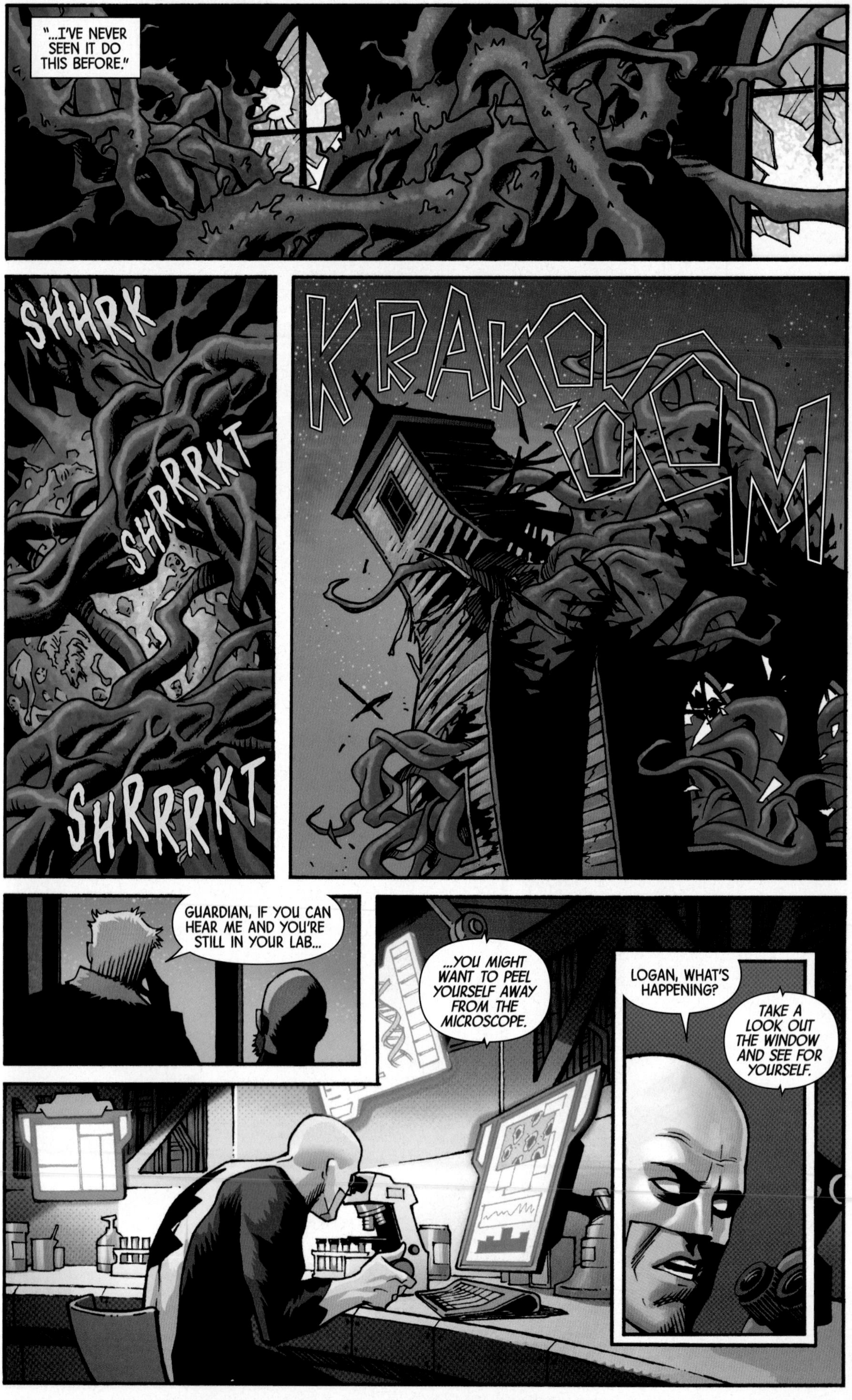
"...I'VE NEVER SEEN IT DO THIS BEFORE."
SHHRK
SHRRRKT
SHRRRKT
KRAKOOOM
GUARDIAN, IF YOU CAN HEAR ME AND YOU'RE STILL IN YOUR LAB...
...YOU MIGHT WANT TO PEEL YOURSELF AWAY FROM THE MICROSCOPE.
LOGAN, WHAT'S HAPPENING?
TAKE A LOOK OUT THE WINDOW AND SEE FOR YOURSELF.

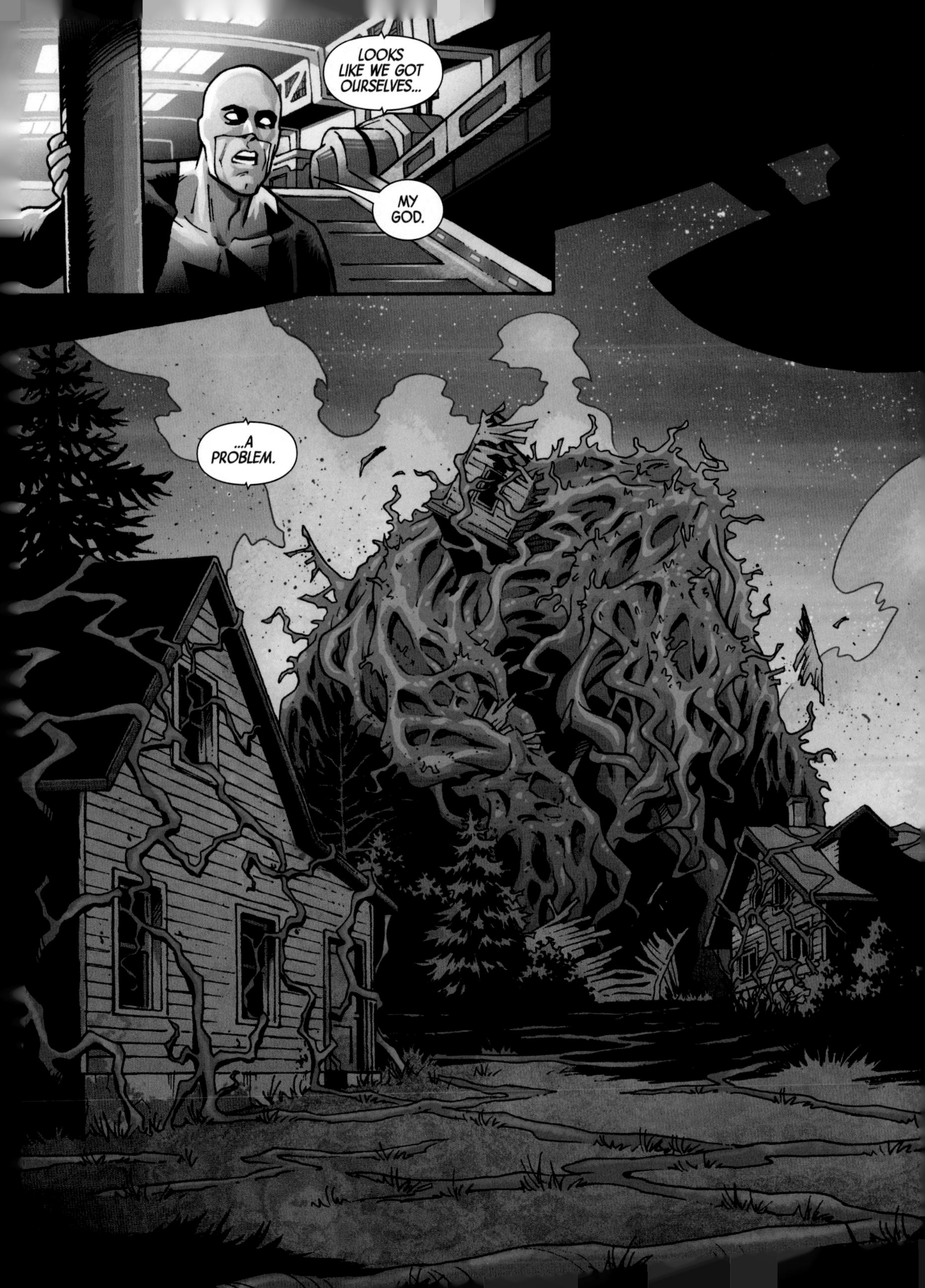
LOOKS LIKE WE GOT OURSELVES...
MY GOD.
...A PROBLEM.

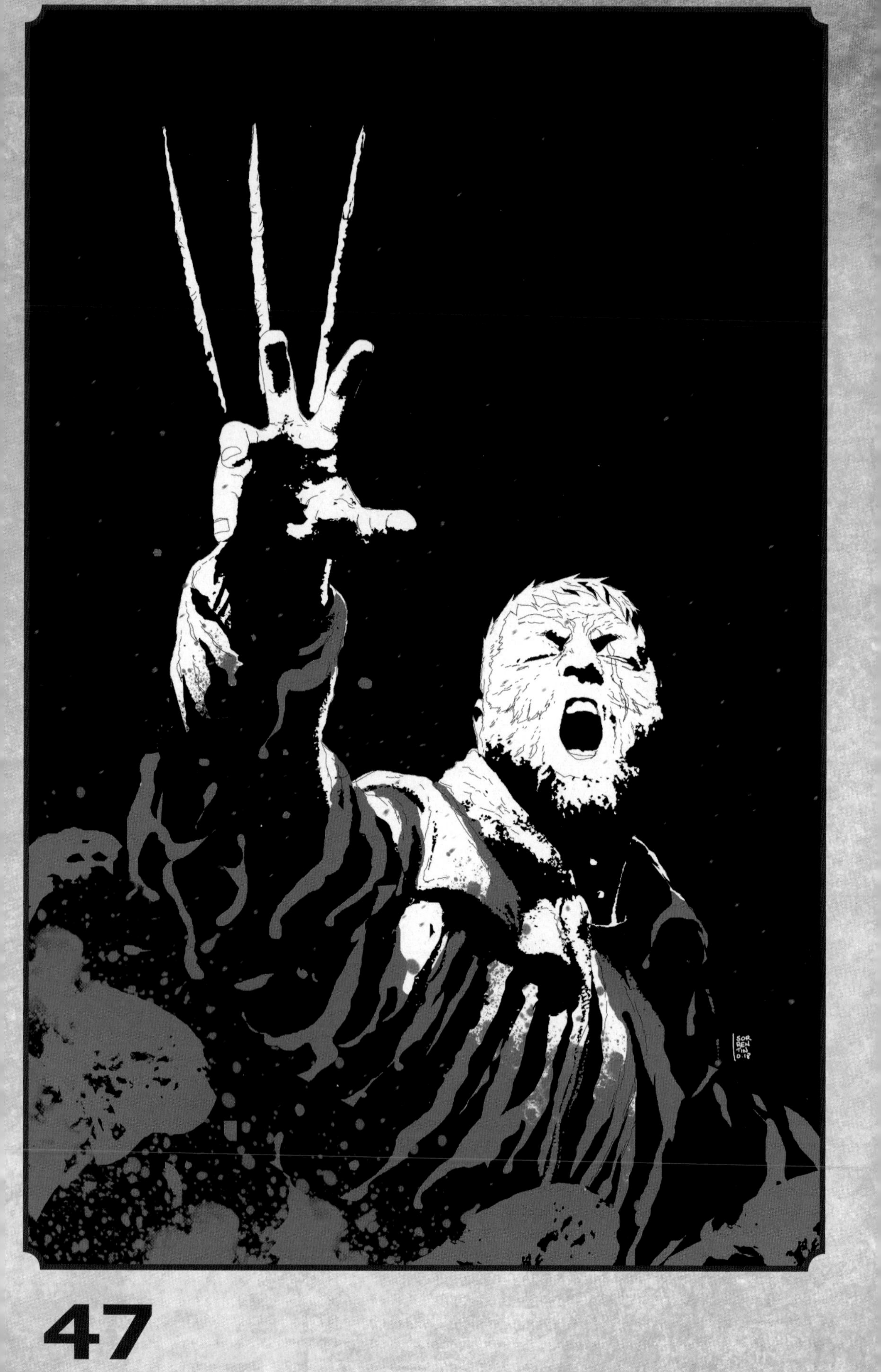

47

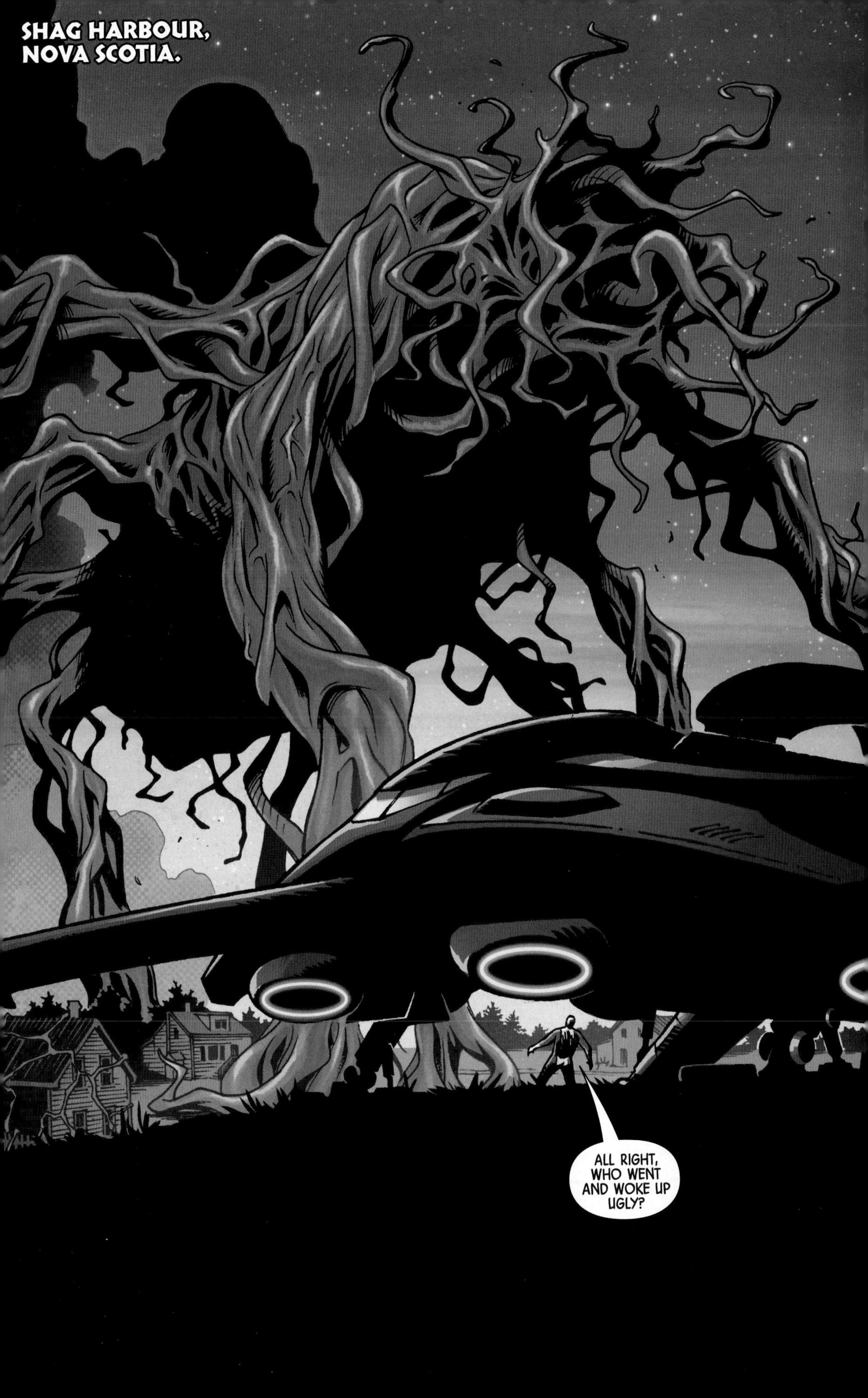
SHAG HARBOUR, NOVA SCOTIA.
ALL RIGHT, WHO WENT AND WOKE UP UGLY?

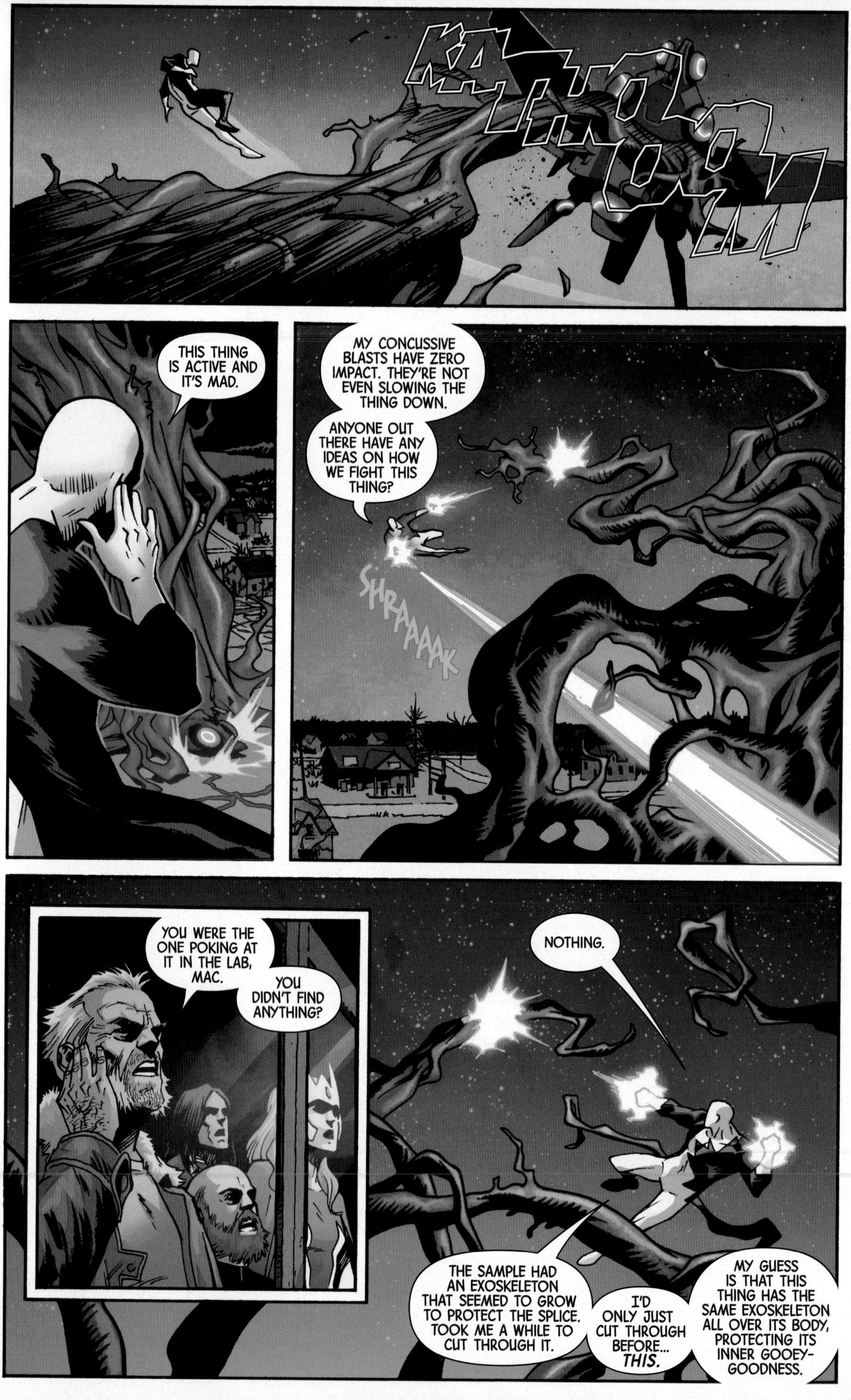
KA-THOOOOM
THIS THING IS ACTIVE AND IT'S MAD.
MY CONCUSSIVE BLASTS HAVE ZERO IMPACT. THEY'RE NOT EVEN SLOWING THE THING DOWN.
ANYONE OUT THERE HAVE ANY IDEAS ON HOW WE FIGHT THIS THING?
SHRAAAAAK
YOU WERE THE ONE POKING AT IT IN THE LAB, MAC.
YOU DIDN'T FIND ANYTHING?
NOTHING.
THE SAMPLE HAD AN EXOSKELETON THAT SEEMED TO GROW TO PROTECT THE SPLICE. TOOK ME A WHILE TO CUT THROUGH IT.
I'D ONLY JUST CUT THROUGH BEFORE... *THIS.*
MY GUESS IS THAT THIS THING HAS THE SAME EXOSKELETON ALL OVER ITS BODY, PROTECTING ITS INNER GOOEY-GOODNESS.

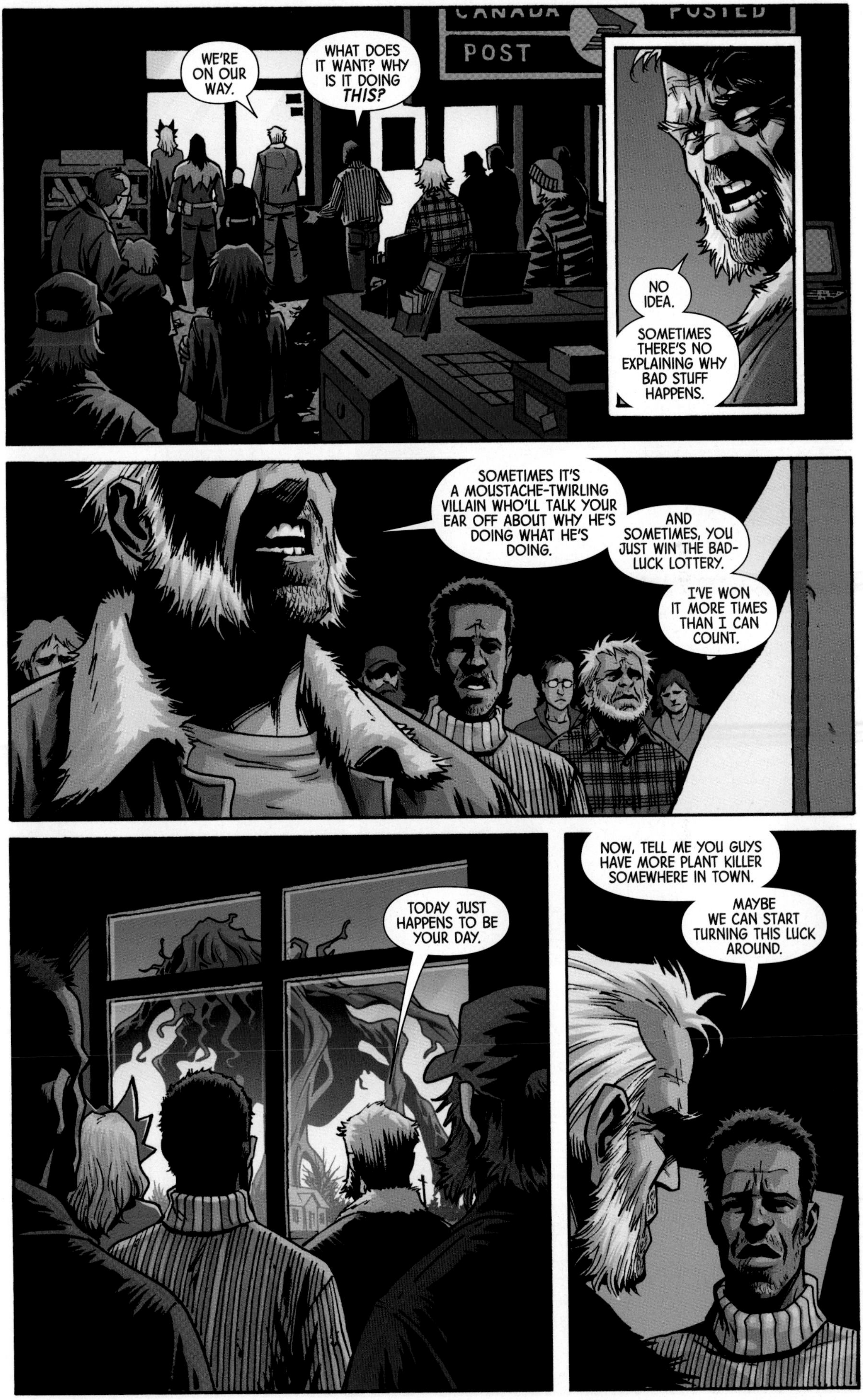
CANADA POST
POSTED
WE'RE ON OUR WAY.
WHAT DOES IT WANT? WHY IS IT DOING THIS?
NO IDEA.
SOMETIMES THERE'S NO EXPLAINING WHY BAD STUFF HAPPENS.
SOMETIMES IT'S A MOUSTACHE-TWIRLING VILLAIN WHO'LL TALK YOUR EAR OFF ABOUT WHY HE'S DOING WHAT HE'S DOING.
AND SOMETIMES, YOU JUST WIN THE BAD-LUCK LOTTERY.
I'VE WON IT MORE TIMES THAN I CAN COUNT.
TODAY JUST HAPPENS TO BE YOUR DAY.
NOW, TELL ME YOU GUYS HAVE MORE PLANT KILLER SOMEWHERE IN TOWN.
MAYBE WE CAN START TURNING THIS LUCK AROUND.

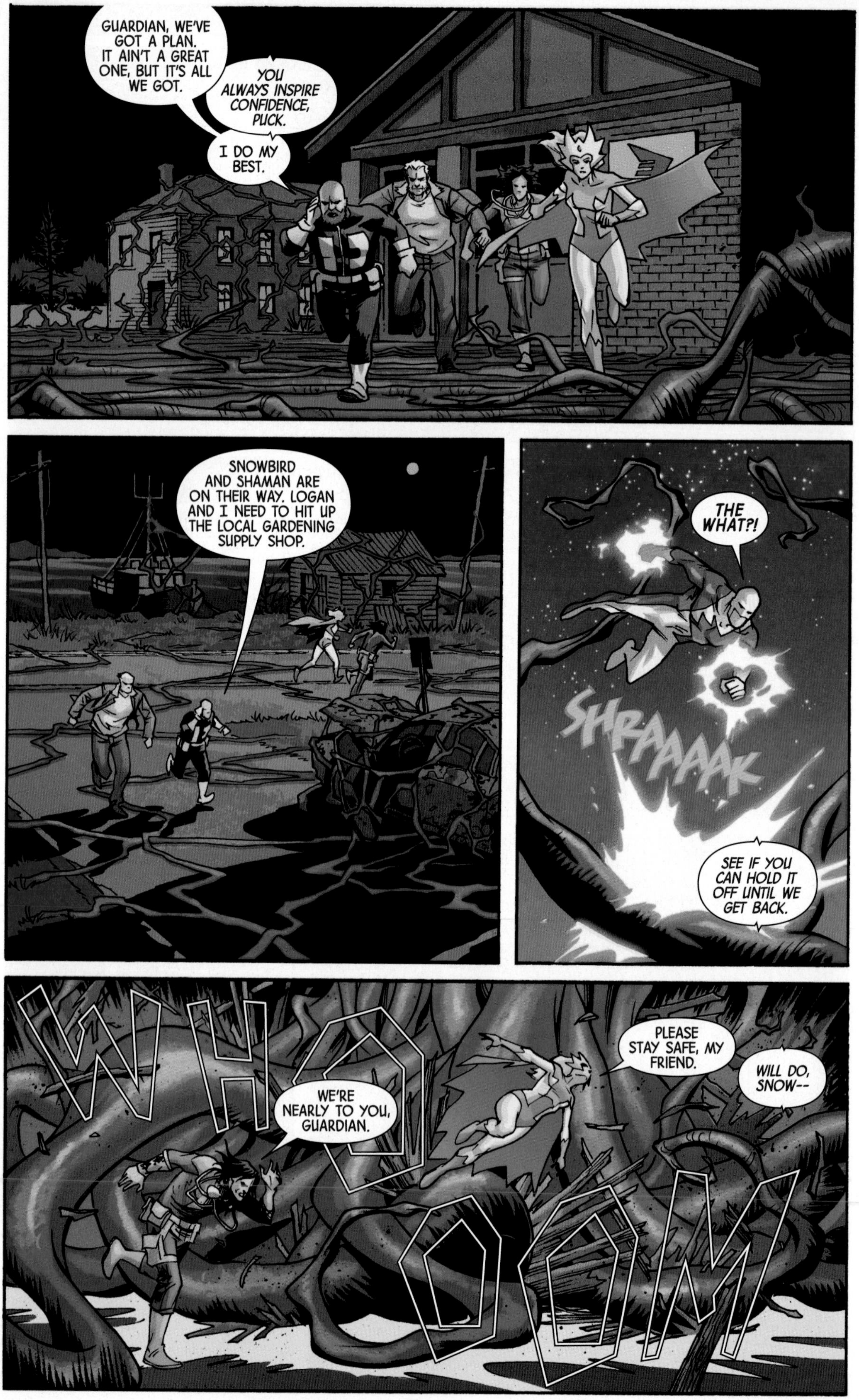
GUARDIAN, WE'VE GOT A PLAN. IT AIN'T A GREAT ONE, BUT IT'S ALL WE GOT.
YOU ALWAYS INSPIRE CONFIDENCE, PUCK.
I DO MY BEST.
SNOWBIRD AND SHAMAN ARE ON THEIR WAY. LOGAN AND I NEED TO HIT UP THE LOCAL GARDENING SUPPLY SHOP.
THE WHAT?!
SHRAAAAK
SEE IF YOU CAN HOLD IT OFF UNTIL WE GET BACK.
WHOOOM
WE'RE NEARLY TO YOU, GUARDIAN.
PLEASE STAY SAFE, MY FRIEND.
WILL DO, SNOW--

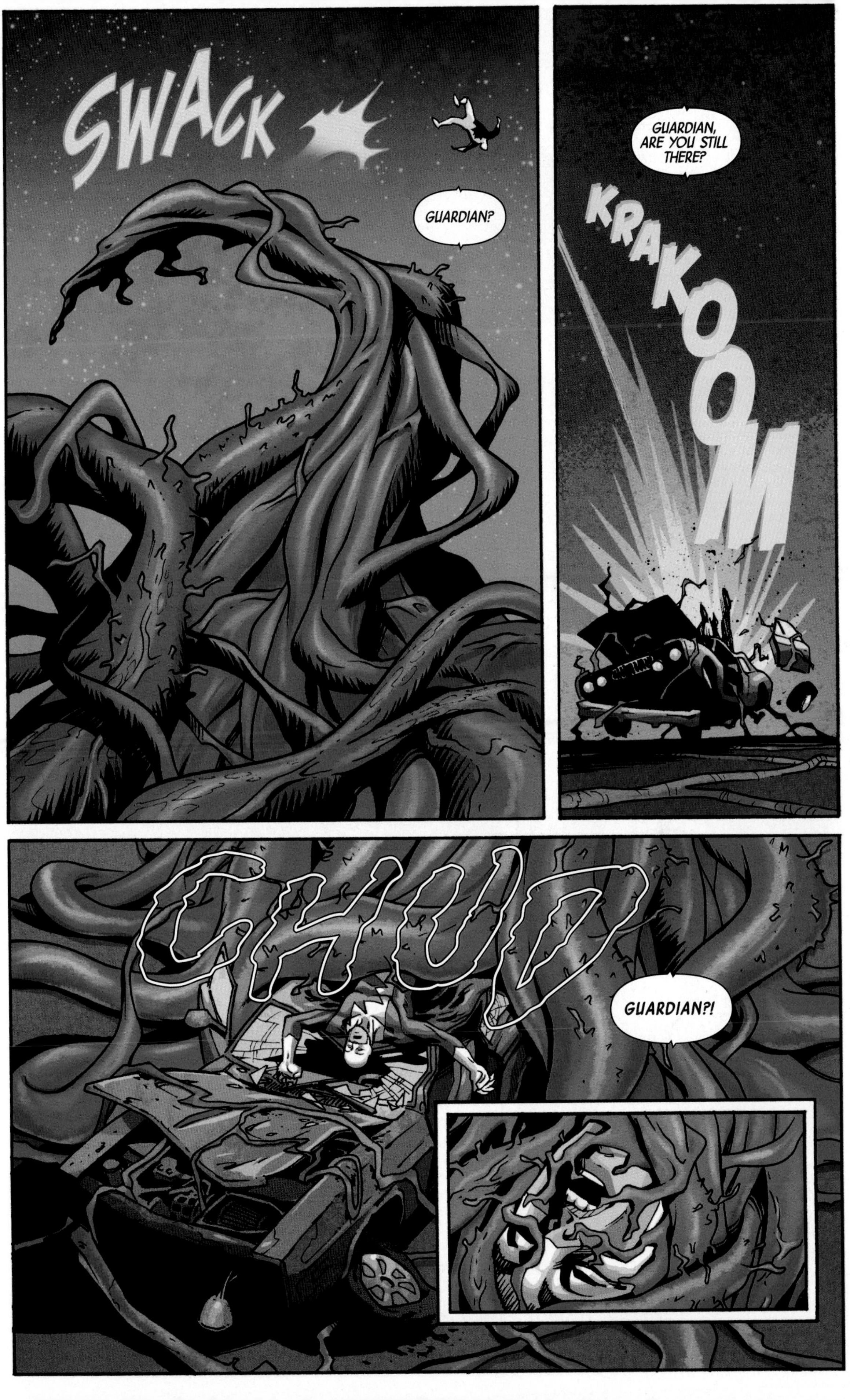
SWACK
GUARDIAN?
GUARDIAN, ARE YOU STILL THERE?
KRAKOOM
CHUD
GUARDIAN?!

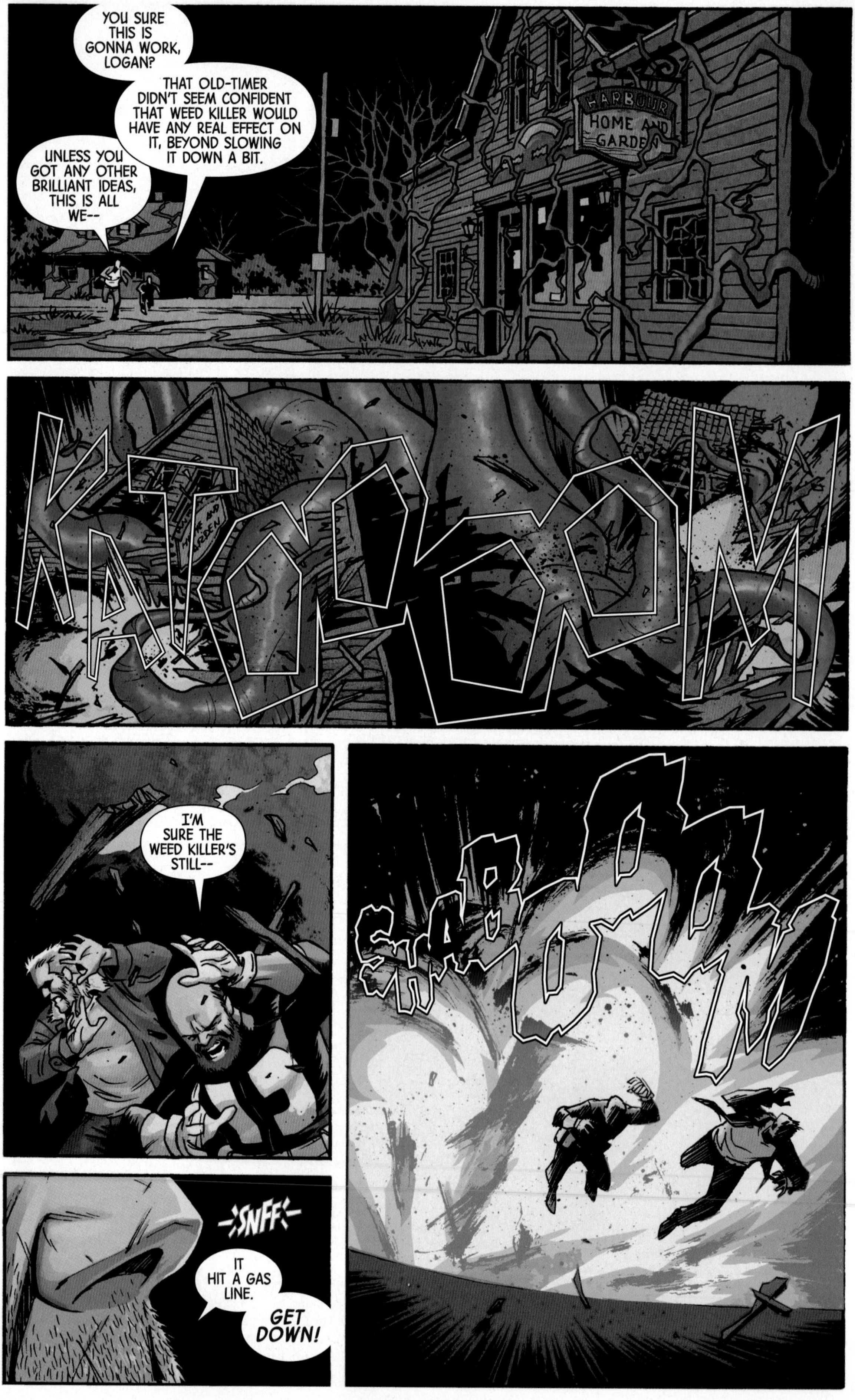

YOU SURE THIS IS GONNA WORK, LOGAN?
THAT OLD-TIMER DIDN'T SEEM CONFIDENT THAT WEED KILLER WOULD HAVE ANY REAL EFFECT ON IT, BEYOND SLOWING IT DOWN A BIT.
UNLESS YOU GOT ANY OTHER BRILLIANT IDEAS, THIS IS ALL WE--
HARBOUR HOME AND GARDEN
KATOOOOOM
I'M SURE THE WEED KILLER'S STILL--
-SNFF-
IT HIT A GAS LINE.
GET DOWN!

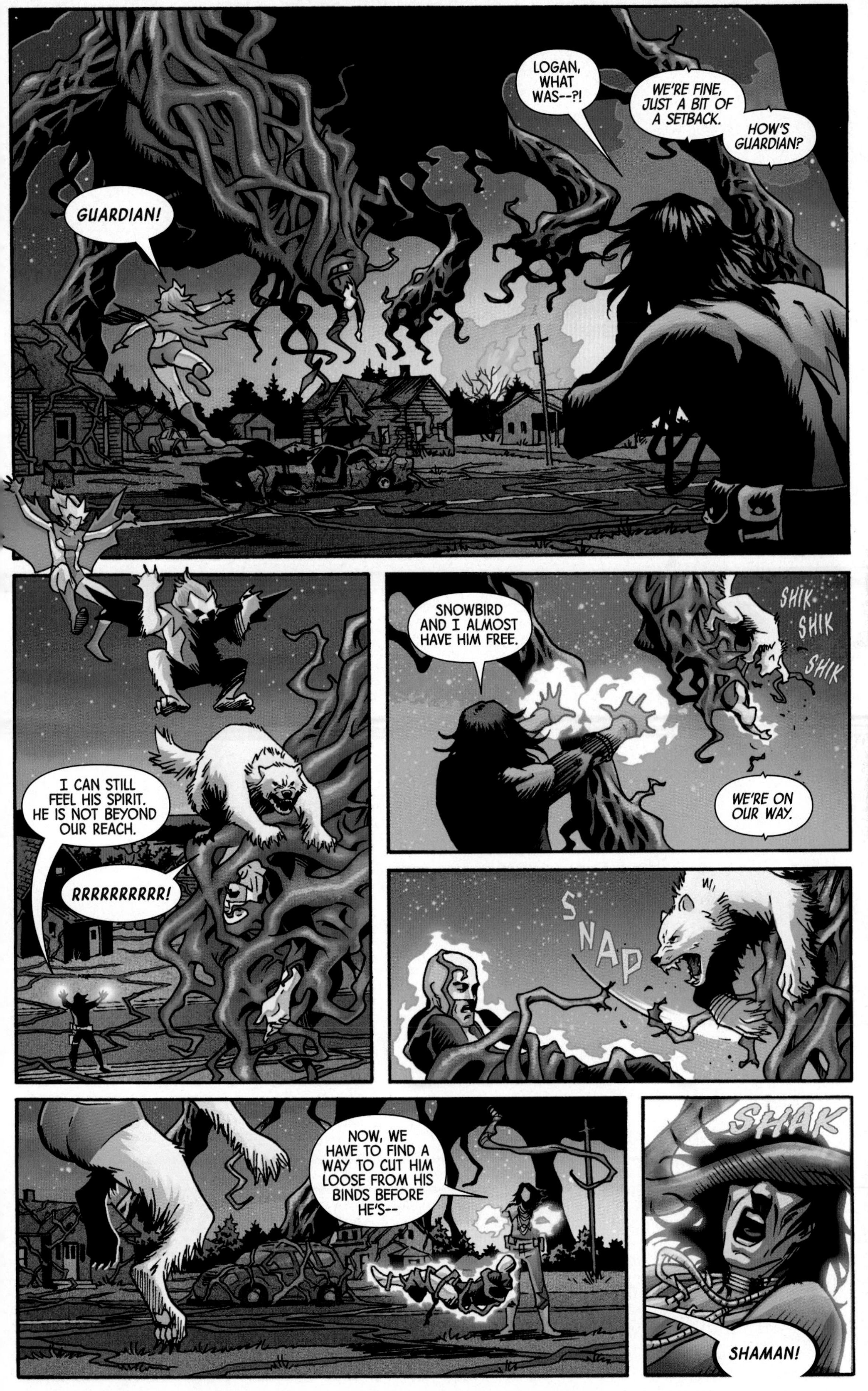

GUARDIAN!
LOGAN, WHAT WAS--?!
WE'RE FINE, JUST A BIT OF A SETBACK.
HOW'S GUARDIAN?
I CAN STILL FEEL HIS SPIRIT. HE IS NOT BEYOND OUR REACH.
RRRRRRRRRR!
SNOWBIRD AND I ALMOST HAVE HIM FREE.
SHIK SHIK SHIK
WE'RE ON OUR WAY.
SNAP
NOW, WE HAVE TO FIND A WAY TO CUT HIM LOOSE FROM HIS BINDS BEFORE HE'S--
SHAK
SHAMAN!

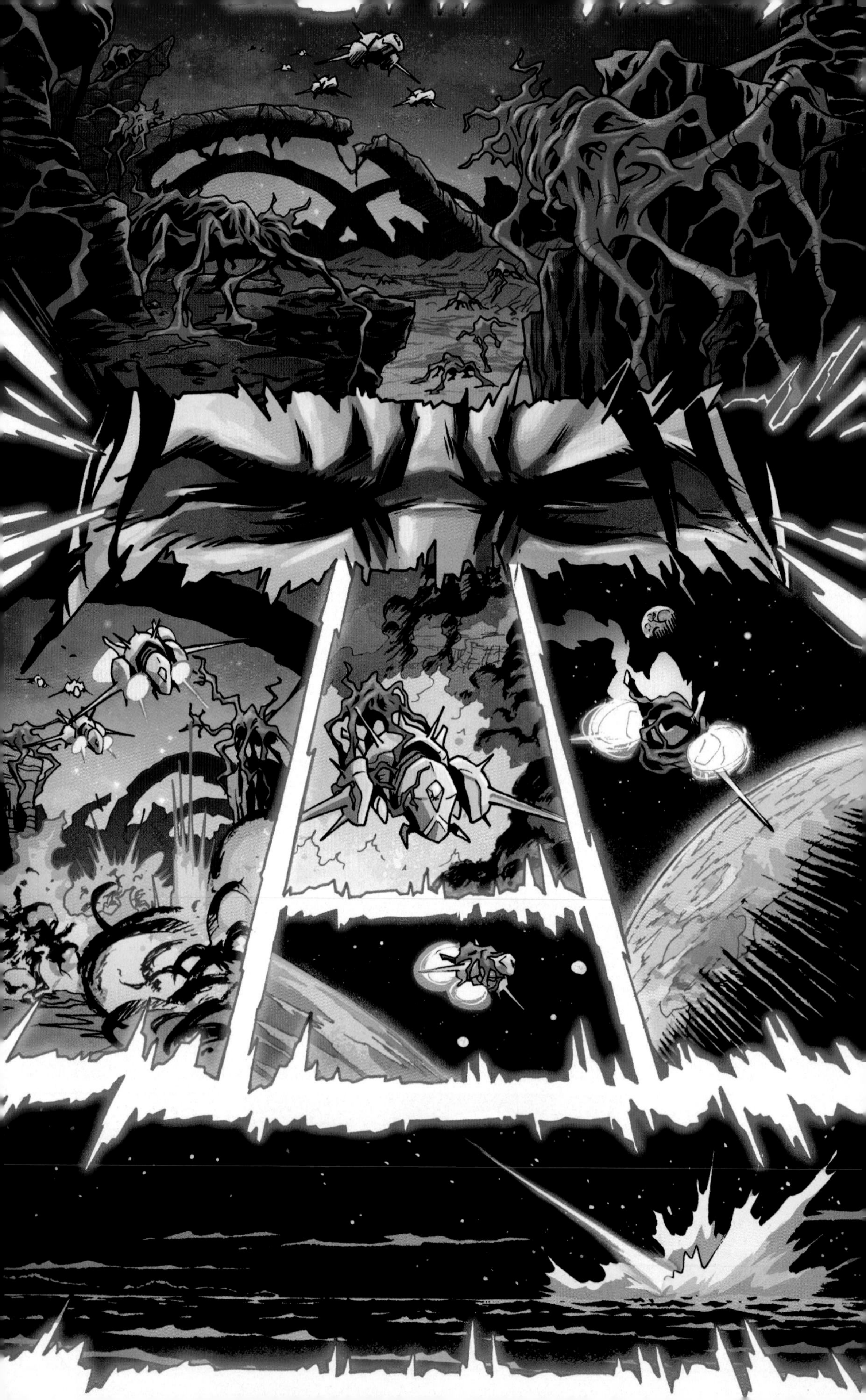

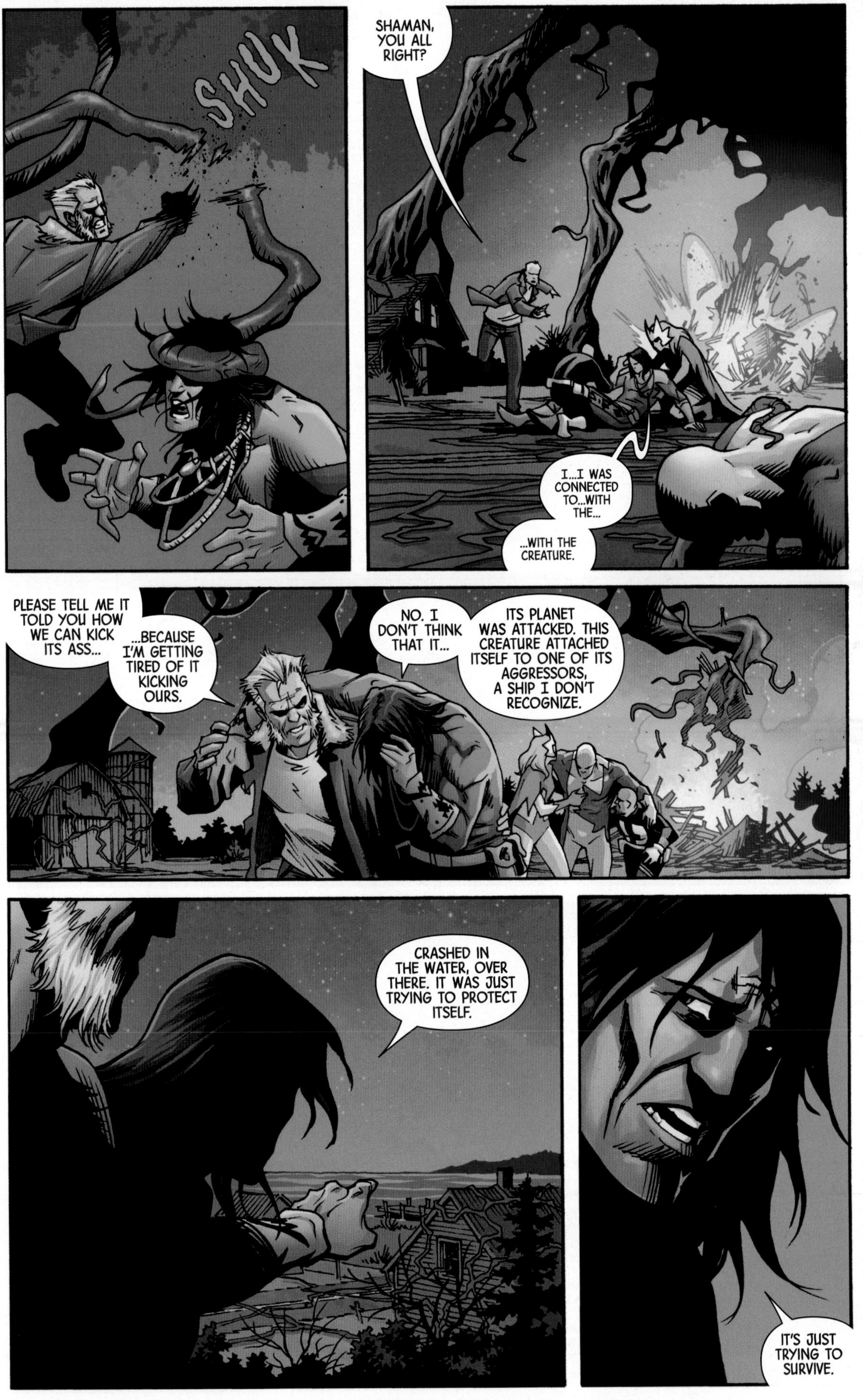
SHUK
SHAMAN, YOU ALL RIGHT?
I...I WAS CONNECTED TO...WITH THE...
...WITH THE CREATURE.
PLEASE TELL ME IT TOLD YOU HOW WE CAN KICK ITS ASS...
...BECAUSE I'M GETTING TIRED OF IT KICKING OURS.
NO. I DON'T THINK THAT IT...
ITS PLANET WAS ATTACKED. THIS CREATURE ATTACHED ITSELF TO ONE OF ITS AGGRESSORS, A SHIP I DON'T RECOGNIZE.
CRASHED IN THE WATER, OVER THERE. IT WAS JUST TRYING TO PROTECT ITSELF.
IT'S JUST TRYING TO SURVIVE.

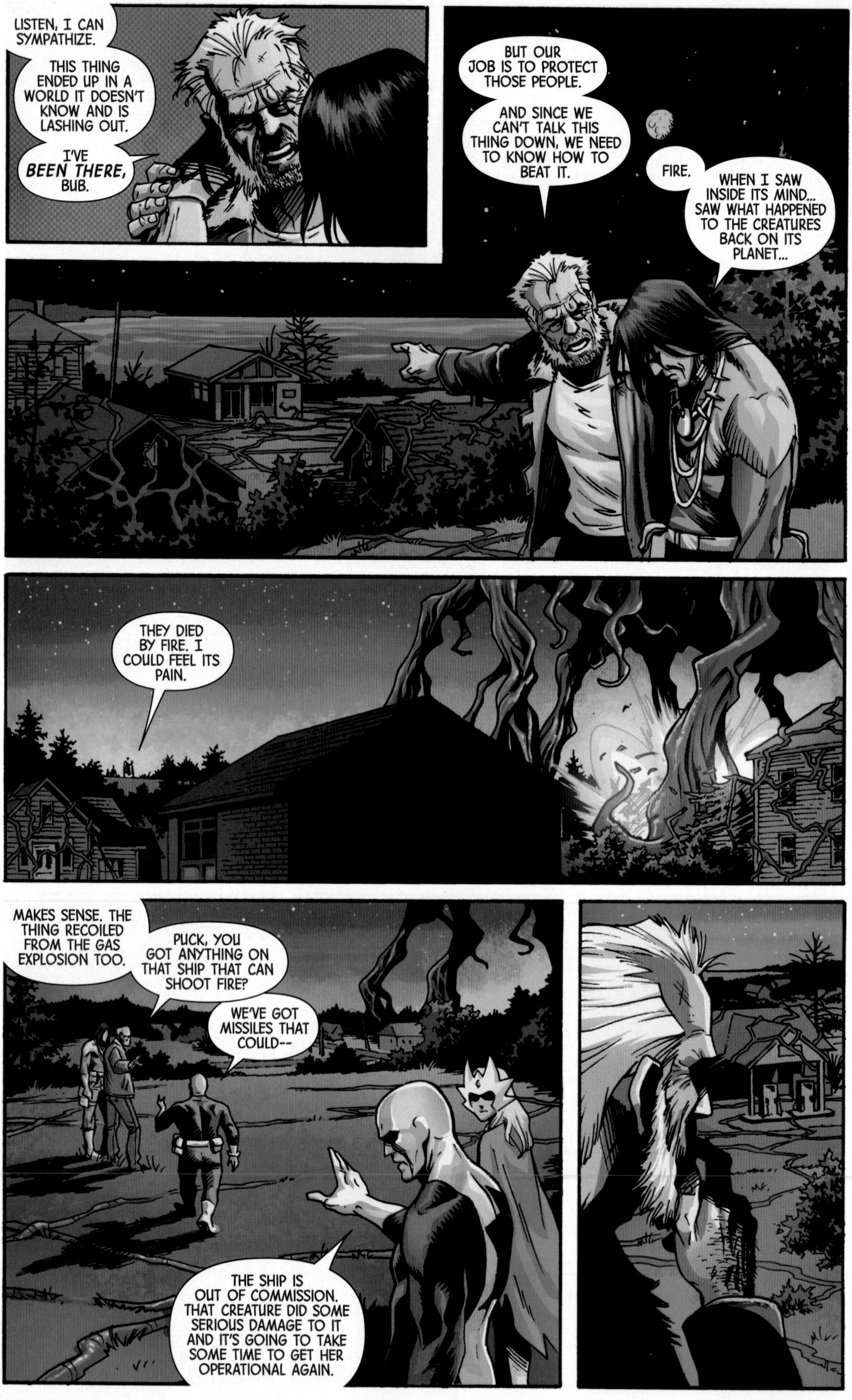
LISTEN, I CAN SYMPATHIZE.
THIS THING ENDED UP IN A WORLD IT DOESN'T KNOW AND IS LASHING OUT.
I'VE *BEEN THERE,* BUB.
BUT OUR JOB IS TO PROTECT THOSE PEOPLE.
AND SINCE WE CAN'T TALK THIS THING DOWN, WE NEED TO KNOW HOW TO BEAT IT.
FIRE.
WHEN I SAW INSIDE ITS MIND... SAW WHAT HAPPENED TO THE CREATURES BACK ON ITS PLANET...
THEY DIED BY FIRE. I COULD FEEL ITS PAIN.
MAKES SENSE. THE THING RECOILED FROM THE GAS EXPLOSION TOO.
PUCK, YOU GOT ANYTHING ON THAT SHIP THAT CAN SHOOT FIRE?
WE'VE GOT MISSILES THAT COULD--
THE SHIP IS OUT OF COMMISSION. THAT CREATURE DID SOME SERIOUS DAMAGE TO IT AND IT'S GOING TO TAKE SOME TIME TO GET HER OPERATIONAL AGAIN.

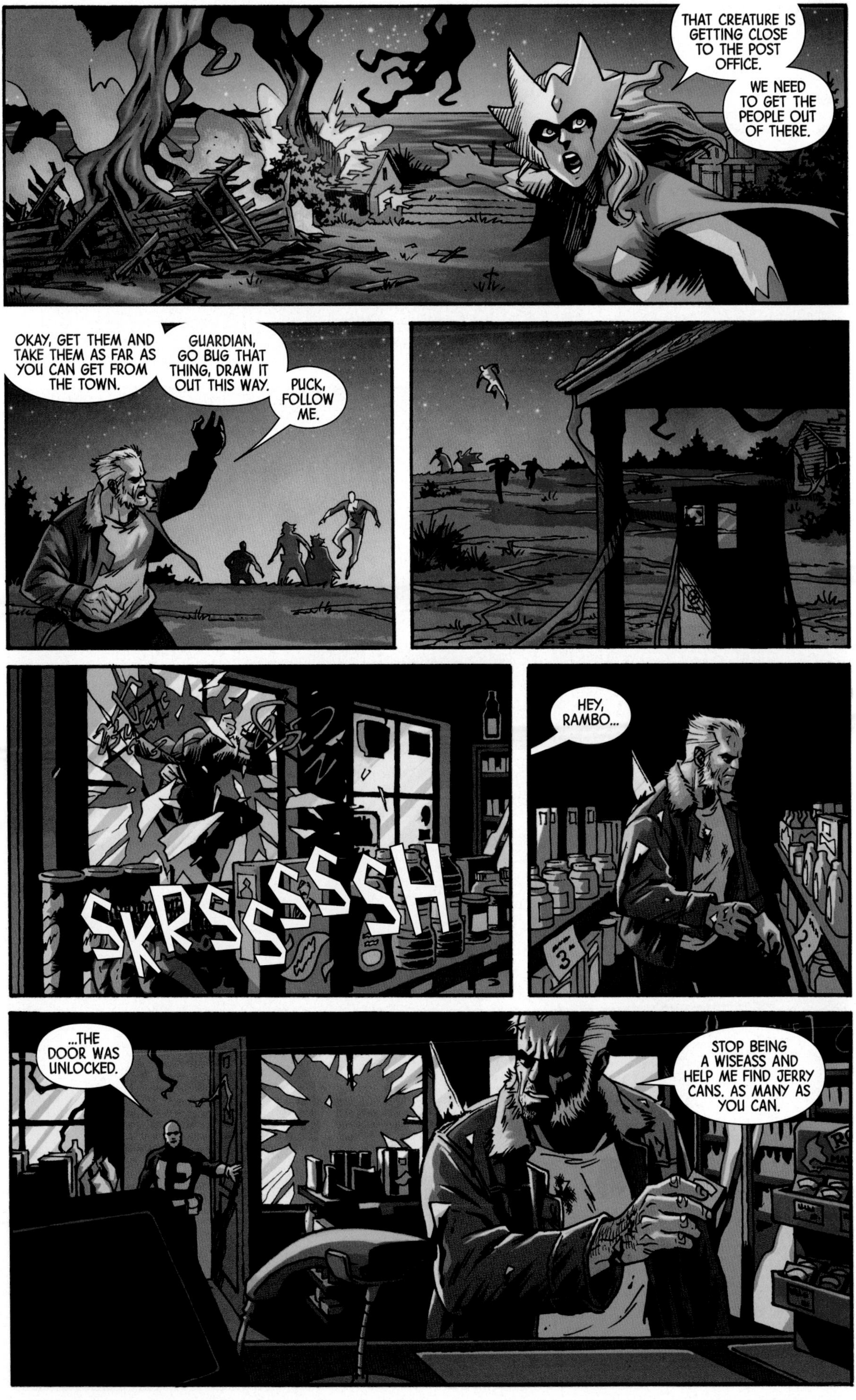
THAT CREATURE IS GETTING CLOSE TO THE POST OFFICE.
WE NEED TO GET THE PEOPLE OUT OF THERE.
OKAY, GET THEM AND TAKE THEM AS FAR AS YOU CAN GET FROM THE TOWN.
GUARDIAN, GO BUG THAT THING, DRAW IT OUT THIS WAY.
PUCK, FOLLOW ME.
SKRSSSSSH
HEY, RAMBO...
...THE DOOR WAS UNLOCKED.
STOP BEING A WISEASS AND HELP ME FIND JERRY CANS. AS MANY AS YOU CAN.

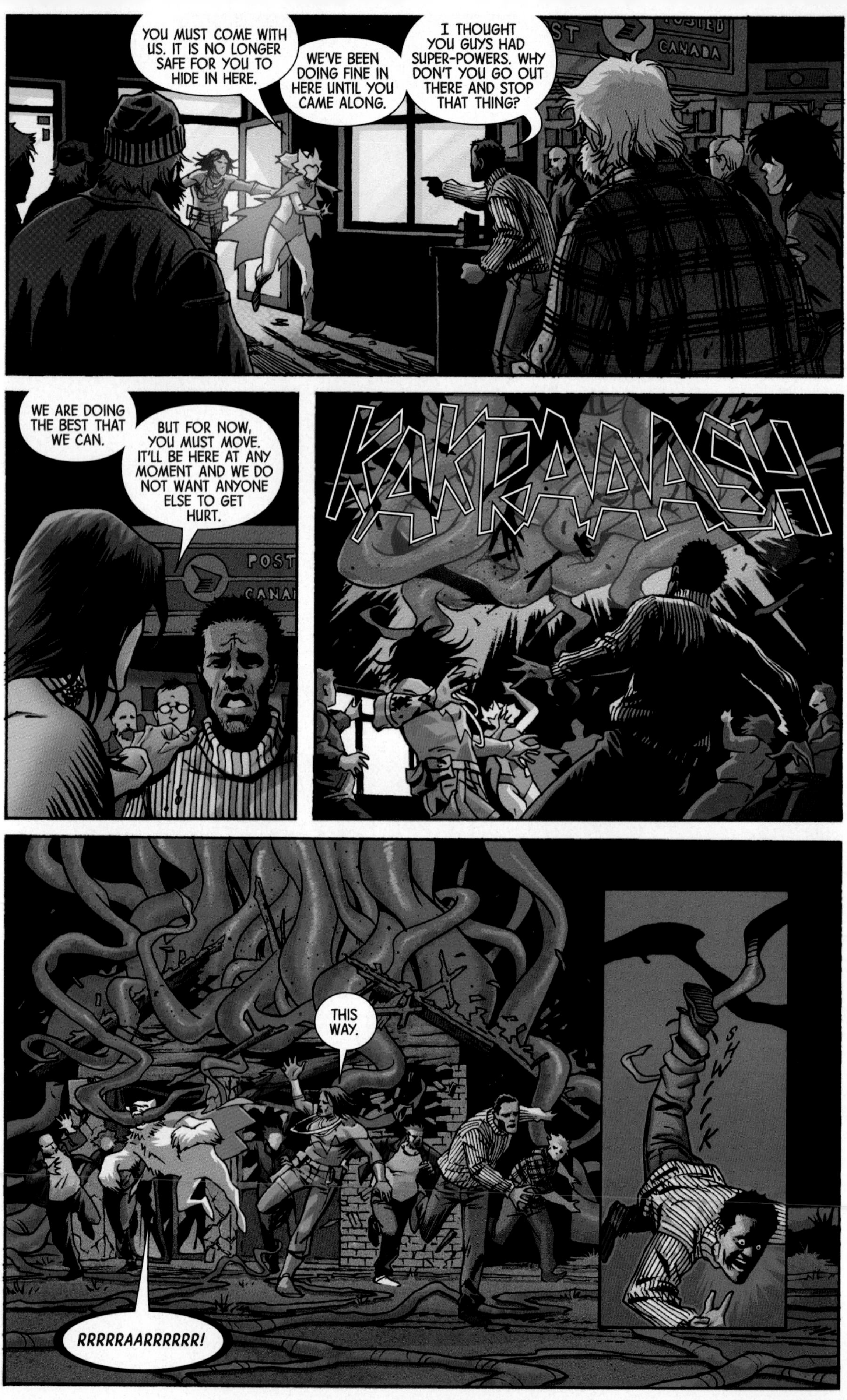
YOU MUST COME WITH US. IT IS NO LONGER SAFE FOR YOU TO HIDE IN HERE.
WE'VE BEEN DOING FINE IN HERE UNTIL YOU CAME ALONG.
I THOUGHT YOU GUYS HAD SUPER-POWERS. WHY DON'T YOU GO OUT THERE AND STOP THAT THING?
POSTED
CANADA
WE ARE DOING THE BEST THAT WE CAN.
BUT FOR NOW, YOU MUST MOVE. IT'LL BE HERE AT ANY MOMENT AND WE DO NOT WANT ANYONE ELSE TO GET HURT.
KAKRAAASH
THIS WAY.
SHWIIIK
RRRRRAARRRRRR!

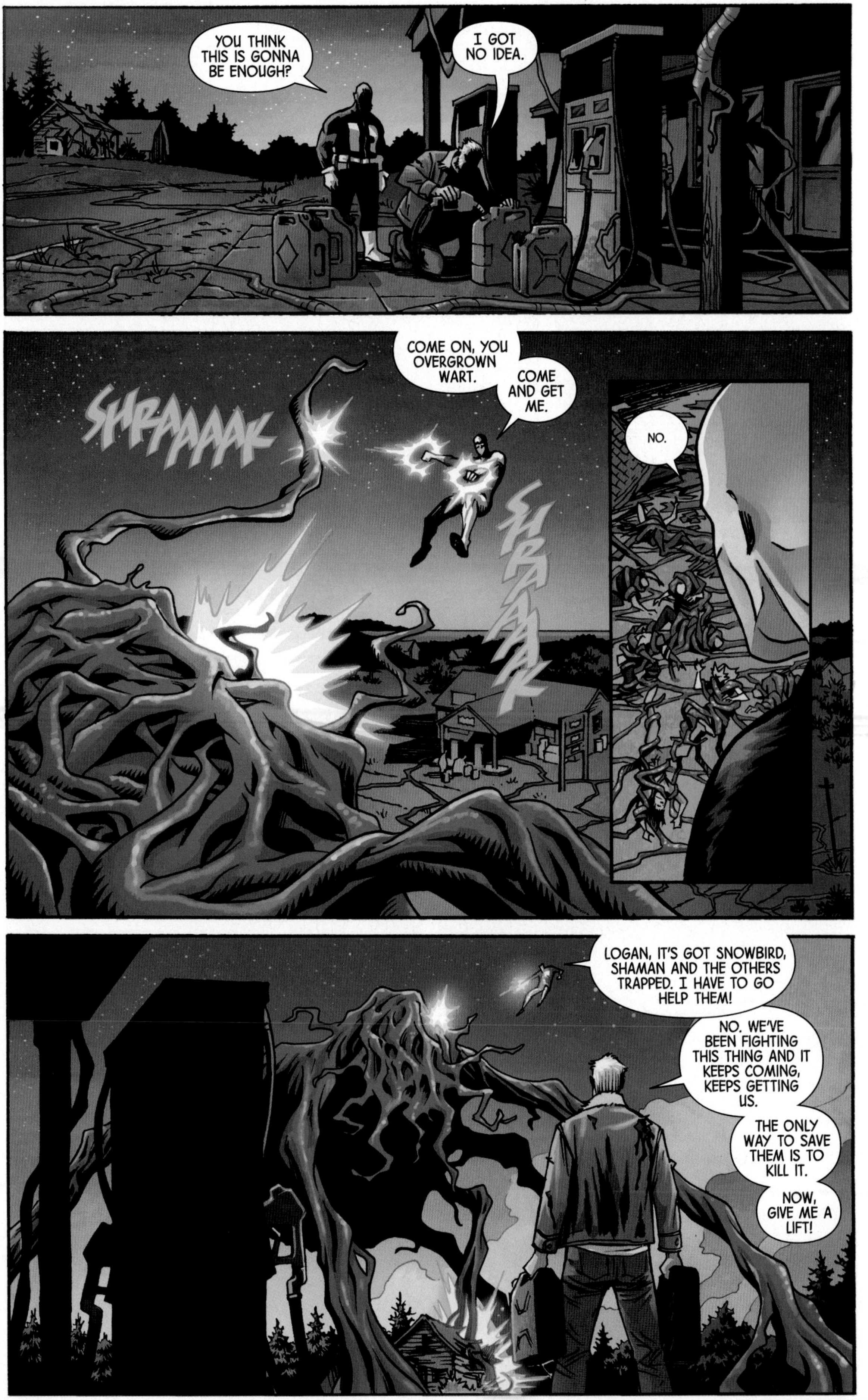
YOU THINK THIS IS GONNA BE ENOUGH?
I GOT NO IDEA.
COME ON, YOU OVERGROWN WART.
COME AND GET ME.
SHRAAAAK
SHRAAAAK
NO.
LOGAN, IT'S GOT SNOWBIRD, SHAMAN AND THE OTHERS TRAPPED. I HAVE TO GO HELP THEM!
NO. WE'VE BEEN FIGHTING THIS THING AND IT KEEPS COMING, KEEPS GETTING US.
THE ONLY WAY TO SAVE THEM IS TO KILL IT.
NOW, GIVE ME A LIFT!

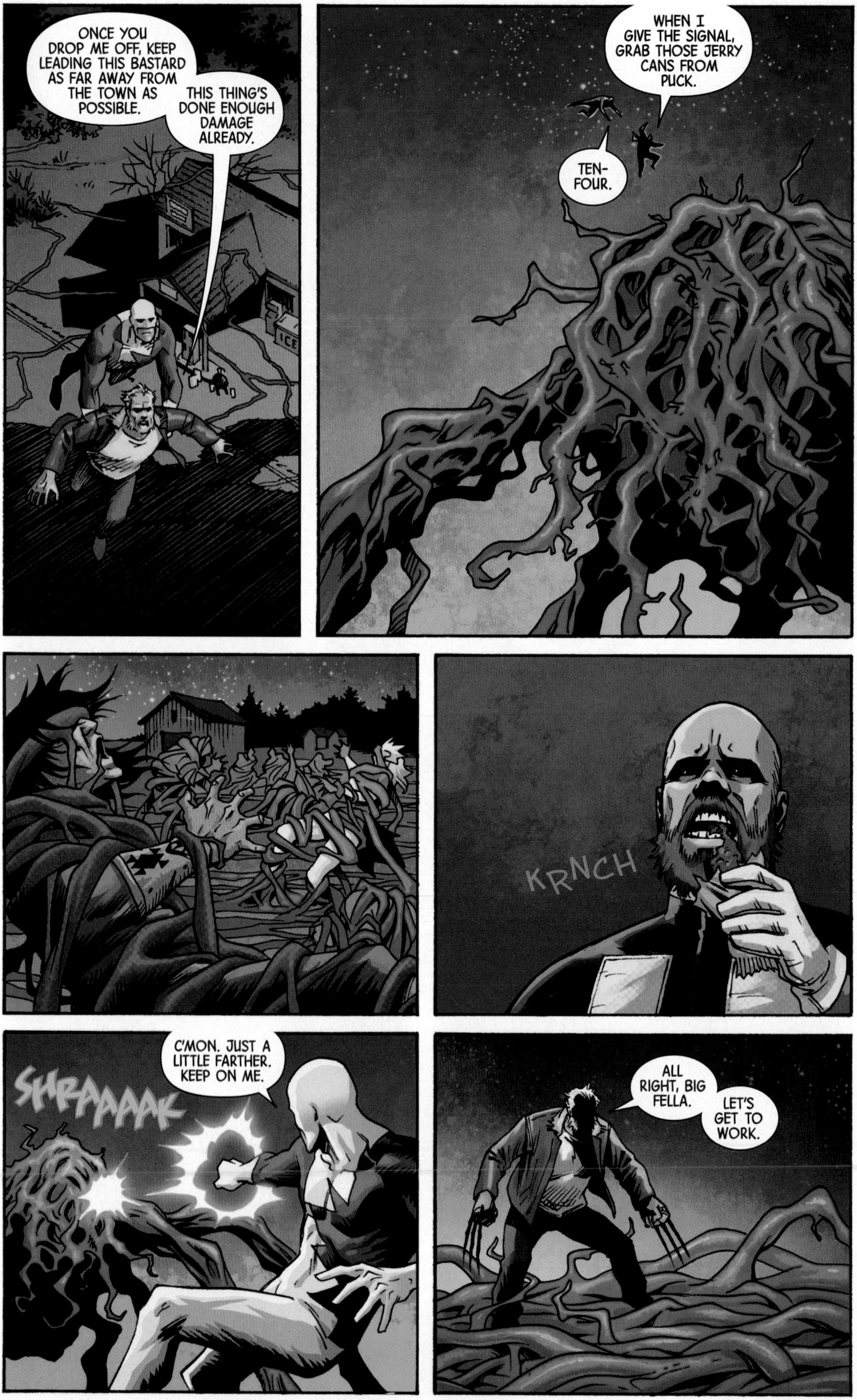
ONCE YOU DROP ME OFF, KEEP LEADING THIS BASTARD AS FAR AWAY FROM THE TOWN AS POSSIBLE.
THIS THING'S DONE ENOUGH DAMAGE ALREADY.
ICE
WHEN I GIVE THE SIGNAL, GRAB THOSE JERRY CANS FROM PUCK.
TEN-FOUR.
KRNCH
C'MON. JUST A LITTLE FARTHER. KEEP ON ME.
SHRAAAAK
ALL RIGHT, BIG FELLA.
LET'S GET TO WORK.

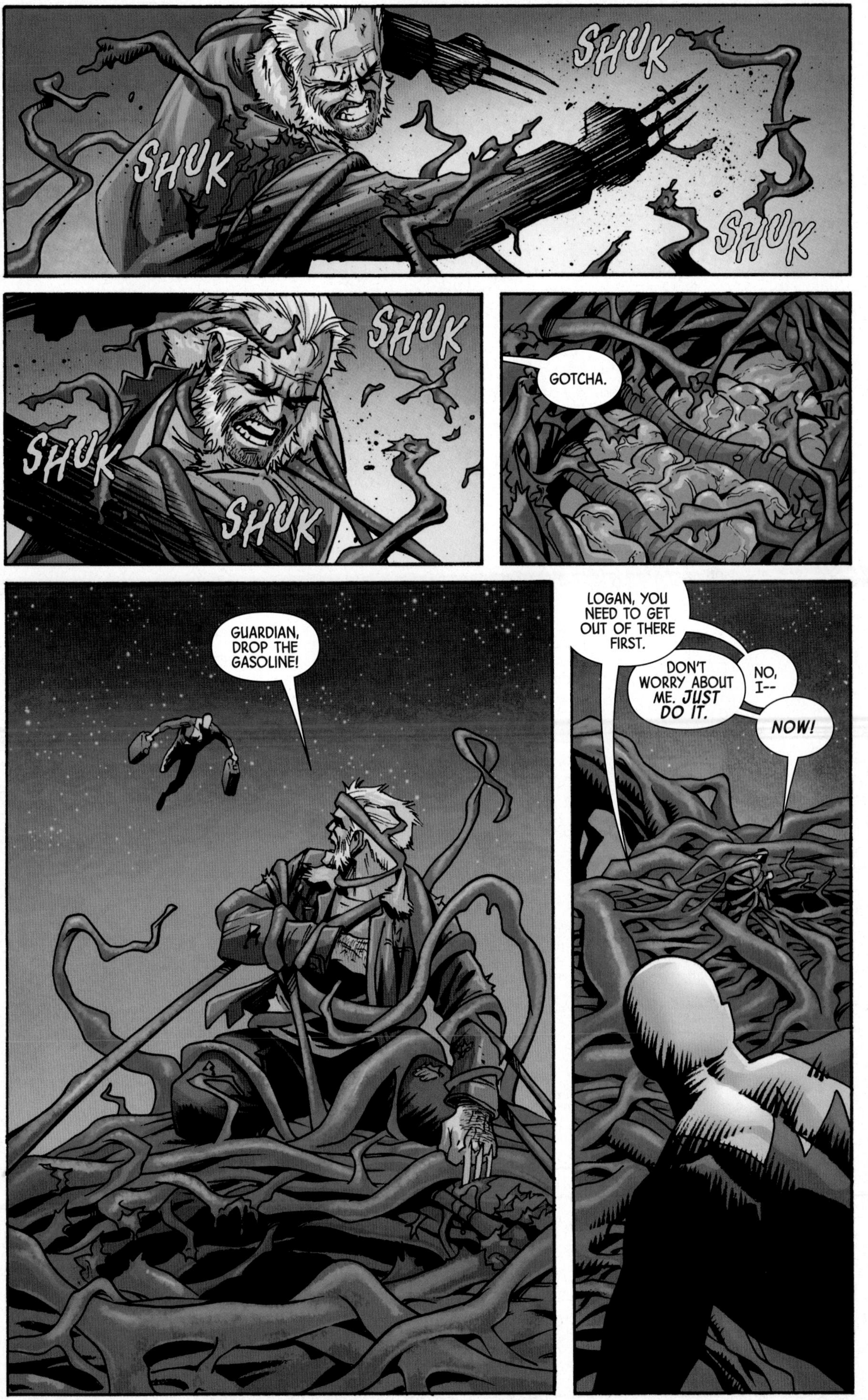
SHUK
SHUK
SHUK
SHUK
SHUK
SHUK
GOTCHA.
GUARDIAN, DROP THE GASOLINE!
LOGAN, YOU NEED TO GET OUT OF THERE FIRST.
NO, I--
DON'T WORRY ABOUT ME. JUST DO IT.
NOW!

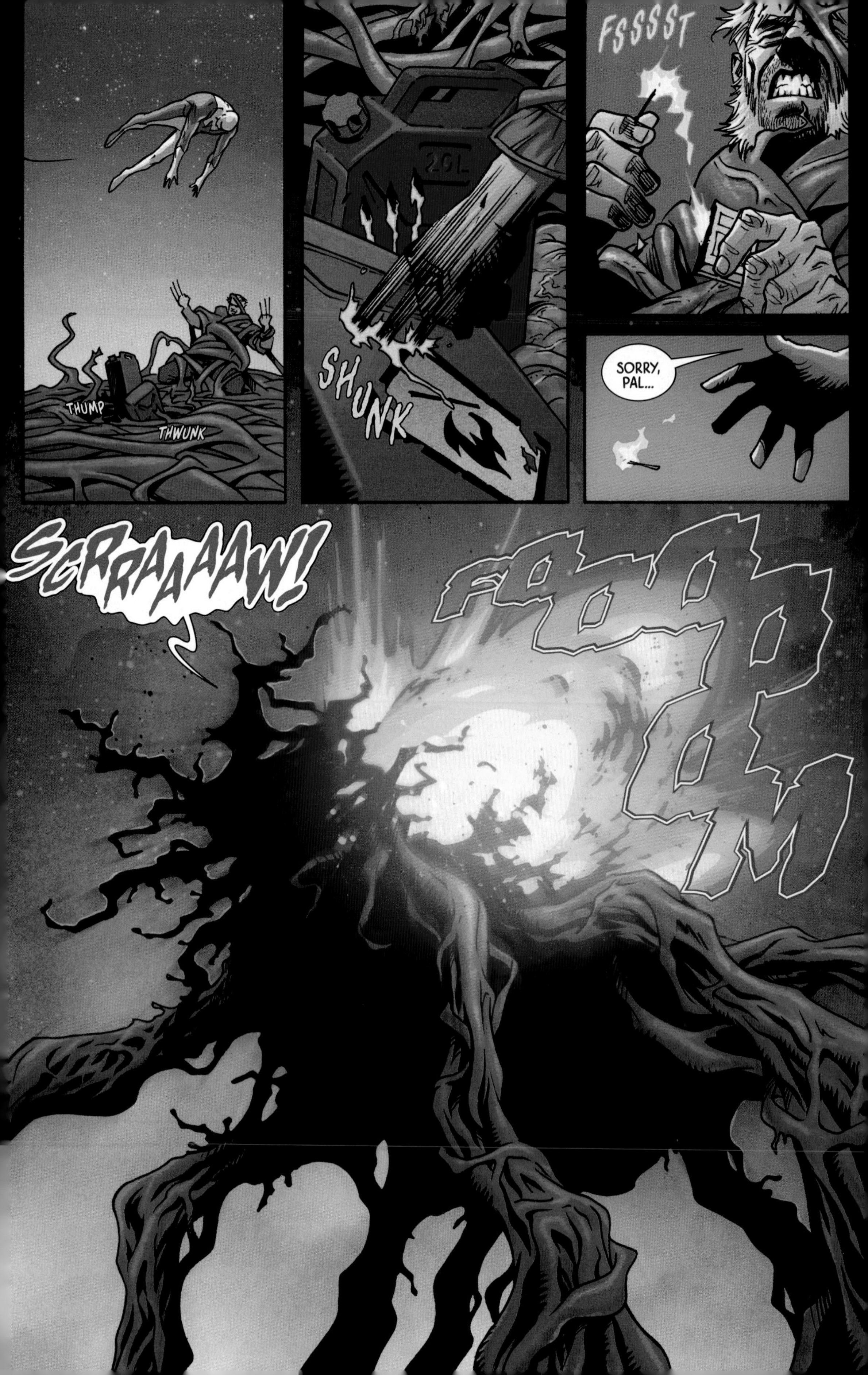
THUMP
THWUNK
SHUNK
FSSSST
SORRY, PAL...
SCRRAAAAW!
FOOOOM

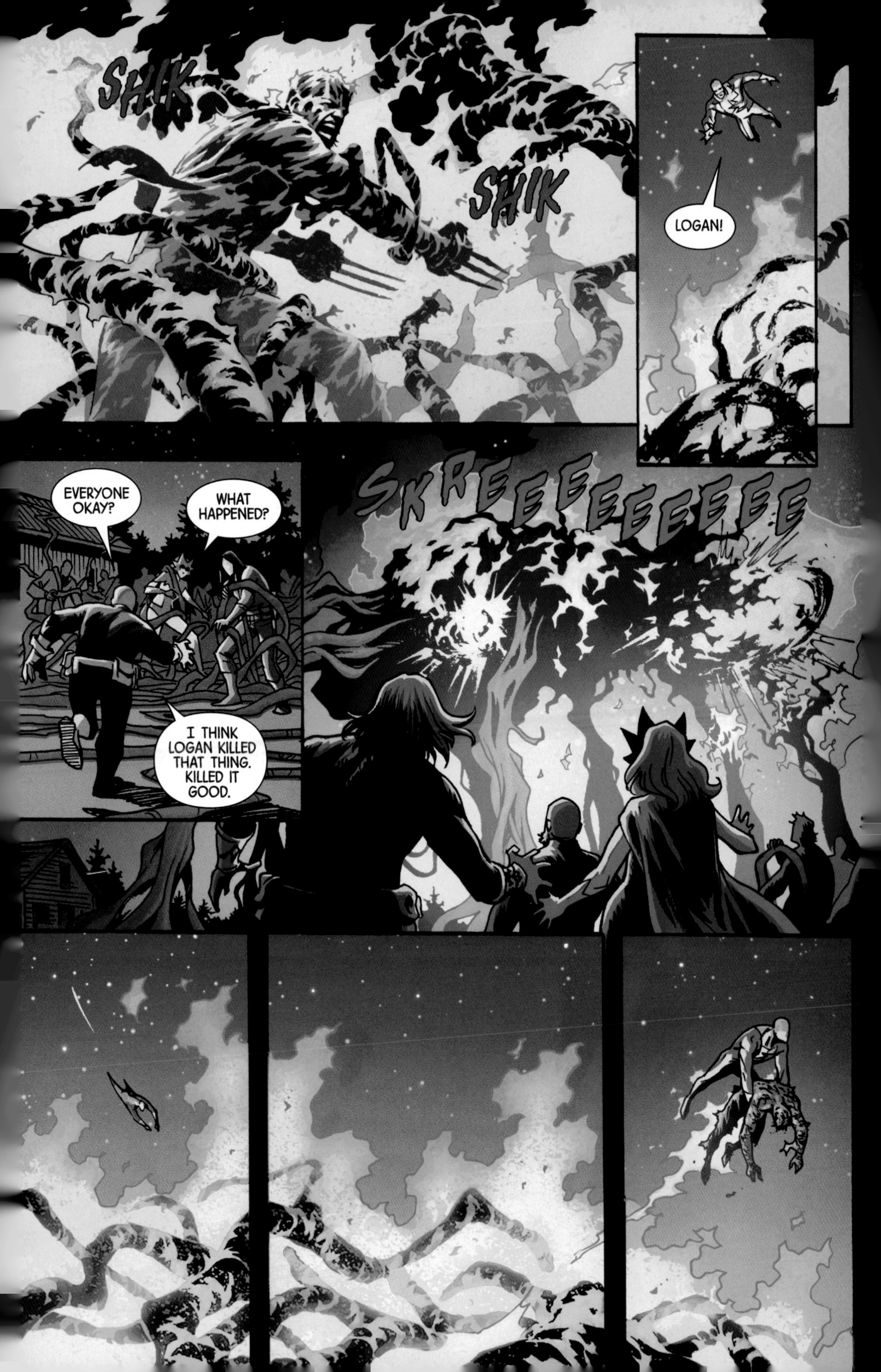
SHIK
SHIK
LOGAN!
EVERYONE OKAY?
WHAT HAPPENED?
I THINK LOGAN KILLED THAT THING. KILLED IT GOOD.
SKREEEEEEEEEEE

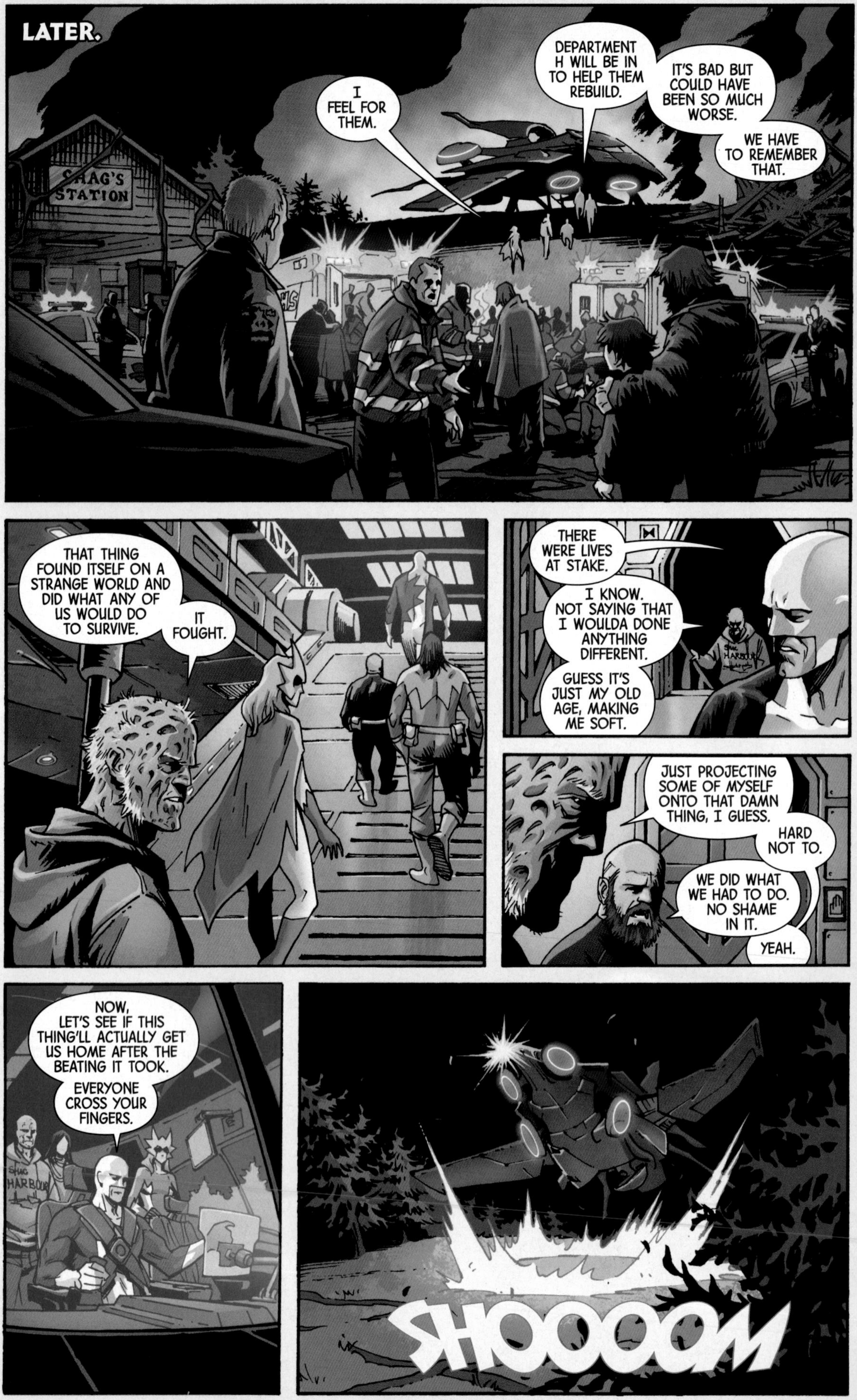

LATER.
I FEEL FOR THEM.
DEPARTMENT H WILL BE IN TO HELP THEM REBUILD.
IT'S BAD BUT COULD HAVE BEEN SO MUCH WORSE.
WE HAVE TO REMEMBER THAT.
SHAG'S STATION
THAT THING FOUND ITSELF ON A STRANGE WORLD AND DID WHAT ANY OF US WOULD DO TO SURVIVE.
IT FOUGHT.
THERE WERE LIVES AT STAKE.
I KNOW. NOT SAYING THAT I WOULDA DONE ANYTHING DIFFERENT.
GUESS IT'S JUST MY OLD AGE, MAKING ME SOFT.
JUST PROJECTING SOME OF MYSELF ONTO THAT DAMN THING, I GUESS.
HARD NOT TO.
WE DID WHAT WE HAD TO DO. NO SHAME IN IT.
YEAH.
NOW, LET'S SEE IF THIS THING'LL ACTUALLY GET US HOME AFTER THE BEATING IT TOOK.
EVERYONE CROSS YOUR FINGERS.
SHOOOOM

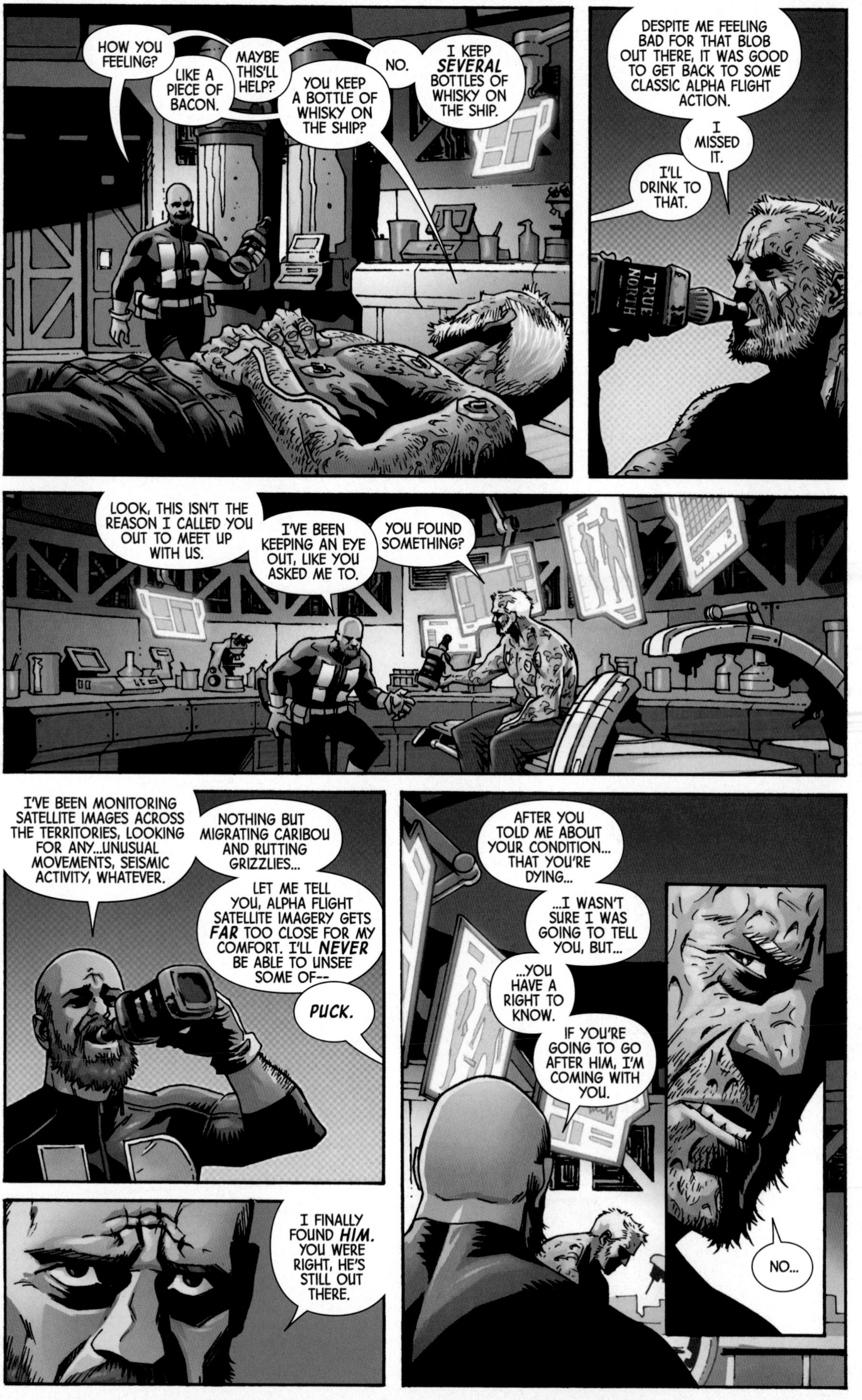
HOW YOU FEELING?
LIKE A PIECE OF BACON.
MAYBE THIS'LL HELP?
YOU KEEP A BOTTLE OF WHISKY ON THE SHIP?
NO.
I KEEP SEVERAL BOTTLES OF WHISKY ON THE SHIP.
DESPITE ME FEELING BAD FOR THAT BLOB OUT THERE, IT WAS GOOD TO GET BACK TO SOME CLASSIC ALPHA FLIGHT ACTION.
I MISSED IT.
I'LL DRINK TO THAT.
TRUE NORTH
LOOK, THIS ISN'T THE REASON I CALLED YOU OUT TO MEET UP WITH US.
I'VE BEEN KEEPING AN EYE OUT, LIKE YOU ASKED ME TO.
YOU FOUND SOMETHING?
I'VE BEEN MONITORING SATELLITE IMAGES ACROSS THE TERRITORIES, LOOKING FOR ANY...UNUSUAL MOVEMENTS, SEISMIC ACTIVITY, WHATEVER.
NOTHING BUT MIGRATING CARIBOU AND RUTTING GRIZZLIES...
LET ME TELL YOU, ALPHA FLIGHT SATELLITE IMAGERY GETS FAR TOO CLOSE FOR MY COMFORT. I'LL NEVER BE ABLE TO UNSEE SOME OF--
PUCK.
I FINALLY FOUND HIM. YOU WERE RIGHT, HE'S STILL OUT THERE.
AFTER YOU TOLD ME ABOUT YOUR CONDITION... THAT YOU'RE DYING...
...I WASN'T SURE I WAS GOING TO TELL YOU, BUT...
...YOU HAVE A RIGHT TO KNOW.
IF YOU'RE GOING TO GO AFTER HIM, I'M COMING WITH YOU.
NO...

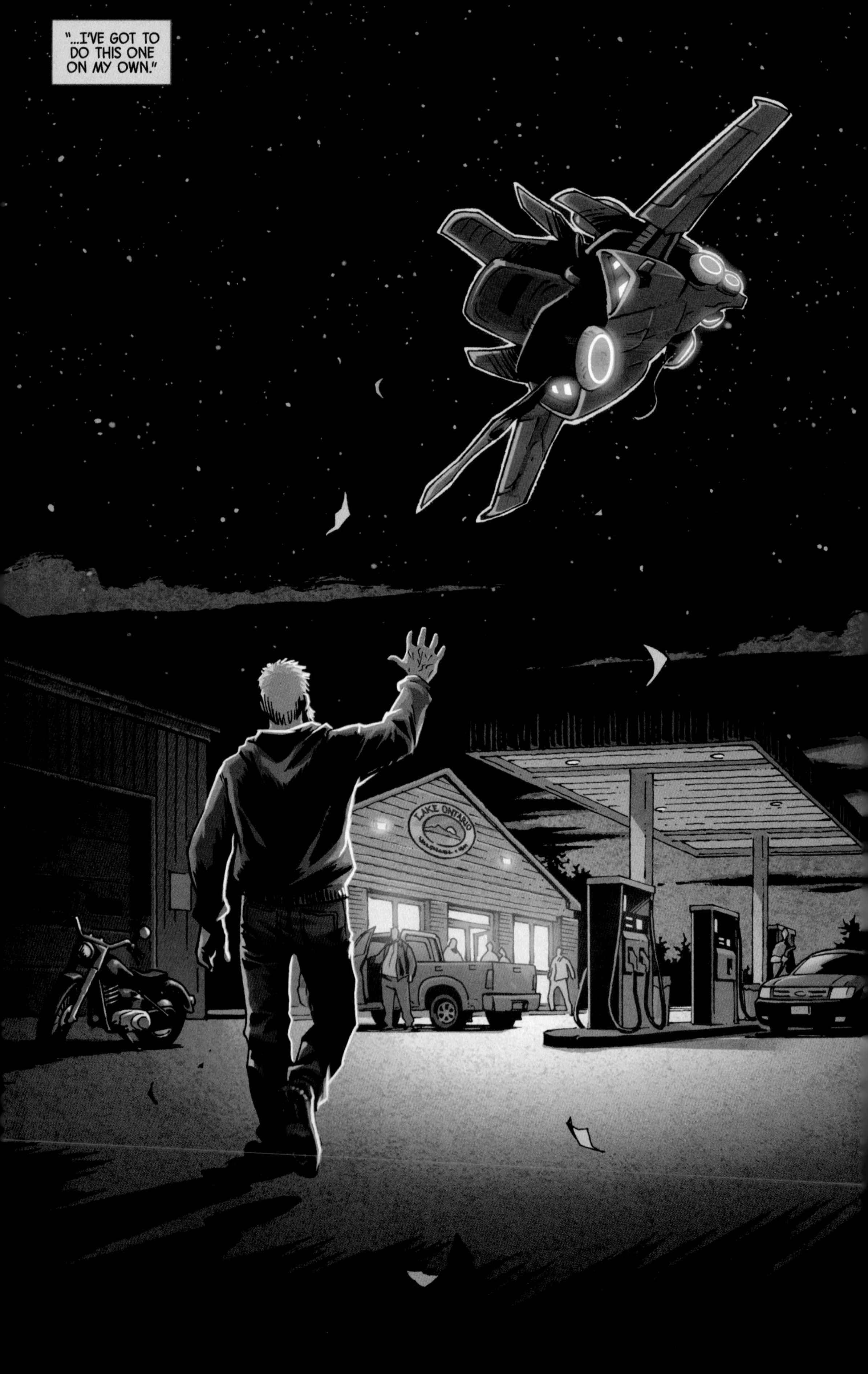
"...I'VE GOT TO DO THIS ONE ON MY OWN."
LAKE ONTARIO

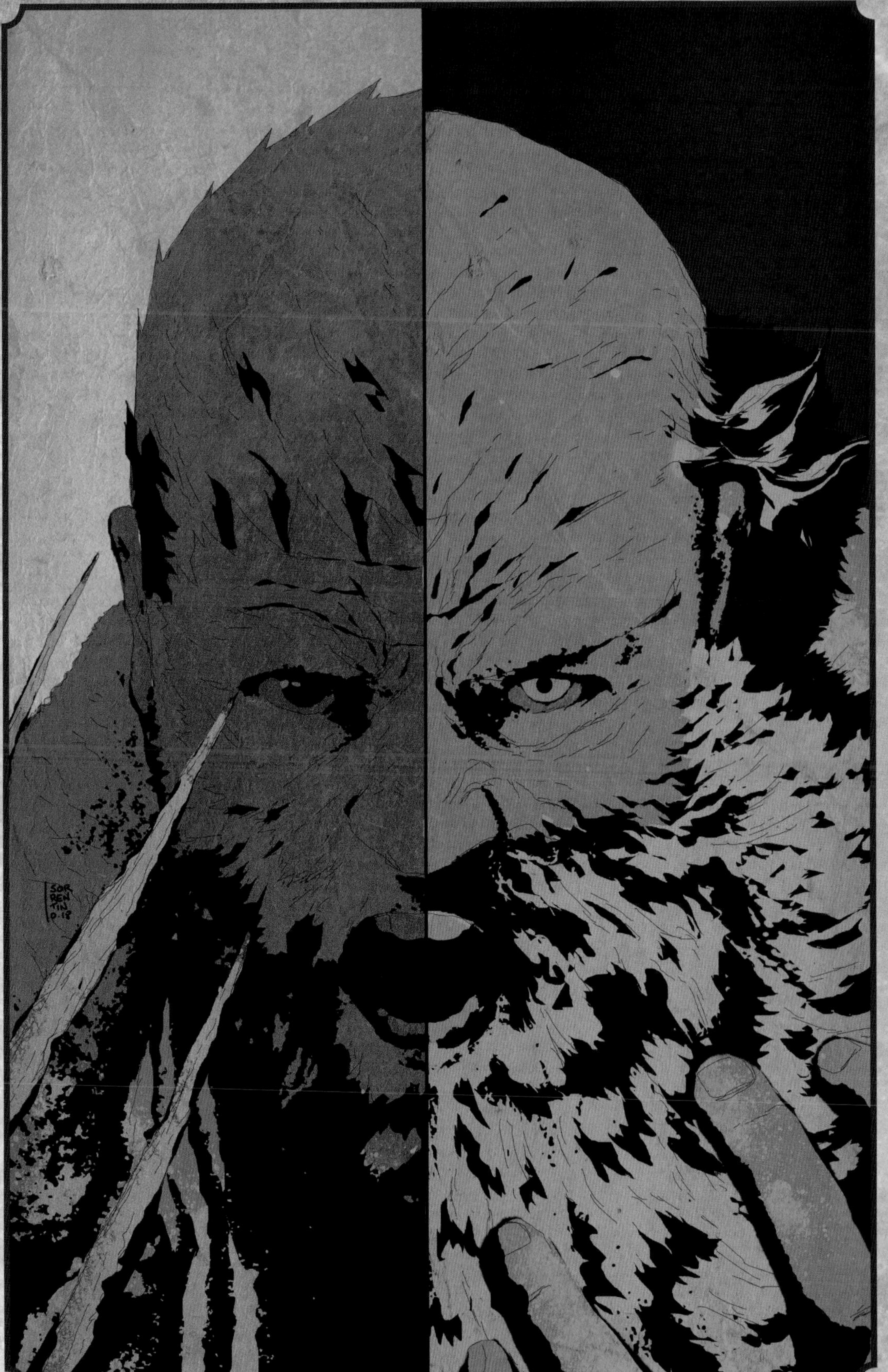

48

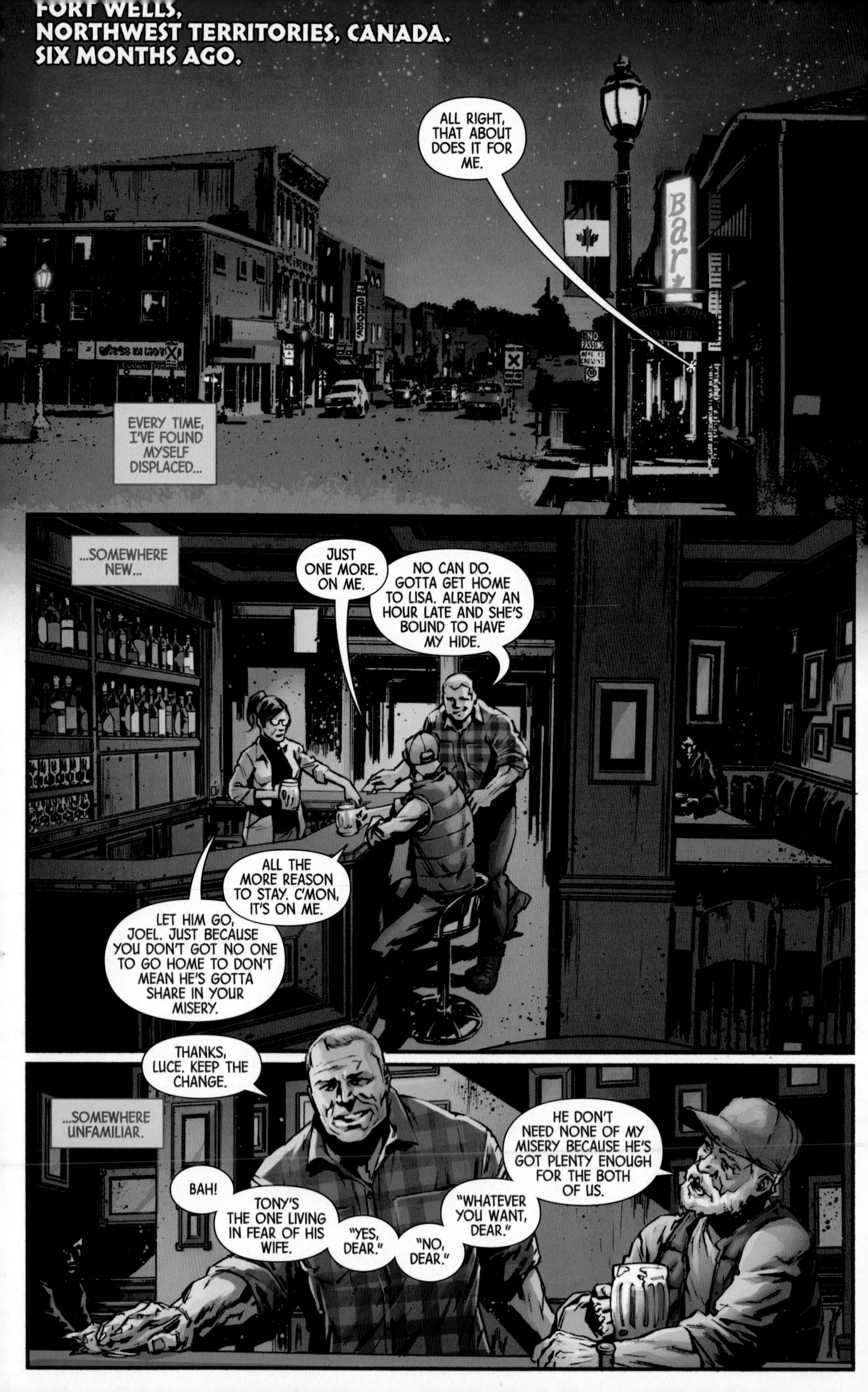
FORT WELLS,
NORTHWEST TERRITORIES, CANADA.
SIX MONTHS AGO.
ALL RIGHT, THAT ABOUT DOES IT FOR ME.
Bar
EVERY TIME, I'VE FOUND MYSELF DISPLACED...
...SOMEWHERE NEW...
JUST ONE MORE. ON ME.
NO CAN DO. GOTTA GET HOME TO LISA. ALREADY AN HOUR LATE AND SHE'S BOUND TO HAVE MY HIDE.
ALL THE MORE REASON TO STAY. C'MON, IT'S ON ME.
LET HIM GO, JOEL. JUST BECAUSE YOU DON'T GOT NO ONE TO GO HOME TO DON'T MEAN HE'S GOTTA SHARE IN YOUR MISERY.
THANKS, LUCE. KEEP THE CHANGE.
...SOMEWHERE UNFAMILIAR.
HE DON'T NEED NONE OF MY MISERY BECAUSE HE'S GOT PLENTY ENOUGH FOR THE BOTH OF US.
BAH!
TONY'S THE ONE LIVING IN FEAR OF HIS WIFE.
"YES, DEAR."
"NO, DEAR."
"WHATEVER YOU WANT, DEAR."

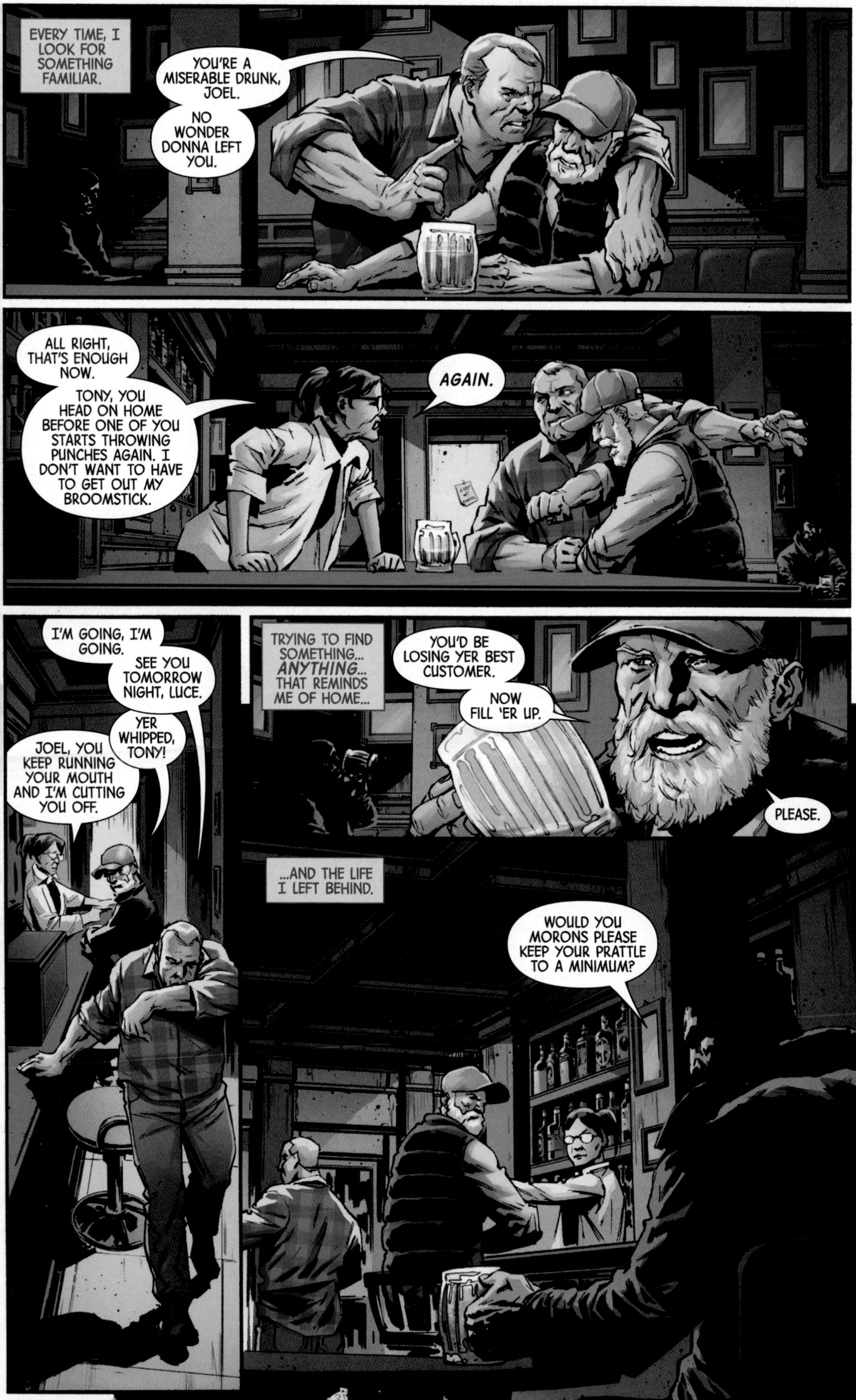
EVERY TIME, I LOOK FOR SOMETHING FAMILIAR.
YOU'RE A MISERABLE DRUNK, JOEL.
NO WONDER DONNA LEFT YOU.
ALL RIGHT, THAT'S ENOUGH NOW.
TONY, YOU HEAD ON HOME BEFORE ONE OF YOU STARTS THROWING PUNCHES AGAIN. I DON'T WANT TO HAVE TO GET OUT MY BROOMSTICK.
AGAIN.
I'M GOING, I'M GOING.
SEE YOU TOMORROW NIGHT, LUCE.
YER WHIPPED, TONY!
JOEL, YOU KEEP RUNNING YOUR MOUTH AND I'M CUTTING YOU OFF.
TRYING TO FIND SOMETHING... ANYTHING... THAT REMINDS ME OF HOME...
YOU'D BE LOSING YER BEST CUSTOMER.
NOW FILL 'ER UP.
PLEASE.
...AND THE LIFE I LEFT BEHIND.
WOULD YOU MORONS PLEASE KEEP YOUR PRATTLE TO A MINIMUM?

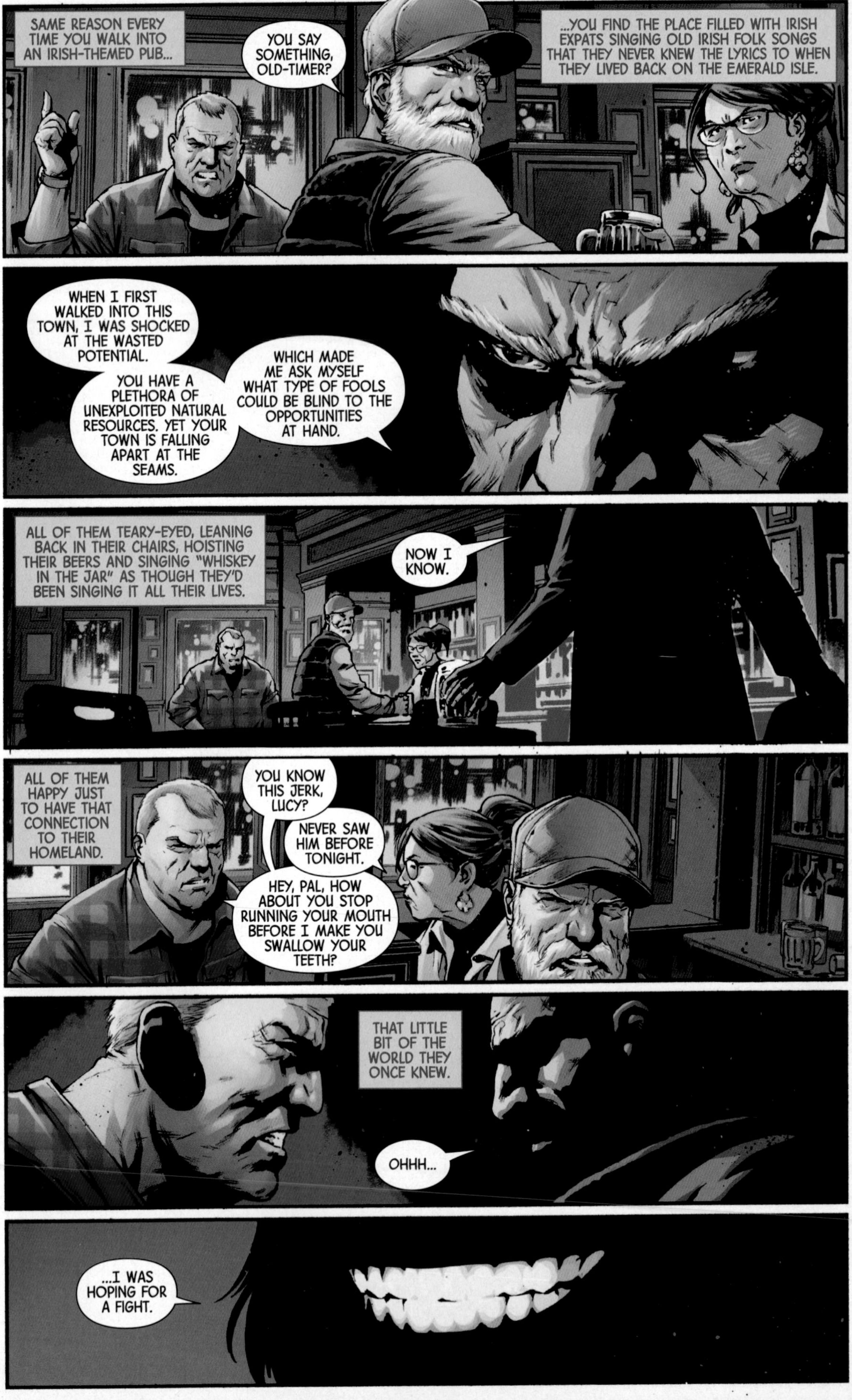
SAME REASON EVERY TIME YOU WALK INTO AN IRISH-THEMED PUB...
YOU SAY SOMETHING, OLD-TIMER?
...YOU FIND THE PLACE FILLED WITH IRISH EXPATS SINGING OLD IRISH FOLK SONGS THAT THEY NEVER KNEW THE LYRICS TO WHEN THEY LIVED BACK ON THE EMERALD ISLE.
WHEN I FIRST WALKED INTO THIS TOWN, I WAS SHOCKED AT THE WASTED POTENTIAL.
YOU HAVE A PLETHORA OF UNEXPLOITED NATURAL RESOURCES. YET YOUR TOWN IS FALLING APART AT THE SEAMS.
WHICH MADE ME ASK MYSELF WHAT TYPE OF FOOLS COULD BE BLIND TO THE OPPORTUNITIES AT HAND.
ALL OF THEM TEARY-EYED, LEANING BACK IN THEIR CHAIRS, HOISTING THEIR BEERS AND SINGING "WHISKEY IN THE JAR" AS THOUGH THEY'D BEEN SINGING IT ALL THEIR LIVES.
NOW I KNOW.
ALL OF THEM HAPPY JUST TO HAVE THAT CONNECTION TO THEIR HOMELAND.
YOU KNOW THIS JERK, LUCY?
NEVER SAW HIM BEFORE TONIGHT.
HEY, PAL, HOW ABOUT YOU STOP RUNNING YOUR MOUTH BEFORE I MAKE YOU SWALLOW YOUR TEETH?
THAT LITTLE BIT OF THE WORLD THEY ONCE KNEW.
OHHH...
...I WAS HOPING FOR A FIGHT.

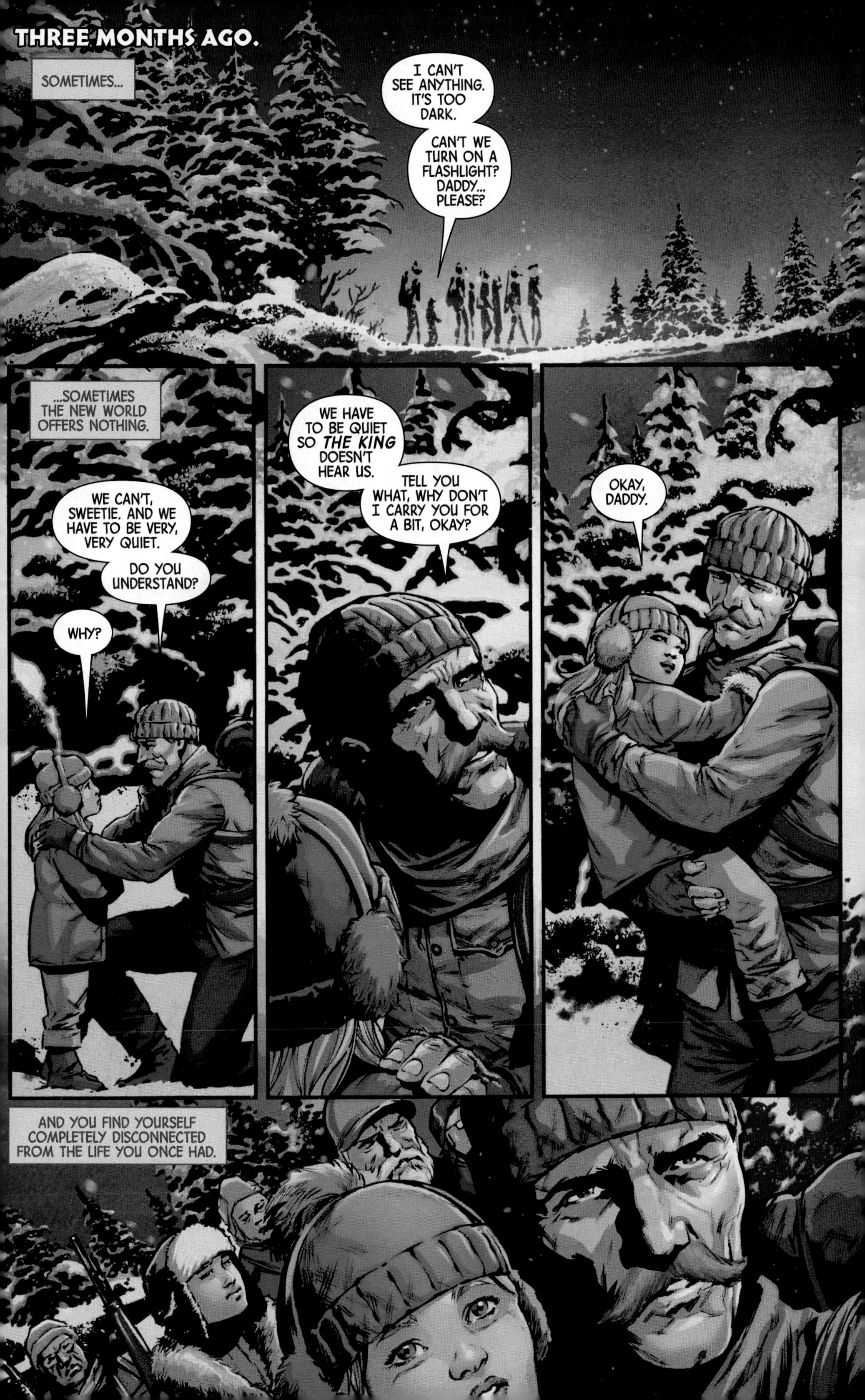
THREE MONTHS AGO.
SOMETIMES...
I CAN'T SEE ANYTHING. IT'S TOO DARK.
CAN'T WE TURN ON A FLASHLIGHT? DADDY... PLEASE?
...SOMETIMES THE NEW WORLD OFFERS NOTHING.
WE CAN'T, SWEETIE. AND WE HAVE TO BE VERY, VERY QUIET.
DO YOU UNDERSTAND?
WHY?
WE HAVE TO BE QUIET SO THE KING DOESN'T HEAR US.
TELL YOU WHAT, WHY DON'T I CARRY YOU FOR A BIT, OKAY?
OKAY, DADDY.
AND YOU FIND YOURSELF COMPLETELY DISCONNECTED FROM THE LIFE YOU ONCE HAD.

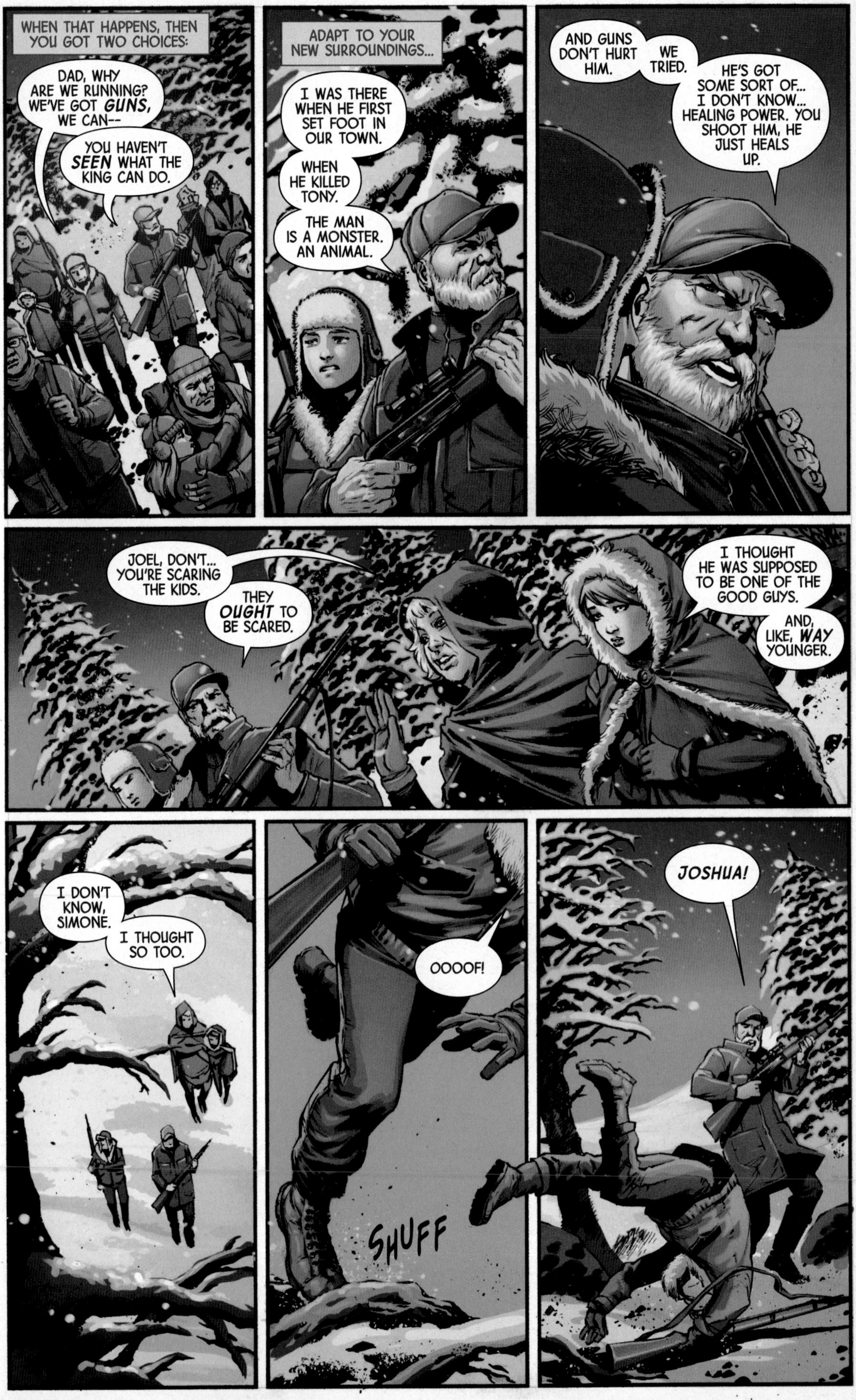
WHEN THAT HAPPENS, THEN YOU GOT TWO CHOICES:
DAD, WHY ARE WE RUNNING? WE'VE GOT GUNS, WE CAN--
YOU HAVEN'T SEEN WHAT THE KING CAN DO.
ADAPT TO YOUR NEW SURROUNDINGS...
I WAS THERE WHEN HE FIRST SET FOOT IN OUR TOWN.
WHEN HE KILLED TONY.
THE MAN IS A MONSTER. AN ANIMAL.
AND GUNS DON'T HURT HIM.
WE TRIED.
HE'S GOT SOME SORT OF... I DON'T KNOW... HEALING POWER. YOU SHOOT HIM, HE JUST HEALS UP.
JOEL, DON'T... YOU'RE SCARING THE KIDS.
THEY OUGHT TO BE SCARED.
I THOUGHT HE WAS SUPPOSED TO BE ONE OF THE GOOD GUYS.
AND, LIKE, WAY YOUNGER.
I DON'T KNOW, SIMONE.
I THOUGHT SO TOO.
OOOOF!
SHUFF
JOSHUA!

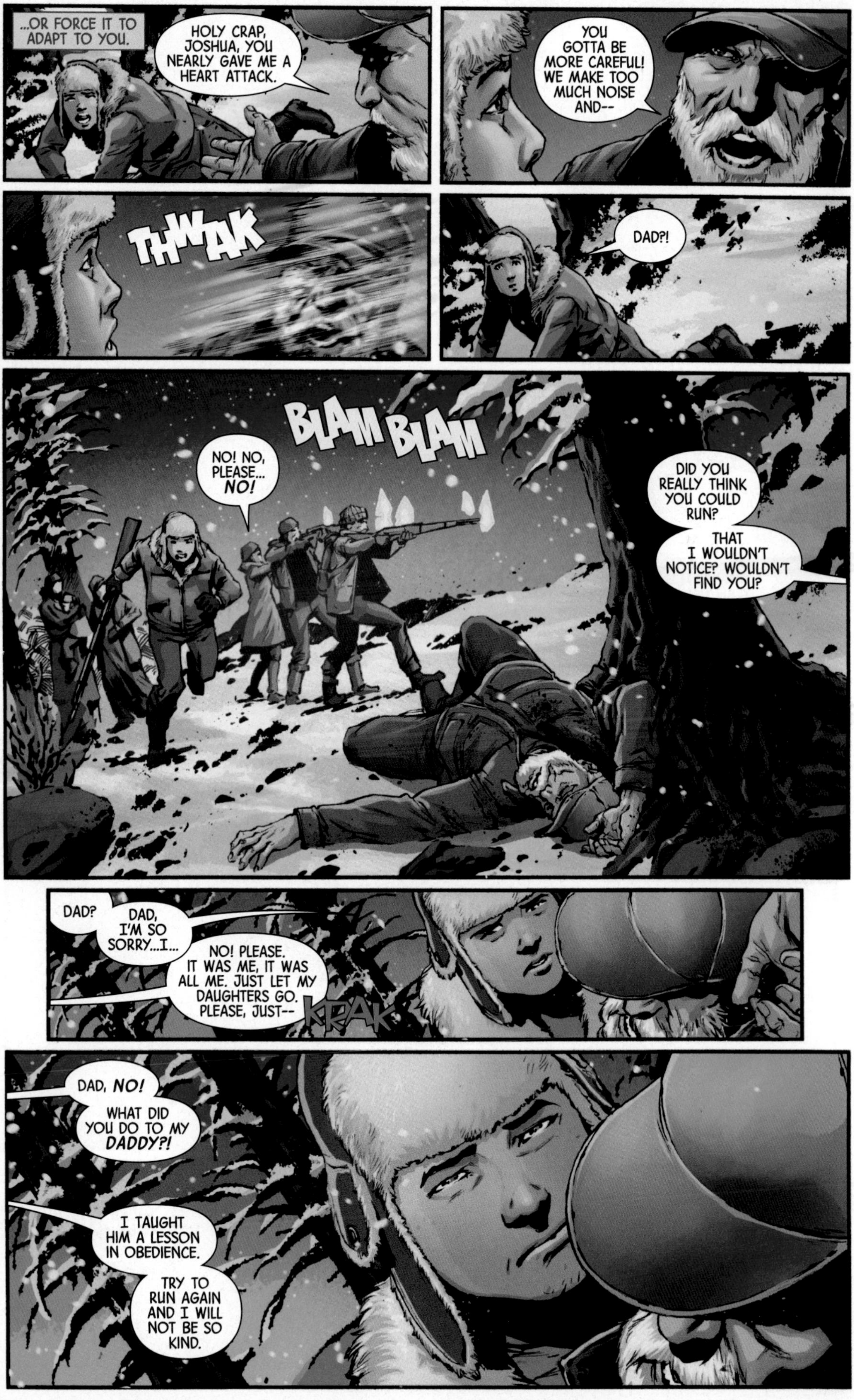
...OR FORCE IT TO ADAPT TO YOU.
HOLY CRAP, JOSHUA, YOU NEARLY GAVE ME A HEART ATTACK.
YOU GOTTA BE MORE CAREFUL! WE MAKE TOO MUCH NOISE AND--
THWAK
DAD?!
BLAM BLAM
NO! NO, PLEASE... NO!
DID YOU REALLY THINK YOU COULD RUN?
THAT I WOULDN'T NOTICE? WOULDN'T FIND YOU?
DAD?
DAD, I'M SO SORRY...I...
NO! PLEASE. IT WAS ME, IT WAS ALL ME. JUST LET MY DAUGHTERS GO. PLEASE, JUST--
KRAK
DAD, NO!
WHAT DID YOU DO TO MY DADDY?!
I TAUGHT HIM A LESSON IN OBEDIENCE.
TRY TO RUN AGAIN AND I WILL NOT BE SO KIND.

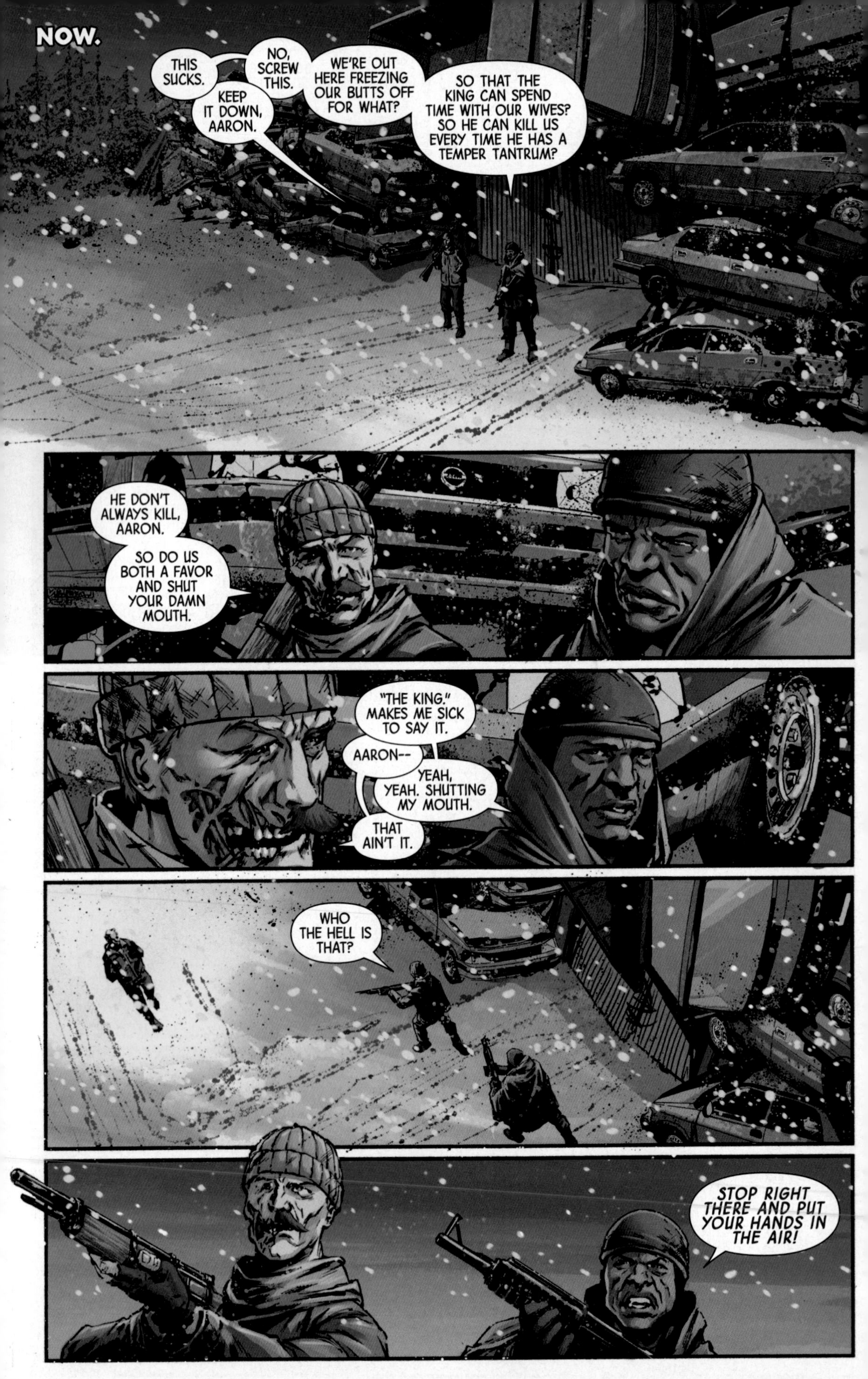
NOW.
THIS SUCKS.
NO, SCREW THIS.
KEEP IT DOWN, AARON.
WE'RE OUT HERE FREEZING OUR BUTTS OFF FOR WHAT?
SO THAT THE KING CAN SPEND TIME WITH OUR WIVES? SO HE CAN KILL US EVERY TIME HE HAS A TEMPER TANTRUM?
HE DON'T ALWAYS KILL, AARON.
SO DO US BOTH A FAVOR AND SHUT YOUR DAMN MOUTH.
"THE KING." MAKES ME SICK TO SAY IT.
AARON--
YEAH, YEAH. SHUTTING MY MOUTH.
THAT AIN'T IT.
WHO THE HELL IS THAT?
STOP RIGHT THERE AND PUT YOUR HANDS IN THE AIR!

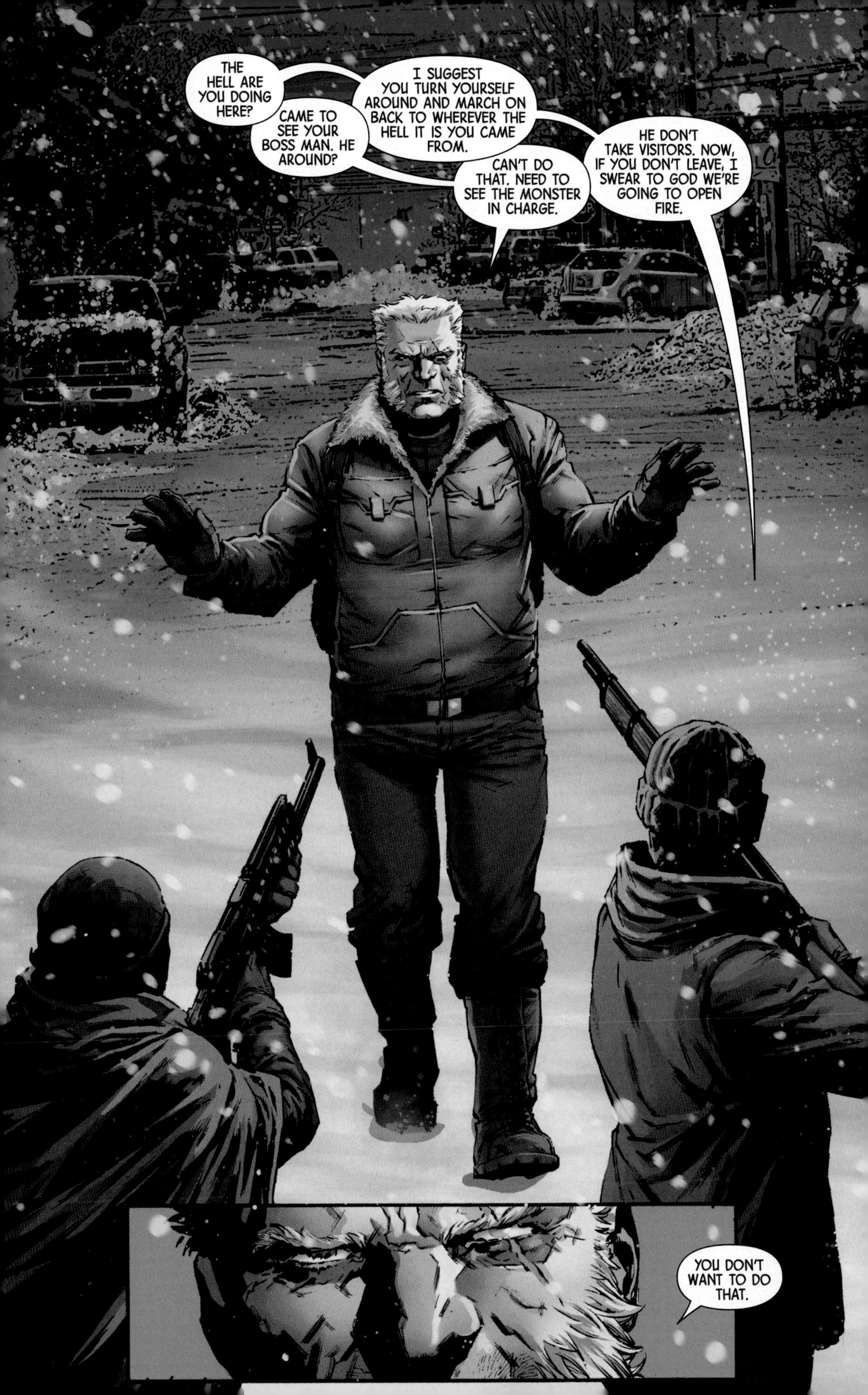
THE HELL ARE YOU DOING HERE?
CAME TO SEE YOUR BOSS MAN. HE AROUND?
I SUGGEST YOU TURN YOURSELF AROUND AND MARCH ON BACK TO WHEREVER THE HELL IT IS YOU CAME FROM.
CAN'T DO THAT. NEED TO SEE THE MONSTER IN CHARGE.
HE DON'T TAKE VISITORS. NOW, IF YOU DON'T LEAVE, I SWEAR TO GOD WE'RE GOING TO OPEN FIRE.
YOU DON'T WANT TO DO THAT.

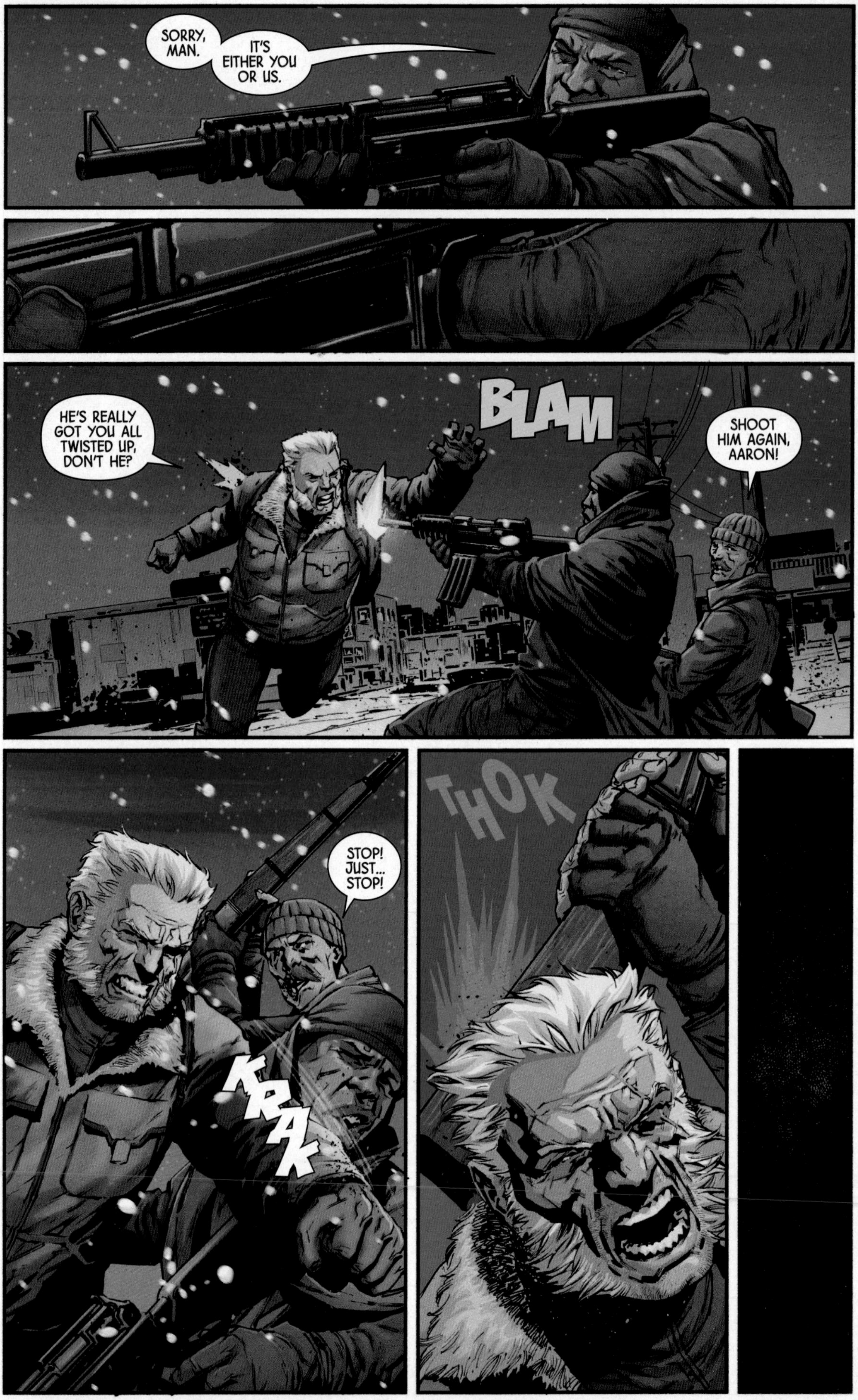
SORRY, MAN.
IT'S EITHER YOU OR US.
BLAM
HE'S REALLY GOT YOU ALL TWISTED UP, DON'T HE?
SHOOT HIM AGAIN, AARON!
STOP! JUST... STOP!
KRAK
THOK

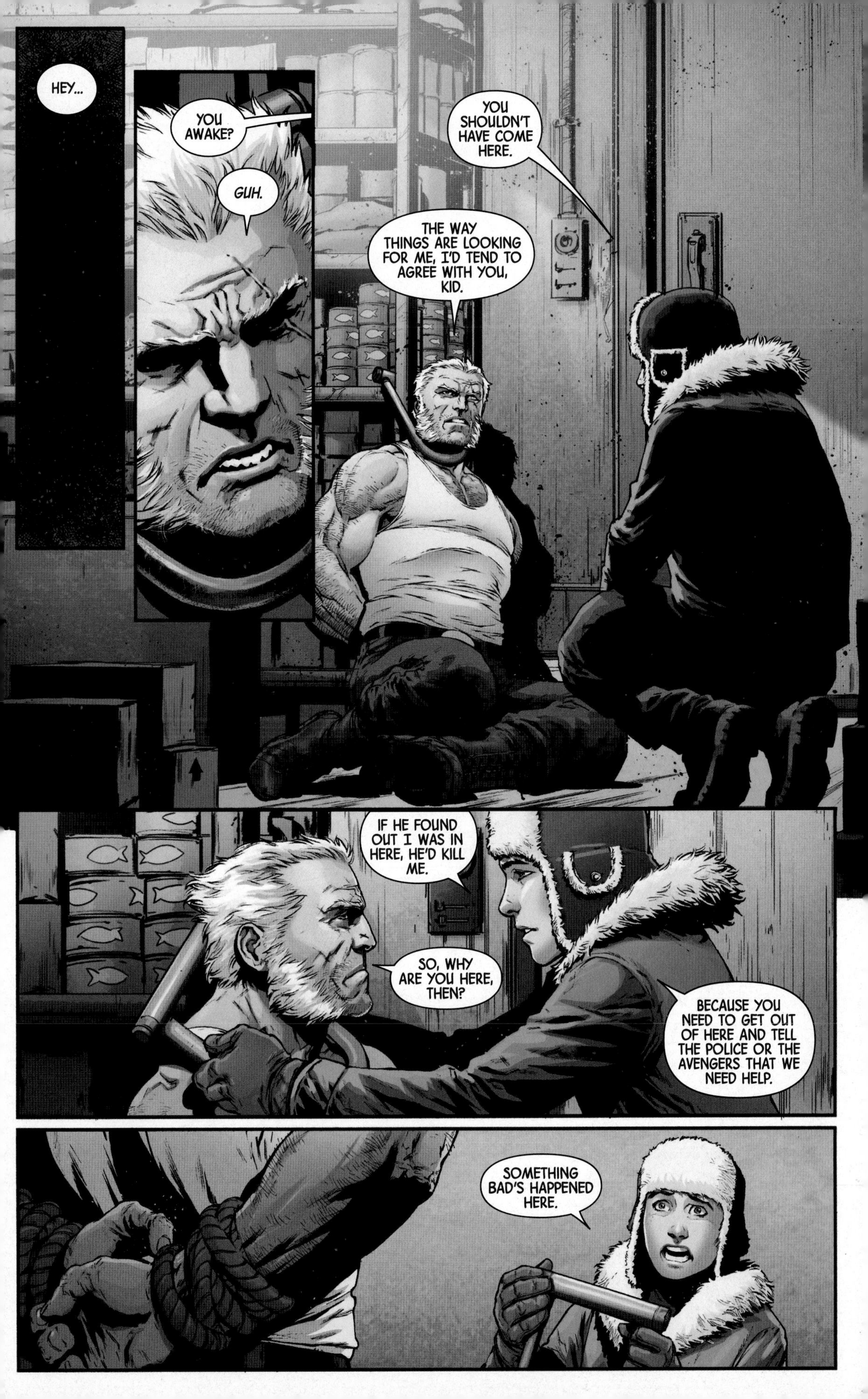
HEY...
YOU AWAKE?
GUH.
YOU SHOULDN'T HAVE COME HERE.
THE WAY THINGS ARE LOOKING FOR ME, I'D TEND TO AGREE WITH YOU, KID.
IF HE FOUND OUT I WAS IN HERE, HE'D KILL ME.
SO, WHY ARE YOU HERE, THEN?
BECAUSE YOU NEED TO GET OUT OF HERE AND TELL THE POLICE OR THE AVENGERS THAT WE NEED HELP.
SOMETHING BAD'S HAPPENED HERE.

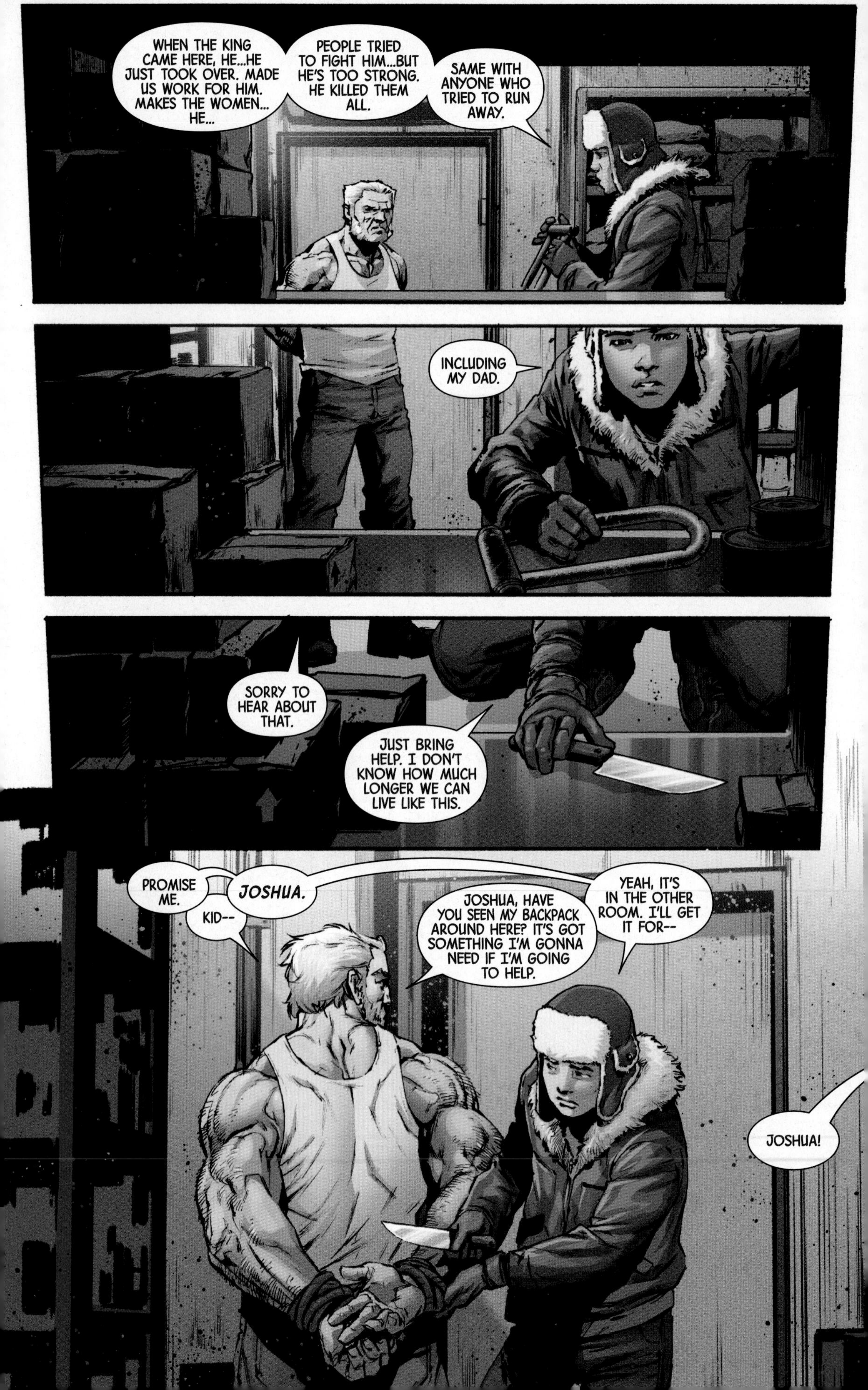
WHEN THE KING CAME HERE, HE...HE JUST TOOK OVER. MADE US WORK FOR HIM. MAKES THE WOMEN... HE...
PEOPLE TRIED TO FIGHT HIM...BUT HE'S TOO STRONG. HE KILLED THEM ALL.
SAME WITH ANYONE WHO TRIED TO RUN AWAY.
INCLUDING MY DAD.
SORRY TO HEAR ABOUT THAT.
JUST BRING HELP. I DON'T KNOW HOW MUCH LONGER WE CAN LIVE LIKE THIS.
PROMISE ME.
KID--
JOSHUA.
JOSHUA, HAVE YOU SEEN MY BACKPACK AROUND HERE? IT'S GOT SOMETHING I'M GONNA NEED IF I'M GOING TO HELP.
YEAH, IT'S IN THE OTHER ROOM. I'LL GET IT FOR--
JOSHUA!

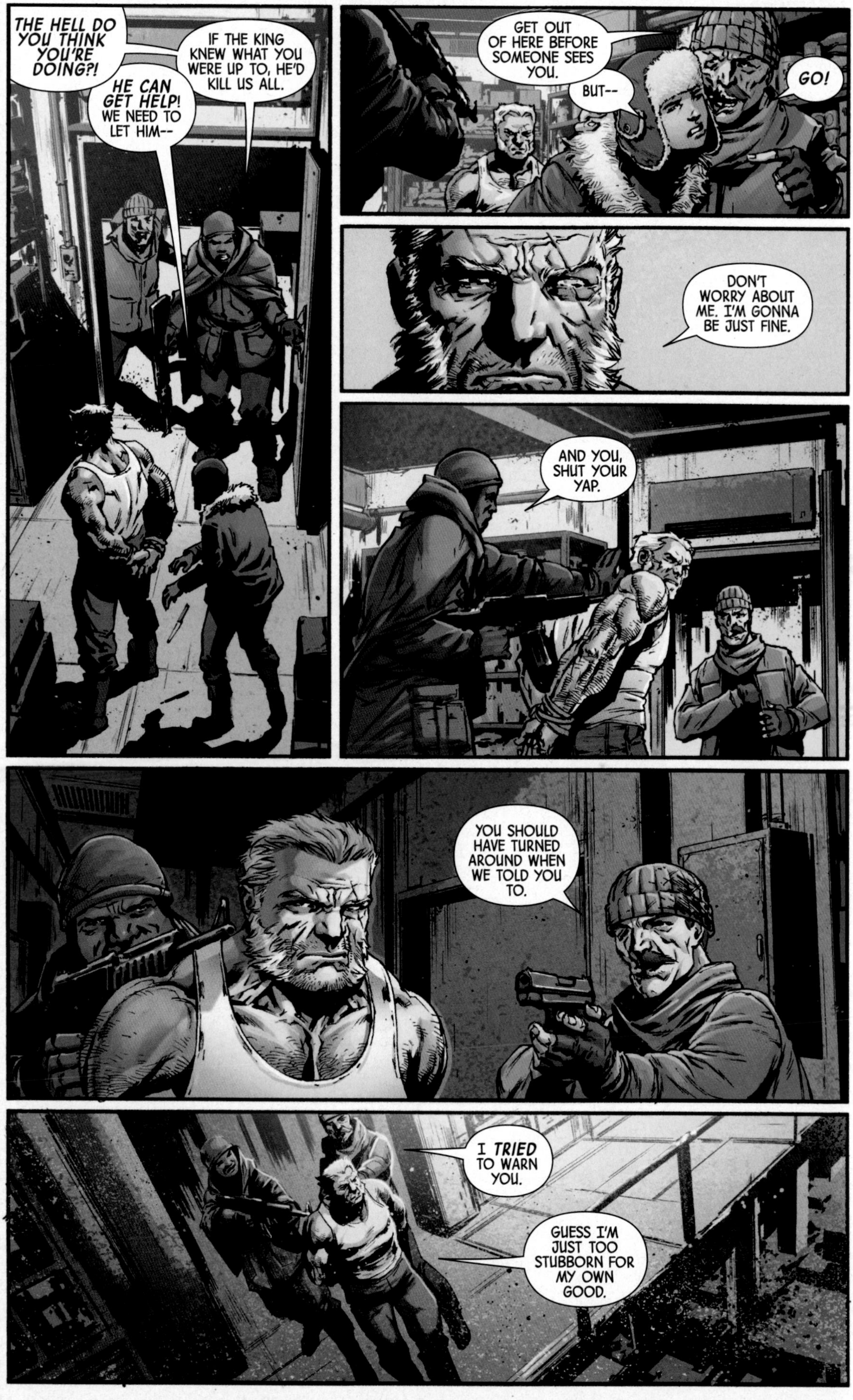
THE HELL DO YOU THINK YOU'RE DOING?!
IF THE KING KNEW WHAT YOU WERE UP TO, HE'D KILL US ALL.
HE CAN GET HELP! WE NEED TO LET HIM--
GET OUT OF HERE BEFORE SOMEONE SEES YOU.
BUT--
GO!
DON'T WORRY ABOUT ME. I'M GONNA BE JUST FINE.
AND YOU, SHUT YOUR YAP.
YOU SHOULD HAVE TURNED AROUND WHEN WE TOLD YOU TO.
I TRIED TO WARN YOU.
GUESS I'M JUST TOO STUBBORN FOR MY OWN GOOD.

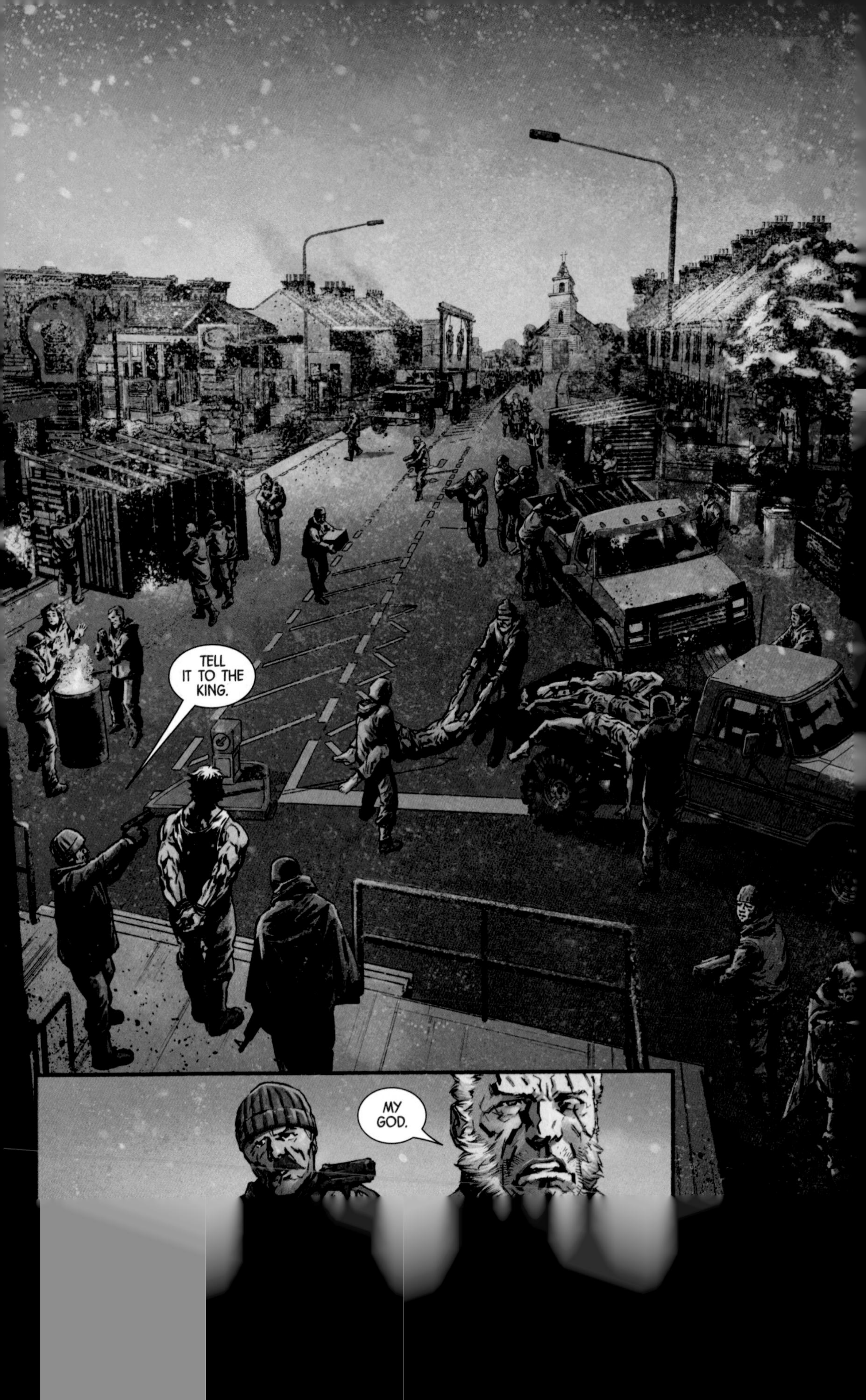
TELL IT TO THE KING.
MY GOD.

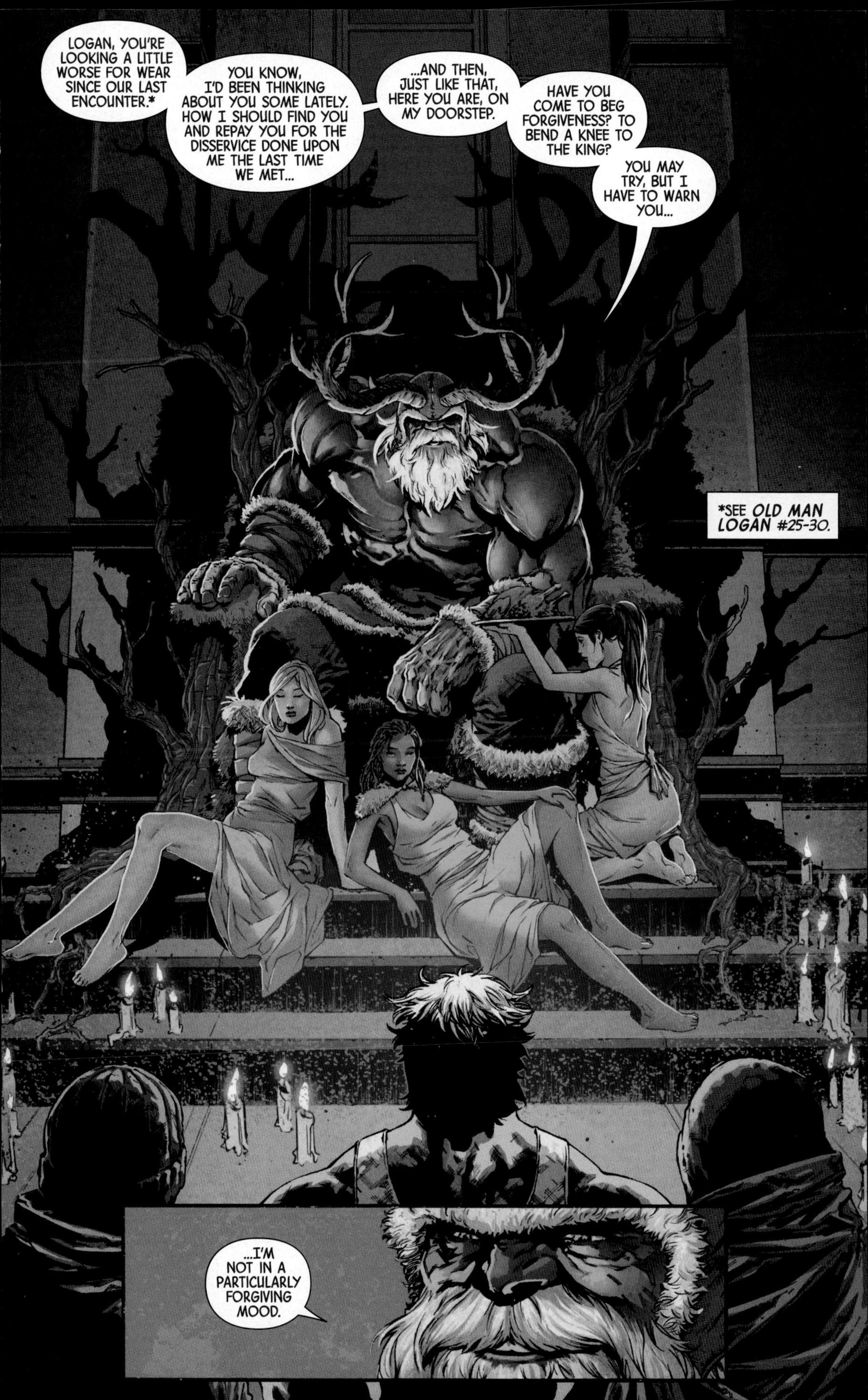
LOGAN, YOU'RE LOOKING A LITTLE WORSE FOR WEAR SINCE OUR LAST ENCOUNTER.*
YOU KNOW, I'D BEEN THINKING ABOUT YOU SOME LATELY. HOW I SHOULD FIND YOU AND REPAY YOU FOR THE DISSERVICE DONE UPON ME THE LAST TIME WE MET...
...AND THEN, JUST LIKE THAT, HERE YOU ARE, ON MY DOORSTEP.
HAVE YOU COME TO BEG FORGIVENESS? TO BEND A KNEE TO THE KING?
YOU MAY TRY, BUT I HAVE TO WARN YOU...
*SEE OLD MAN LOGAN #25-30.
...I'M NOT IN A PARTICULARLY FORGIVING MOOD.

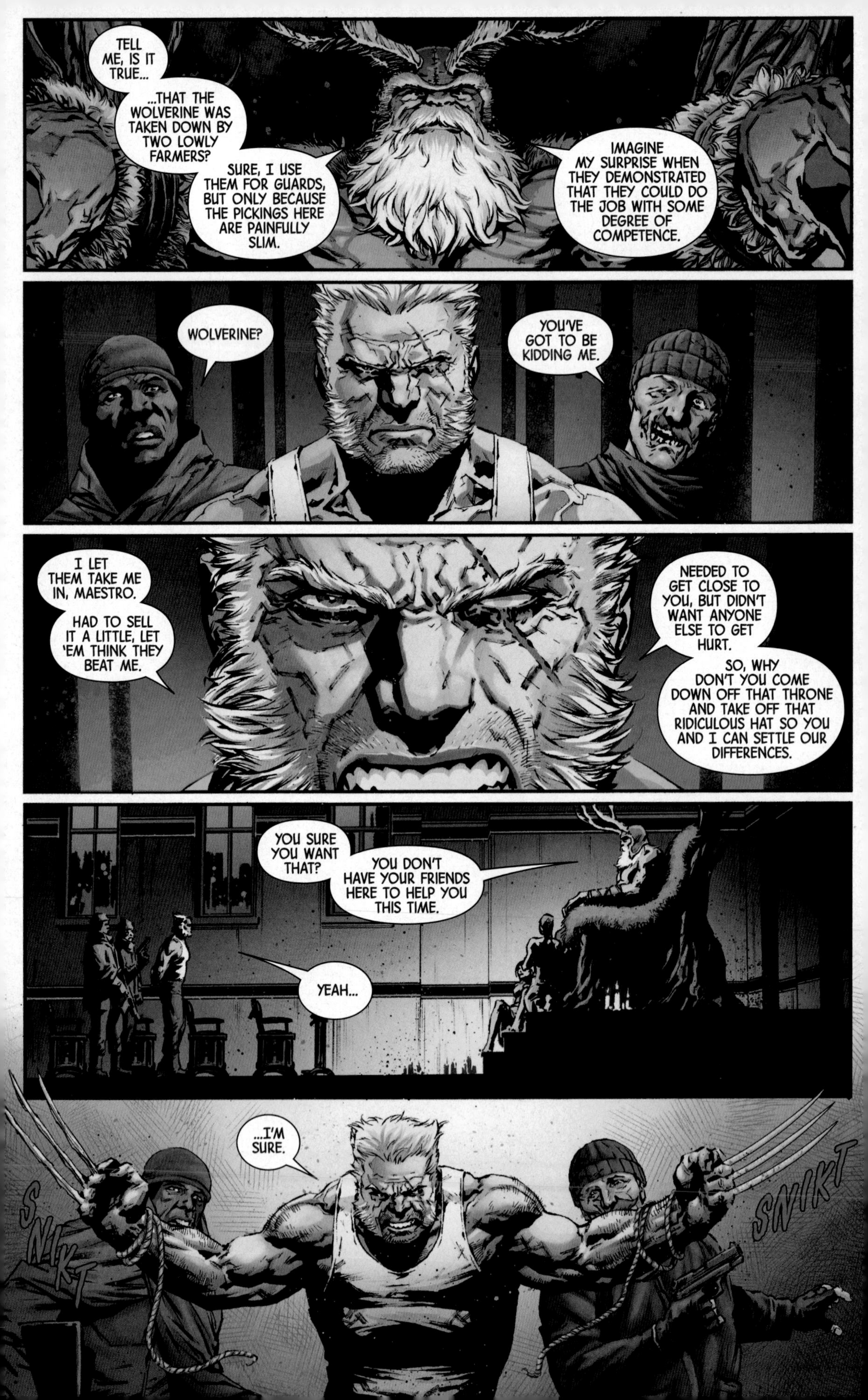
TELL ME, IS IT TRUE...
...THAT THE WOLVERINE WAS TAKEN DOWN BY TWO LOWLY FARMERS?
SURE, I USE THEM FOR GUARDS, BUT ONLY BECAUSE THE PICKINGS HERE ARE PAINFULLY SLIM.
IMAGINE MY SURPRISE WHEN THEY DEMONSTRATED THAT THEY COULD DO THE JOB WITH SOME DEGREE OF COMPETENCE.
WOLVERINE?
YOU'VE GOT TO BE KIDDING ME.
I LET THEM TAKE ME IN, MAESTRO.
HAD TO SELL IT A LITTLE, LET 'EM THINK THEY BEAT ME.
NEEDED TO GET CLOSE TO YOU, BUT DIDN'T WANT ANYONE ELSE TO GET HURT.
SO, WHY DON'T YOU COME DOWN OFF THAT THRONE AND TAKE OFF THAT RIDICULOUS HAT SO YOU AND I CAN SETTLE OUR DIFFERENCES.
YOU SURE YOU WANT THAT?
YOU DON'T HAVE YOUR FRIENDS HERE TO HELP YOU THIS TIME.
YEAH...
...I'M SURE.
SNIKT
SNIKT

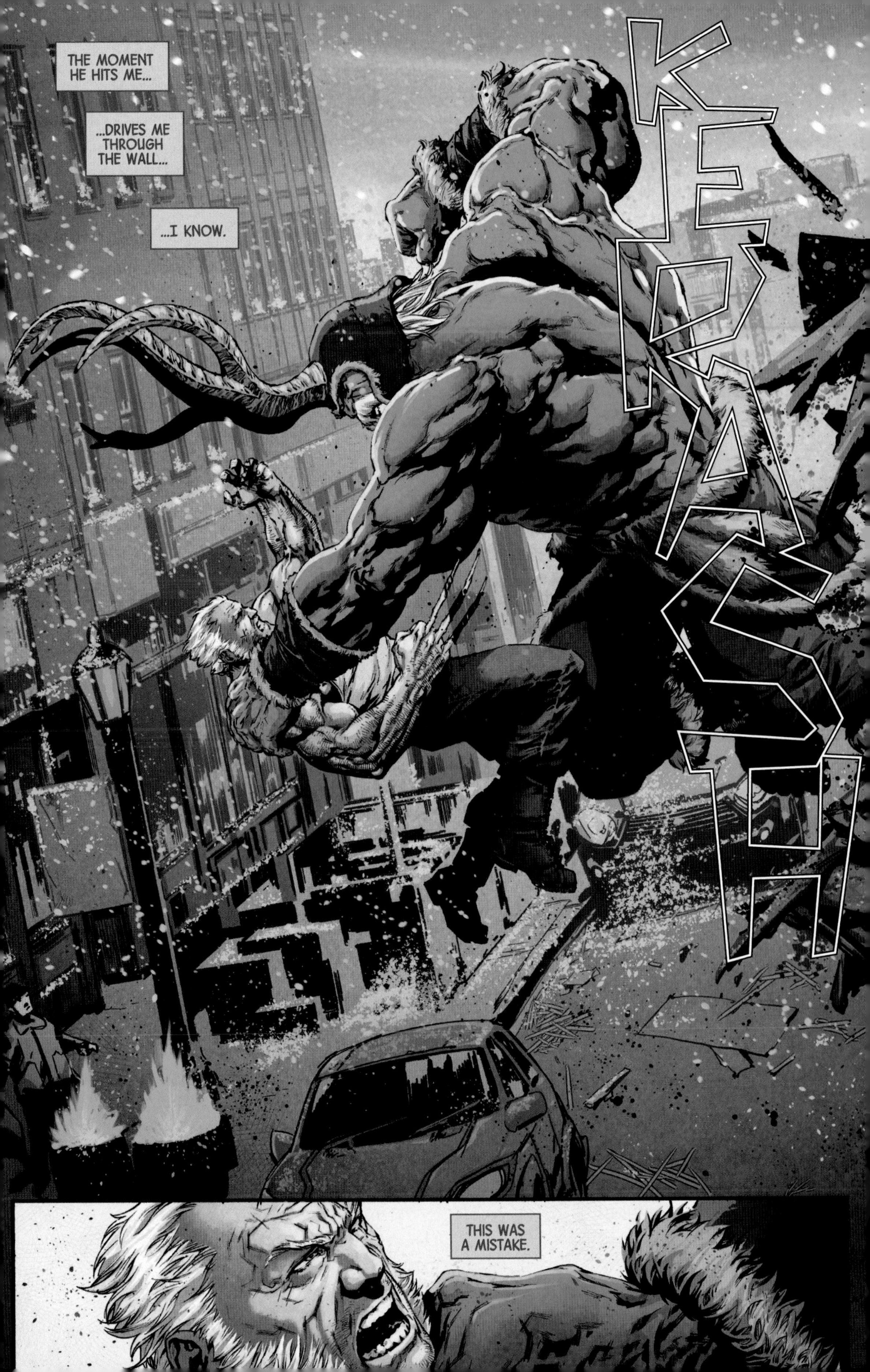
THE MOMENT HE HITS ME...
...DRIVES ME THROUGH THE WALL...
...I KNOW.
THIS WAS A MISTAKE.

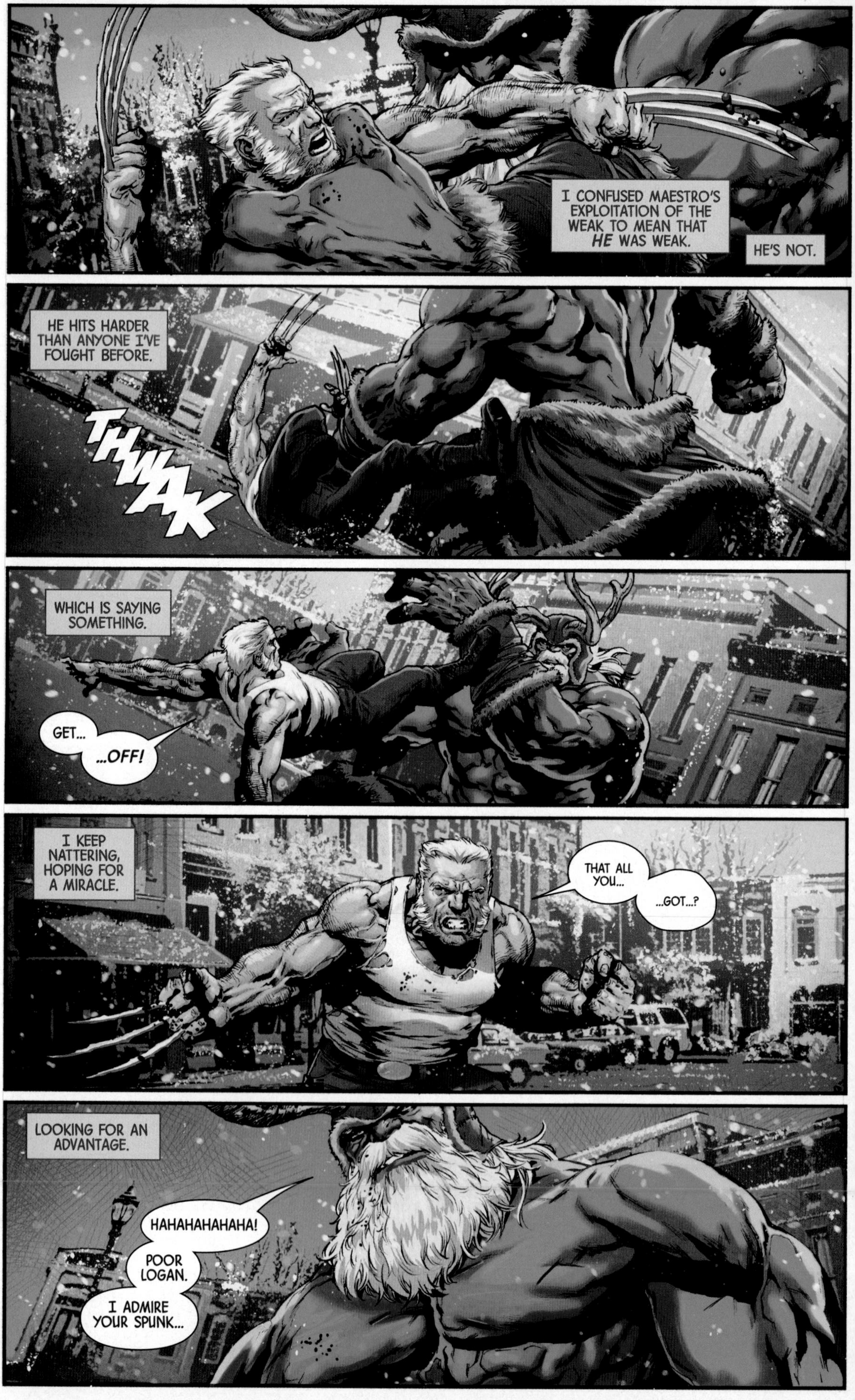
I CONFUSED MAESTRO'S EXPLOITATION OF THE WEAK TO MEAN THAT *HE* WAS WEAK.
HE'S NOT.
HE HITS HARDER THAN ANYONE I'VE FOUGHT BEFORE.
THWAK
WHICH IS SAYING SOMETHING.
GET...
...OFF!
I KEEP NATTERING, HOPING FOR A MIRACLE.
THAT ALL YOU...
...GOT...?
LOOKING FOR AN ADVANTAGE.
HAHAHAHAHAHA!
POOR LOGAN.
I ADMIRE YOUR SPUNK...

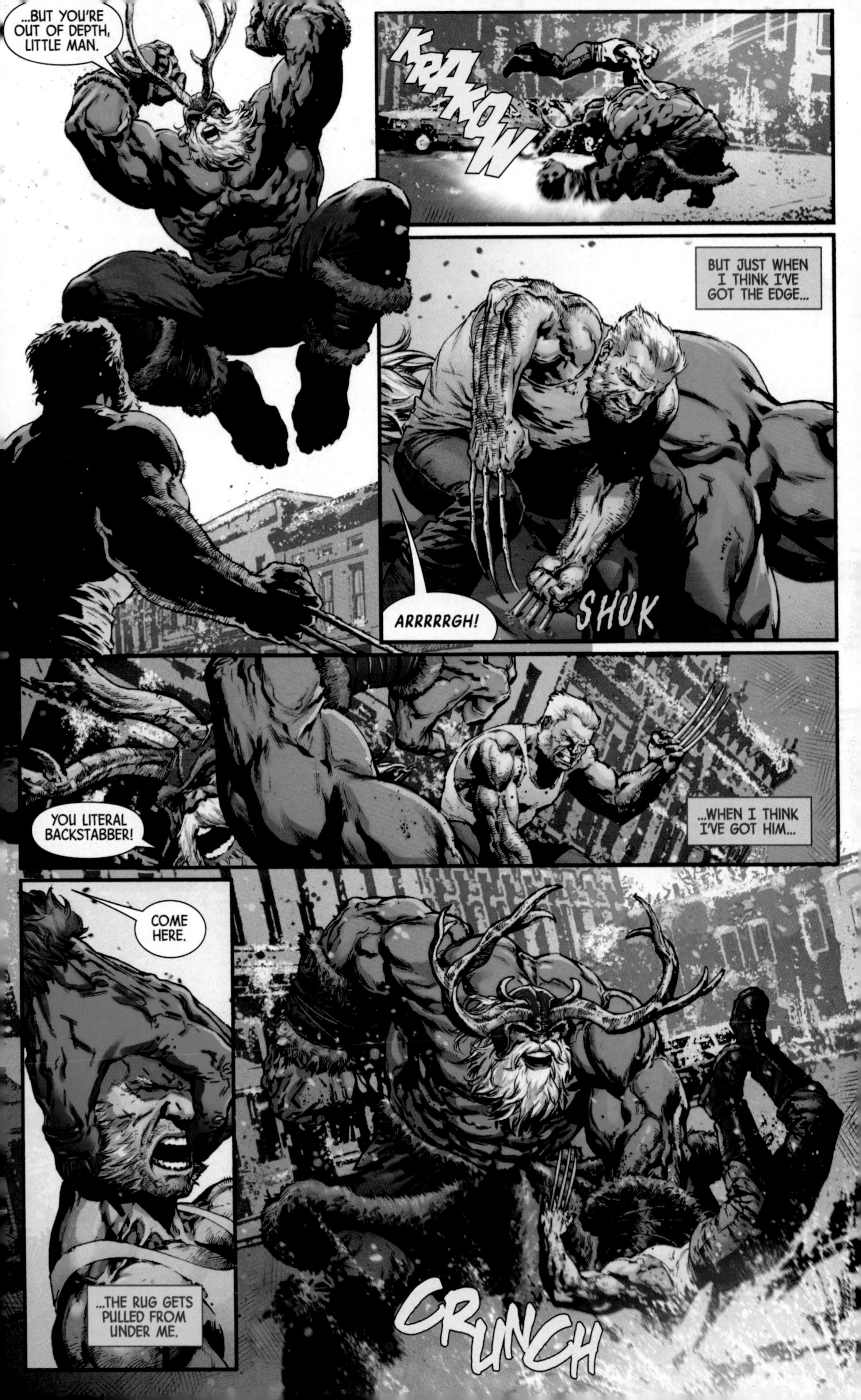
...BUT YOU'RE OUT OF DEPTH, LITTLE MAN.
KRAKOW
BUT JUST WHEN I THINK I'VE GOT THE EDGE...
ARRRRRGH!
SHUK
YOU LITERAL BACKSTABBER!
...WHEN I THINK I'VE GOT HIM...
COME HERE.
...THE RUG GETS PULLED FROM UNDER ME.
CRUNCH

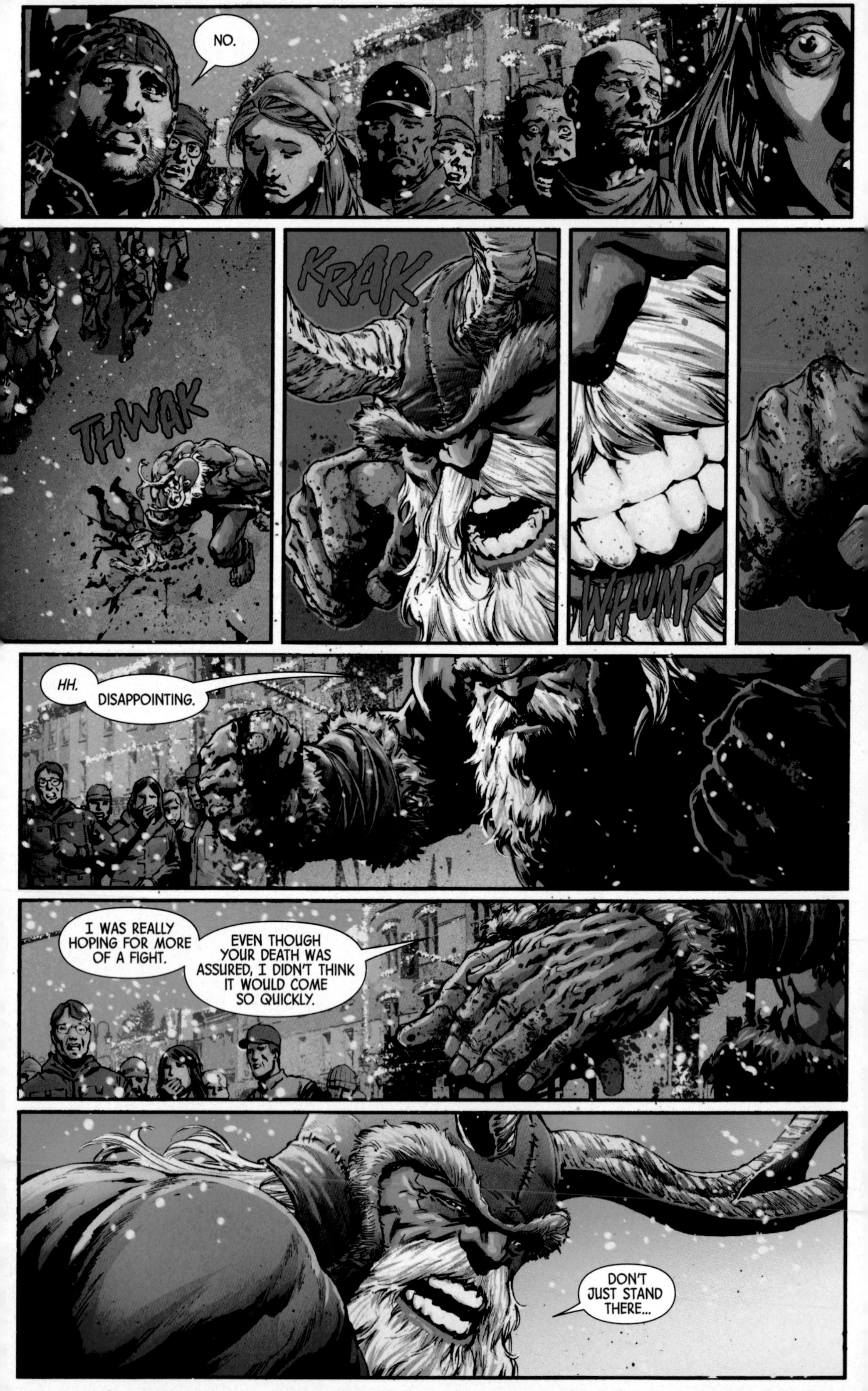
NO.
THWAK
KRAK
WHUMP
HH.
DISAPPOINTING.
I WAS REALLY HOPING FOR MORE OF A FIGHT.
EVEN THOUGH YOUR DEATH WAS ASSURED, I DIDN'T THINK IT WOULD COME SO QUICKLY.
DON'T JUST STAND THERE...

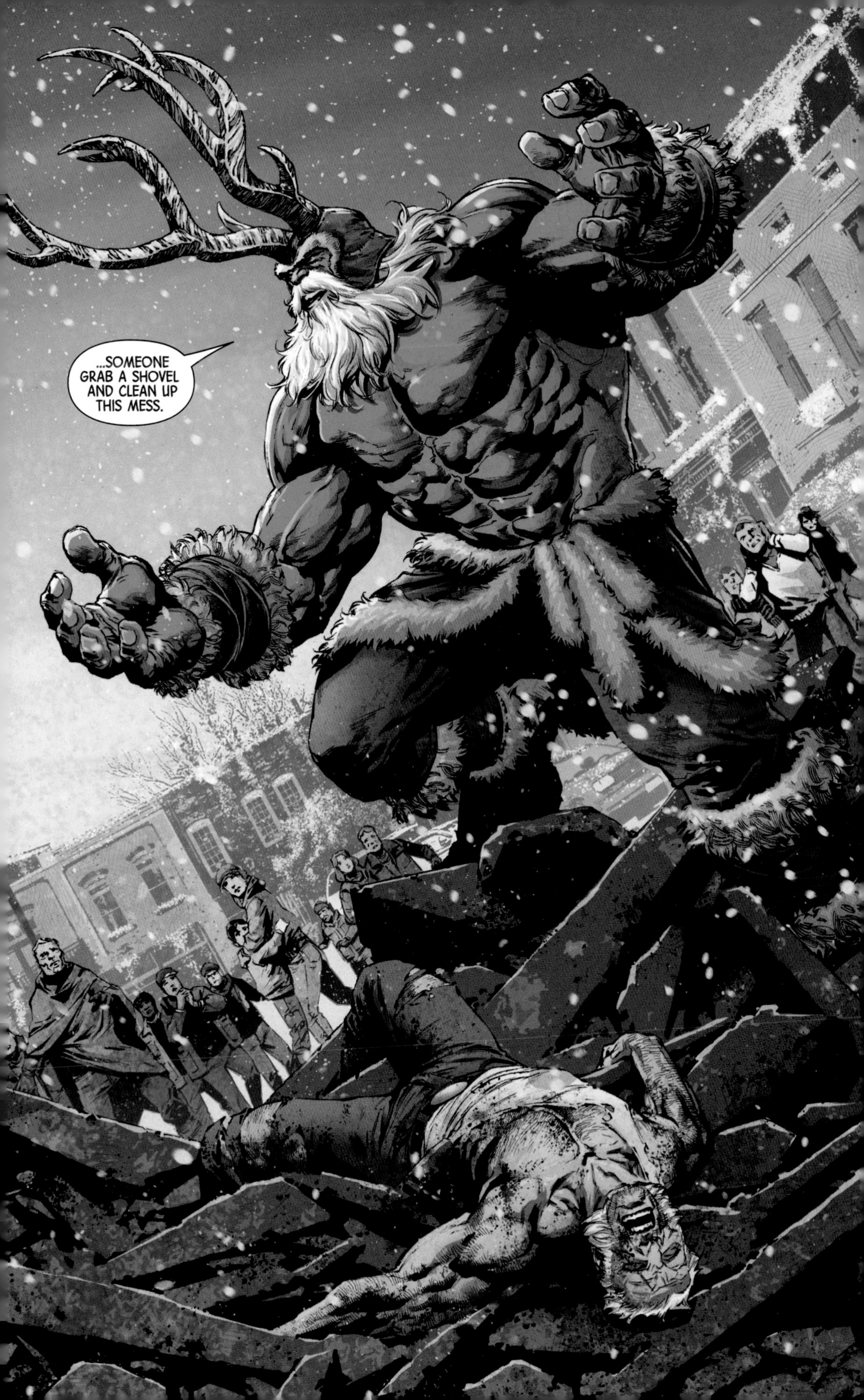
...SOMEONE GRAB A SHOVEL AND CLEAN UP THIS MESS.

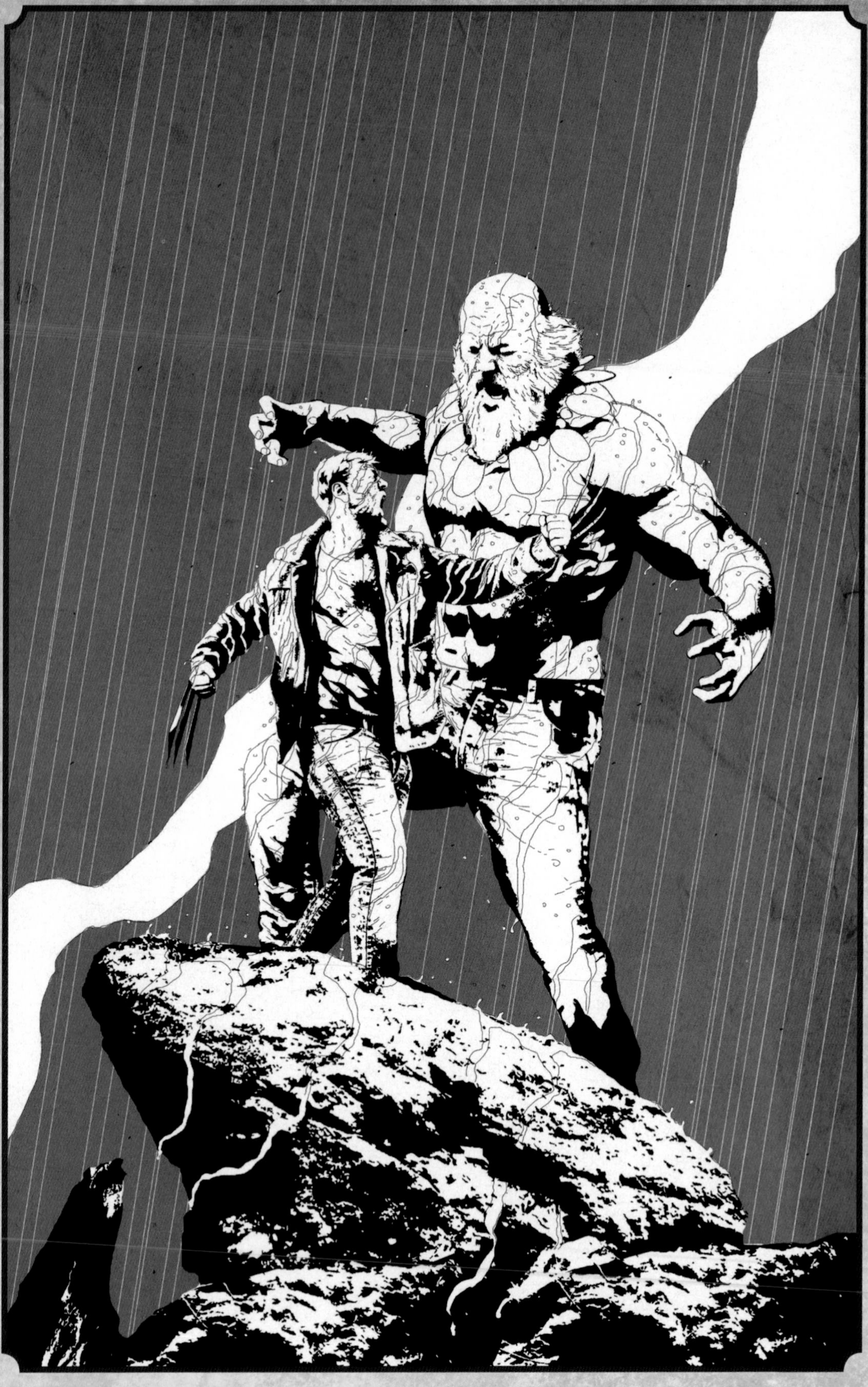

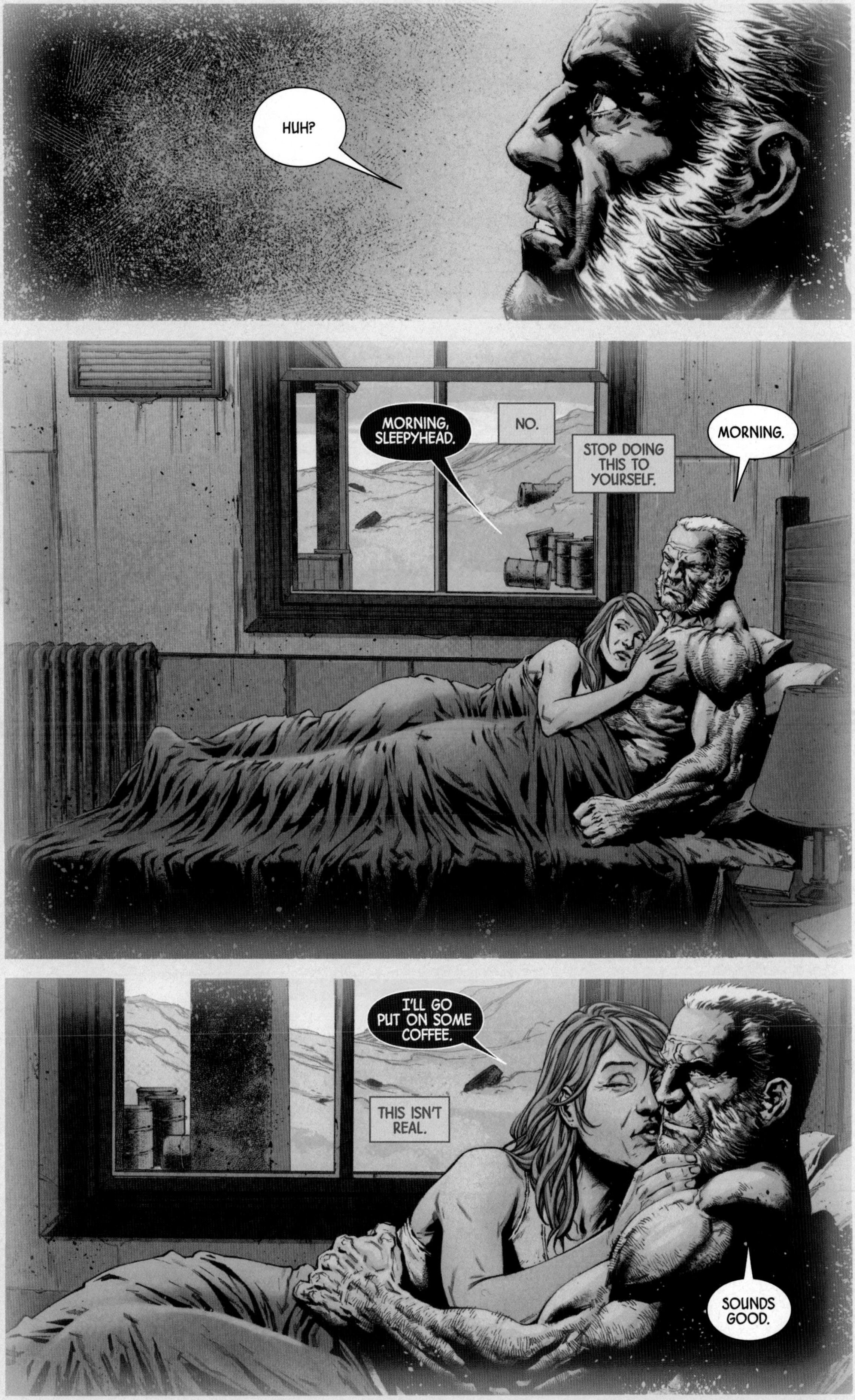
HUH?
MORNING, SLEEPYHEAD.
NO.
STOP DOING THIS TO YOURSELF.
MORNING.
I'LL GO PUT ON SOME COFFEE.
THIS ISN'T REAL.
SOUNDS GOOD.

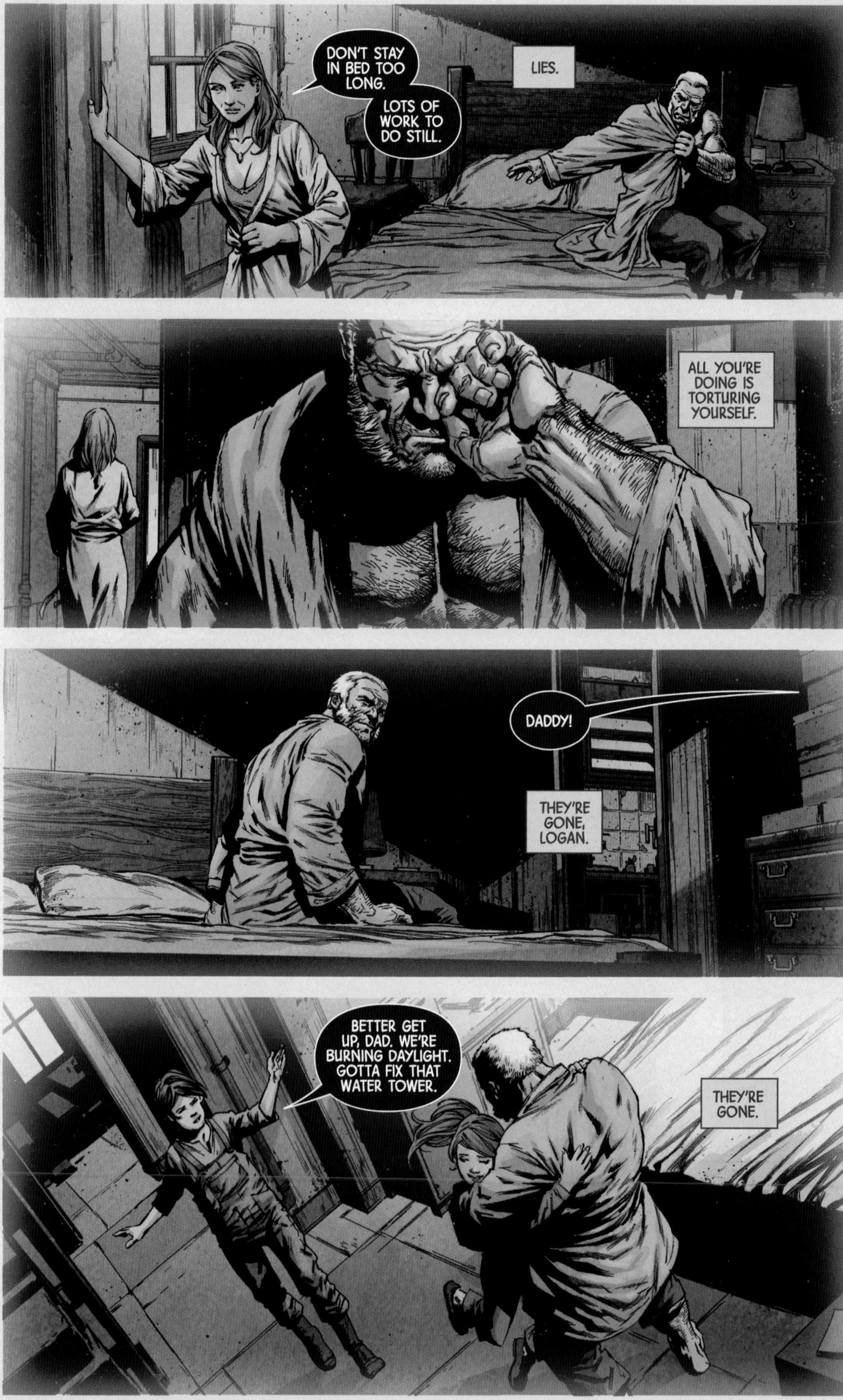
DON'T STAY IN BED TOO LONG.
LOTS OF WORK TO DO STILL.
LIES.
ALL YOU'RE DOING IS TORTURING YOURSELF.
DADDY!
THEY'RE GONE, LOGAN.
BETTER GET UP, DAD. WE'RE BURNING DAYLIGHT. GOTTA FIX THAT WATER TOWER.
THEY'RE GONE.

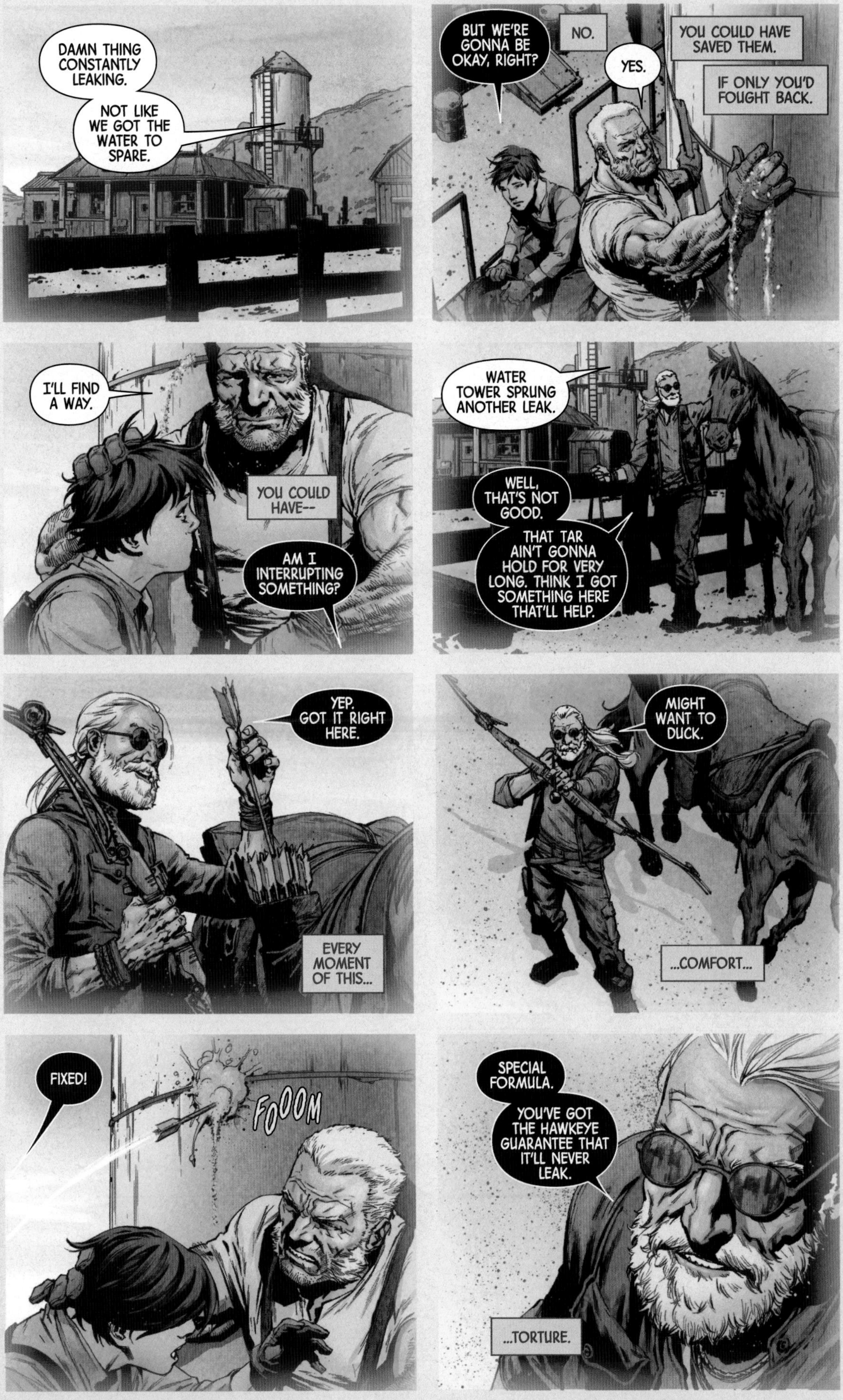
DAMN THING CONSTANTLY LEAKING.
NOT LIKE WE GOT THE WATER TO SPARE.
BUT WE'RE GONNA BE OKAY, RIGHT?
NO.
YES.
YOU COULD HAVE SAVED THEM.
IF ONLY YOU'D FOUGHT BACK.
I'LL FIND A WAY.
YOU COULD HAVE--
AM I INTERRUPTING SOMETHING?
WATER TOWER SPRUNG ANOTHER LEAK.
WELL, THAT'S NOT GOOD.
THAT TAR AIN'T GONNA HOLD FOR VERY LONG. THINK I GOT SOMETHING HERE THAT'LL HELP.
YEP. GOT IT RIGHT HERE.
EVERY MOMENT OF THIS...
MIGHT WANT TO DUCK.
...COMFORT...
FIXED!
FOOOM
SPECIAL FORMULA.
YOU'VE GOT THE HAWKEYE GUARANTEE THAT IT'LL NEVER LEAK.
...TORTURE.

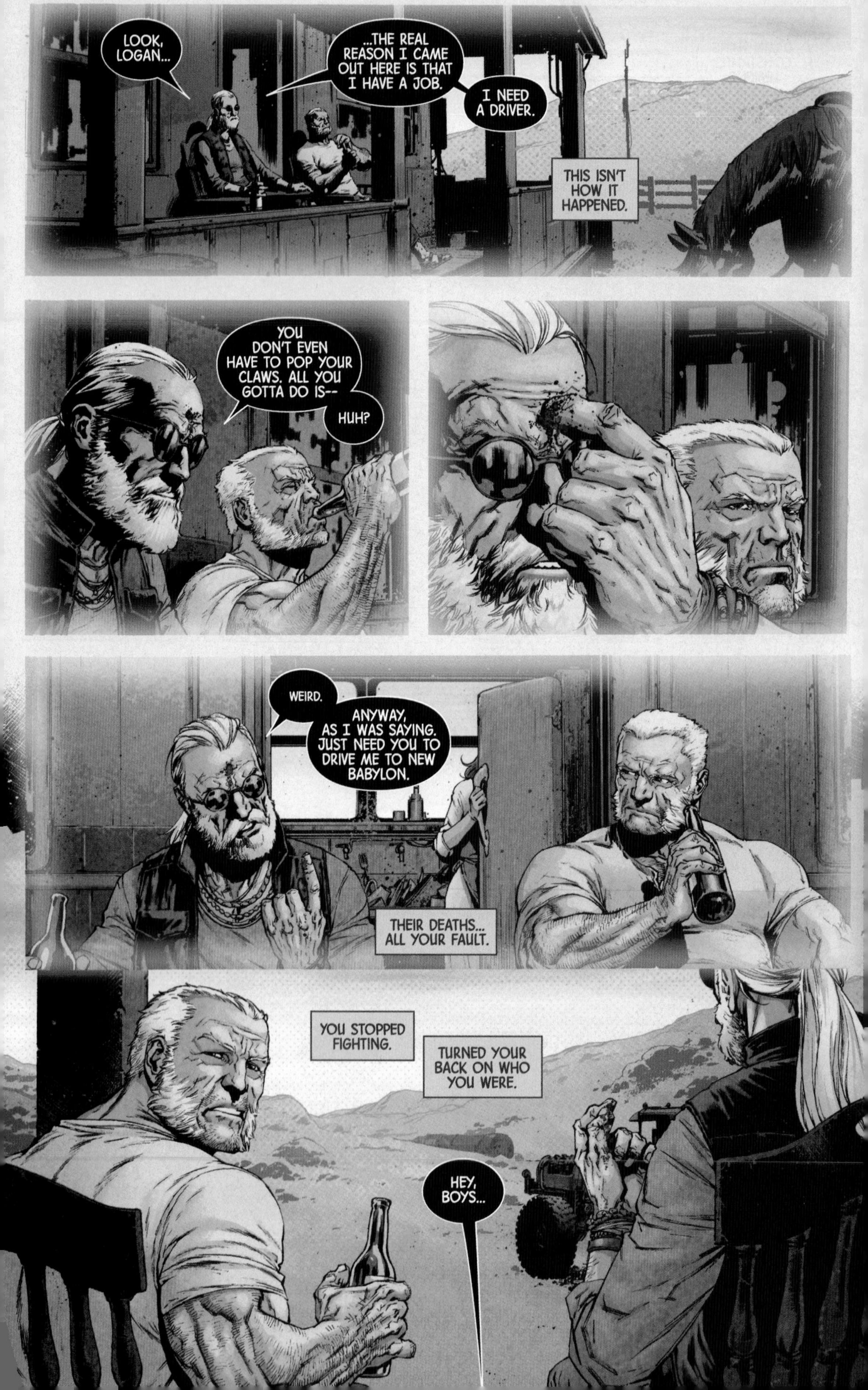
LOOK, LOGAN...
...THE REAL REASON I CAME OUT HERE IS THAT I HAVE A JOB.
I NEED A DRIVER.
THIS ISN'T HOW IT HAPPENED.
YOU DON'T EVEN HAVE TO POP YOUR CLAWS. ALL YOU GOTTA DO IS--
HUH?
WEIRD.
ANYWAY, AS I WAS SAYING. JUST NEED YOU TO DRIVE ME TO NEW BABYLON.
THEIR DEATHS... ALL YOUR FAULT.
YOU STOPPED FIGHTING.
TURNED YOUR BACK ON WHO YOU WERE.
HEY, BOYS...

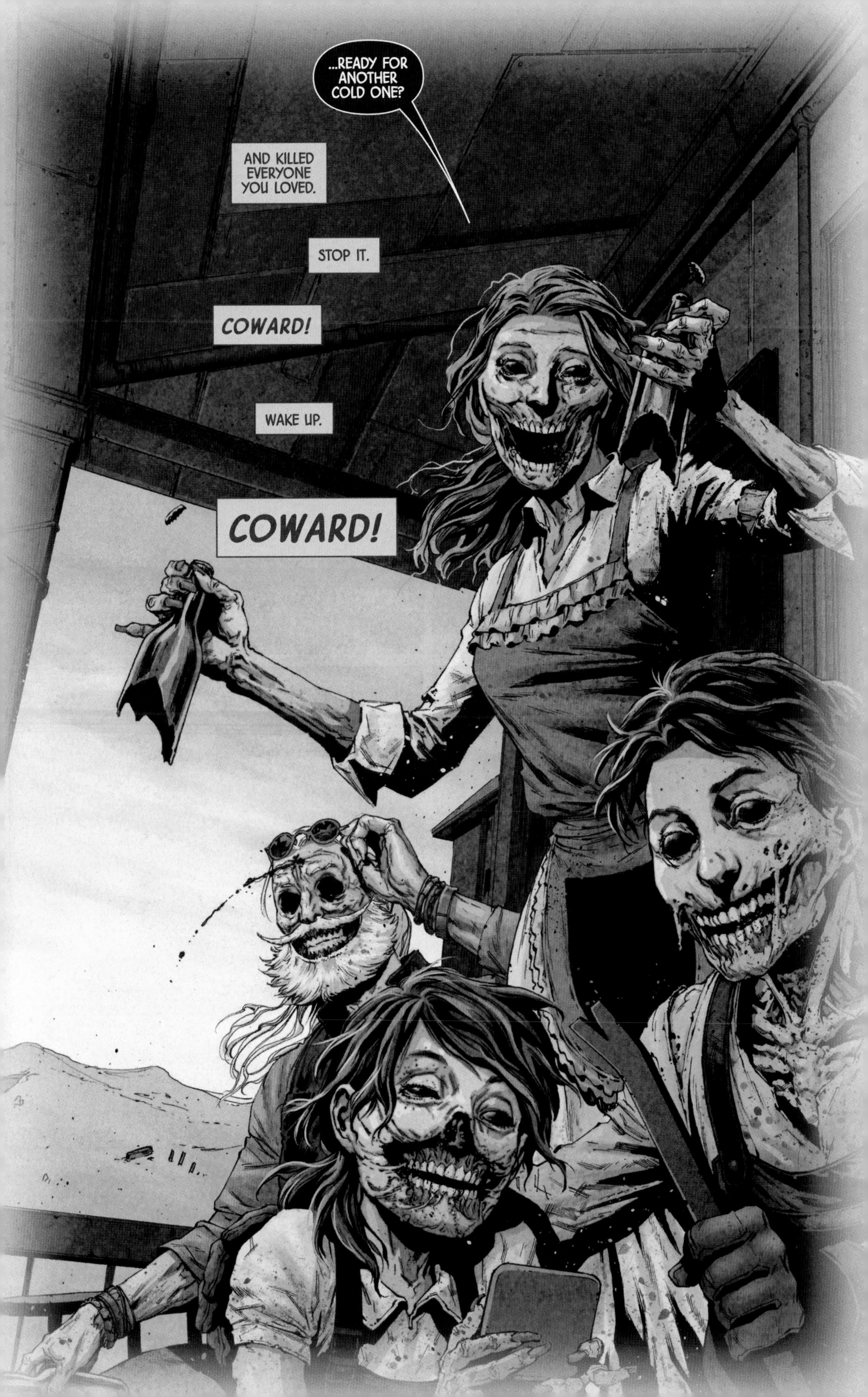

...READY FOR ANOTHER COLD ONE?
AND KILLED EVERYONE YOU LOVED.
STOP IT.
COWARD!
WAKE UP.
COWARD!

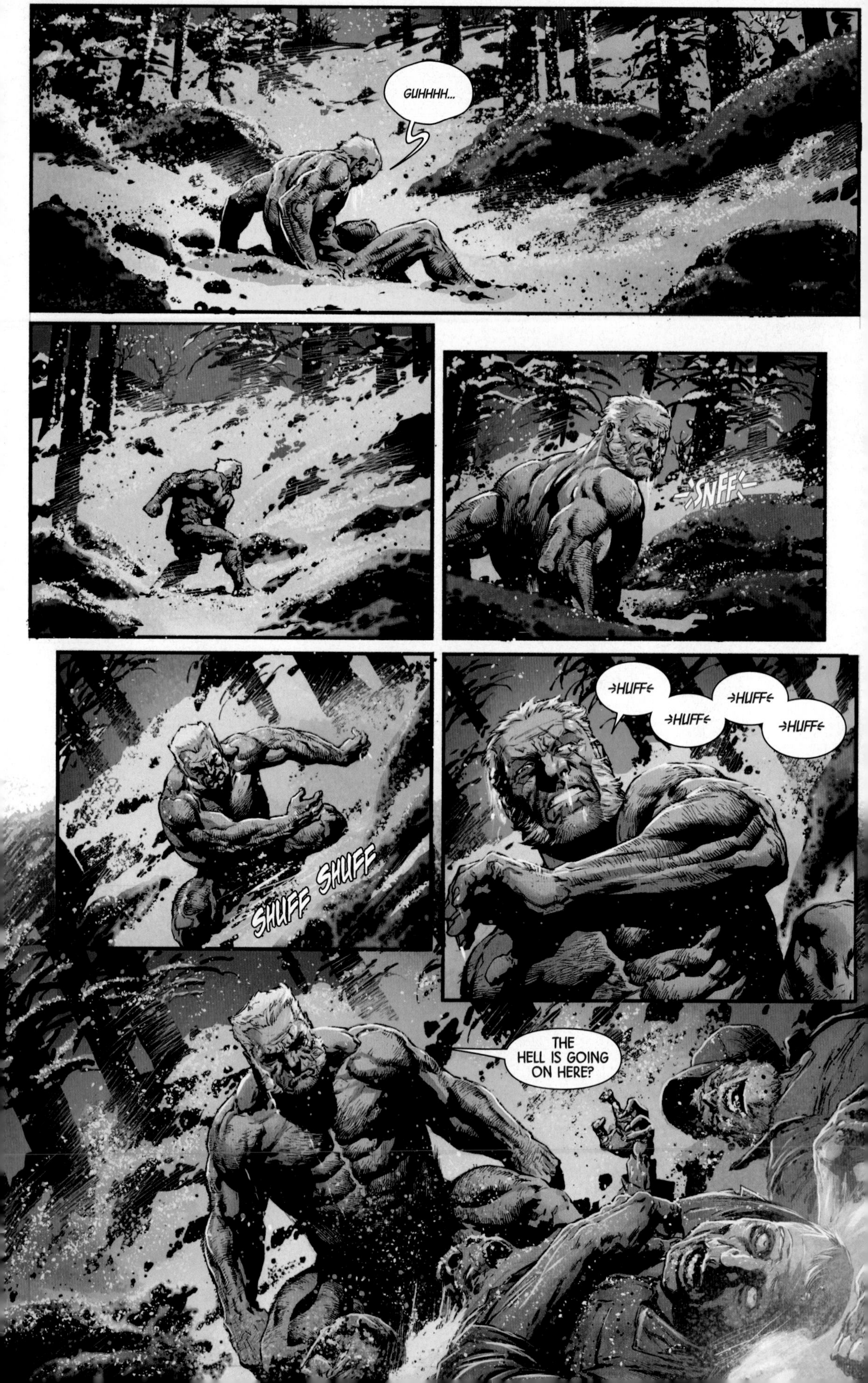
GUHHHH...
SNFF
SHUFF SHUFF
HUFF
HUFF
HUFF
HUFF
THE HELL IS GOING ON HERE?

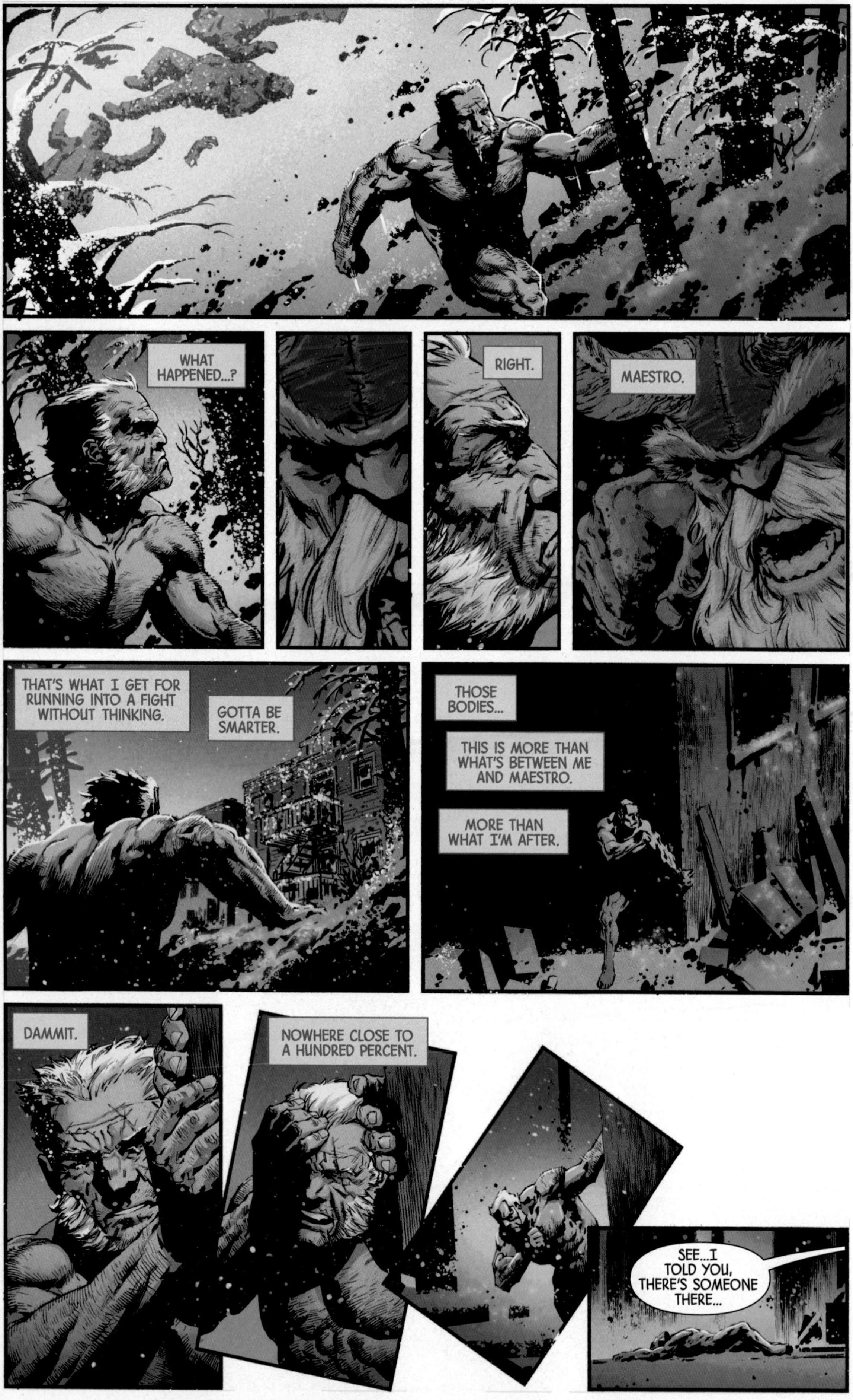
WHAT HAPPENED...?
RIGHT.
MAESTRO.
THAT'S WHAT I GET FOR RUNNING INTO A FIGHT WITHOUT THINKING.
GOTTA BE SMARTER.
THOSE BODIES...
THIS IS MORE THAN WHAT'S BETWEEN ME AND MAESTRO.
MORE THAN WHAT I'M AFTER.
DAMMIT.
NOWHERE CLOSE TO A HUNDRED PERCENT.
SEE...I TOLD YOU, THERE'S SOMEONE THERE...

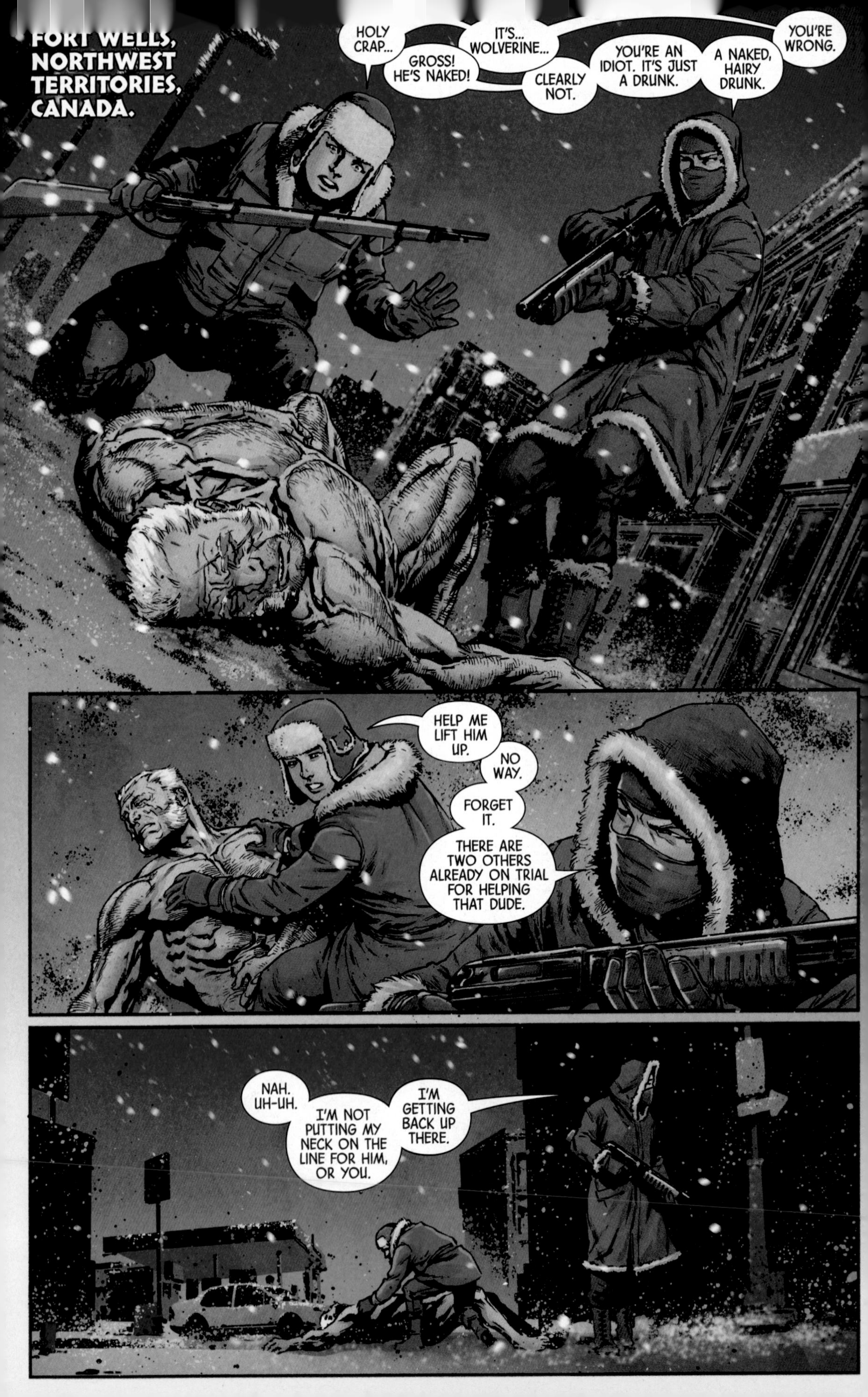
FORT WELLS, NORTHWEST TERRITORIES, CANADA.
HOLY CRAP...
IT'S... WOLVERINE...
YOU'RE WRONG.
GROSS! HE'S NAKED!
CLEARLY NOT.
YOU'RE AN IDIOT. IT'S JUST A DRUNK.
A NAKED, HAIRY DRUNK.
HELP ME LIFT HIM UP.
NO WAY.
FORGET IT.
THERE ARE TWO OTHERS ALREADY ON TRIAL FOR HELPING THAT DUDE.
NAH. UH-UH.
I'M NOT PUTTING MY NECK ON THE LINE FOR HIM, OR YOU.
I'M GETTING BACK UP THERE.

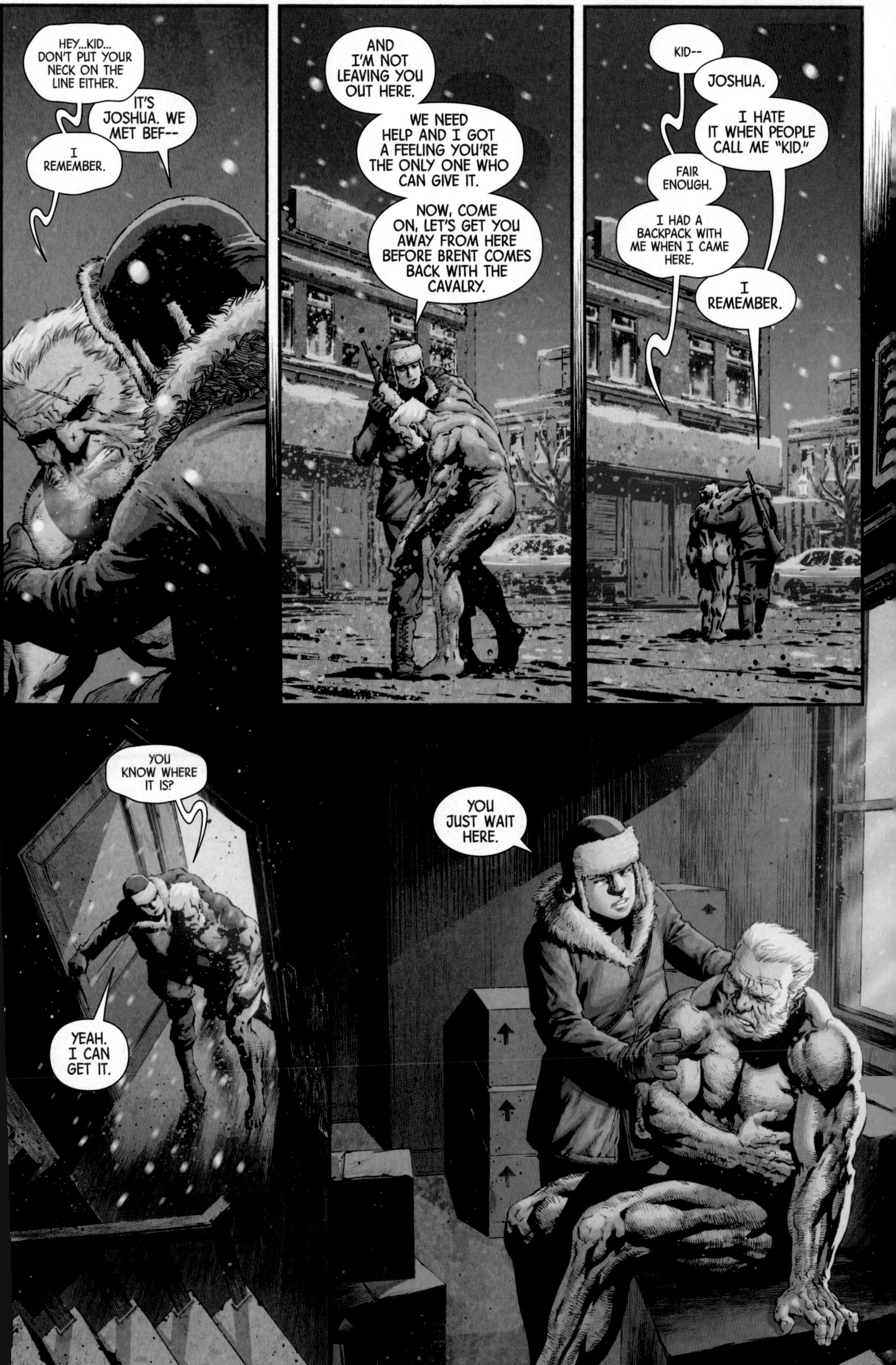
HEY...KID... DON'T PUT YOUR NECK ON THE LINE EITHER.
IT'S JOSHUA. WE MET BEF--
I REMEMBER.
AND I'M NOT LEAVING YOU OUT HERE.
WE NEED HELP AND I GOT A FEELING YOU'RE THE ONLY ONE WHO CAN GIVE IT.
NOW, COME ON, LET'S GET YOU AWAY FROM HERE BEFORE BRENT COMES BACK WITH THE CAVALRY.
KID--
JOSHUA.
I HATE IT WHEN PEOPLE CALL ME "KID."
FAIR ENOUGH.
I HAD A BACKPACK WITH ME WHEN I CAME HERE.
I REMEMBER.
YOU KNOW WHERE IT IS?
YEAH. I CAN GET IT.
YOU JUST WAIT HERE.

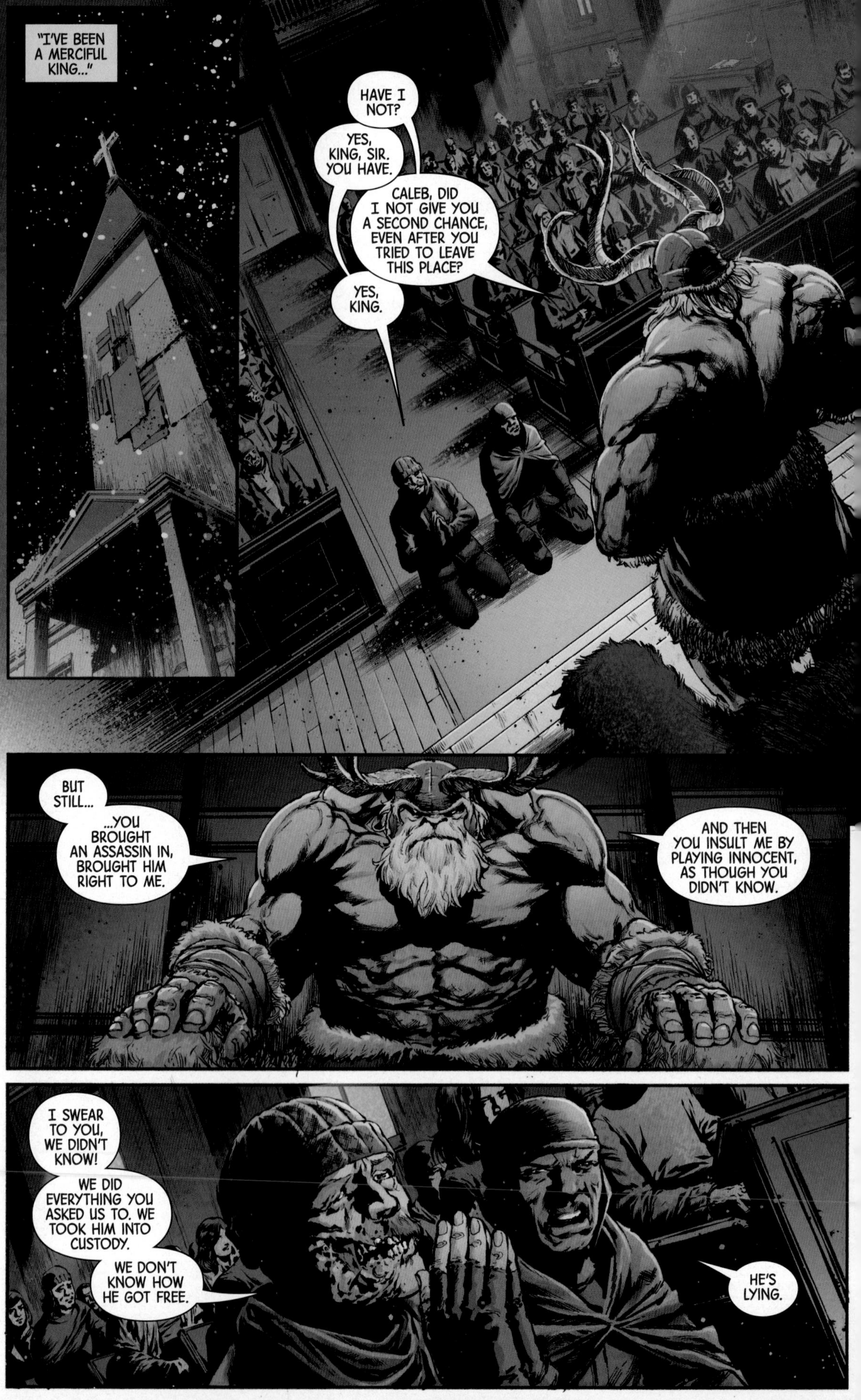
"I'VE BEEN A MERCIFUL KING..."
HAVE I NOT?
YES, KING, SIR. YOU HAVE.
CALEB, DID I NOT GIVE YOU A SECOND CHANCE, EVEN AFTER YOU TRIED TO LEAVE THIS PLACE?
YES, KING.
BUT STILL...
...YOU BROUGHT AN ASSASSIN IN, BROUGHT HIM RIGHT TO ME.
AND THEN YOU INSULT ME BY PLAYING INNOCENT, AS THOUGH YOU DIDN'T KNOW.
I SWEAR TO YOU, WE DIDN'T KNOW!
WE DID EVERYTHING YOU ASKED US TO. WE TOOK HIM INTO CUSTODY.
WE DON'T KNOW HOW HE GOT FREE.
HE'S LYING.

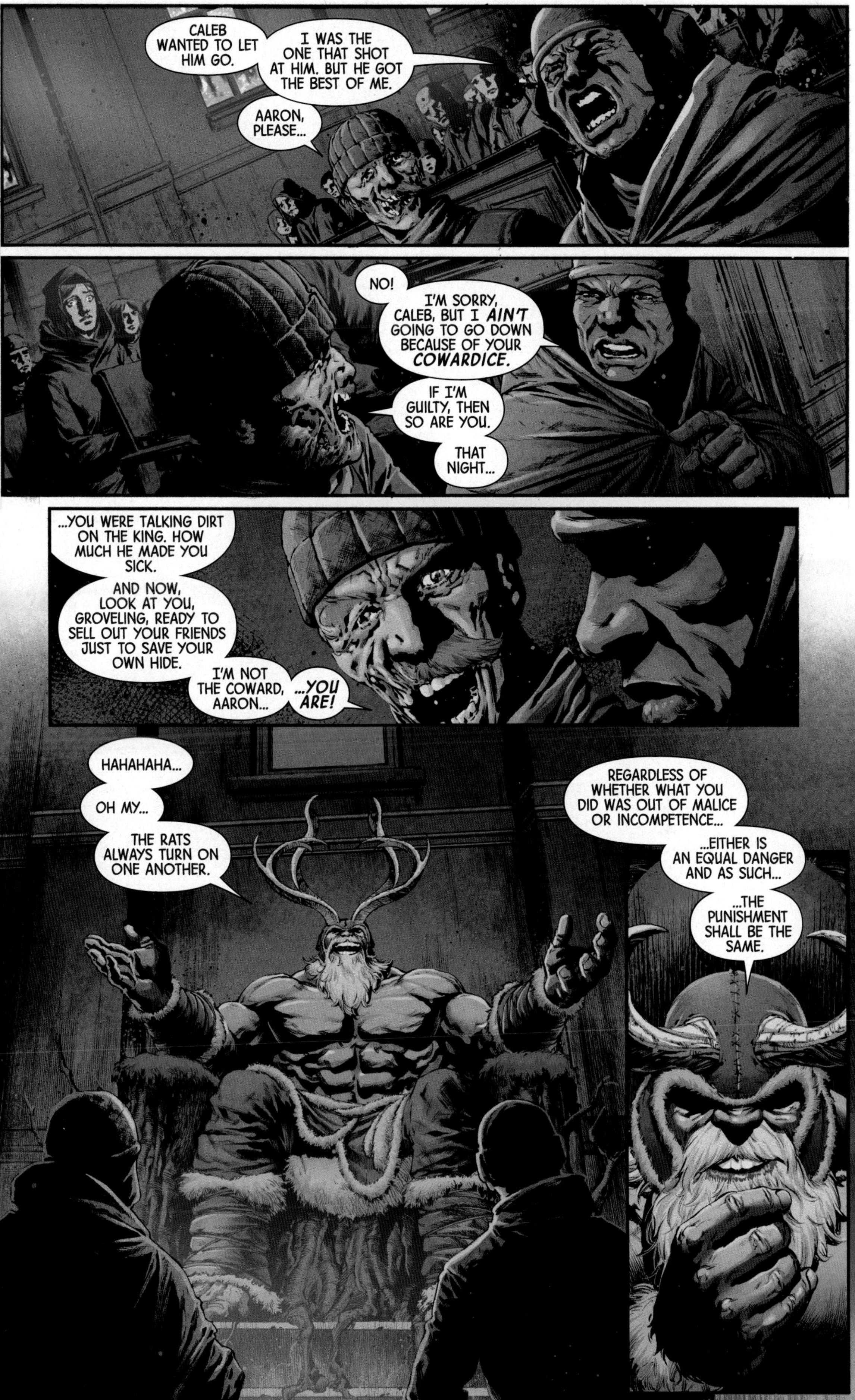
CALEB WANTED TO LET HIM GO.
I WAS THE ONE THAT SHOT AT HIM. BUT HE GOT THE BEST OF ME.
AARON, PLEASE...
NO!
I'M SORRY, CALEB, BUT I AIN'T GOING TO GO DOWN BECAUSE OF YOUR COWARDICE.
IF I'M GUILTY, THEN SO ARE YOU.
THAT NIGHT...
...YOU WERE TALKING DIRT ON THE KING. HOW MUCH HE MADE YOU SICK.
AND NOW, LOOK AT YOU, GROVELING, READY TO SELL OUT YOUR FRIENDS JUST TO SAVE YOUR OWN HIDE.
I'M NOT THE COWARD, AARON...
...YOU ARE!
HAHAHAHA...
OH MY...
THE RATS ALWAYS TURN ON ONE ANOTHER.
REGARDLESS OF WHETHER WHAT YOU DID WAS OUT OF MALICE OR INCOMPETENCE...
...EITHER IS AN EQUAL DANGER AND AS SUCH...
...THE PUNISHMENT SHALL BE THE SAME.

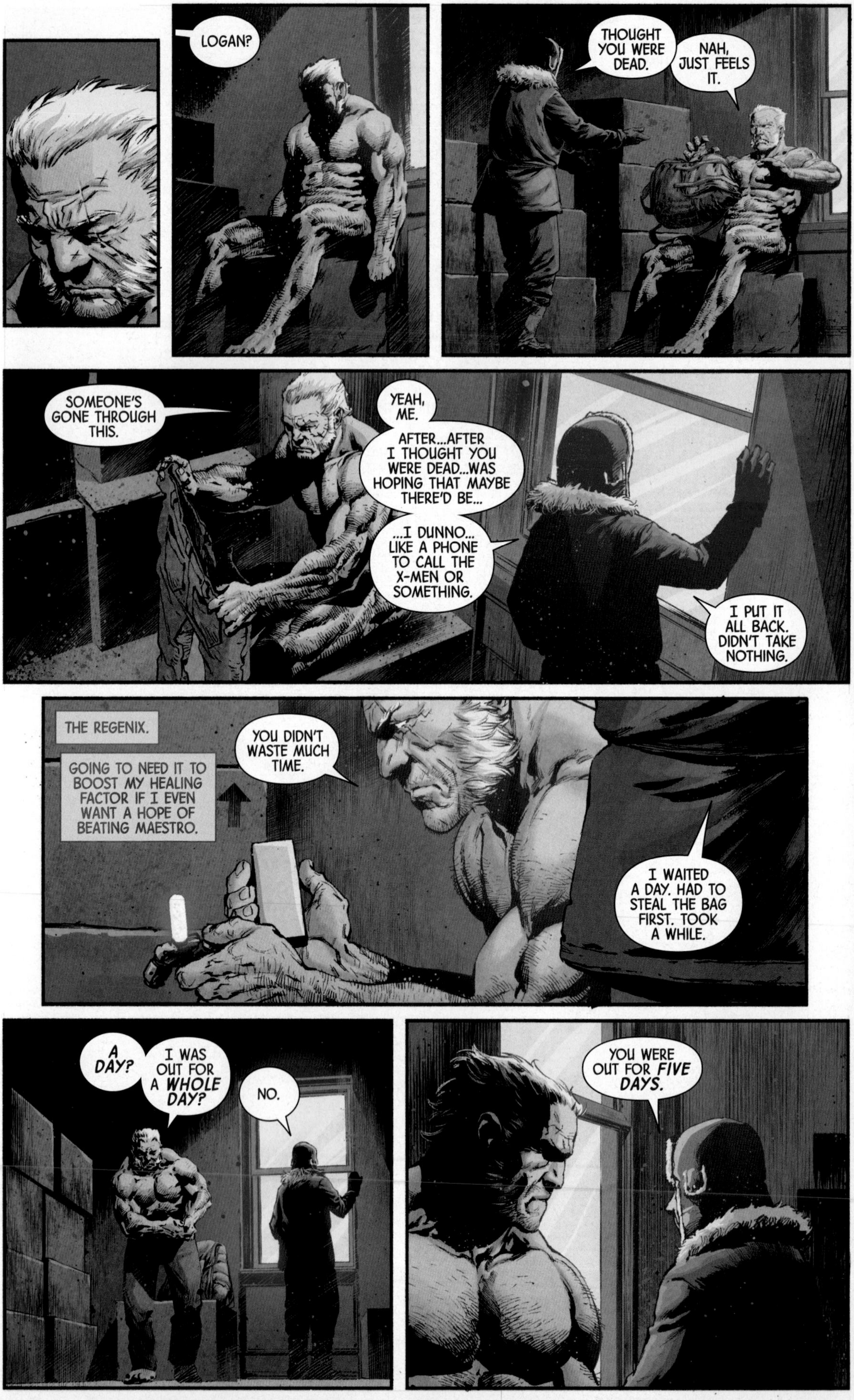
LOGAN?
THOUGHT YOU WERE DEAD.
NAH, JUST FEELS IT.
SOMEONE'S GONE THROUGH THIS.
YEAH, ME.
AFTER...AFTER I THOUGHT YOU WERE DEAD...WAS HOPING THAT MAYBE THERE'D BE...
...I DUNNO... LIKE A PHONE TO CALL THE X-MEN OR SOMETHING.
I PUT IT ALL BACK. DIDN'T TAKE NOTHING.
THE REGENIX.
GOING TO NEED IT TO BOOST MY HEALING FACTOR IF I EVEN WANT A HOPE OF BEATING MAESTRO.
YOU DIDN'T WASTE MUCH TIME.
I WAITED A DAY. HAD TO STEAL THE BAG FIRST. TOOK A WHILE.
A DAY?
I WAS OUT FOR A WHOLE DAY?
NO.
YOU WERE OUT FOR FIVE DAYS.

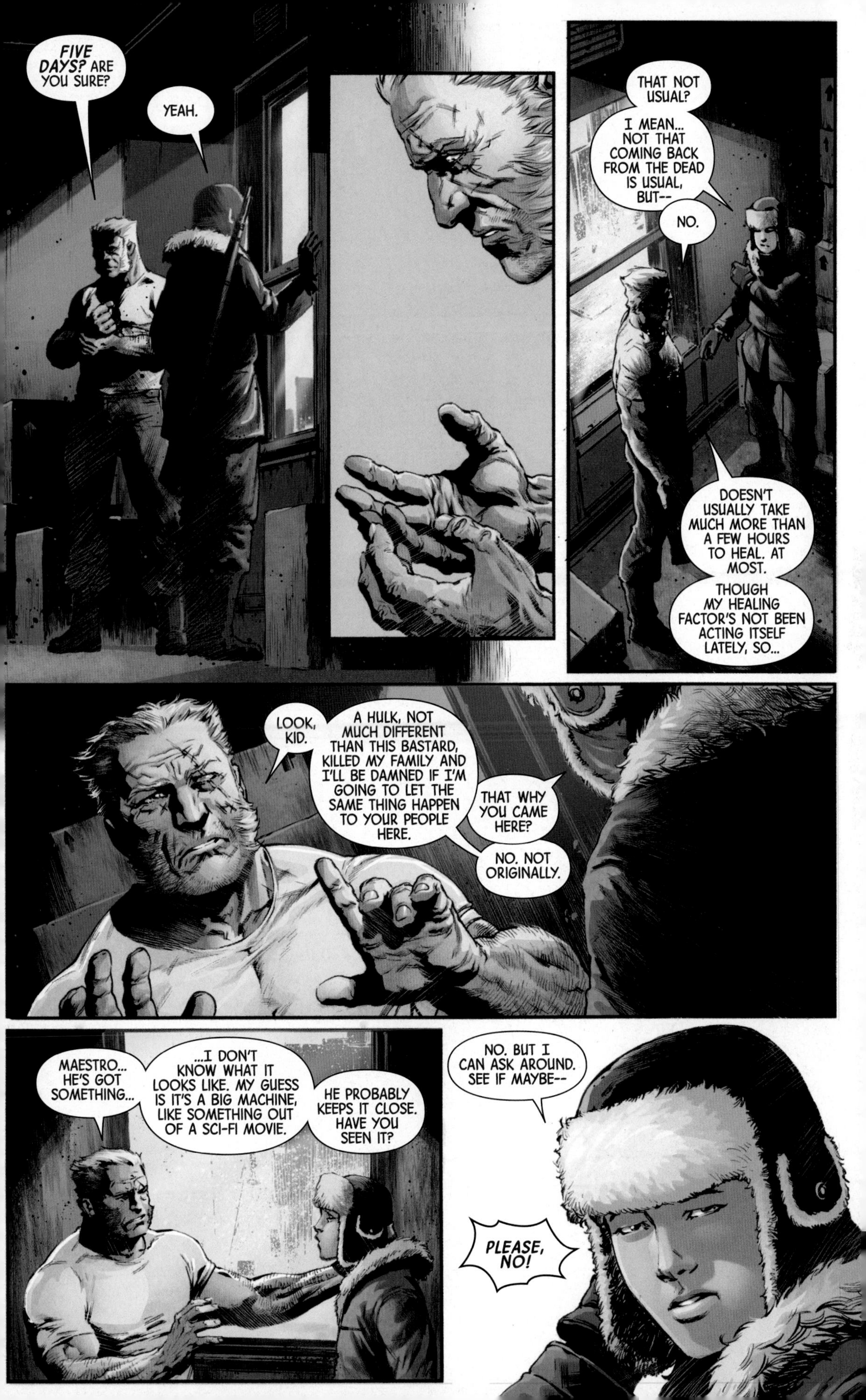

FIVE DAYS? ARE YOU SURE?
YEAH.
THAT NOT USUAL?
I MEAN... NOT THAT COMING BACK FROM THE DEAD IS USUAL, BUT--
NO.
DOESN'T USUALLY TAKE MUCH MORE THAN A FEW HOURS TO HEAL. AT MOST.
THOUGH MY HEALING FACTOR'S NOT BEEN ACTING ITSELF LATELY, SO...
LOOK, KID.
A HULK, NOT MUCH DIFFERENT THAN THIS BASTARD, KILLED MY FAMILY AND I'LL BE DAMNED IF I'M GOING TO LET THE SAME THING HAPPEN TO YOUR PEOPLE HERE.
THAT WHY YOU CAME HERE?
NO. NOT ORIGINALLY.
MAESTRO... HE'S GOT SOMETHING...
...I DON'T KNOW WHAT IT LOOKS LIKE. MY GUESS IS IT'S A BIG MACHINE, LIKE SOMETHING OUT OF A SCI-FI MOVIE.
HE PROBABLY KEEPS IT CLOSE. HAVE YOU SEEN IT?
NO. BUT I CAN ASK AROUND. SEE IF MAYBE--
PLEASE, NO!

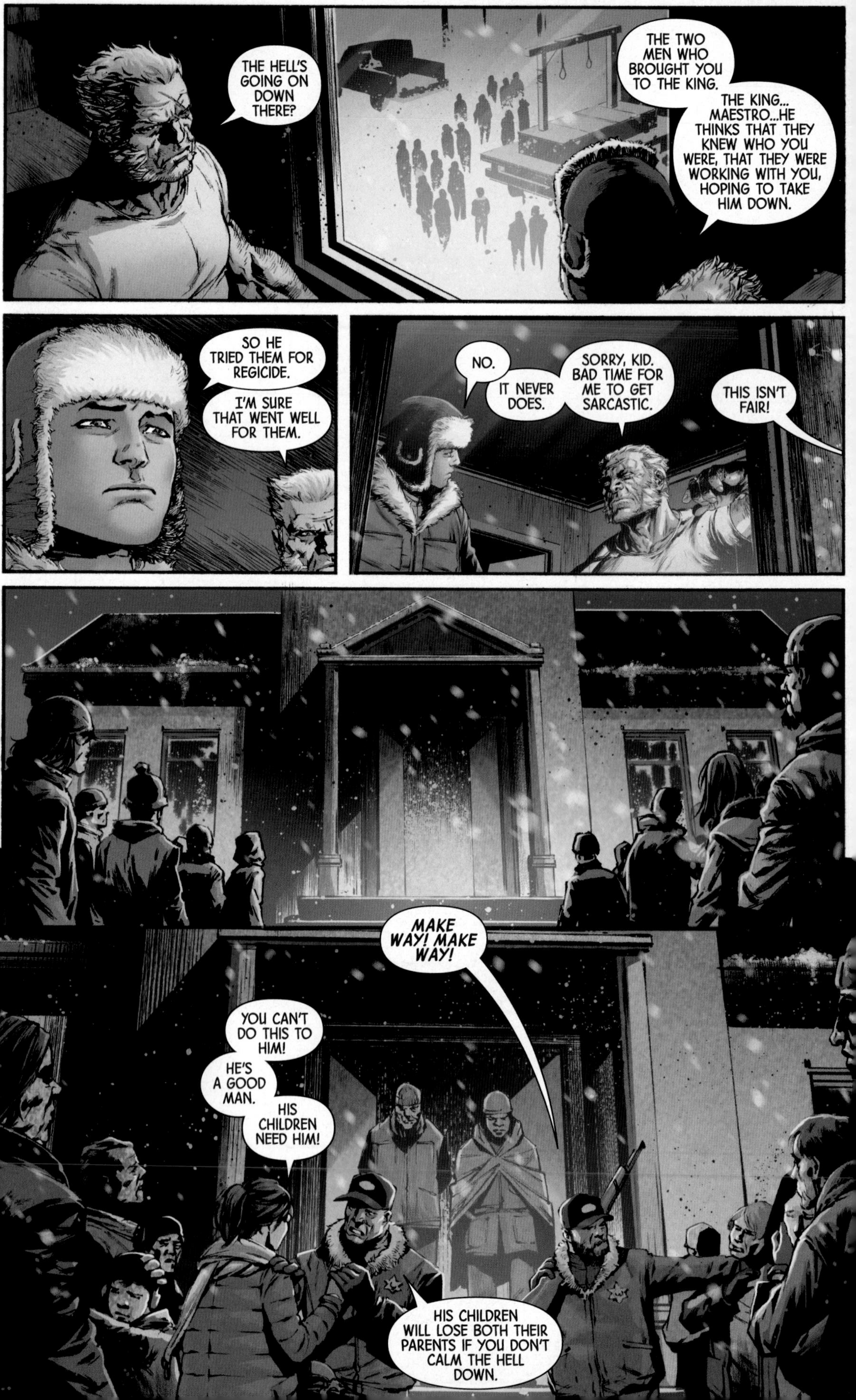
THE HELL'S GOING ON DOWN THERE?
THE TWO MEN WHO BROUGHT YOU TO THE KING.
THE KING... MAESTRO...HE THINKS THAT THEY KNEW WHO YOU WERE, THAT THEY WERE WORKING WITH YOU, HOPING TO TAKE HIM DOWN.
SO HE TRIED THEM FOR REGICIDE.
I'M SURE THAT WENT WELL FOR THEM.
NO.
IT NEVER DOES.
SORRY, KID. BAD TIME FOR ME TO GET SARCASTIC.
THIS ISN'T FAIR!
MAKE WAY! MAKE WAY!
YOU CAN'T DO THIS TO HIM!
HE'S A GOOD MAN.
HIS CHILDREN NEED HIM!
HIS CHILDREN WILL LOSE BOTH THEIR PARENTS IF YOU DON'T CALM THE HELL DOWN.

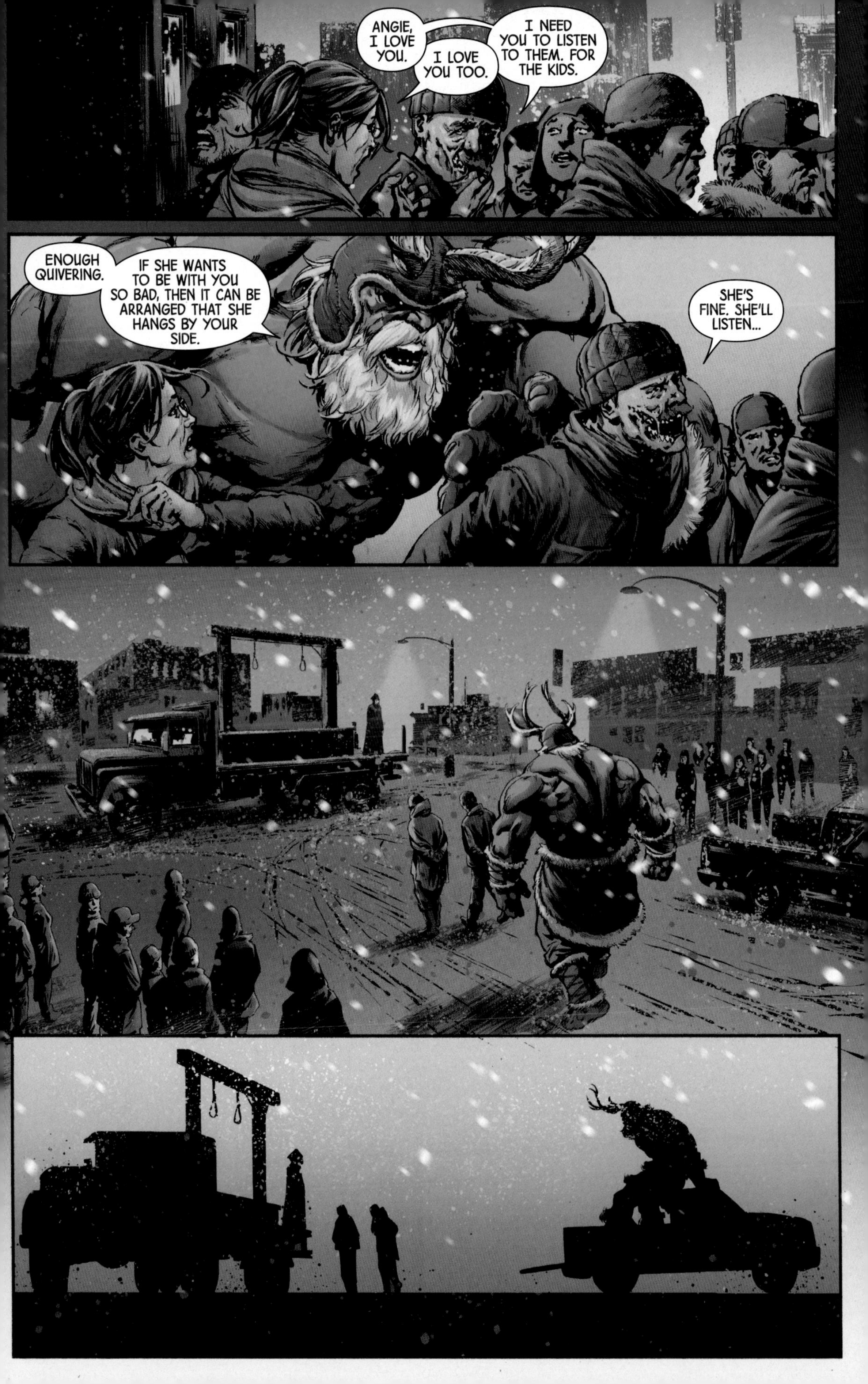
ANGIE, I LOVE YOU.
I LOVE YOU TOO.
I NEED YOU TO LISTEN TO THEM. FOR THE KIDS.
ENOUGH QUIVERING.
IF SHE WANTS TO BE WITH YOU SO BAD, THEN IT CAN BE ARRANGED THAT SHE HANGS BY YOUR SIDE.
SHE'S FINE. SHE'LL LISTEN...

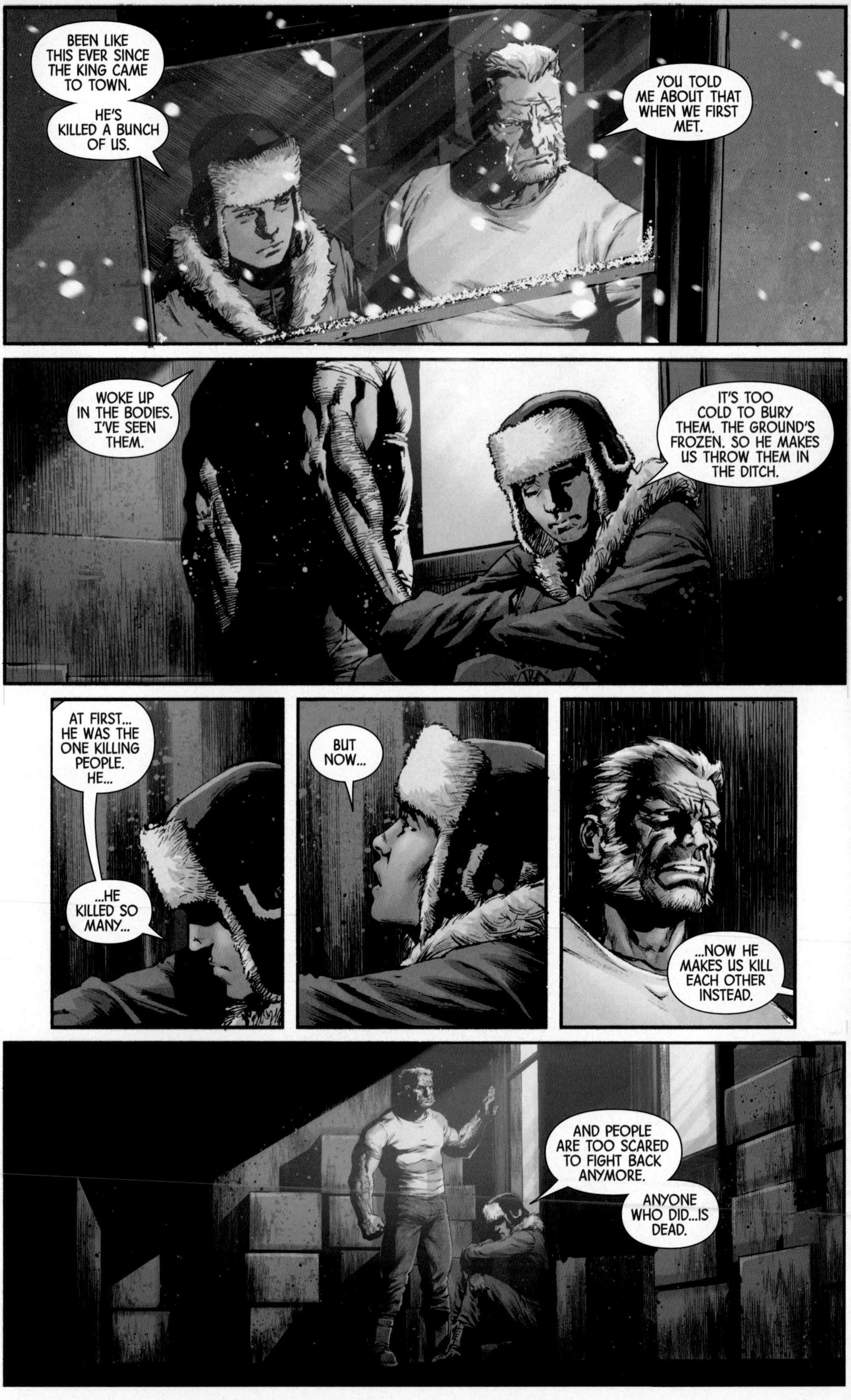
BEEN LIKE THIS EVER SINCE THE KING CAME TO TOWN.
HE'S KILLED A BUNCH OF US.
YOU TOLD ME ABOUT THAT WHEN WE FIRST MET.
WOKE UP IN THE BODIES. I'VE SEEN THEM.
IT'S TOO COLD TO BURY THEM. THE GROUND'S FROZEN. SO HE MAKES US THROW THEM IN THE DITCH.
AT FIRST... HE WAS THE ONE KILLING PEOPLE. HE...
...HE KILLED SO MANY...
BUT NOW...
...NOW HE MAKES US KILL EACH OTHER INSTEAD.
AND PEOPLE ARE TOO SCARED TO FIGHT BACK ANYMORE.
ANYONE WHO DID...IS DEAD.

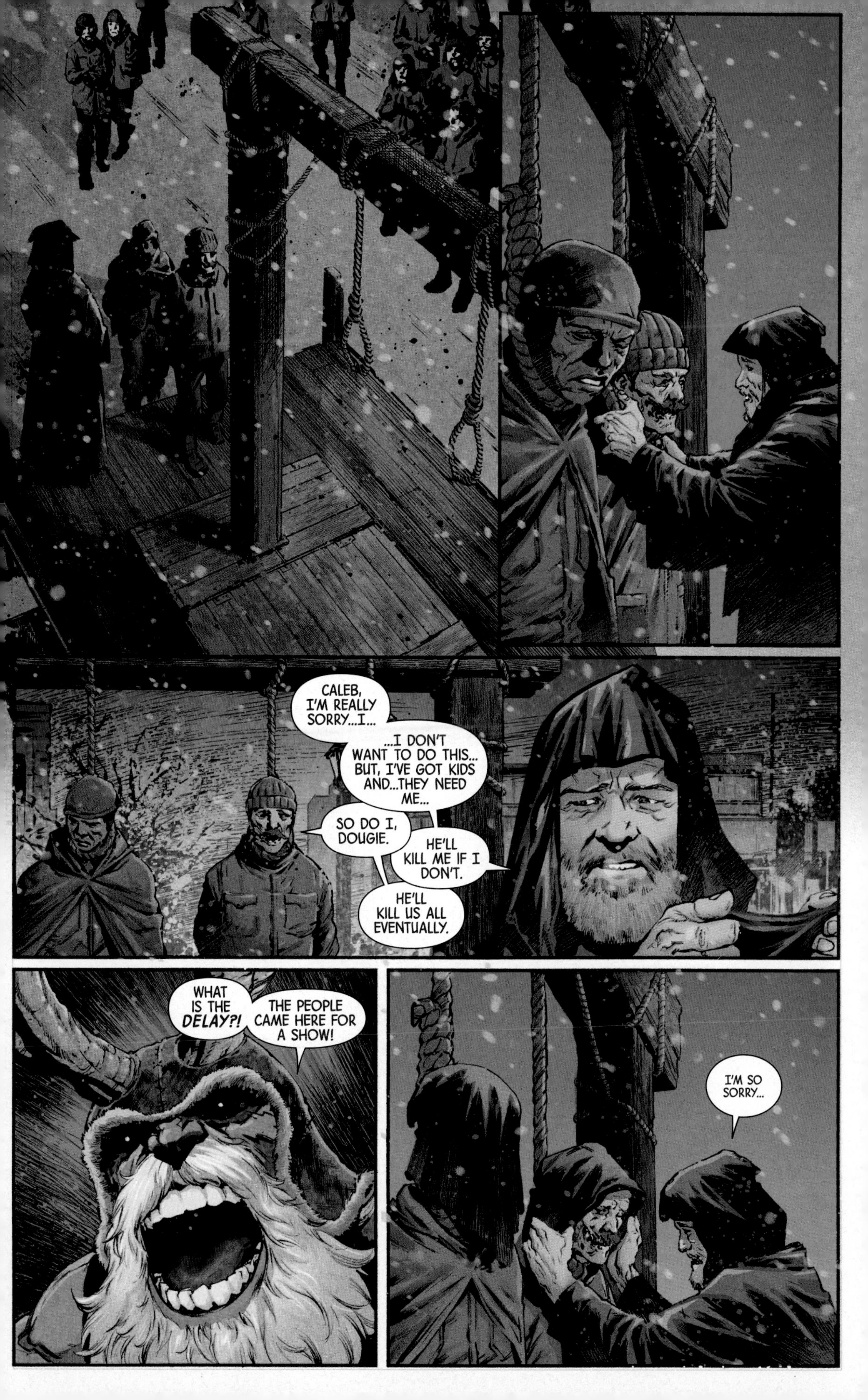

CALEB, I'M REALLY SORRY...I...
...I DON'T WANT TO DO THIS... BUT, I'VE GOT KIDS AND...THEY NEED ME...
SO DO I, DOUGIE.
HE'LL KILL ME IF I DON'T.
HE'LL KILL US ALL EVENTUALLY.
WHAT IS THE *DELAY?!*
THE PEOPLE CAME HERE FOR A SHOW!
I'M SO SORRY...

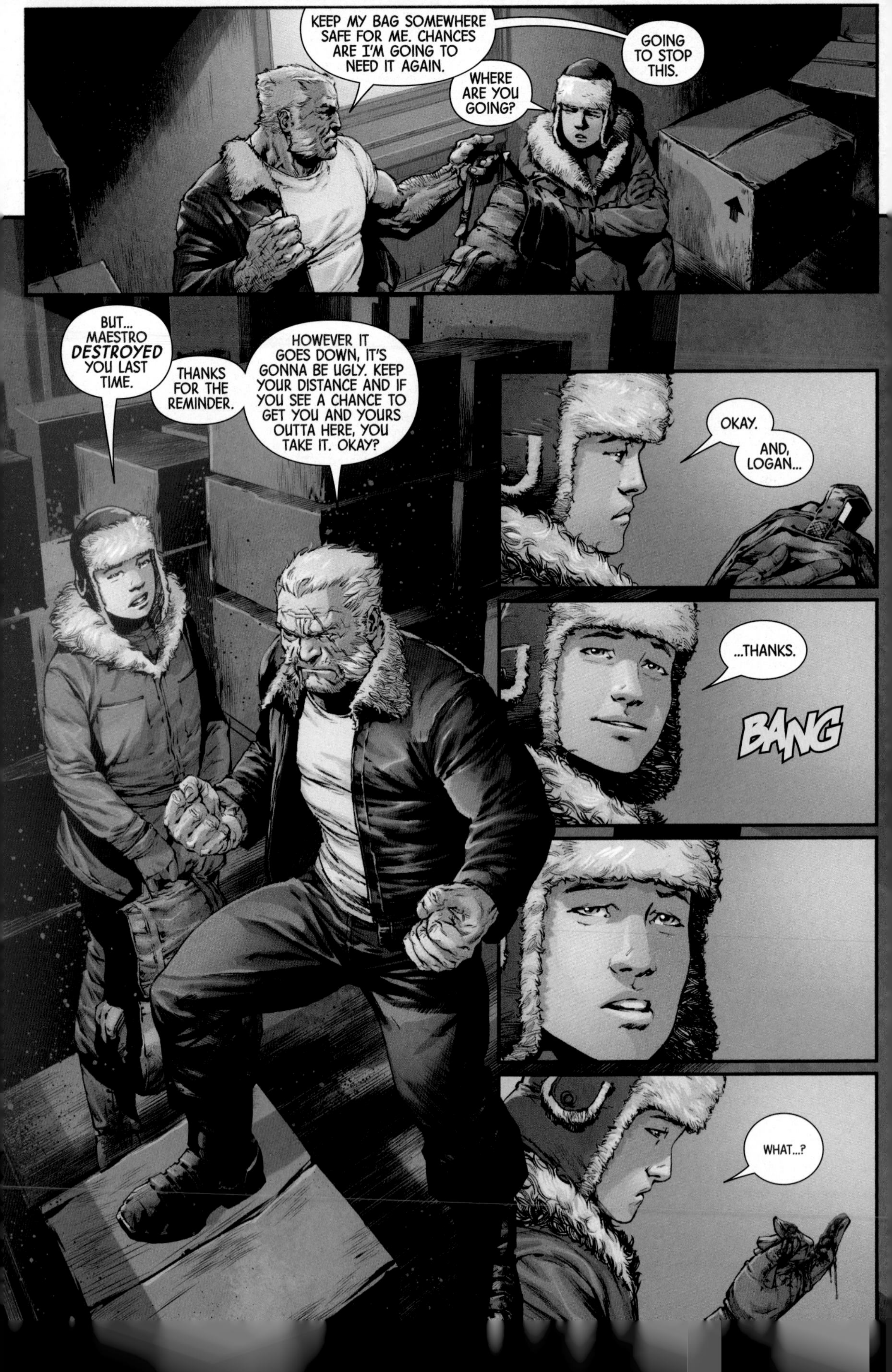
KEEP MY BAG SOMEWHERE SAFE FOR ME. CHANCES ARE I'M GOING TO NEED IT AGAIN.
WHERE ARE YOU GOING?
GOING TO STOP THIS.
BUT... MAESTRO DESTROYED YOU LAST TIME.
THANKS FOR THE REMINDER.
HOWEVER IT GOES DOWN, IT'S GONNA BE UGLY. KEEP YOUR DISTANCE AND IF YOU SEE A CHANCE TO GET YOU AND YOURS OUTTA HERE, YOU TAKE IT. OKAY?
OKAY.
AND, LOGAN...
...THANKS.
BANG
WHAT...?

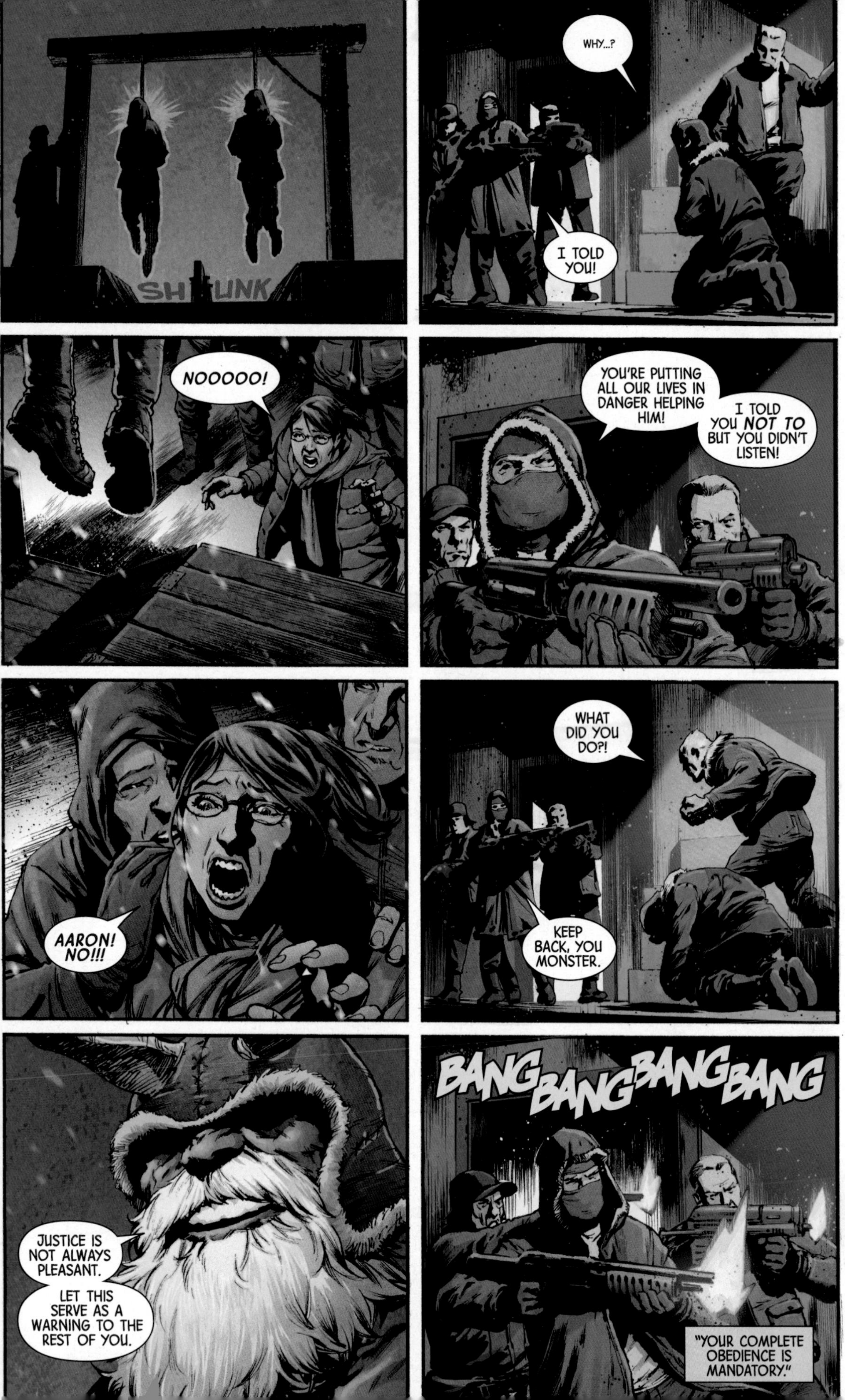

SHTUNK
WHY...?
I TOLD YOU!
NOOOOO!
YOU'RE PUTTING ALL OUR LIVES IN DANGER HELPING HIM!
I TOLD YOU NOT TO BUT YOU DIDN'T LISTEN!
AARON! NO!!!
WHAT DID YOU DO?!
KEEP BACK, YOU MONSTER.
JUSTICE IS NOT ALWAYS PLEASANT.
LET THIS SERVE AS A WARNING TO THE REST OF YOU.
BANG BANG BANG BANG
"YOUR COMPLETE OBEDIENCE IS MANDATORY."

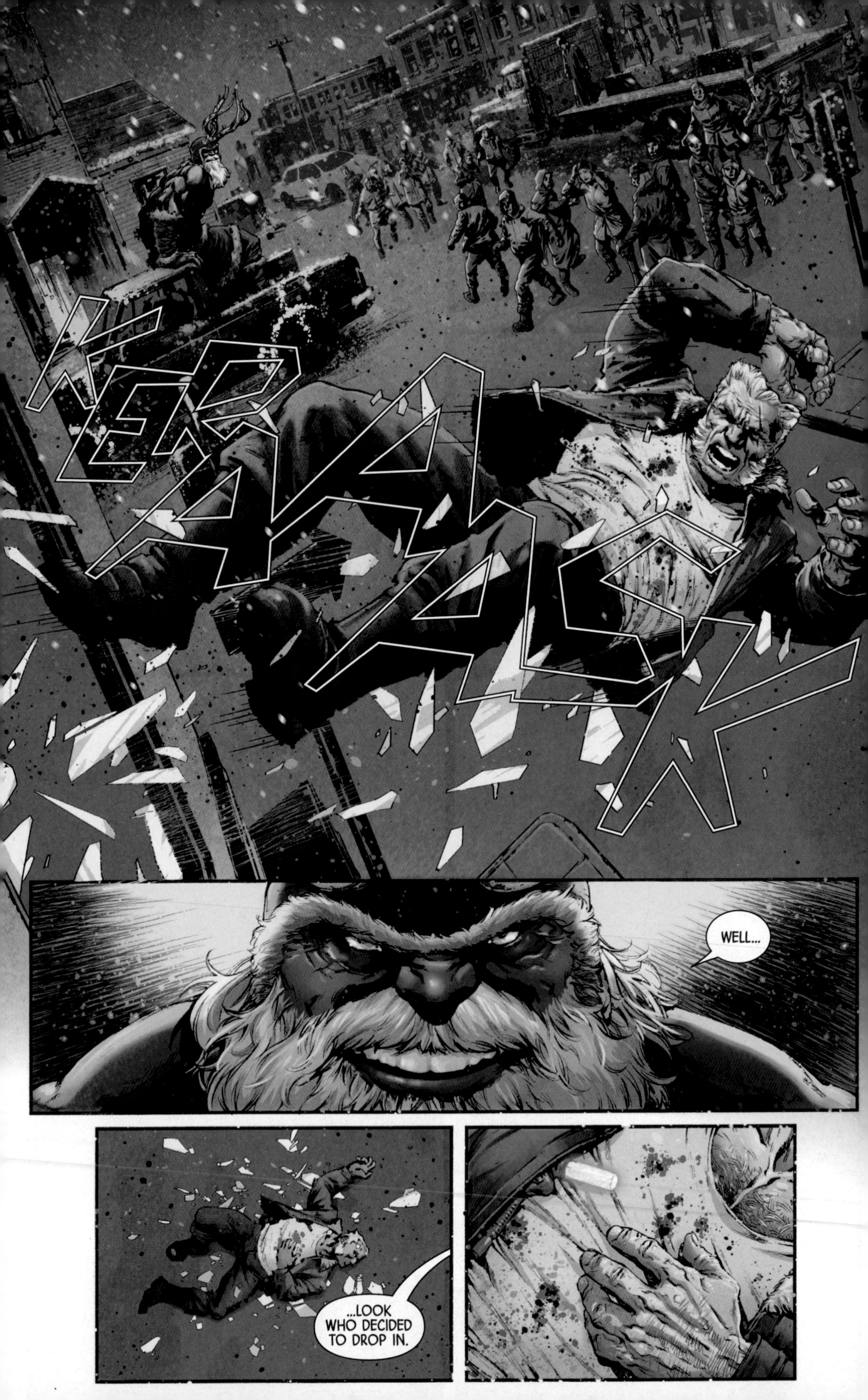
KERRAACK
WELL...
...LOOK WHO DECIDED TO DROP IN.

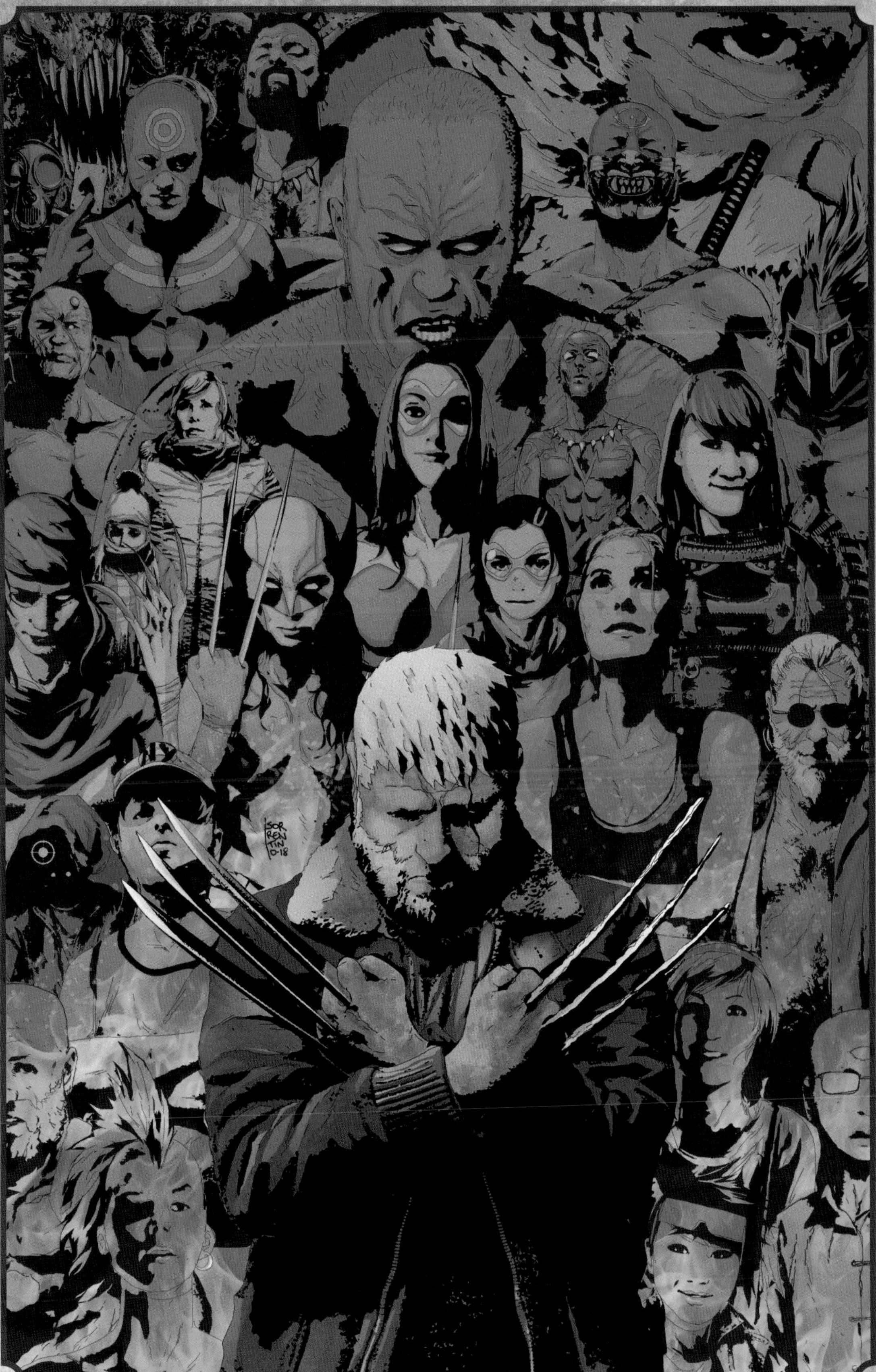

50

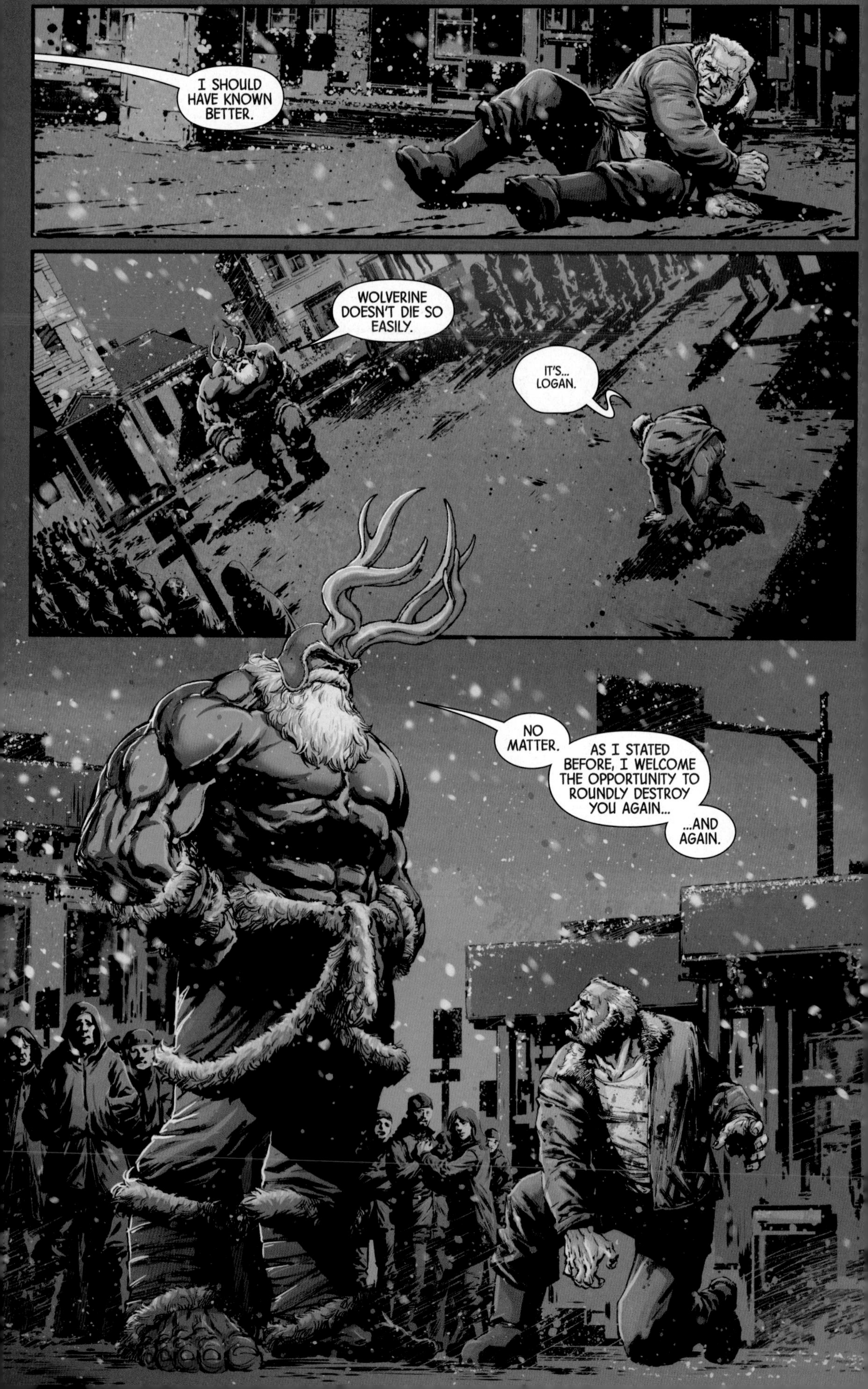
I SHOULD HAVE KNOWN BETTER.
WOLVERINE DOESN'T DIE SO EASILY.
IT'S... LOGAN.
NO MATTER.
AS I STATED BEFORE, I WELCOME THE OPPORTUNITY TO ROUNDLY DESTROY YOU AGAIN...
...AND AGAIN.

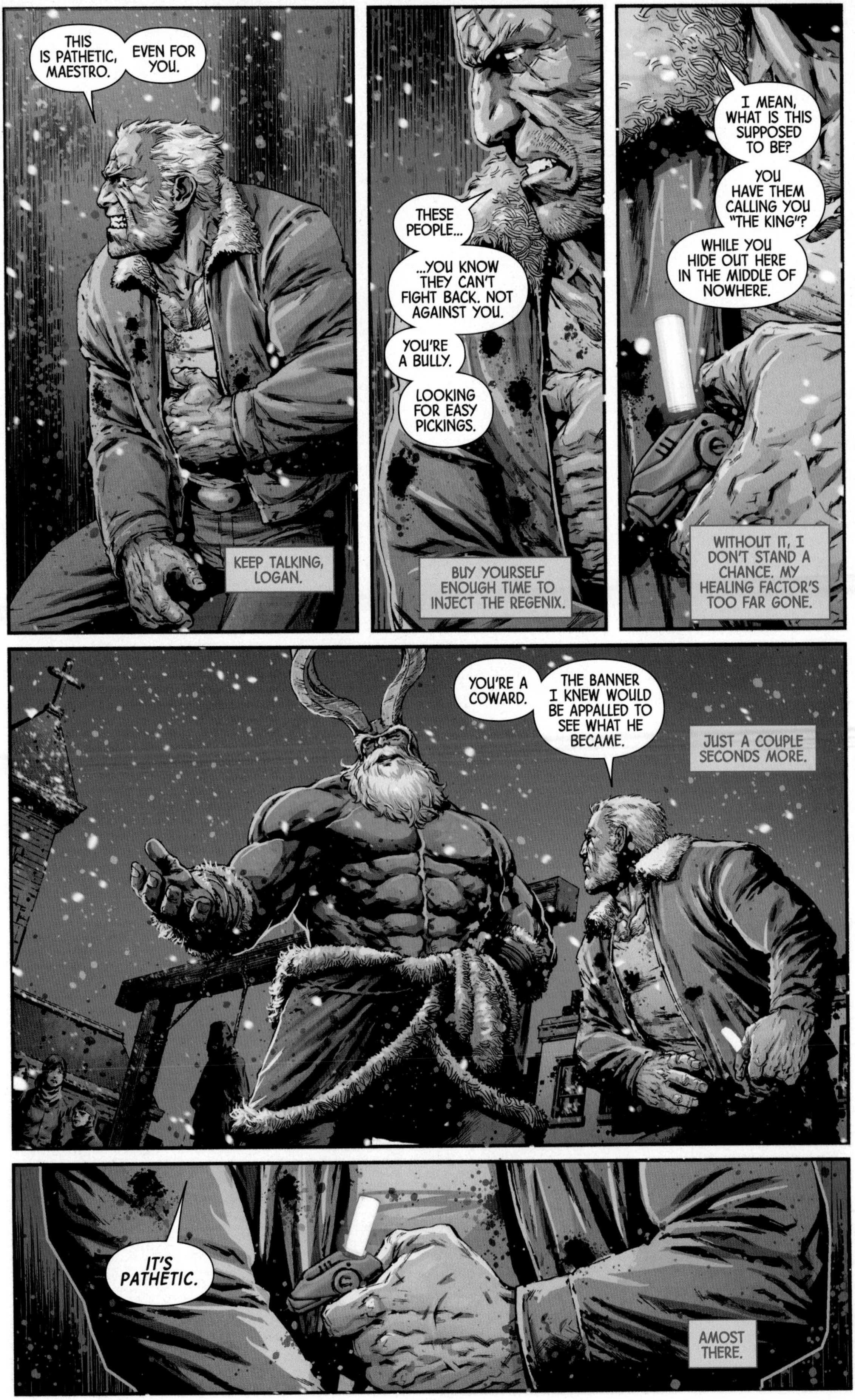
THIS IS PATHETIC, MAESTRO.
EVEN FOR YOU.
KEEP TALKING, LOGAN.
THESE PEOPLE...
...YOU KNOW THEY CAN'T FIGHT BACK. NOT AGAINST YOU.
YOU'RE A BULLY.
LOOKING FOR EASY PICKINGS.
BUY YOURSELF ENOUGH TIME TO INJECT THE REGENIX.
I MEAN, WHAT IS THIS SUPPOSED TO BE?
YOU HAVE THEM CALLING YOU "THE KING"?
WHILE YOU HIDE OUT HERE IN THE MIDDLE OF NOWHERE.
WITHOUT IT, I DON'T STAND A CHANCE. MY HEALING FACTOR'S TOO FAR GONE.
YOU'RE A COWARD.
THE BANNER I KNEW WOULD BE APPALLED TO SEE WHAT HE BECAME.
JUST A COUPLE SECONDS MORE.
IT'S PATHETIC.
AMOST THERE.

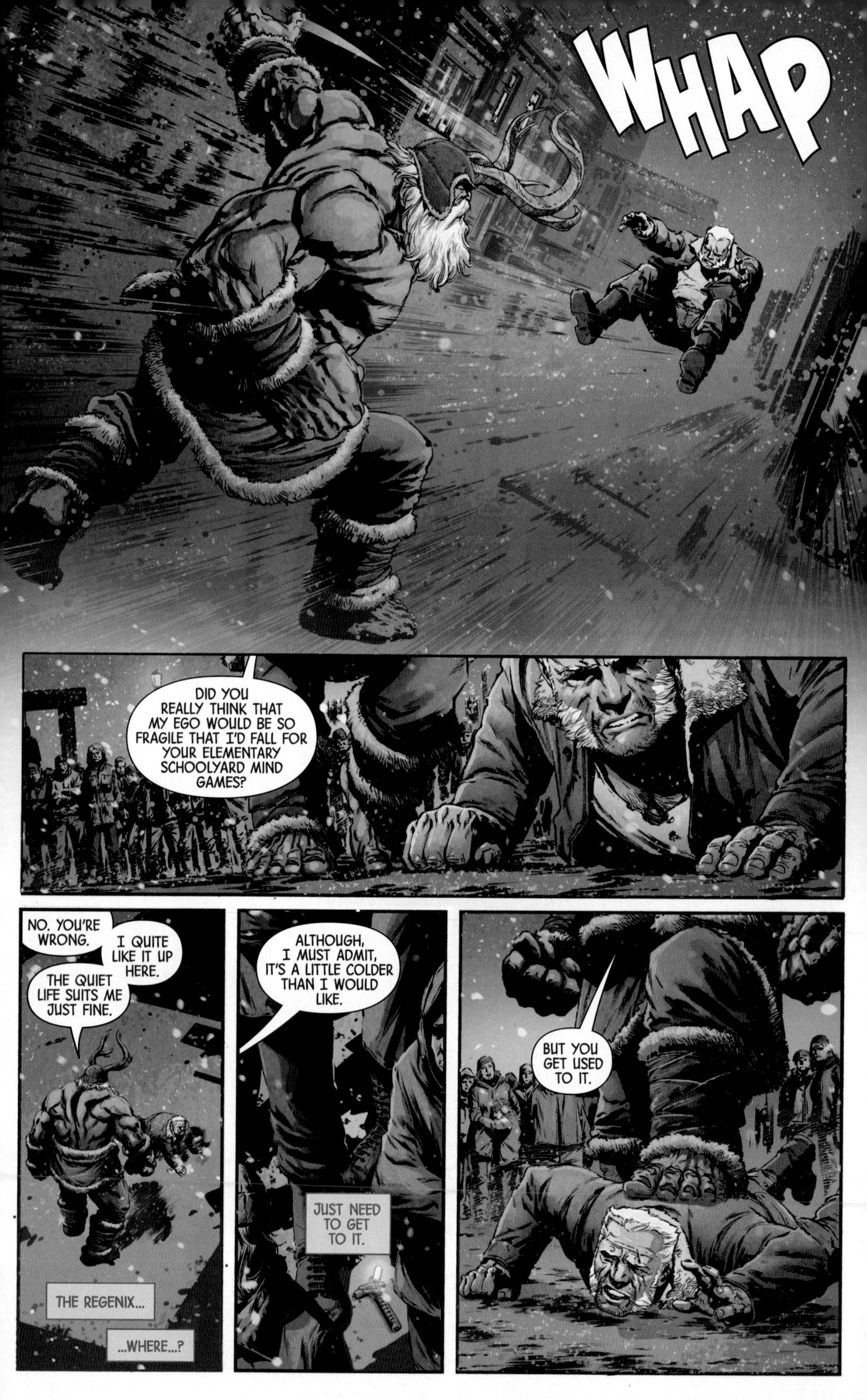
WHAP
DID YOU REALLY THINK THAT MY EGO WOULD BE SO FRAGILE THAT I'D FALL FOR YOUR ELEMENTARY SCHOOLYARD MIND GAMES?
NO. YOU'RE WRONG.
I QUITE LIKE IT UP HERE.
THE QUIET LIFE SUITS ME JUST FINE.
THE REGENIX...
...WHERE...?
ALTHOUGH, I MUST ADMIT, IT'S A LITTLE COLDER THAN I WOULD LIKE.
JUST NEED TO GET TO IT.
BUT YOU GET USED TO IT.

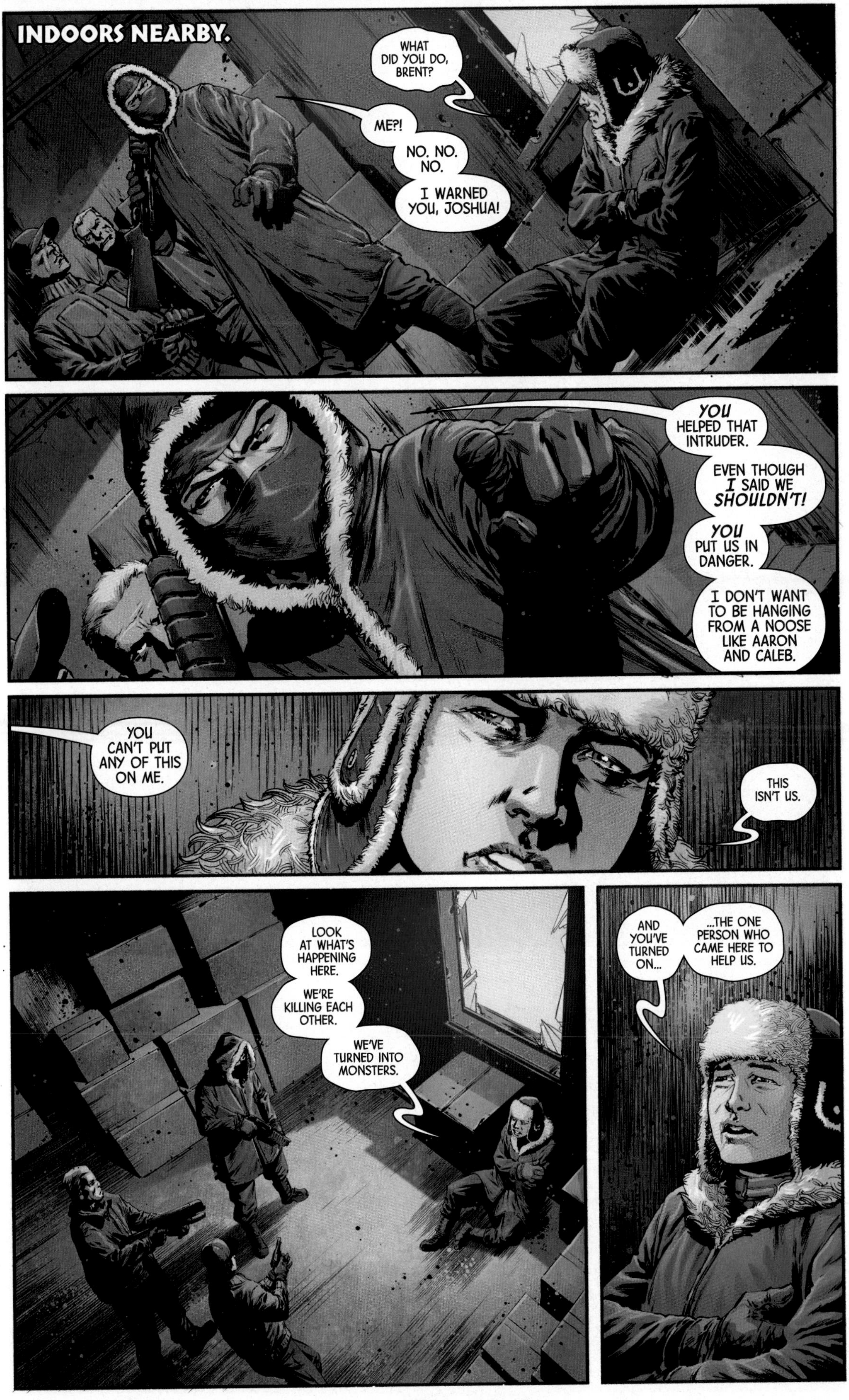

INDOORS NEARBY.
WHAT DID YOU DO, BRENT?
ME?!
NO. NO. NO.
I WARNED YOU, JOSHUA!
YOU HELPED THAT INTRUDER.
EVEN THOUGH I SAID WE SHOULDN'T!
YOU PUT US IN DANGER.
I DON'T WANT TO BE HANGING FROM A NOOSE LIKE AARON AND CALEB.
YOU CAN'T PUT ANY OF THIS ON ME.
THIS ISN'T US.
LOOK AT WHAT'S HAPPENING HERE.
WE'RE KILLING EACH OTHER.
WE'VE TURNED INTO MONSTERS.
AND YOU'VE TURNED ON...
...THE ONE PERSON WHO CAME HERE TO HELP US.

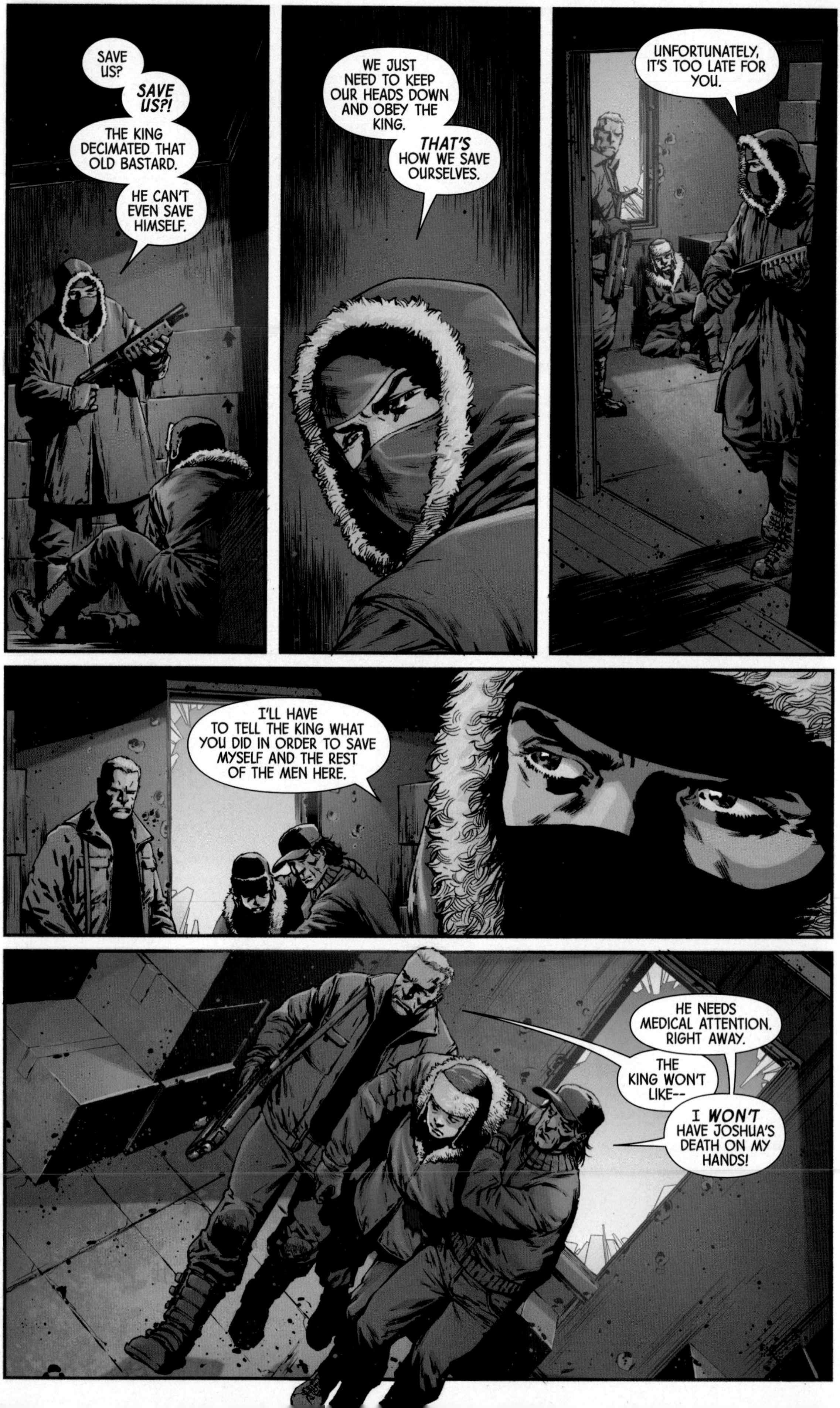
SAVE US?
SAVE US?!
THE KING DECIMATED THAT OLD BASTARD.
HE CAN'T EVEN SAVE HIMSELF.
WE JUST NEED TO KEEP OUR HEADS DOWN AND OBEY THE KING.
THAT'S HOW WE SAVE OURSELVES.
UNFORTUNATELY, IT'S TOO LATE FOR YOU.
I'LL HAVE TO TELL THE KING WHAT YOU DID IN ORDER TO SAVE MYSELF AND THE REST OF THE MEN HERE.
HE NEEDS MEDICAL ATTENTION. RIGHT AWAY.
THE KING WON'T LIKE--
I WON'T HAVE JOSHUA'S DEATH ON MY HANDS!

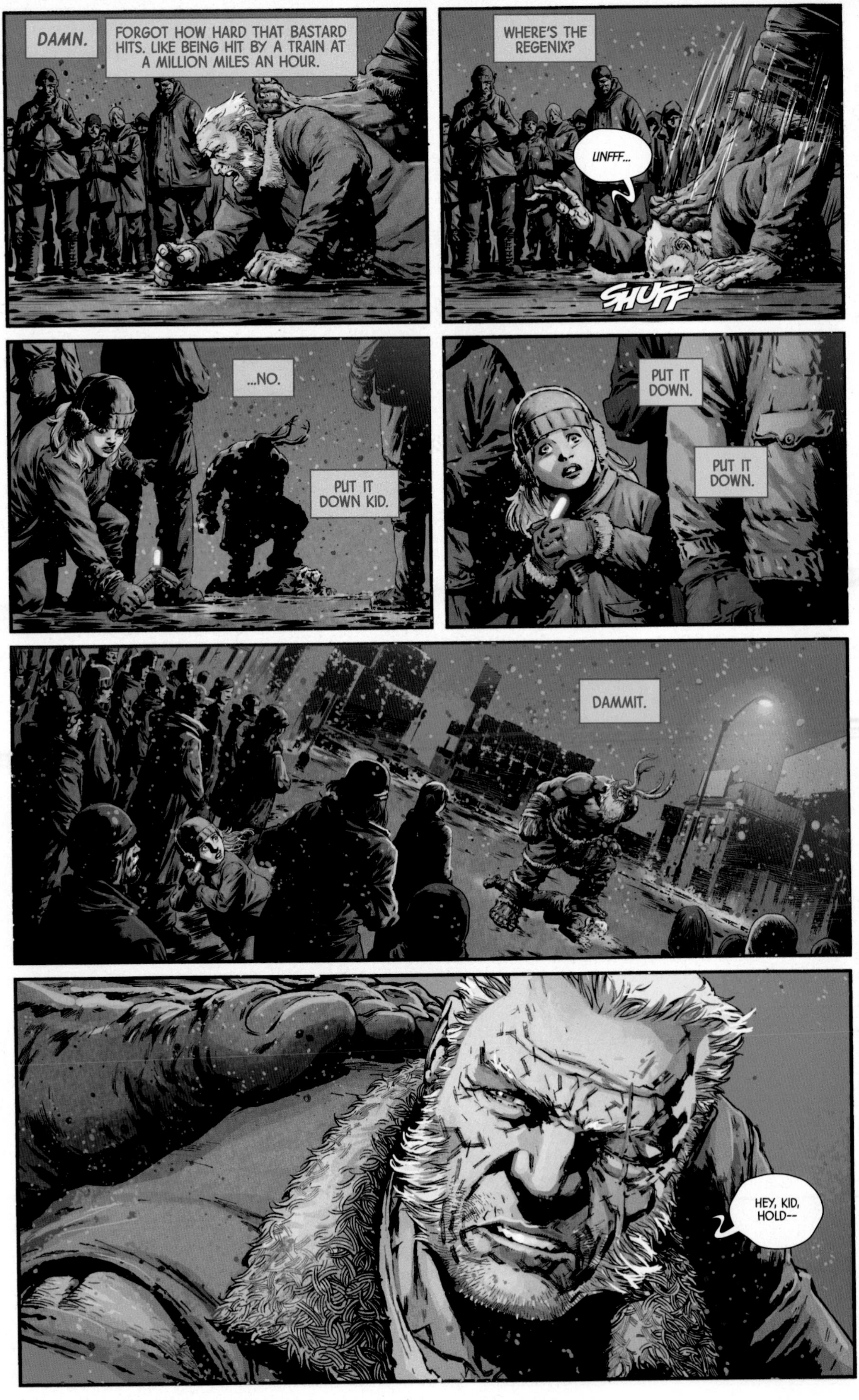
DAMN.
FORGOT HOW HARD THAT BASTARD HITS. LIKE BEING HIT BY A TRAIN AT A MILLION MILES AN HOUR.
WHERE'S THE REGENIX?
UNFFF...
SHUFF
...NO.
PUT IT DOWN KID.
PUT IT DOWN.
PUT IT DOWN.
DAMMIT.
HEY, KID, HOLD--

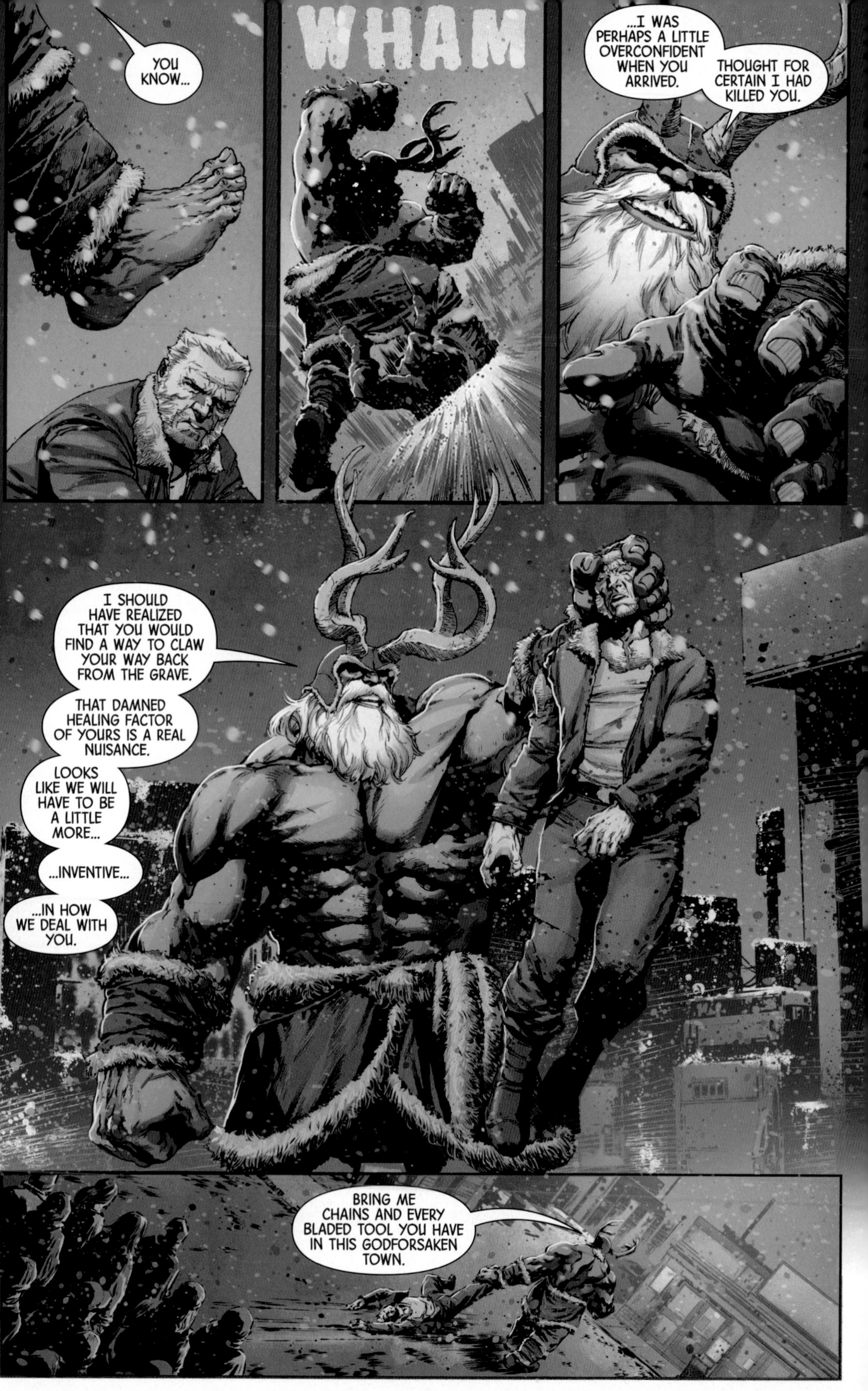
YOU KNOW...
WHAM
...I WAS PERHAPS A LITTLE OVERCONFIDENT WHEN YOU ARRIVED.
THOUGHT FOR CERTAIN I HAD KILLED YOU.
I SHOULD HAVE REALIZED THAT YOU WOULD FIND A WAY TO CLAW YOUR WAY BACK FROM THE GRAVE.
THAT DAMNED HEALING FACTOR OF YOURS IS A REAL NUISANCE.
LOOKS LIKE WE WILL HAVE TO BE A LITTLE MORE...
...INVENTIVE...
...IN HOW WE DEAL WITH YOU.
BRING ME CHAINS AND EVERY BLADED TOOL YOU HAVE IN THIS GODFORSAKEN TOWN.

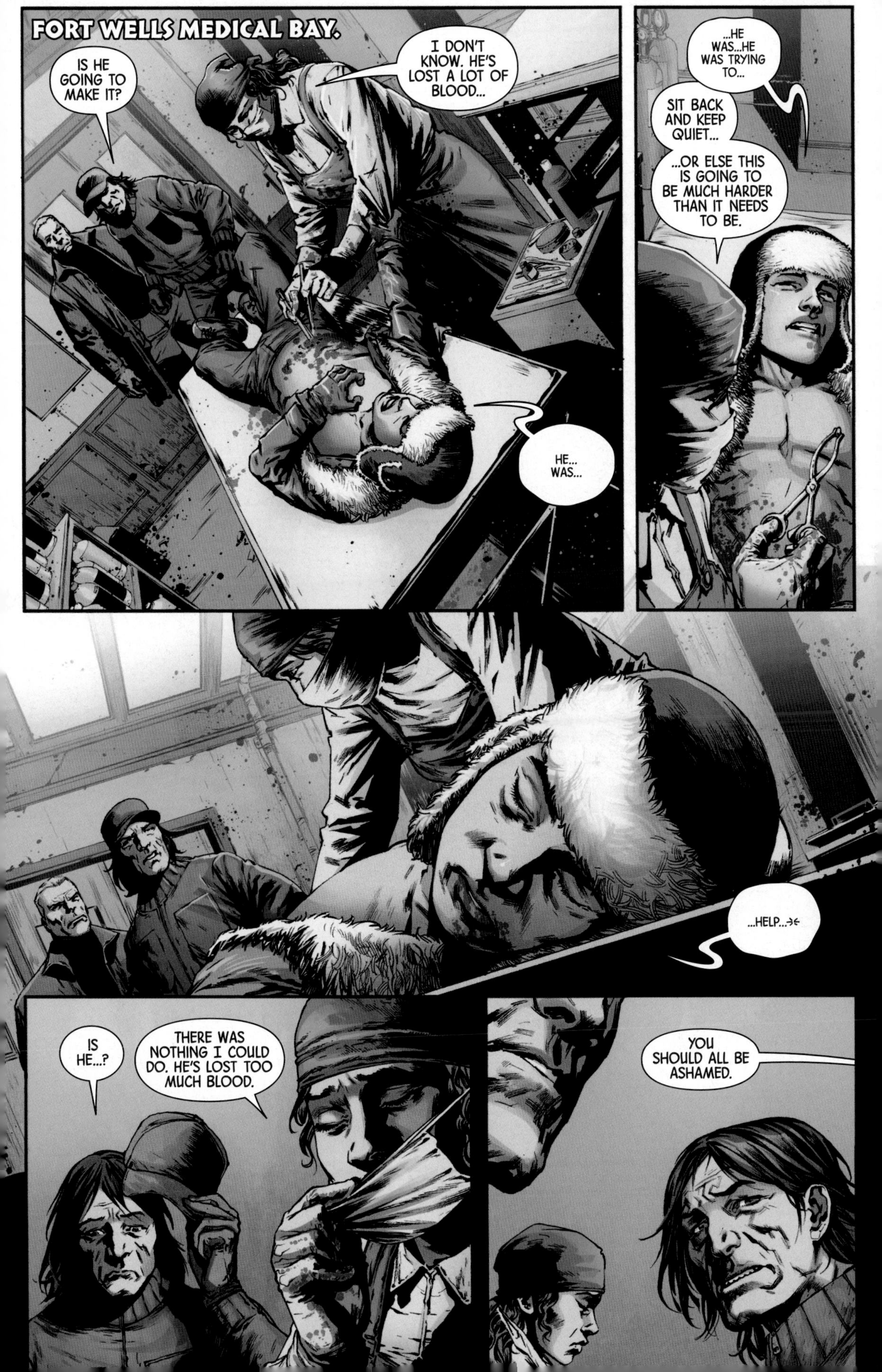
FORT WELLS MEDICAL BAY.
IS HE GOING TO MAKE IT?
I DON'T KNOW. HE'S LOST A LOT OF BLOOD...
HE... WAS...
...HE WAS...HE WAS TRYING TO...
SIT BACK AND KEEP QUIET...
...OR ELSE THIS IS GOING TO BE MUCH HARDER THAN IT NEEDS TO BE.
...HELP...
IS HE...?
THERE WAS NOTHING I COULD DO. HE'S LOST TOO MUCH BLOOD.
YOU SHOULD ALL BE ASHAMED.

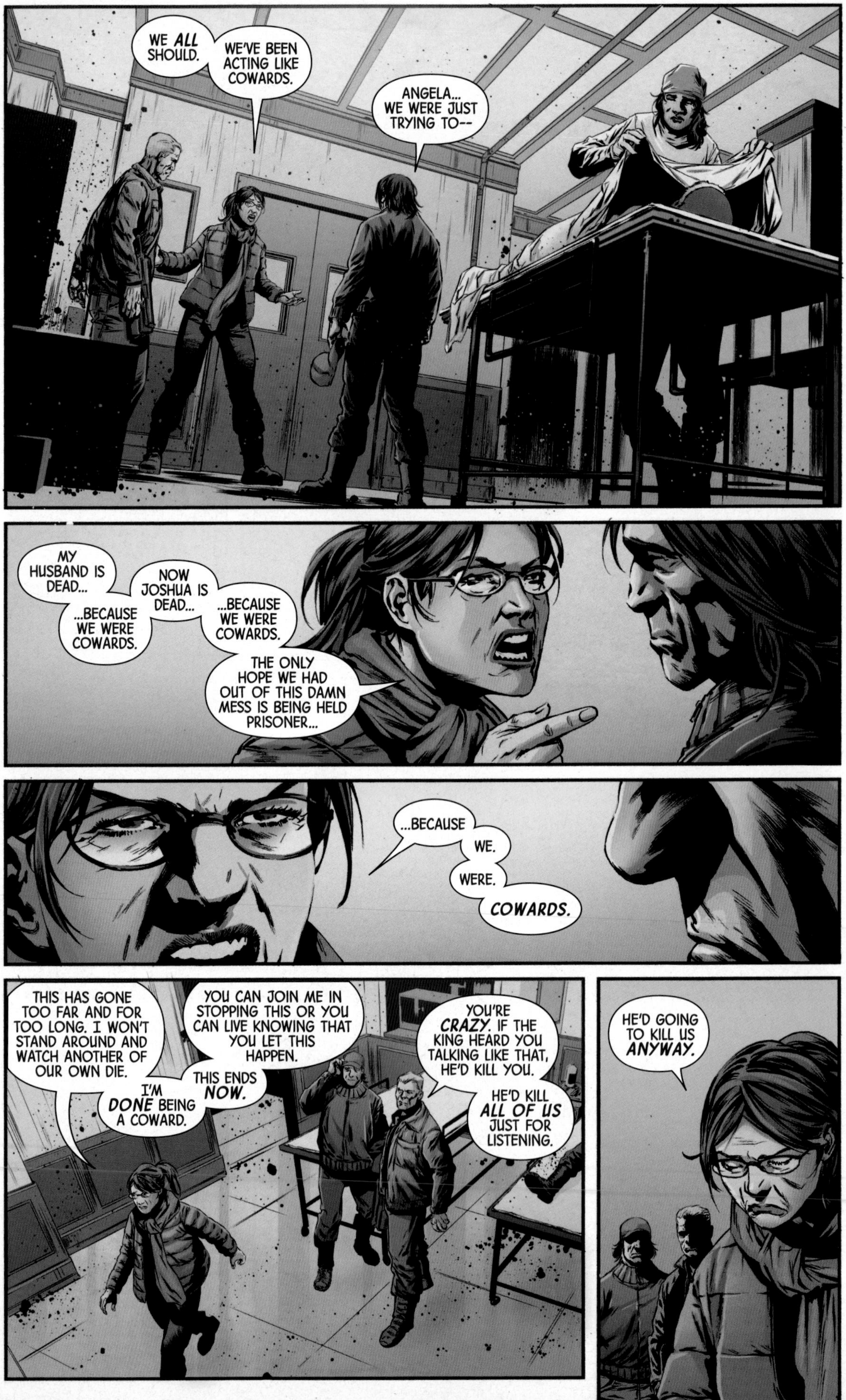
WE ALL SHOULD.
WE'VE BEEN ACTING LIKE COWARDS.
ANGELA... WE WERE JUST TRYING TO--
MY HUSBAND IS DEAD...
...BECAUSE WE WERE COWARDS.
NOW JOSHUA IS DEAD...
...BECAUSE WE WERE COWARDS.
THE ONLY HOPE WE HAD OUT OF THIS DAMN MESS IS BEING HELD PRISONER...
...BECAUSE
WE.
WERE.
COWARDS.
THIS HAS GONE TOO FAR AND FOR TOO LONG. I WON'T STAND AROUND AND WATCH ANOTHER OF OUR OWN DIE.
I'M DONE BEING A COWARD.
YOU CAN JOIN ME IN STOPPING THIS OR YOU CAN LIVE KNOWING THAT YOU LET THIS HAPPEN.
THIS ENDS NOW.
YOU'RE CRAZY. IF THE KING HEARD YOU TALKING LIKE THAT, HE'D KILL YOU.
HE'D KILL ALL OF US JUST FOR LISTENING.
HE'D GOING TO KILL US ANYWAY.

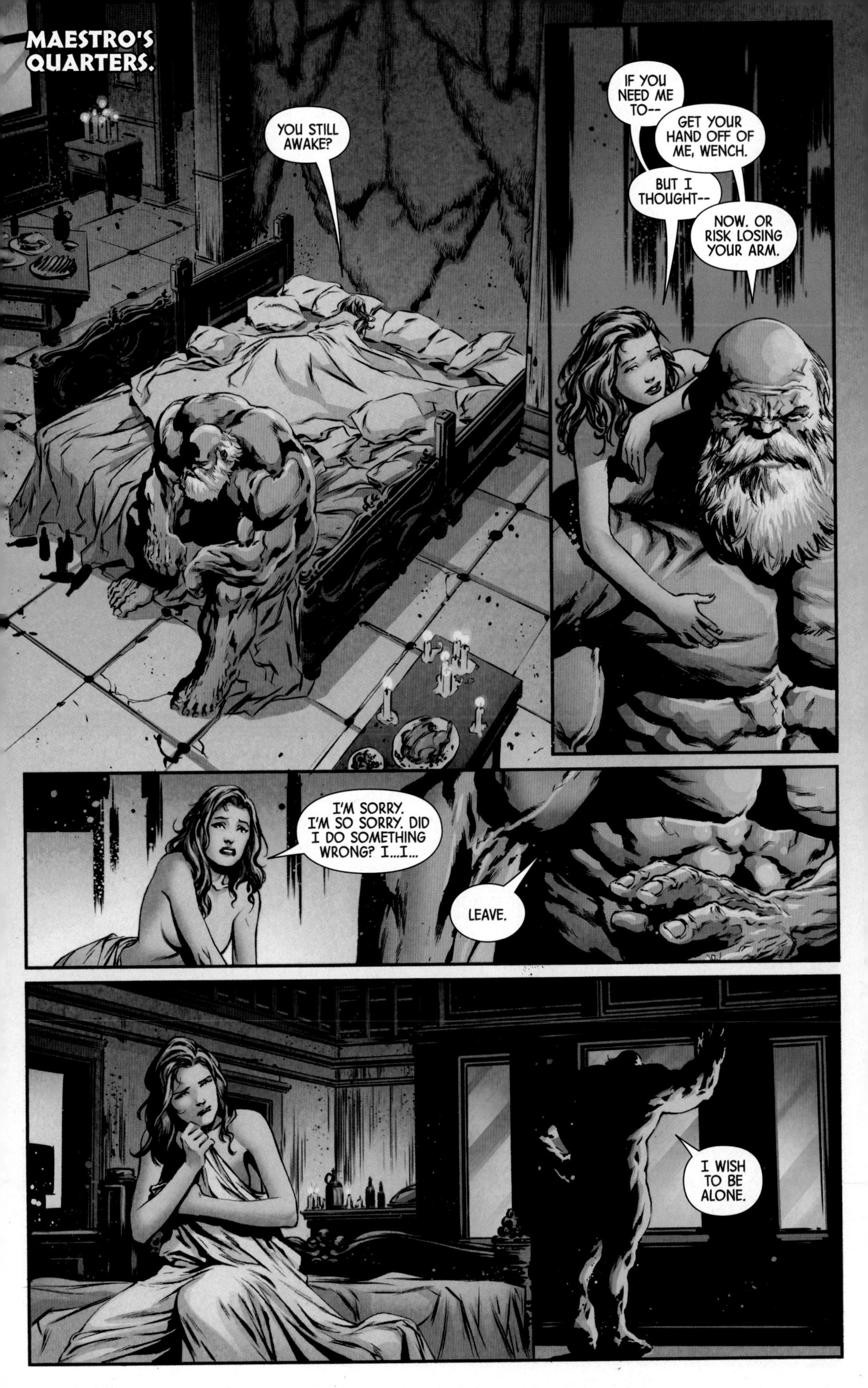
MAESTRO'S QUARTERS.
YOU STILL AWAKE?
IF YOU NEED ME TO--
GET YOUR HAND OFF OF ME, WENCH.
BUT I THOUGHT--
NOW. OR RISK LOSING YOUR ARM.
I'M SORRY. I'M SO SORRY. DID I DO SOMETHING WRONG? I...I...
LEAVE.
I WISH TO BE ALONE.

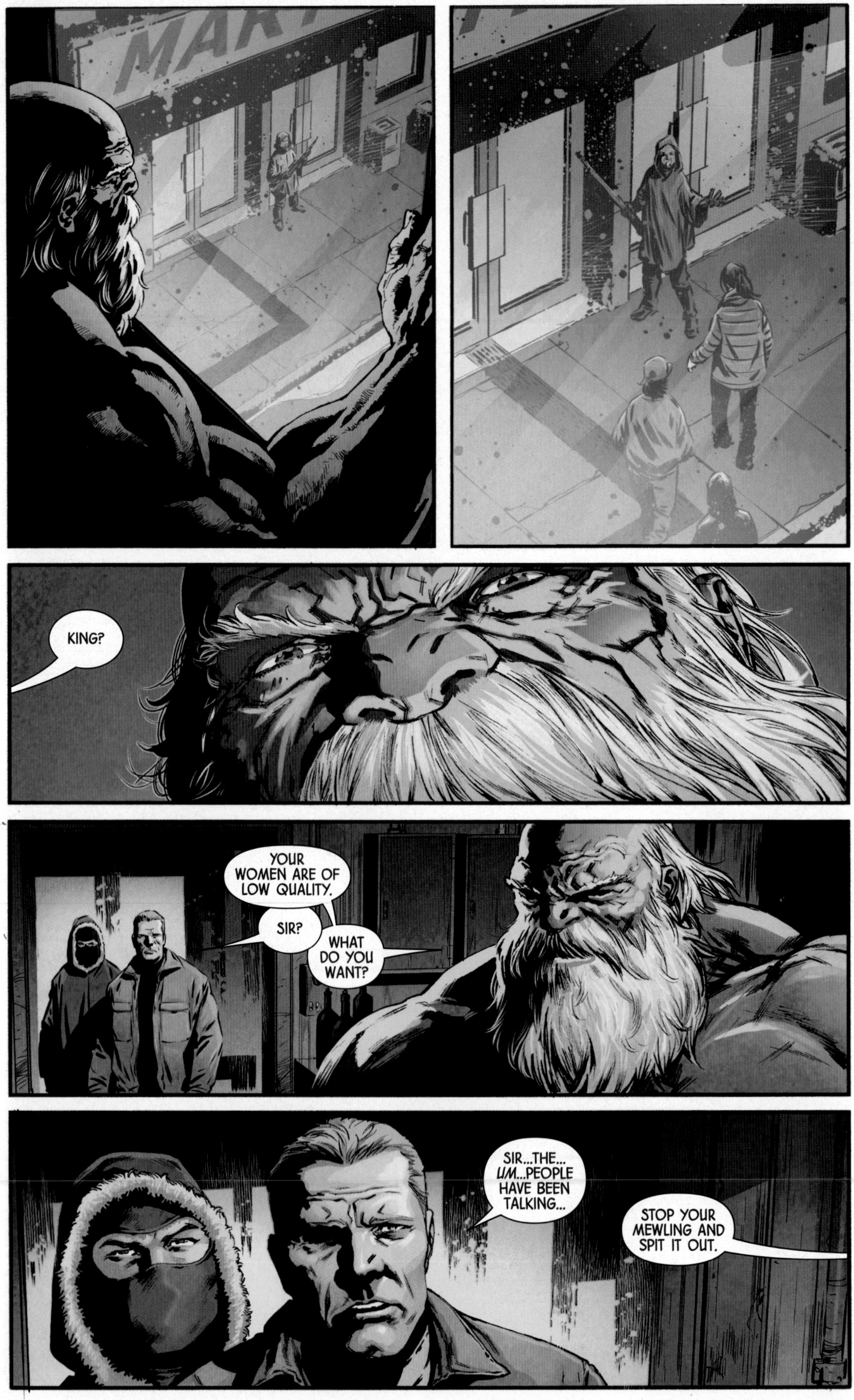
KING?
YOUR WOMEN ARE OF LOW QUALITY.
SIR?
WHAT DO YOU WANT?
SIR...THE... UM...PEOPLE HAVE BEEN TALKING...
STOP YOUR MEWLING AND SPIT IT OUT.

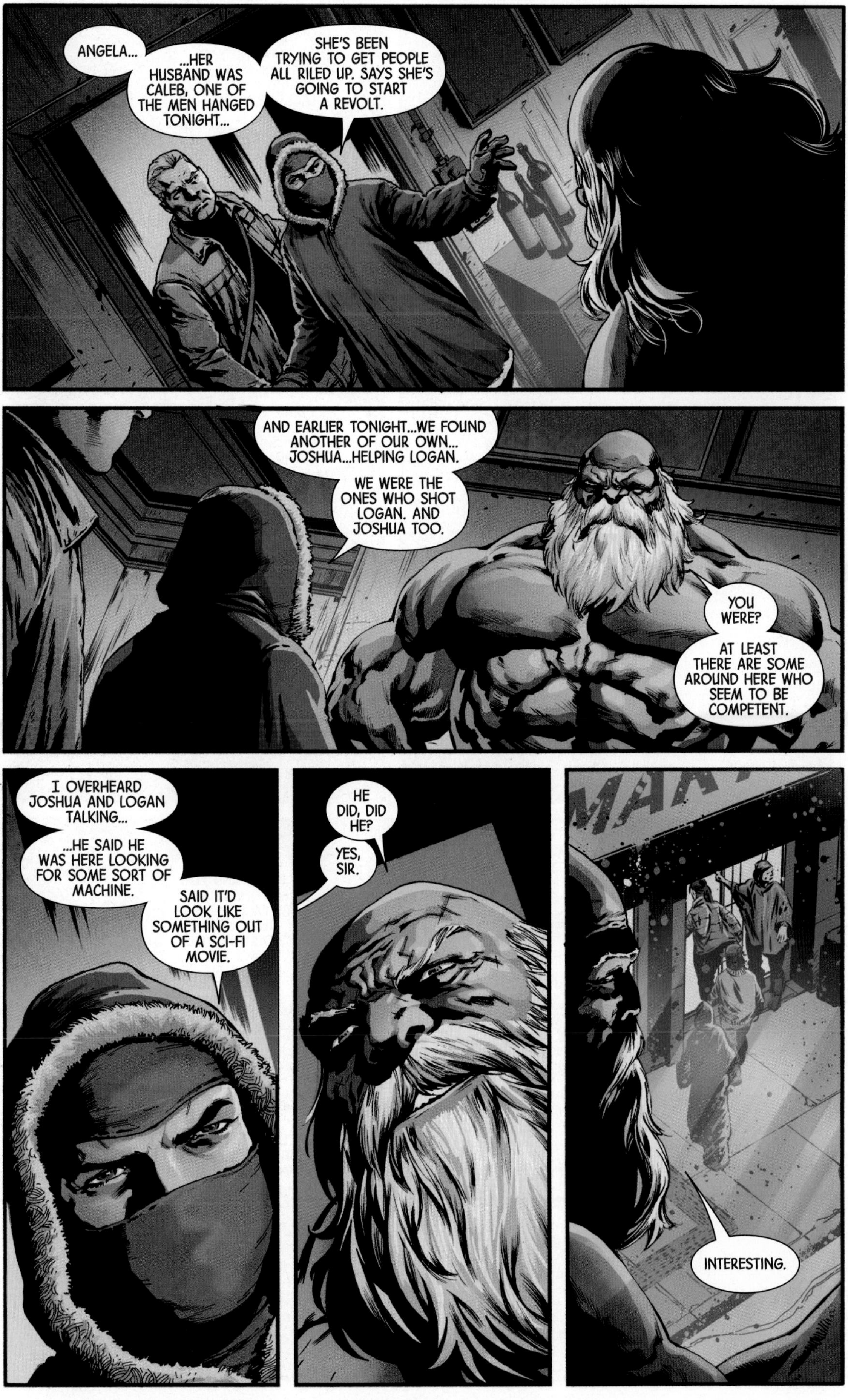
ANGELA...
...HER HUSBAND WAS CALEB, ONE OF THE MEN HANGED TONIGHT...
SHE'S BEEN TRYING TO GET PEOPLE ALL RILED UP. SAYS SHE'S GOING TO START A REVOLT.
AND EARLIER TONIGHT...WE FOUND ANOTHER OF OUR OWN... JOSHUA...HELPING LOGAN.
WE WERE THE ONES WHO SHOT LOGAN. AND JOSHUA TOO.
YOU WERE?
AT LEAST THERE ARE SOME AROUND HERE WHO SEEM TO BE COMPETENT.
I OVERHEARD JOSHUA AND LOGAN TALKING...
...HE SAID HE WAS HERE LOOKING FOR SOME SORT OF MACHINE.
SAID IT'D LOOK LIKE SOMETHING OUT OF A SCI-FI MOVIE.
HE DID, DID HE?
YES, SIR.
INTERESTING.

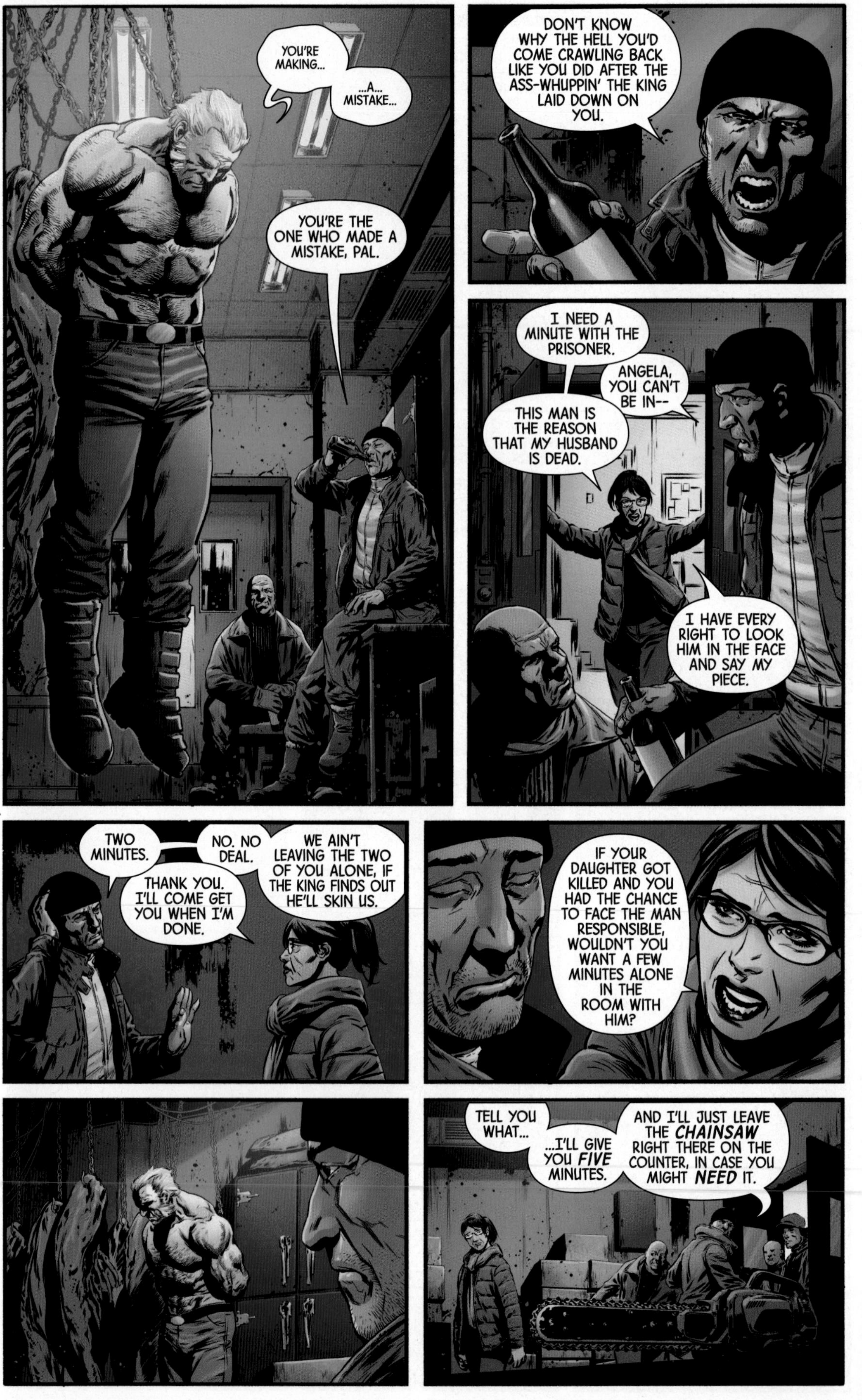
YOU'RE MAKING...
...A... MISTAKE...
YOU'RE THE ONE WHO MADE A MISTAKE, PAL.
DON'T KNOW WHY THE HELL YOU'D COME CRAWLING BACK LIKE YOU DID AFTER THE ASS-WHUPPIN' THE KING LAID DOWN ON YOU.
I NEED A MINUTE WITH THE PRISONER.
ANGELA, YOU CAN'T BE IN--
THIS MAN IS THE REASON THAT MY HUSBAND IS DEAD.
I HAVE EVERY RIGHT TO LOOK HIM IN THE FACE AND SAY MY PIECE.
TWO MINUTES.
NO. NO DEAL.
WE AIN'T LEAVING THE TWO OF YOU ALONE, IF THE KING FINDS OUT HE'LL SKIN US.
THANK YOU. I'LL COME GET YOU WHEN I'M DONE.
IF YOUR DAUGHTER GOT KILLED AND YOU HAD THE CHANCE TO FACE THE MAN RESPONSIBLE, WOULDN'T YOU WANT A FEW MINUTES ALONE IN THE ROOM WITH HIM?
TELL YOU WHAT...
...I'LL GIVE YOU FIVE MINUTES.
AND I'LL JUST LEAVE THE CHAINSAW RIGHT THERE ON THE COUNTER, IN CASE YOU MIGHT NEED IT.

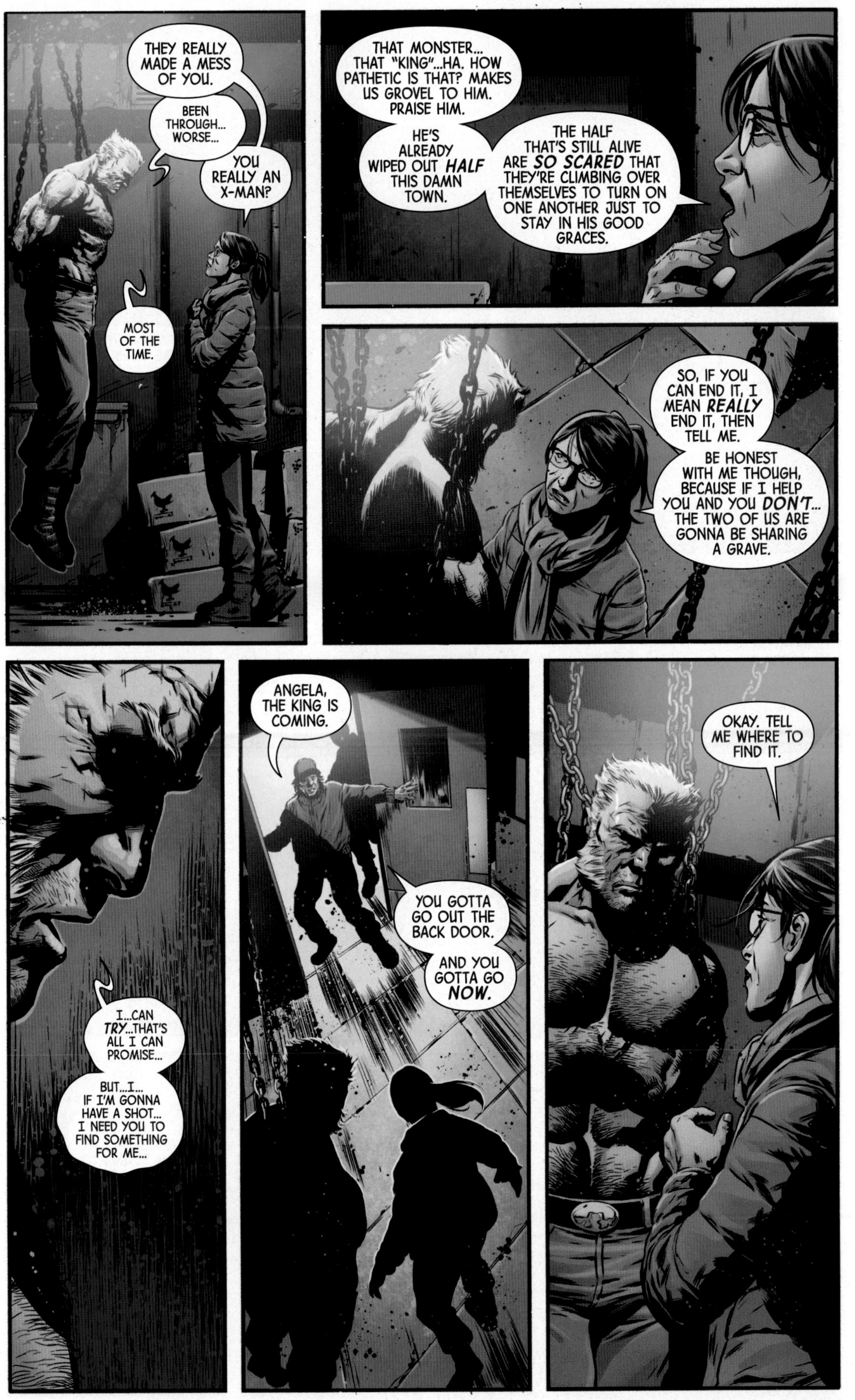
THEY REALLY MADE A MESS OF YOU.
BEEN THROUGH... WORSE...
YOU REALLY AN X-MAN?
MOST OF THE TIME.
THAT MONSTER... THAT "KING"...HA. HOW PATHETIC IS THAT? MAKES US GROVEL TO HIM. PRAISE HIM.
HE'S ALREADY WIPED OUT HALF THIS DAMN TOWN.
THE HALF THAT'S STILL ALIVE ARE SO SCARED THAT THEY'RE CLIMBING OVER THEMSELVES TO TURN ON ONE ANOTHER JUST TO STAY IN HIS GOOD GRACES.
SO, IF YOU CAN END IT, I MEAN REALLY END IT, THEN TELL ME.
BE HONEST WITH ME THOUGH, BECAUSE IF I HELP YOU AND YOU DON'T... THE TWO OF US ARE GONNA BE SHARING A GRAVE.
I...CAN TRY...THAT'S ALL I CAN PROMISE...
BUT...I... IF I'M GONNA HAVE A SHOT... I NEED YOU TO FIND SOMETHING FOR ME...
ANGELA, THE KING IS COMING.
YOU GOTTA GO OUT THE BACK DOOR.
AND YOU GOTTA GO NOW.
OKAY. TELL ME WHERE TO FIND IT.

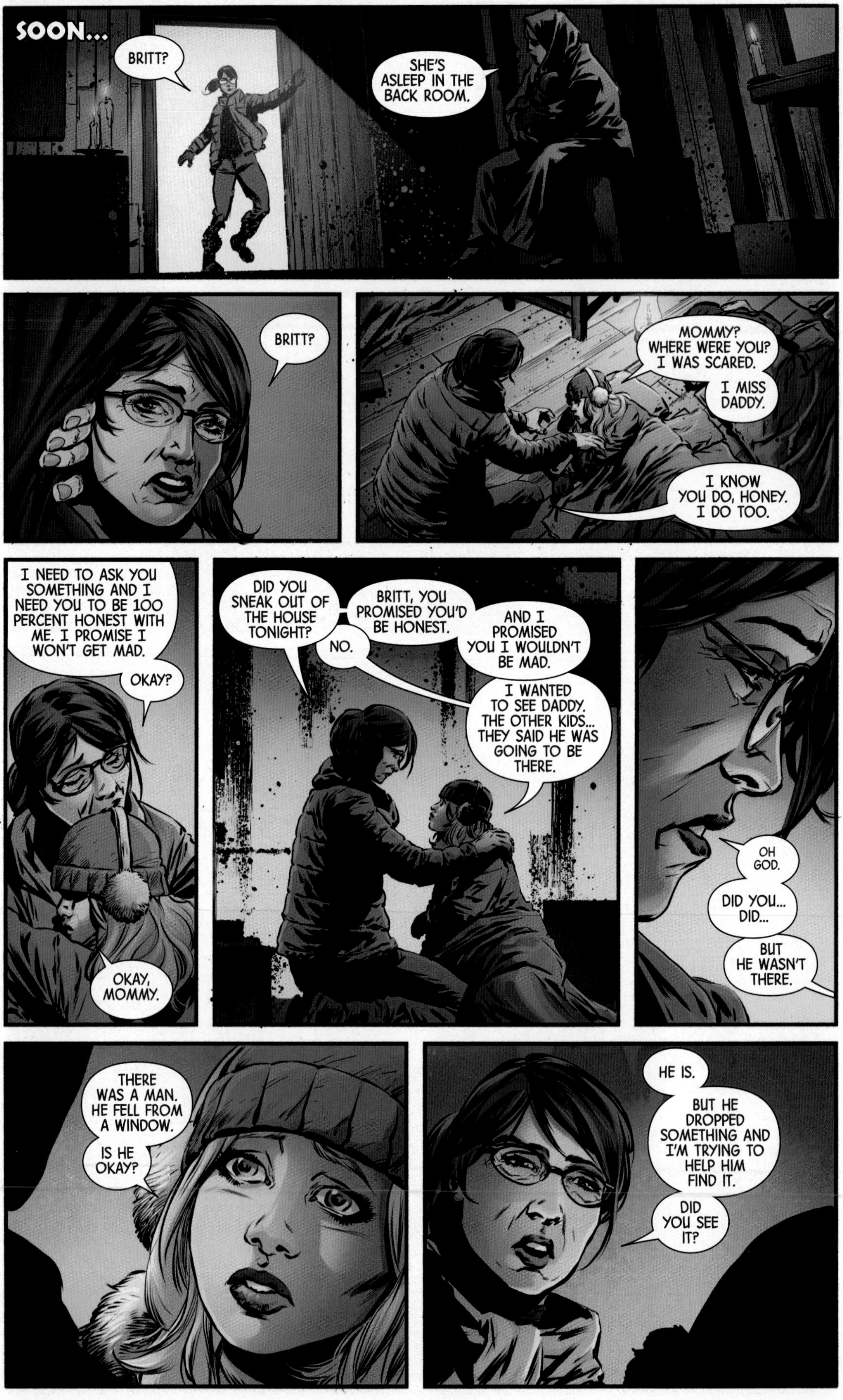
SOON...
BRITT?
SHE'S ASLEEP IN THE BACK ROOM.
BRITT?
MOMMY? WHERE WERE YOU? I WAS SCARED.
I MISS DADDY.
I KNOW YOU DO, HONEY. I DO TOO.
I NEED TO ASK YOU SOMETHING AND I NEED YOU TO BE 100 PERCENT HONEST WITH ME. I PROMISE I WON'T GET MAD.
OKAY?
OKAY, MOMMY.
DID YOU SNEAK OUT OF THE HOUSE TONIGHT?
NO.
BRITT, YOU PROMISED YOU'D BE HONEST.
AND I PROMISED YOU I WOULDN'T BE MAD.
I WANTED TO SEE DADDY. THE OTHER KIDS... THEY SAID HE WAS GOING TO BE THERE.
OH GOD.
DID YOU... DID...
BUT HE WASN'T THERE.
THERE WAS A MAN. HE FELL FROM A WINDOW.
IS HE OKAY?
HE IS.
BUT HE DROPPED SOMETHING AND I'M TRYING TO HELP HIM FIND IT.
DID YOU SEE IT?

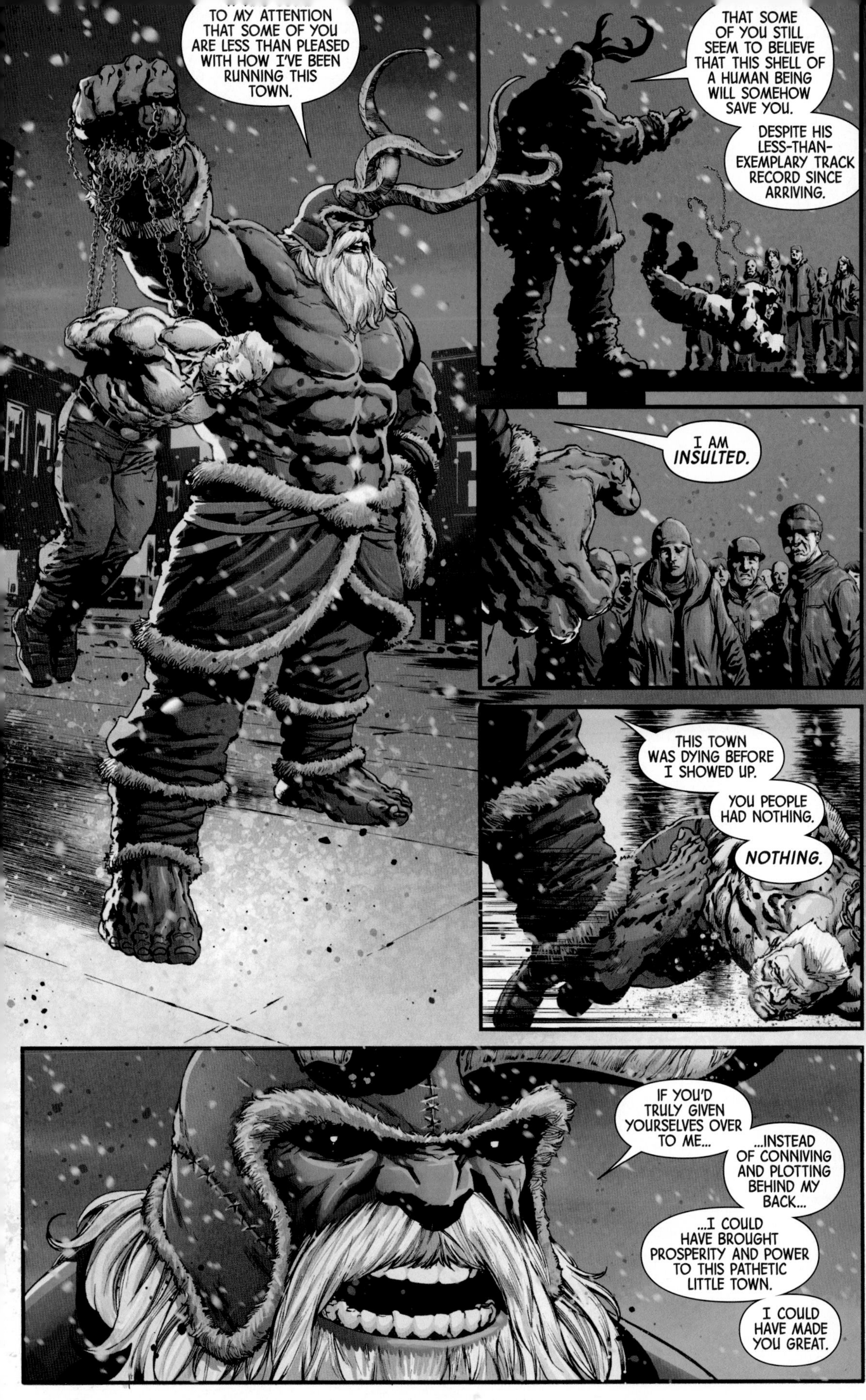
TO MY ATTENTION THAT SOME OF YOU ARE LESS THAN PLEASED WITH HOW I'VE BEEN RUNNING THIS TOWN.
THAT SOME OF YOU STILL SEEM TO BELIEVE THAT THIS SHELL OF A HUMAN BEING WILL SOMEHOW SAVE YOU.
DESPITE HIS LESS-THAN-EXEMPLARY TRACK RECORD SINCE ARRIVING.
I AM *INSULTED.*
THIS TOWN WAS DYING BEFORE I SHOWED UP.
YOU PEOPLE HAD NOTHING.
NOTHING.
IF YOU'D TRULY GIVEN YOURSELVES OVER TO ME...
...INSTEAD OF CONNIVING AND PLOTTING BEHIND MY BACK...
...I COULD HAVE BROUGHT PROSPERITY AND POWER TO THIS PATHETIC LITTLE TOWN.
I COULD HAVE MADE YOU GREAT.

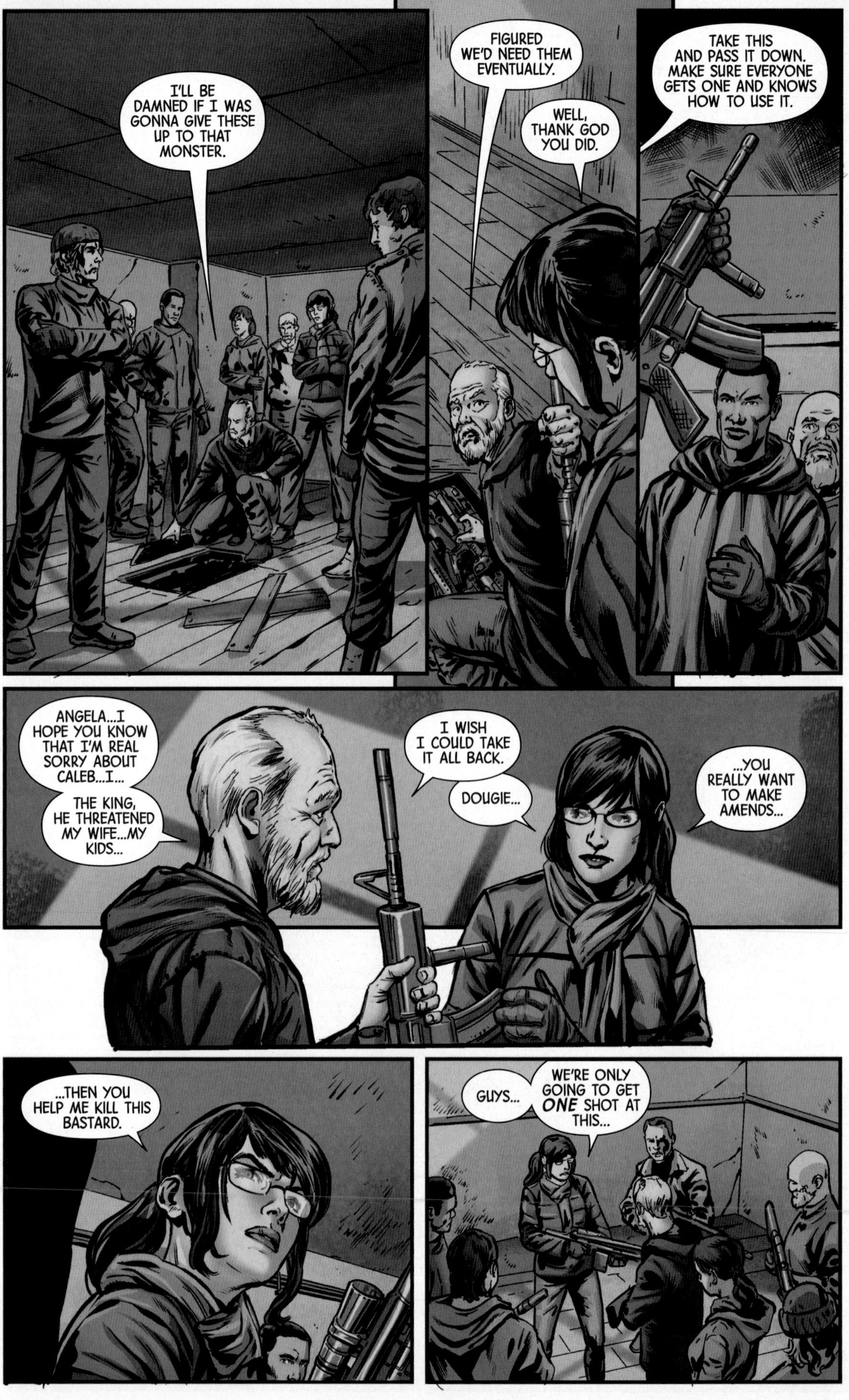
I'LL BE DAMNED IF I WAS GONNA GIVE THESE UP TO THAT MONSTER.
FIGURED WE'D NEED THEM EVENTUALLY.
WELL, THANK GOD YOU DID.
TAKE THIS AND PASS IT DOWN. MAKE SURE EVERYONE GETS ONE AND KNOWS HOW TO USE IT.
ANGELA...I HOPE YOU KNOW THAT I'M REAL SORRY ABOUT CALEB...I...
THE KING, HE THREATENED MY WIFE...MY KIDS...
I WISH I COULD TAKE IT ALL BACK.
DOUGIE...
...YOU REALLY WANT TO MAKE AMENDS...
...THEN YOU HELP ME KILL THIS BASTARD.
GUYS...
WE'RE ONLY GOING TO GET ***ONE*** SHOT AT THIS...

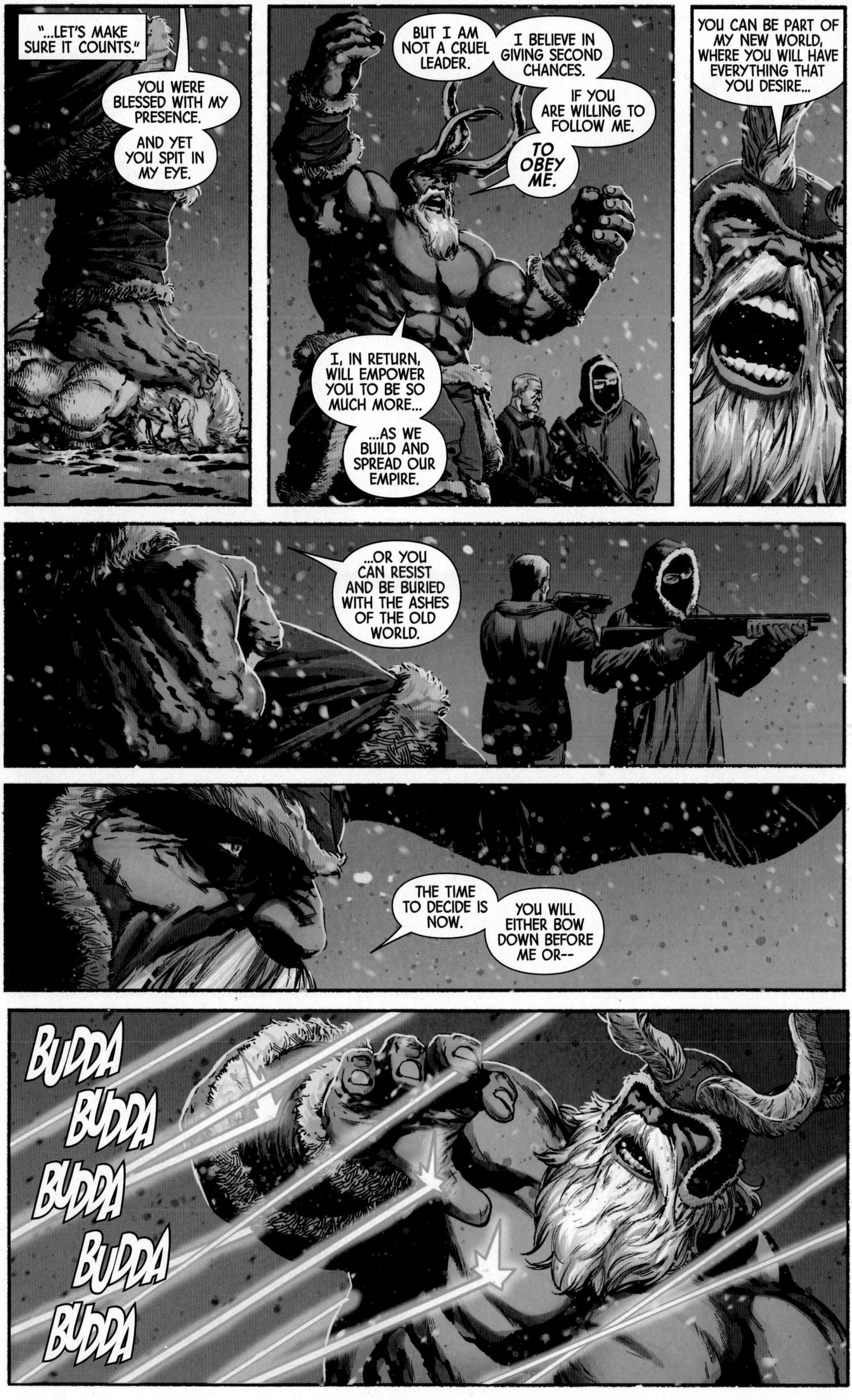
"...LET'S MAKE SURE IT COUNTS."
YOU WERE BLESSED WITH MY PRESENCE.
AND YET YOU SPIT IN MY EYE.
BUT I AM NOT A CRUEL LEADER.
I BELIEVE IN GIVING SECOND CHANCES.
IF YOU ARE WILLING TO FOLLOW ME.
TO OBEY ME.
I, IN RETURN, WILL EMPOWER YOU TO BE SO MUCH MORE...
...AS WE BUILD AND SPREAD OUR EMPIRE.
YOU CAN BE PART OF MY NEW WORLD, WHERE YOU WILL HAVE EVERYTHING THAT YOU DESIRE...
...OR YOU CAN RESIST AND BE BURIED WITH THE ASHES OF THE OLD WORLD.
THE TIME TO DECIDE IS NOW.
YOU WILL EITHER BOW DOWN BEFORE ME OR--
BUDDA
BUDDA
BUDDA
BUDDA
BUDDA

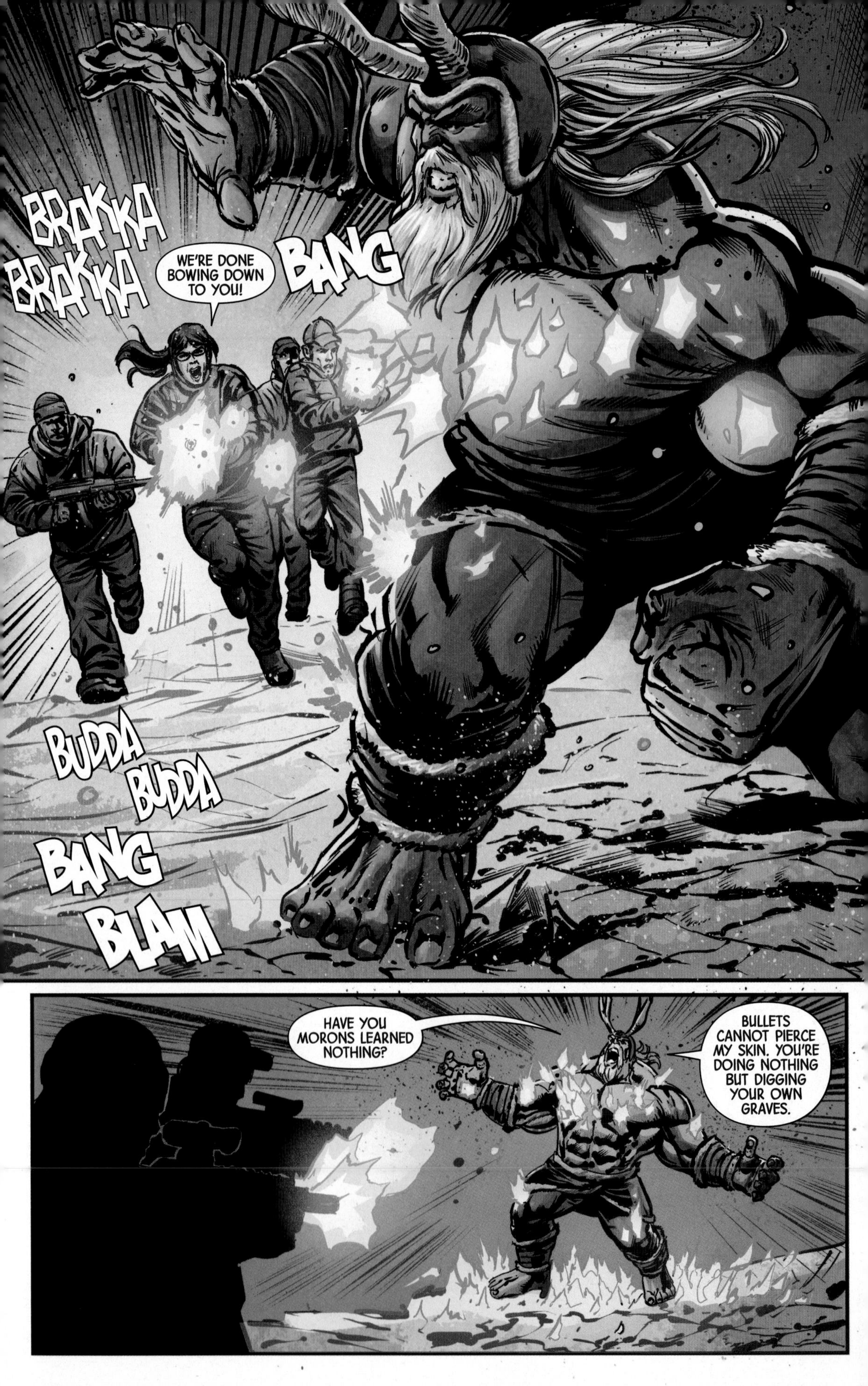
BRAKKA
BRAKKA
WE'RE DONE BOWING DOWN TO YOU!
BANG
BUDDA
BUDDA
BANG
BLAM
HAVE YOU MORONS LEARNED NOTHING?
BULLETS CANNOT PIERCE MY SKIN. YOU'RE DOING NOTHING BUT DIGGING YOUR OWN GRAVES.

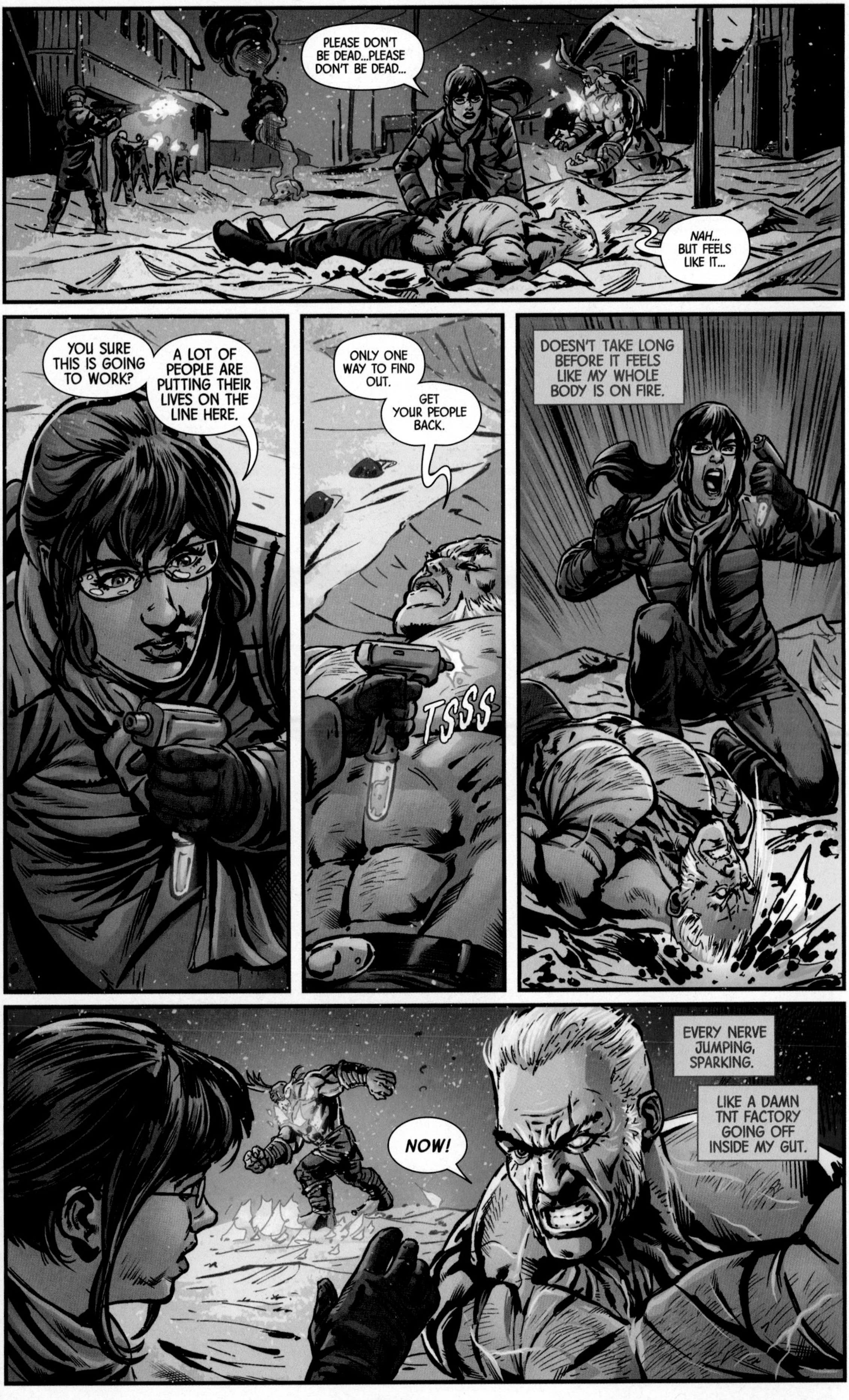
PLEASE DON'T BE DEAD...PLEASE DON'T BE DEAD...
NAH... BUT FEELS LIKE IT...
YOU SURE THIS IS GOING TO WORK?
A LOT OF PEOPLE ARE PUTTING THEIR LIVES ON THE LINE HERE.
ONLY ONE WAY TO FIND OUT.
GET YOUR PEOPLE BACK.
TSSS
DOESN'T TAKE LONG BEFORE IT FEELS LIKE MY WHOLE BODY IS ON FIRE.
EVERY NERVE JUMPING, SPARKING.
LIKE A DAMN TNT FACTORY GOING OFF INSIDE MY GUT.
NOW!

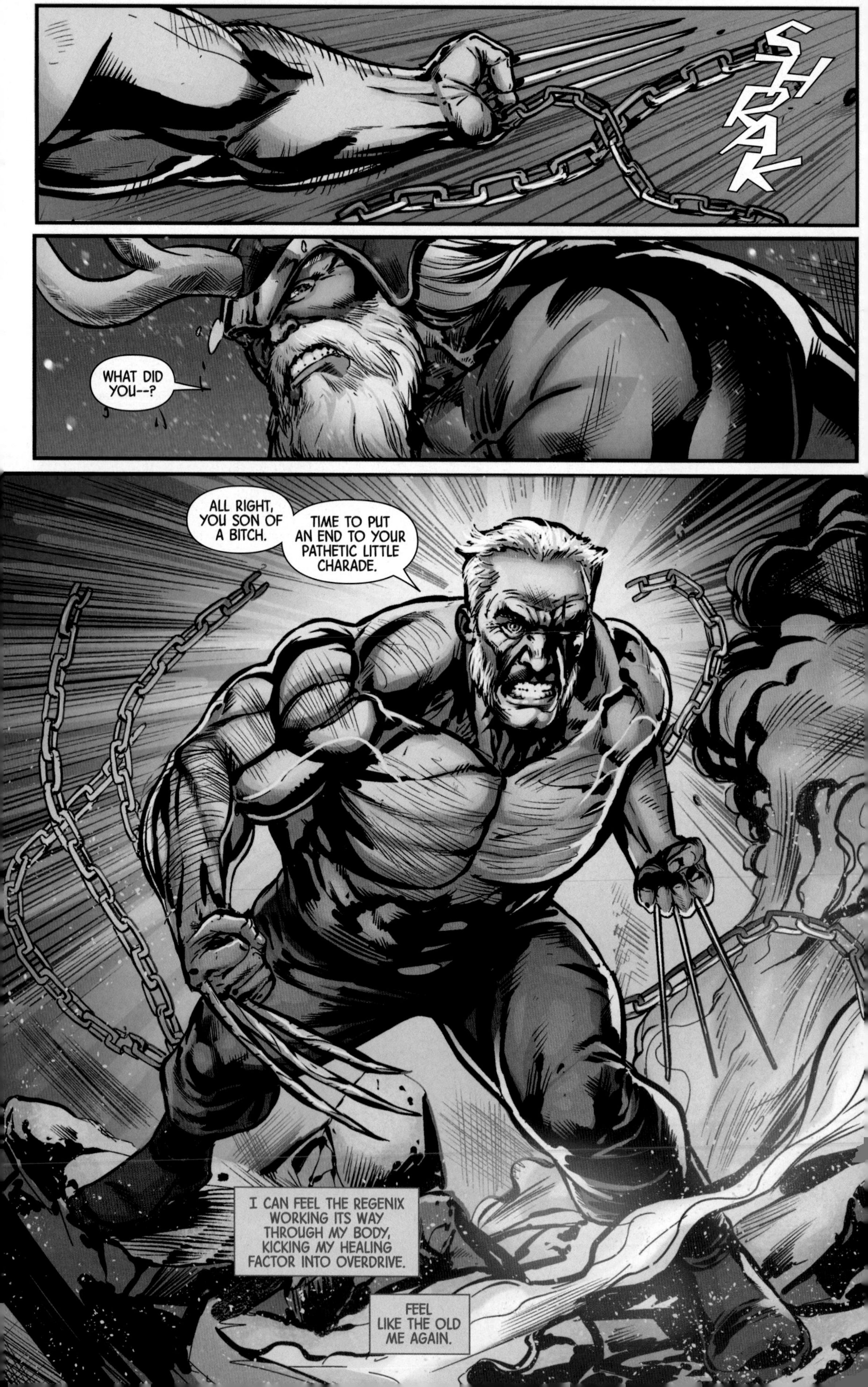
SHRAK
WHAT DID YOU--?
ALL RIGHT, YOU SON OF A BITCH.
TIME TO PUT AN END TO YOUR PATHETIC LITTLE CHARADE.
I CAN FEEL THE REGENIX WORKING ITS WAY THROUGH MY BODY, KICKING MY HEALING FACTOR INTO OVERDRIVE.
FEEL LIKE THE OLD ME AGAIN.

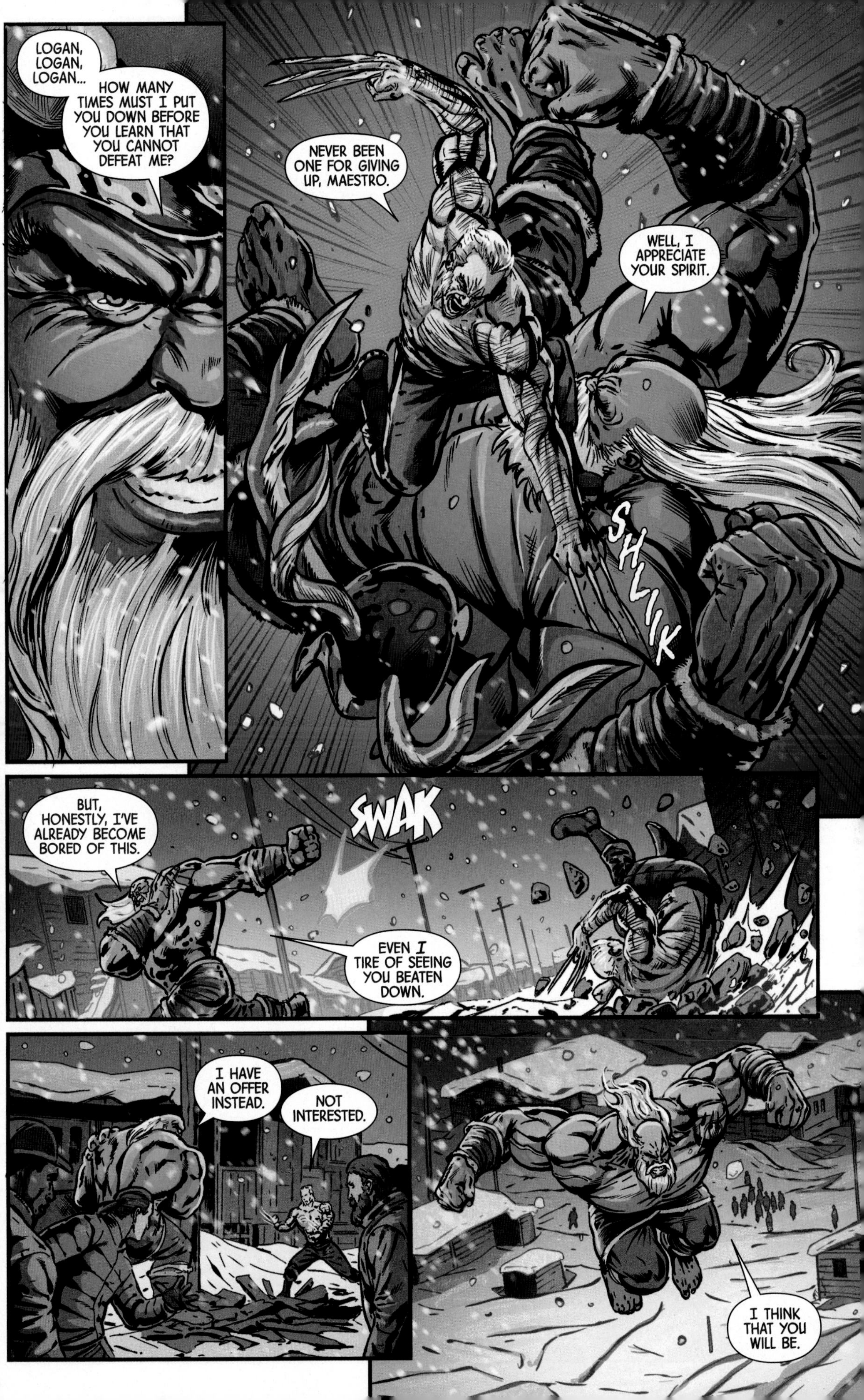
LOGAN, LOGAN, LOGAN...
HOW MANY TIMES MUST I PUT YOU DOWN BEFORE YOU LEARN THAT YOU CANNOT DEFEAT ME?
NEVER BEEN ONE FOR GIVING UP, MAESTRO.
WELL, I APPRECIATE YOUR SPIRIT.
SHLIIK
BUT, HONESTLY, I'VE ALREADY BECOME BORED OF THIS.
SWAK
EVEN I TIRE OF SEEING YOU BEATEN DOWN.
I HAVE AN OFFER INSTEAD.
NOT INTERESTED.
I THINK THAT YOU WILL BE.

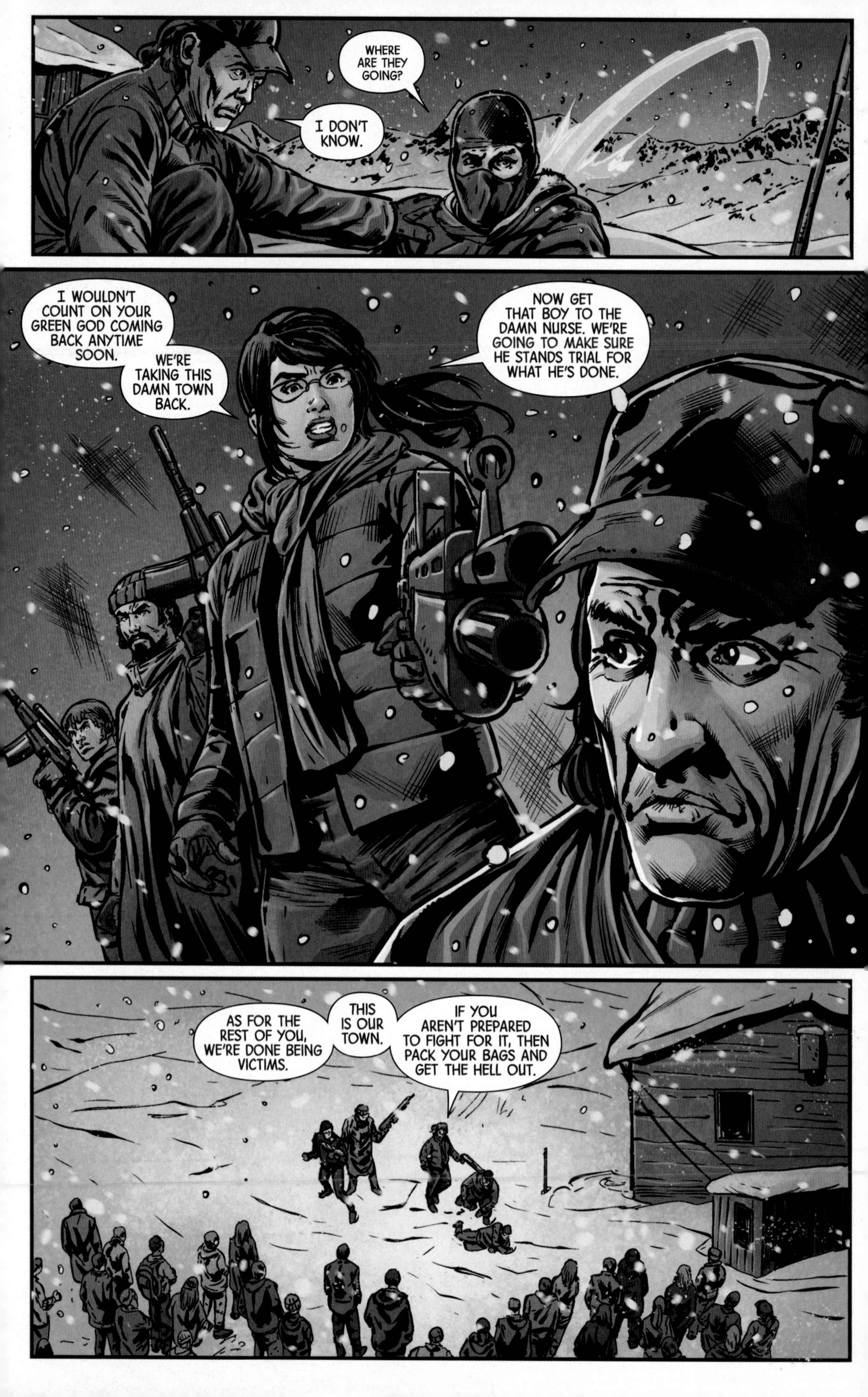
WHERE ARE THEY GOING?
I DON'T KNOW.
I WOULDN'T COUNT ON YOUR GREEN GOD COMING BACK ANYTIME SOON.
WE'RE TAKING THIS DAMN TOWN BACK.
NOW GET THAT BOY TO THE DAMN NURSE. WE'RE GOING TO MAKE SURE HE STANDS TRIAL FOR WHAT HE'S DONE.
AS FOR THE REST OF YOU, WE'RE DONE BEING VICTIMS.
THIS IS OUR TOWN.
IF YOU AREN'T PREPARED TO FIGHT FOR IT, THEN PACK YOUR BAGS AND GET THE HELL OUT.

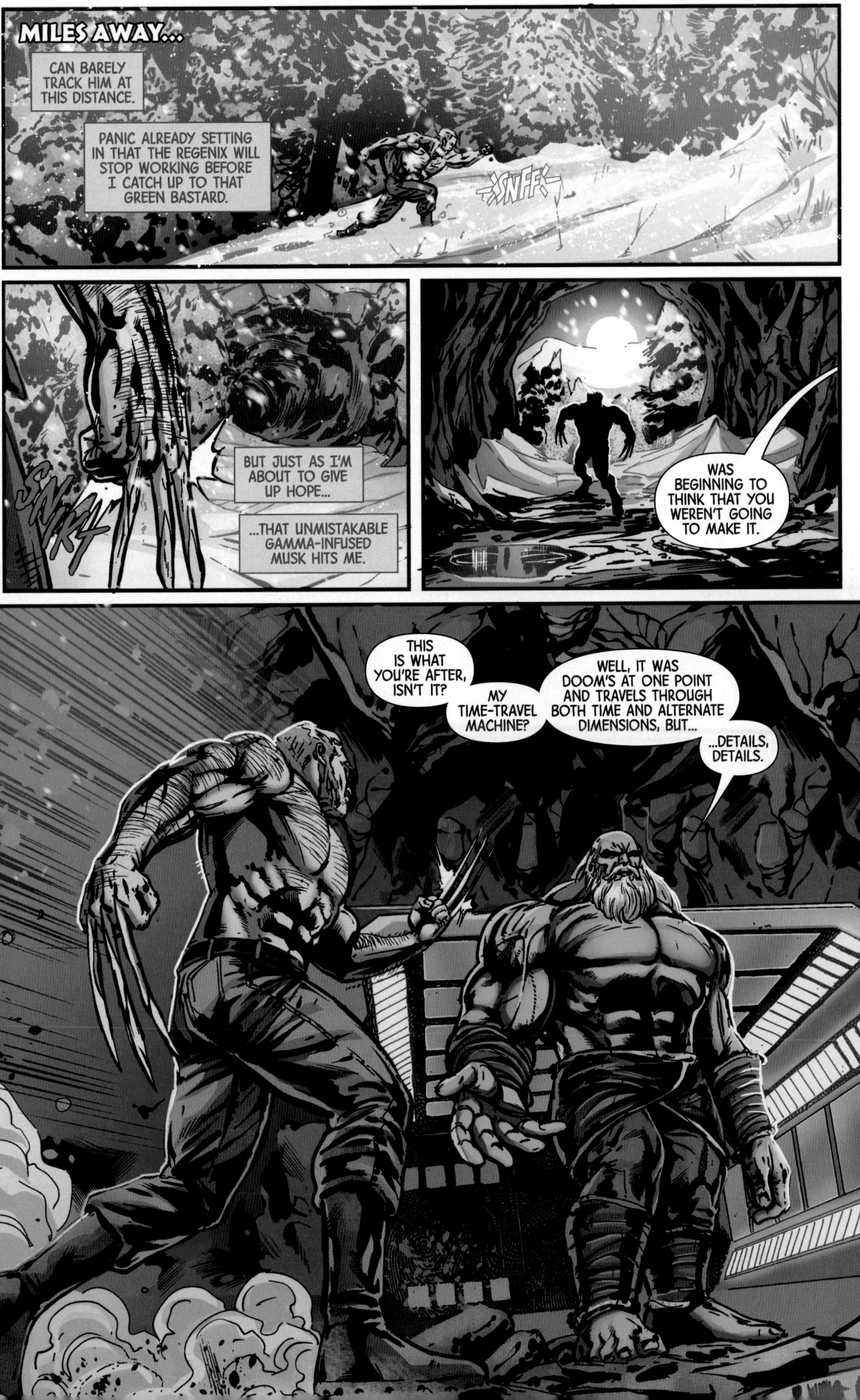
MILES AWAY...
CAN BARELY TRACK HIM AT THIS DISTANCE.
PANIC ALREADY SETTING IN THAT THE REGENIX WILL STOP WORKING BEFORE I CATCH UP TO THAT GREEN BASTARD.
SNFF
SNIKT
BUT JUST AS I'M ABOUT TO GIVE UP HOPE...
...THAT UNMISTAKABLE GAMMA-INFUSED MUSK HITS ME.
WAS BEGINNING TO THINK THAT YOU WEREN'T GOING TO MAKE IT.
THIS IS WHAT YOU'RE AFTER, ISN'T IT?
MY TIME-TRAVEL MACHINE?
WELL, IT WAS DOOM'S AT ONE POINT AND TRAVELS THROUGH BOTH TIME AND ALTERNATE DIMENSIONS, BUT...
...DETAILS, DETAILS.

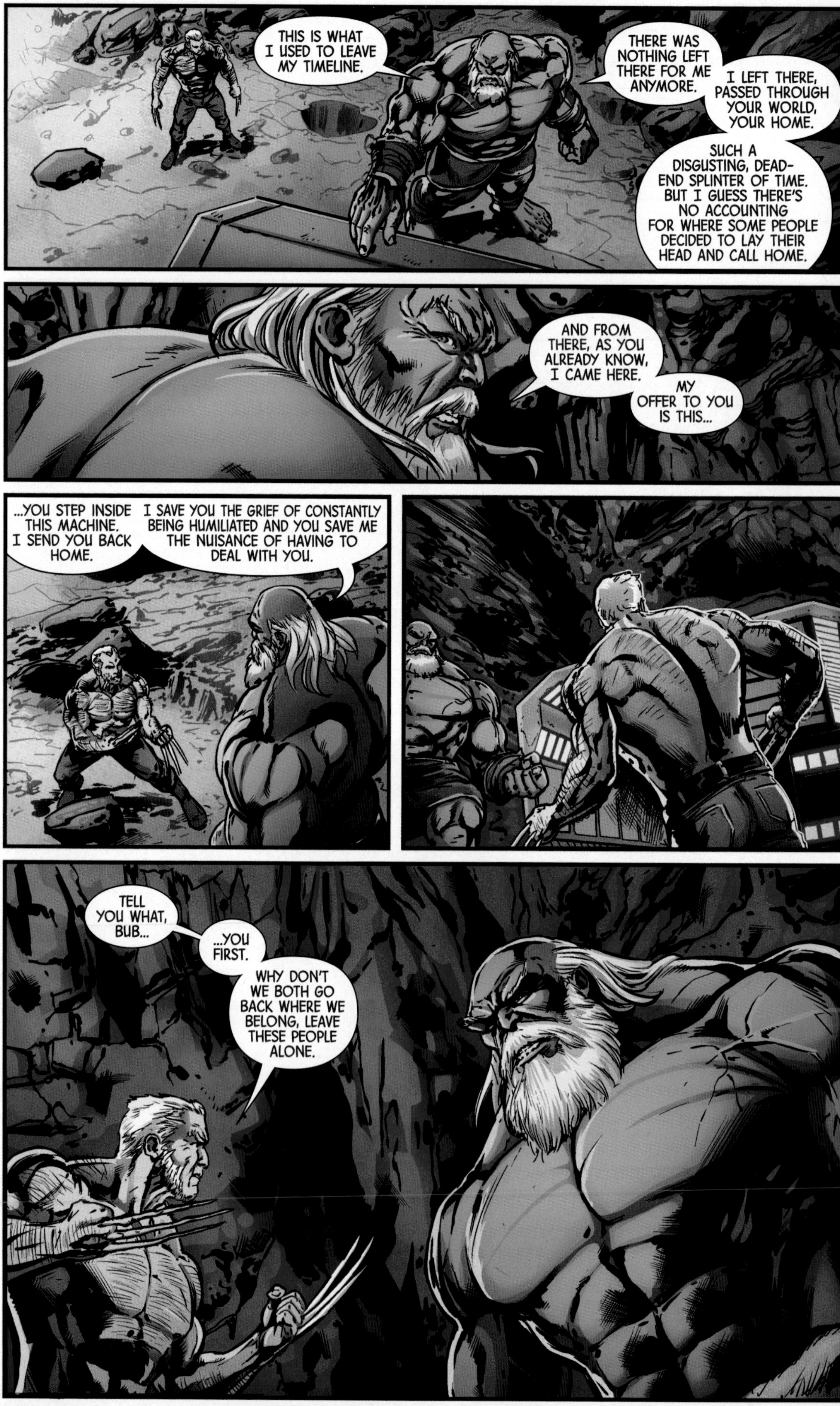
THIS IS WHAT I USED TO LEAVE MY TIMELINE.
THERE WAS NOTHING LEFT THERE FOR ME ANYMORE.
I LEFT THERE, PASSED THROUGH YOUR WORLD, YOUR HOME.
SUCH A DISGUSTING, DEAD-END SPLINTER OF TIME. BUT I GUESS THERE'S NO ACCOUNTING FOR WHERE SOME PEOPLE DECIDED TO LAY THEIR HEAD AND CALL HOME.
AND FROM THERE, AS YOU ALREADY KNOW, I CAME HERE.
MY OFFER TO YOU IS THIS...
...YOU STEP INSIDE THIS MACHINE. I SEND YOU BACK HOME.
I SAVE YOU THE GRIEF OF CONSTANTLY BEING HUMILIATED AND YOU SAVE ME THE NUISANCE OF HAVING TO DEAL WITH YOU.
TELL YOU WHAT, BUB...
...YOU FIRST.
WHY DON'T WE BOTH GO BACK WHERE WE BELONG, LEAVE THESE PEOPLE ALONE.

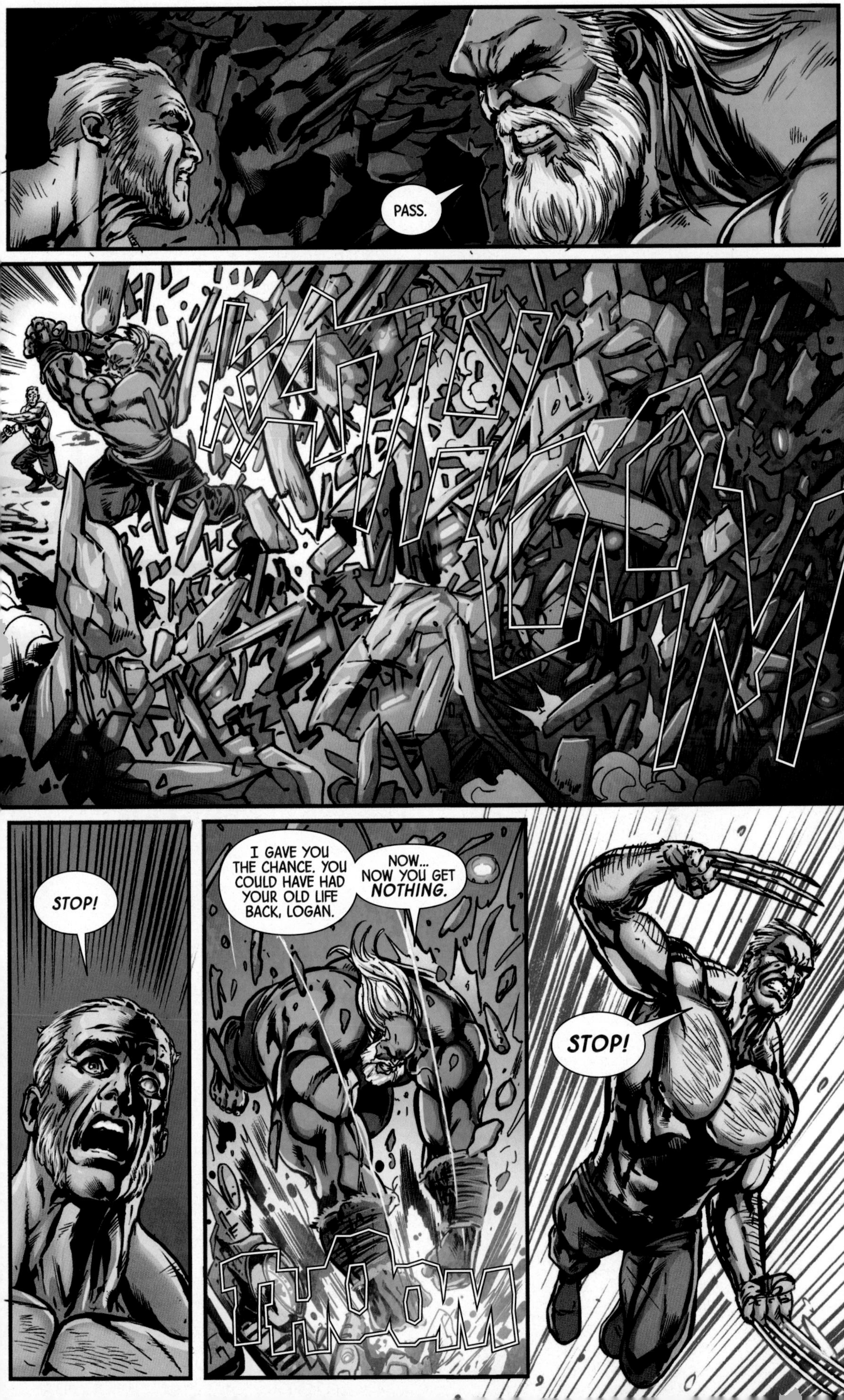
PASS.
KRA-TH-OOM
STOP!
I GAVE YOU THE CHANCE. YOU COULD HAVE HAD YOUR OLD LIFE BACK, LOGAN.
NOW... NOW YOU GET NOTHING.
THOOM
STOP!

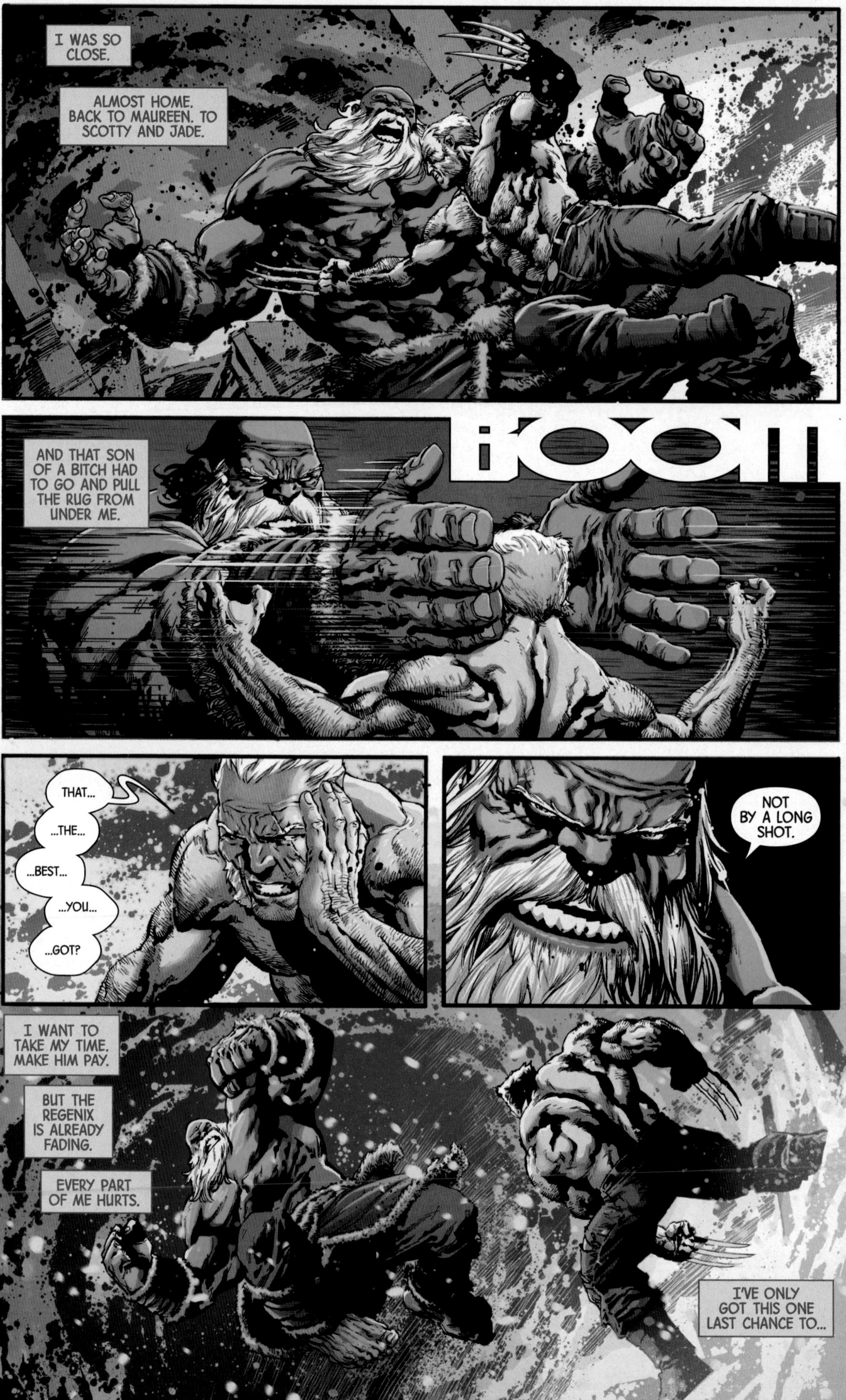
I WAS SO CLOSE.
ALMOST HOME. BACK TO MAUREEN. TO SCOTTY AND JADE.
BOOM
AND THAT SON OF A BITCH HAD TO GO AND PULL THE RUG FROM UNDER ME.
THAT...
...THE...
...BEST...
...YOU...
...GOT?
NOT BY A LONG SHOT.
I WANT TO TAKE MY TIME. MAKE HIM PAY.
BUT THE REGENIX IS ALREADY FADING.
EVERY PART OF ME HURTS.
I'VE ONLY GOT THIS ONE LAST CHANCE TO...

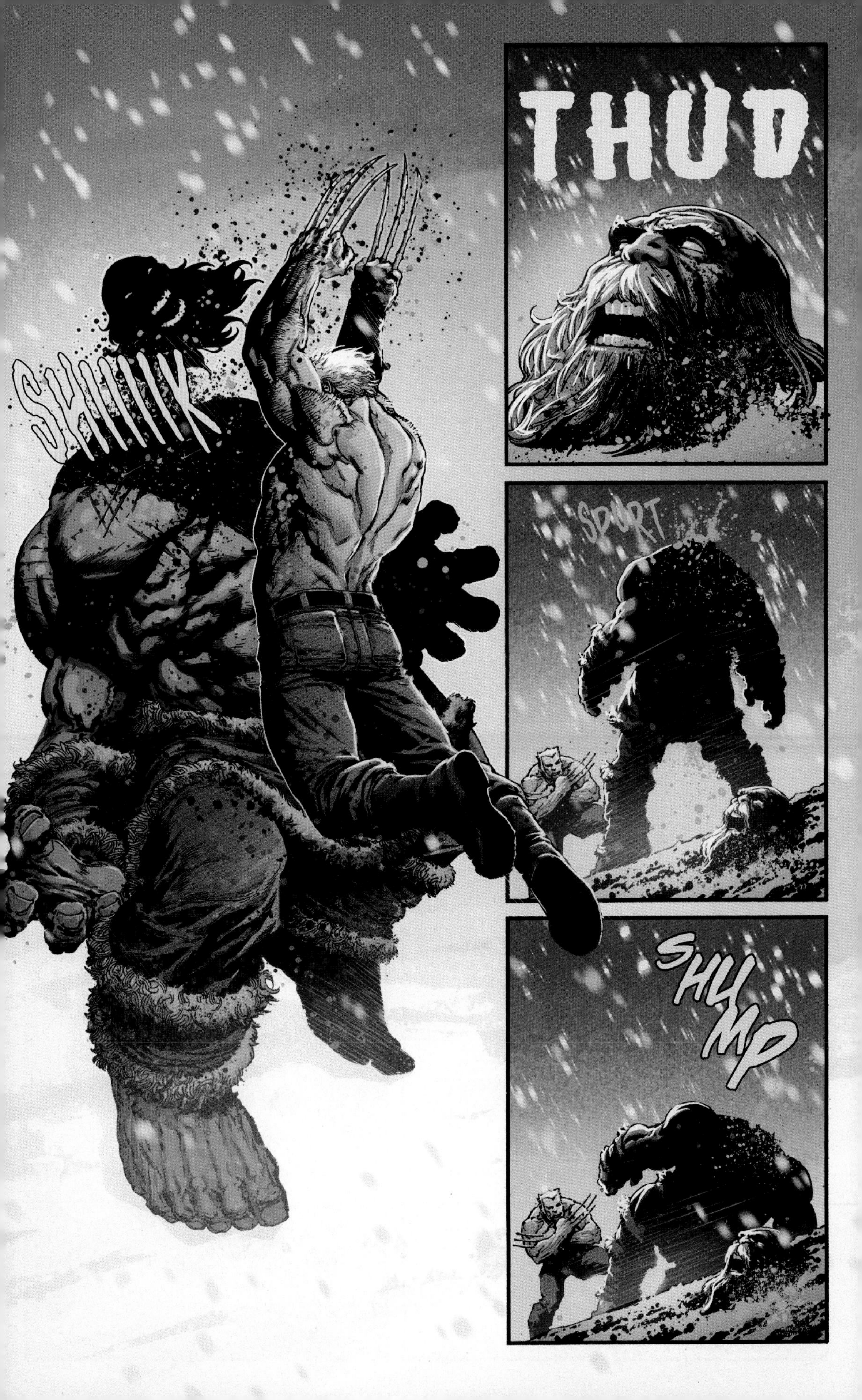
SHHHK
THUD
SPURT
SHUMP

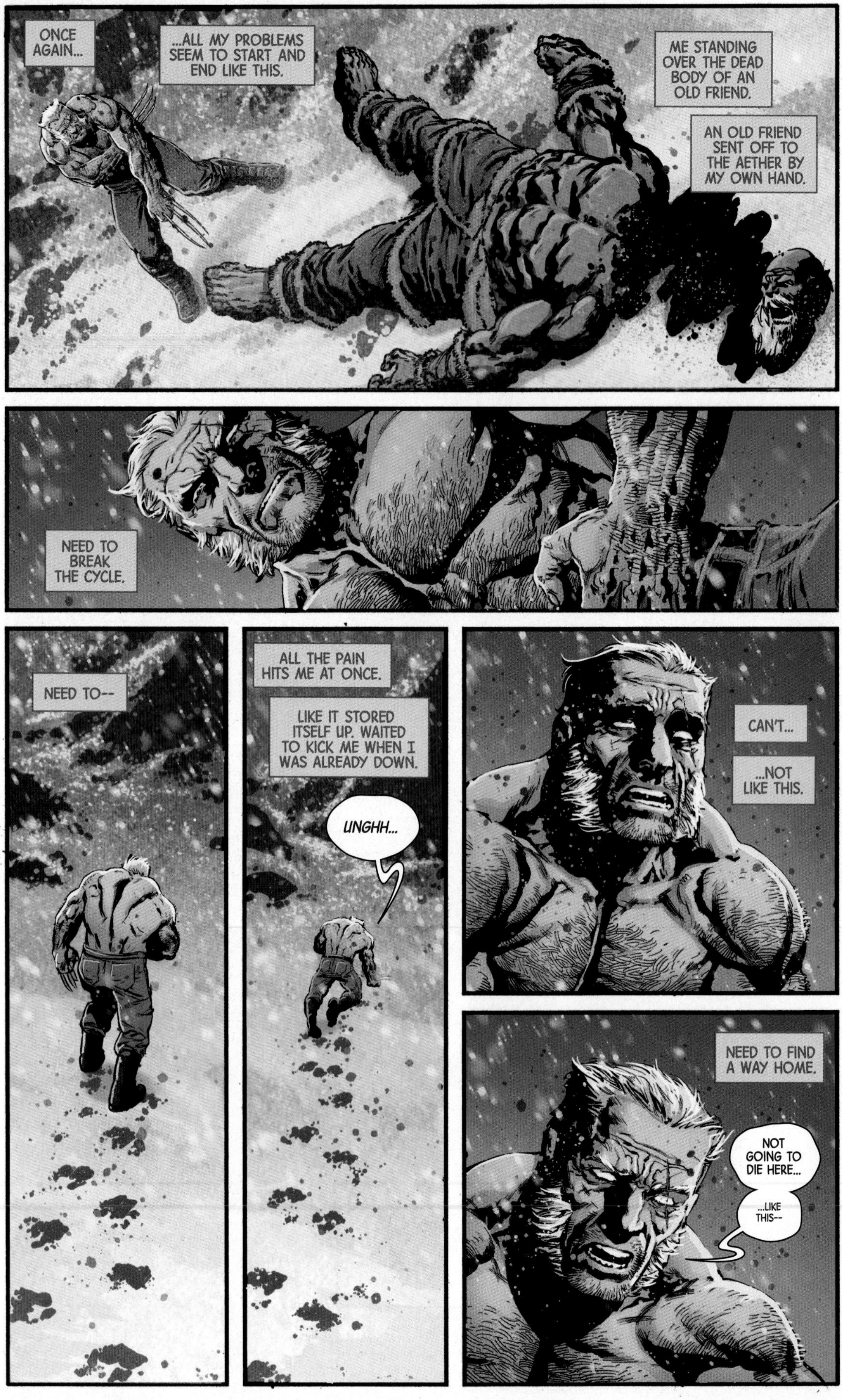
ONCE AGAIN...
...ALL MY PROBLEMS SEEM TO START AND END LIKE THIS.
ME STANDING OVER THE DEAD BODY OF AN OLD FRIEND.
AN OLD FRIEND SENT OFF TO THE AETHER BY MY OWN HAND.
NEED TO BREAK THE CYCLE.
NEED TO--
ALL THE PAIN HITS ME AT ONCE.
LIKE IT STORED ITSELF UP. WAITED TO KICK ME WHEN I WAS ALREADY DOWN.
UNGHH...
CAN'T...
...NOT LIKE THIS.
NEED TO FIND A WAY HOME.
NOT GOING TO DIE HERE...
...LIKE THIS--

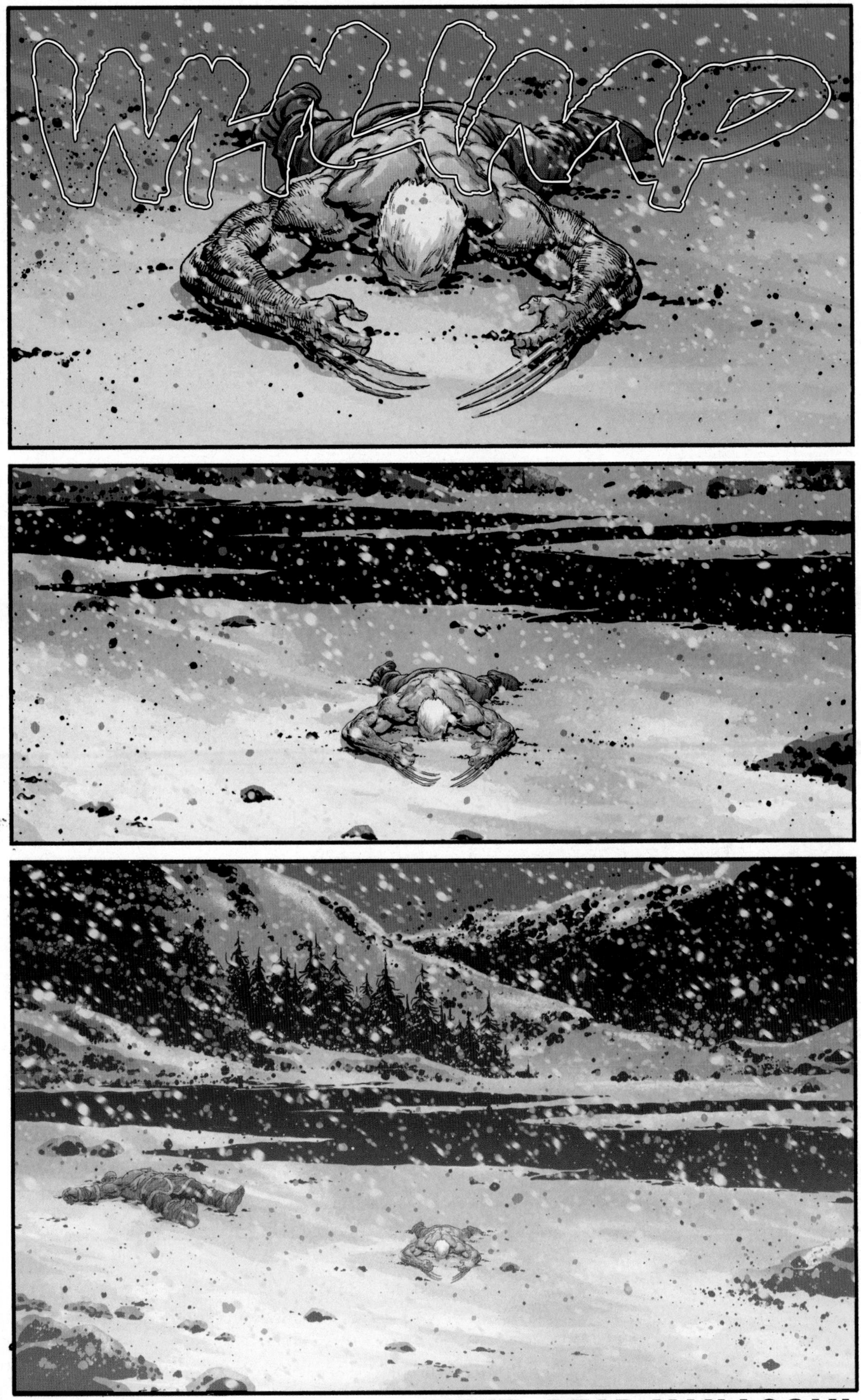
WHUMP

NEXT: *DEAD MAN LOGAN*

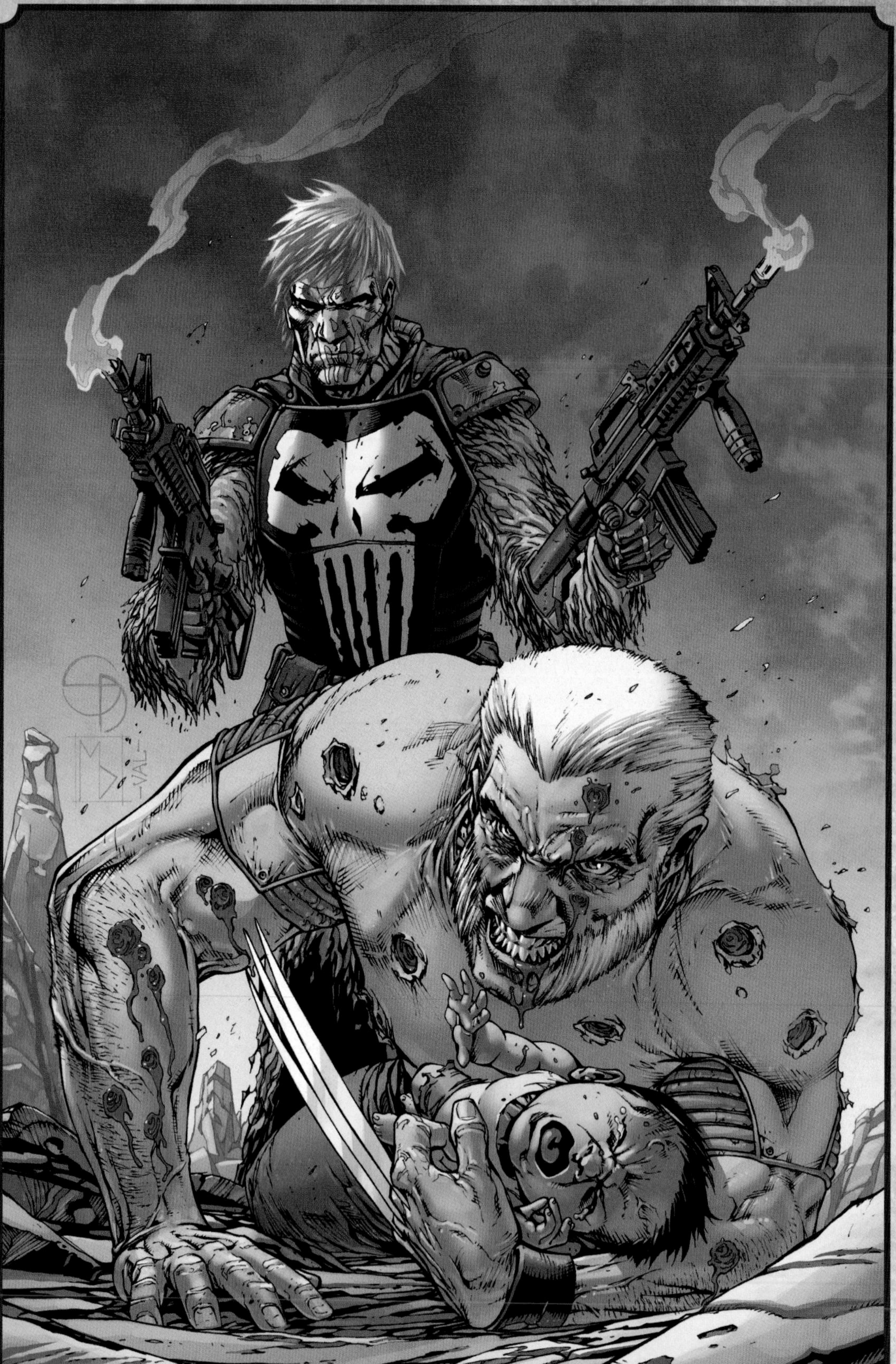

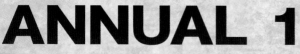

ANNUAL 1

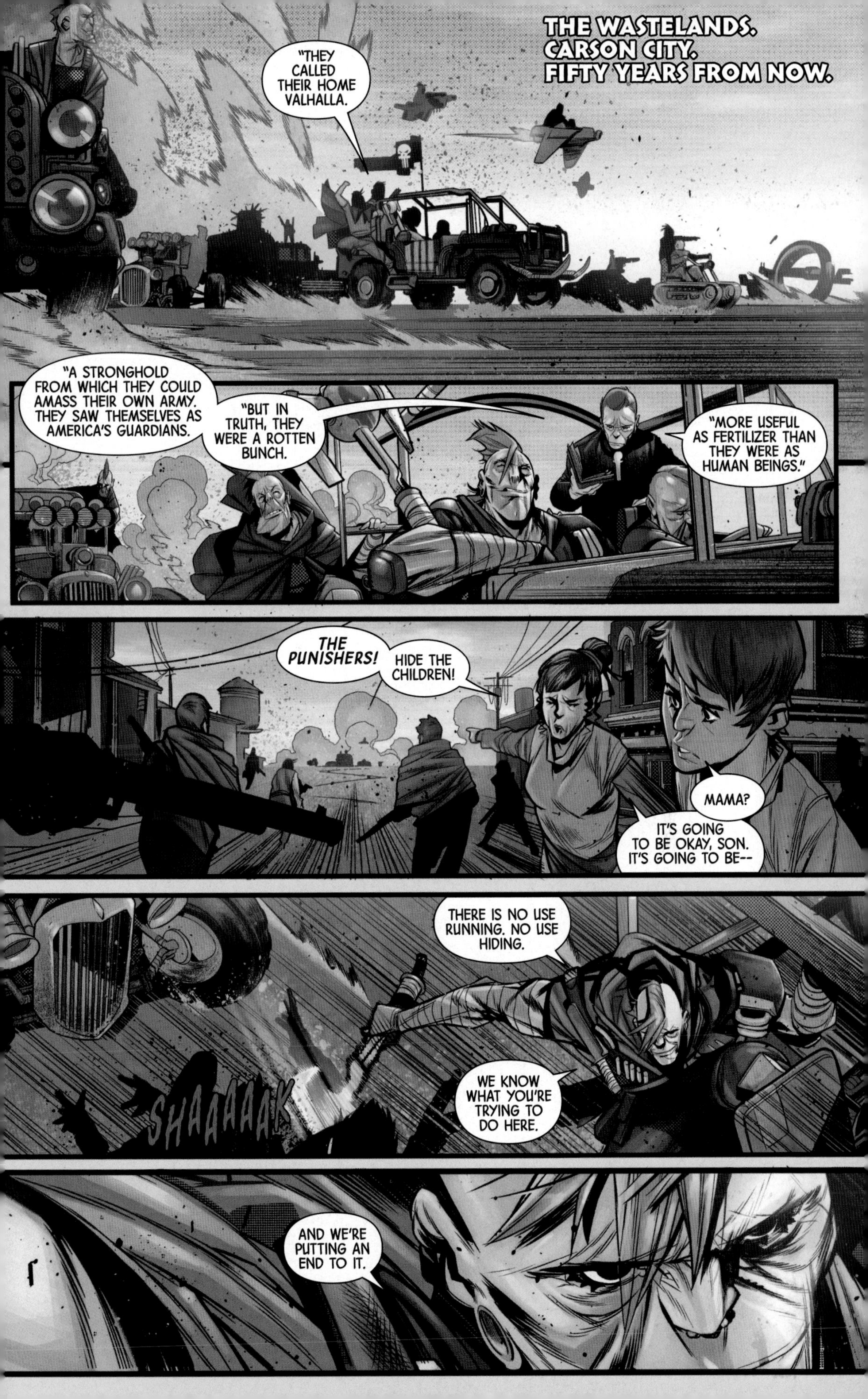
THE WASTELANDS.
CARSON CITY.
FIFTY YEARS FROM NOW.
"THEY CALLED THEIR HOME VALHALLA.
"A STRONGHOLD FROM WHICH THEY COULD AMASS THEIR OWN ARMY. THEY SAW THEMSELVES AS AMERICA'S GUARDIANS.
"BUT IN TRUTH, THEY WERE A ROTTEN BUNCH.
"MORE USEFUL AS FERTILIZER THAN THEY WERE AS HUMAN BEINGS."
THE PUNISHERS!
HIDE THE CHILDREN!
MAMA?
IT'S GOING TO BE OKAY, SON. IT'S GOING TO BE--
THERE IS NO USE RUNNING. NO USE HIDING.
SHAAAAAK
WE KNOW WHAT YOU'RE TRYING TO DO HERE.
AND WE'RE PUTTING AN END TO IT.

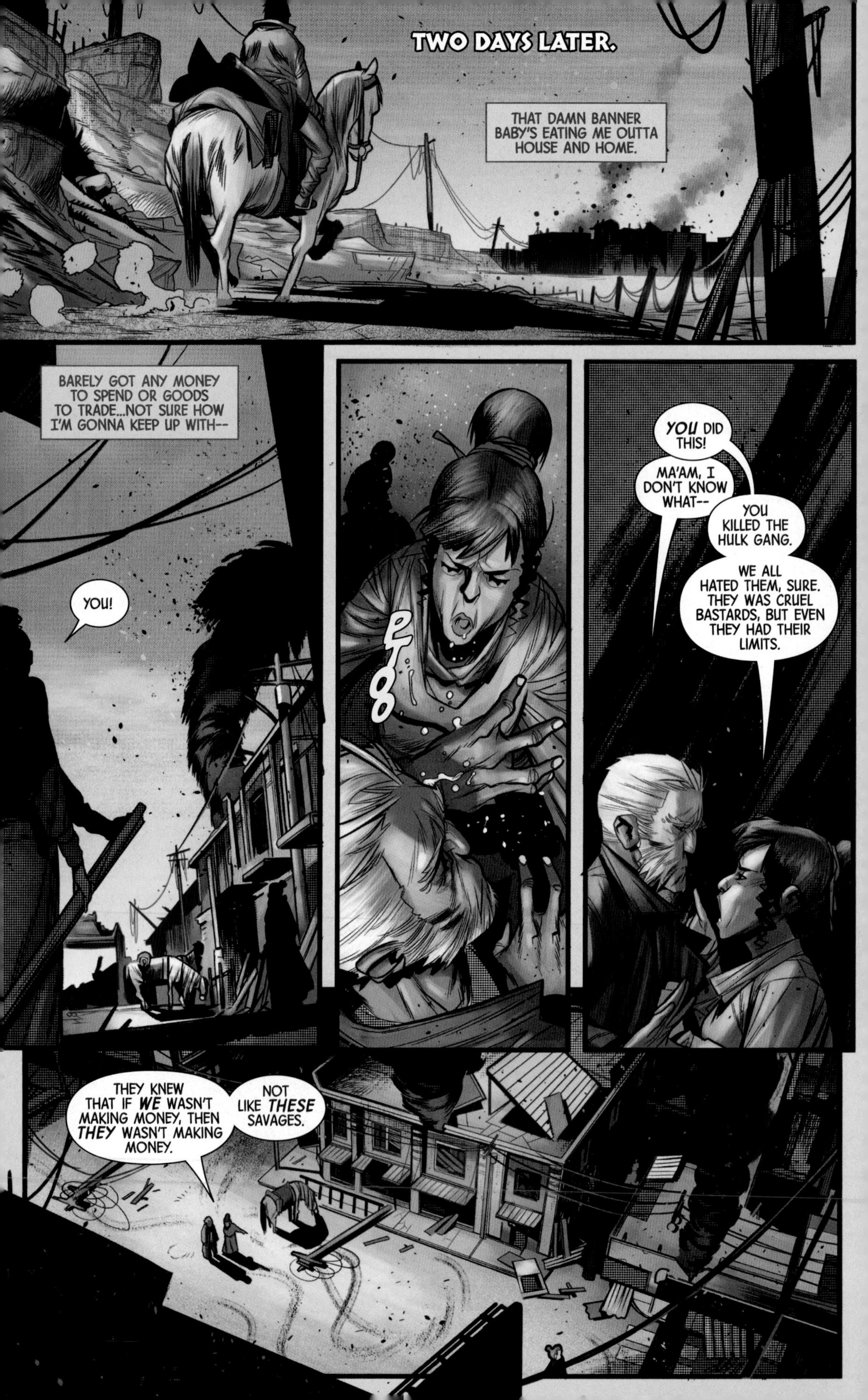
TWO DAYS LATER.
THAT DAMN BANNER BABY'S EATING ME OUTTA HOUSE AND HOME.
BARELY GOT ANY MONEY TO SPEND OR GOODS TO TRADE...NOT SURE HOW I'M GONNA KEEP UP WITH--
YOU!
YOU DID THIS!
MA'AM, I DON'T KNOW WHAT--
YOU KILLED THE HULK GANG.
WE ALL HATED THEM, SURE. THEY WAS CRUEL BASTARDS, BUT EVEN THEY HAD THEIR LIMITS.
THEY KNEW THAT IF WE WASN'T MAKING MONEY, THEN THEY WASN'T MAKING MONEY.
NOT LIKE THESE SAVAGES.

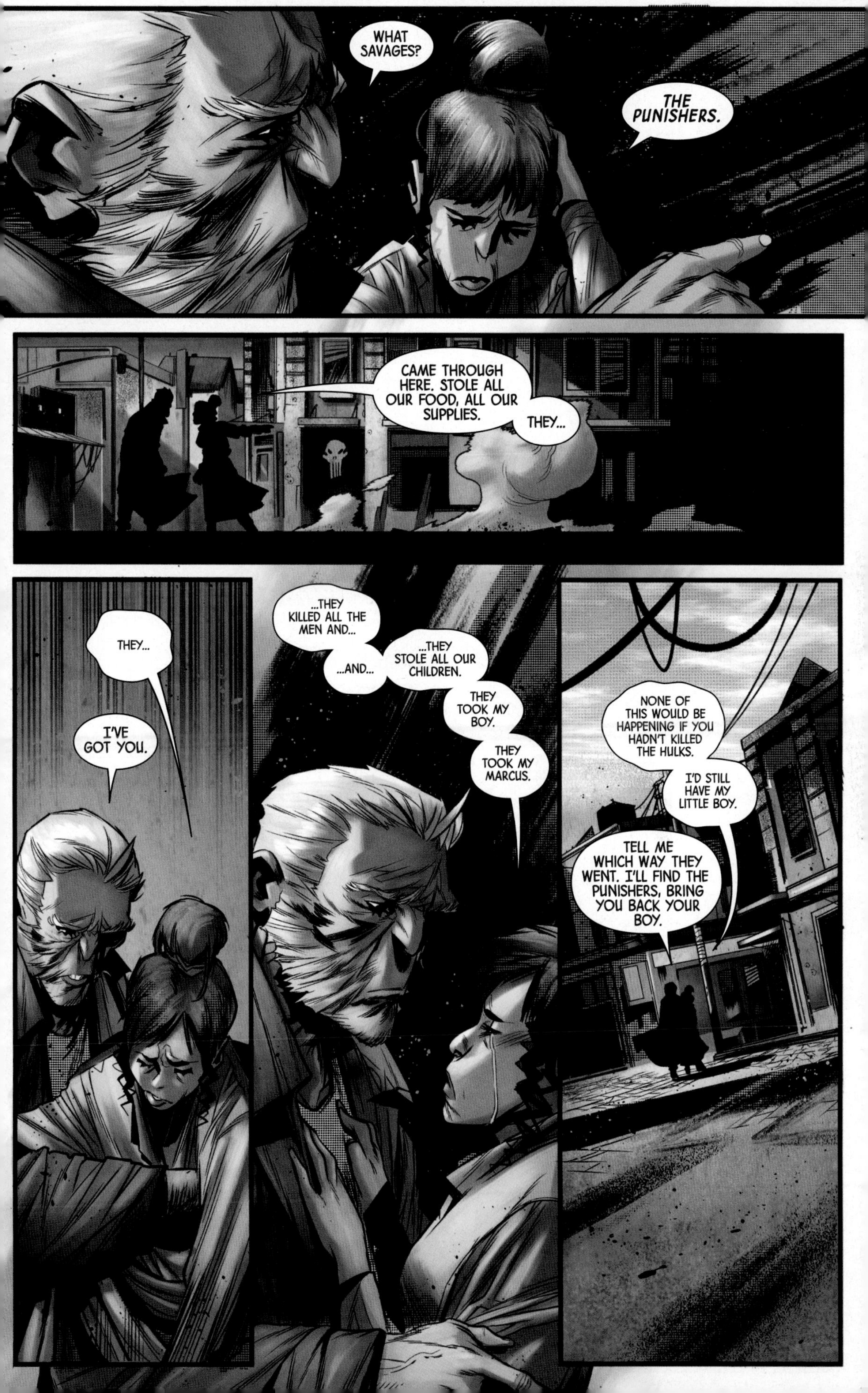
WHAT SAVAGES?
THE PUNISHERS.
CAME THROUGH HERE. STOLE ALL OUR FOOD, ALL OUR SUPPLIES.
THEY...
THEY...
I'VE GOT YOU.
...THEY KILLED ALL THE MEN AND...
...AND...
...THEY STOLE ALL OUR CHILDREN.
THEY TOOK MY BOY.
THEY TOOK MY MARCUS.
NONE OF THIS WOULD BE HAPPENING IF YOU HADN'T KILLED THE HULKS.
I'D STILL HAVE MY LITTLE BOY.
TELL ME WHICH WAY THEY WENT. I'LL FIND THE PUNISHERS, BRING YOU BACK YOUR BOY.

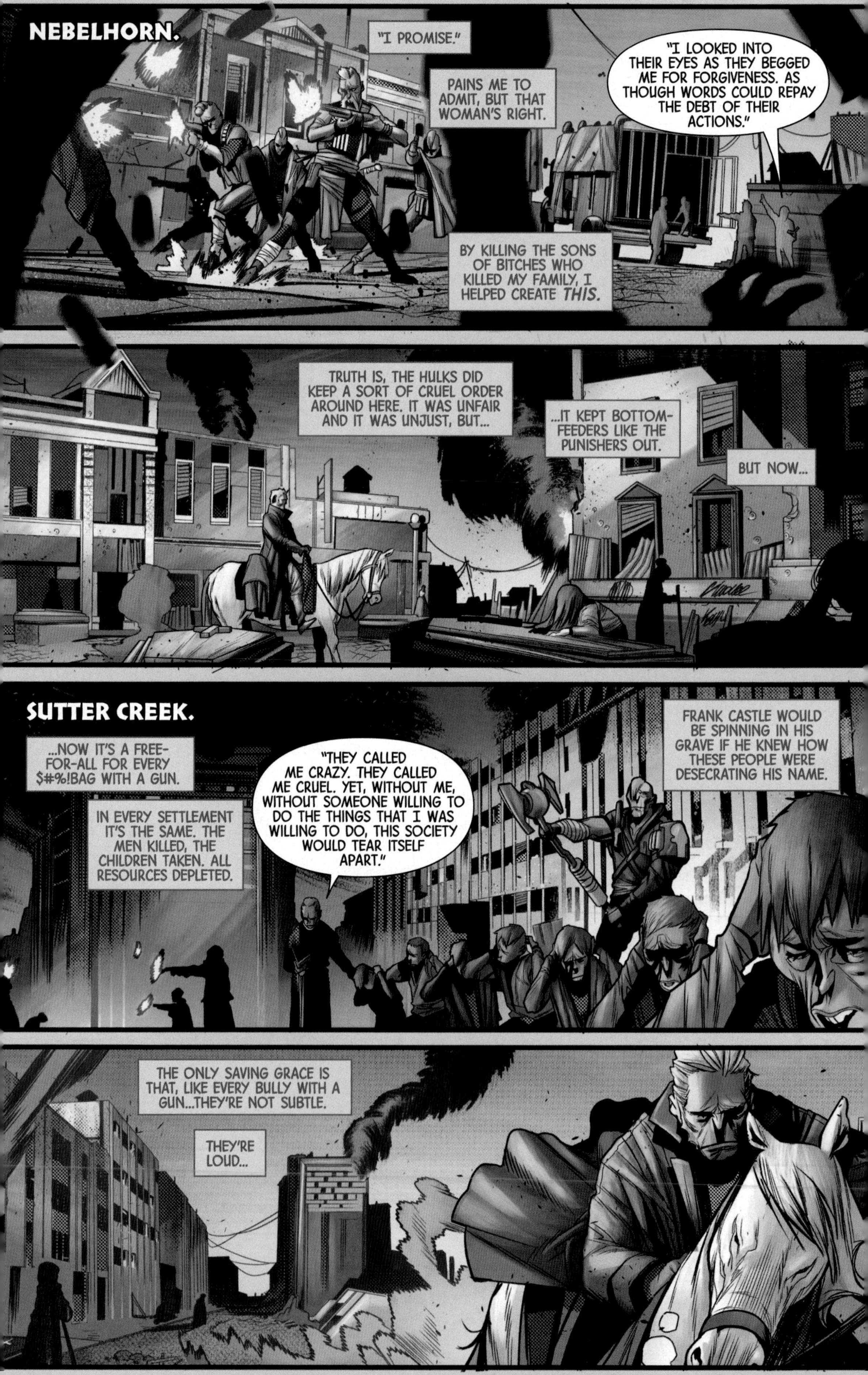
NEBELHORN.
"I PROMISE."
PAINS ME TO ADMIT, BUT THAT WOMAN'S RIGHT.
"I LOOKED INTO THEIR EYES AS THEY BEGGED ME FOR FORGIVENESS. AS THOUGH WORDS COULD REPAY THE DEBT OF THEIR ACTIONS."
BY KILLING THE SONS OF BITCHES WHO KILLED MY FAMILY, I HELPED CREATE *THIS.*
TRUTH IS, THE HULKS DID KEEP A SORT OF CRUEL ORDER AROUND HERE. IT WAS UNFAIR AND IT WAS UNJUST, BUT...
...IT KEPT BOTTOM-FEEDERS LIKE THE PUNISHERS OUT.
BUT NOW...
SUTTER CREEK.
...NOW IT'S A FREE-FOR-ALL FOR EVERY $#%!BAG WITH A GUN.
IN EVERY SETTLEMENT IT'S THE SAME. THE MEN KILLED, THE CHILDREN TAKEN. ALL RESOURCES DEPLETED.
"THEY CALLED ME CRAZY. THEY CALLED ME CRUEL. YET, WITHOUT ME, WITHOUT SOMEONE WILLING TO DO THE THINGS THAT I WAS WILLING TO DO, THIS SOCIETY WOULD TEAR ITSELF APART."
FRANK CASTLE WOULD BE SPINNING IN HIS GRAVE IF HE KNEW HOW THESE PEOPLE WERE DESECRATING HIS NAME.
THE ONLY SAVING GRACE IS THAT, LIKE EVERY BULLY WITH A GUN...THEY'RE NOT SUBTLE.
THEY'RE LOUD...

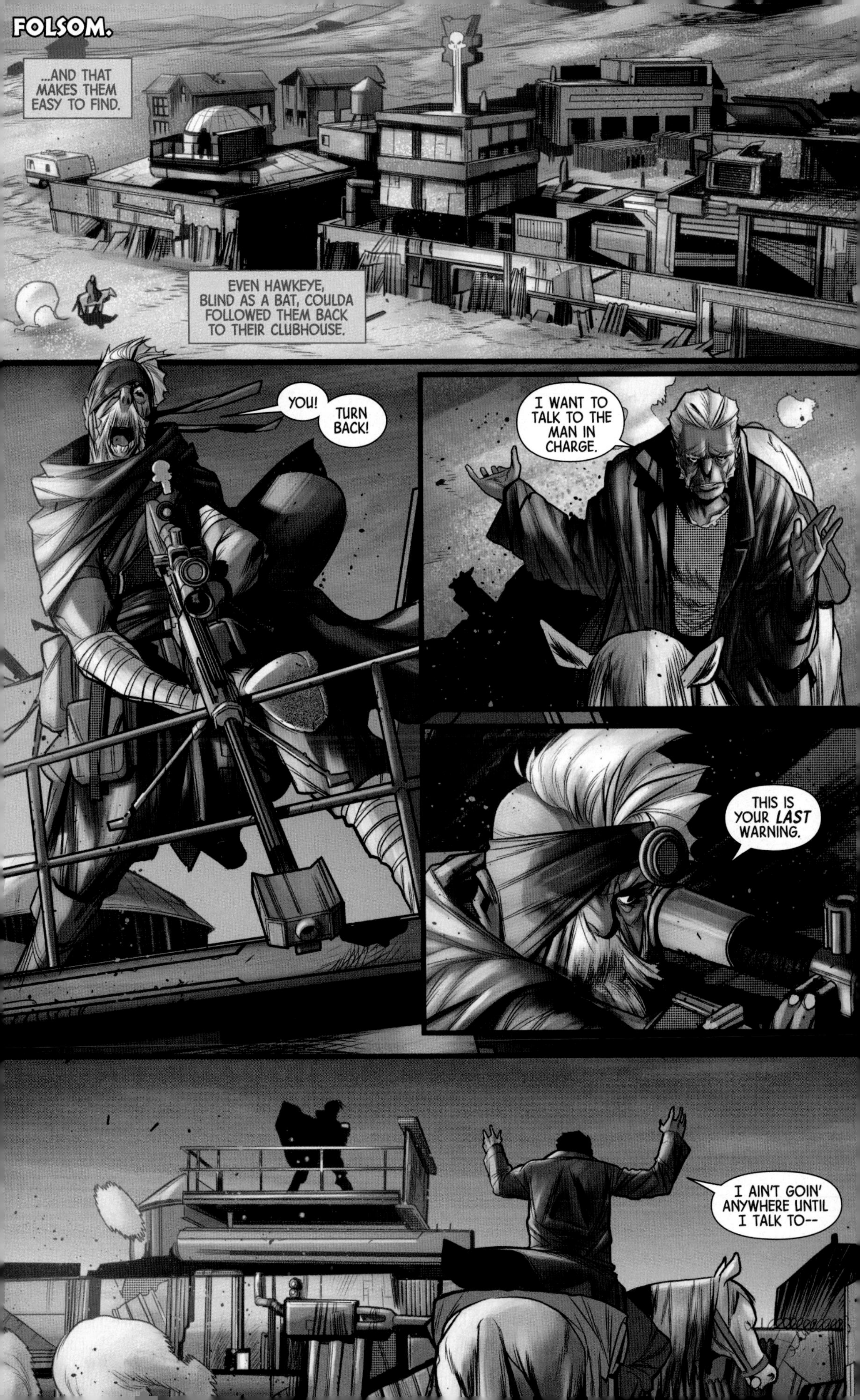
FOLSOM.
...AND THAT MAKES THEM EASY TO FIND.
EVEN HAWKEYE, BLIND AS A BAT, COULDA FOLLOWED THEM BACK TO THEIR CLUBHOUSE.
YOU!
TURN BACK!
I WANT TO TALK TO THE MAN IN CHARGE.
THIS IS YOUR LAST WARNING.
I AIN'T GOIN' ANYWHERE UNTIL I TALK TO--

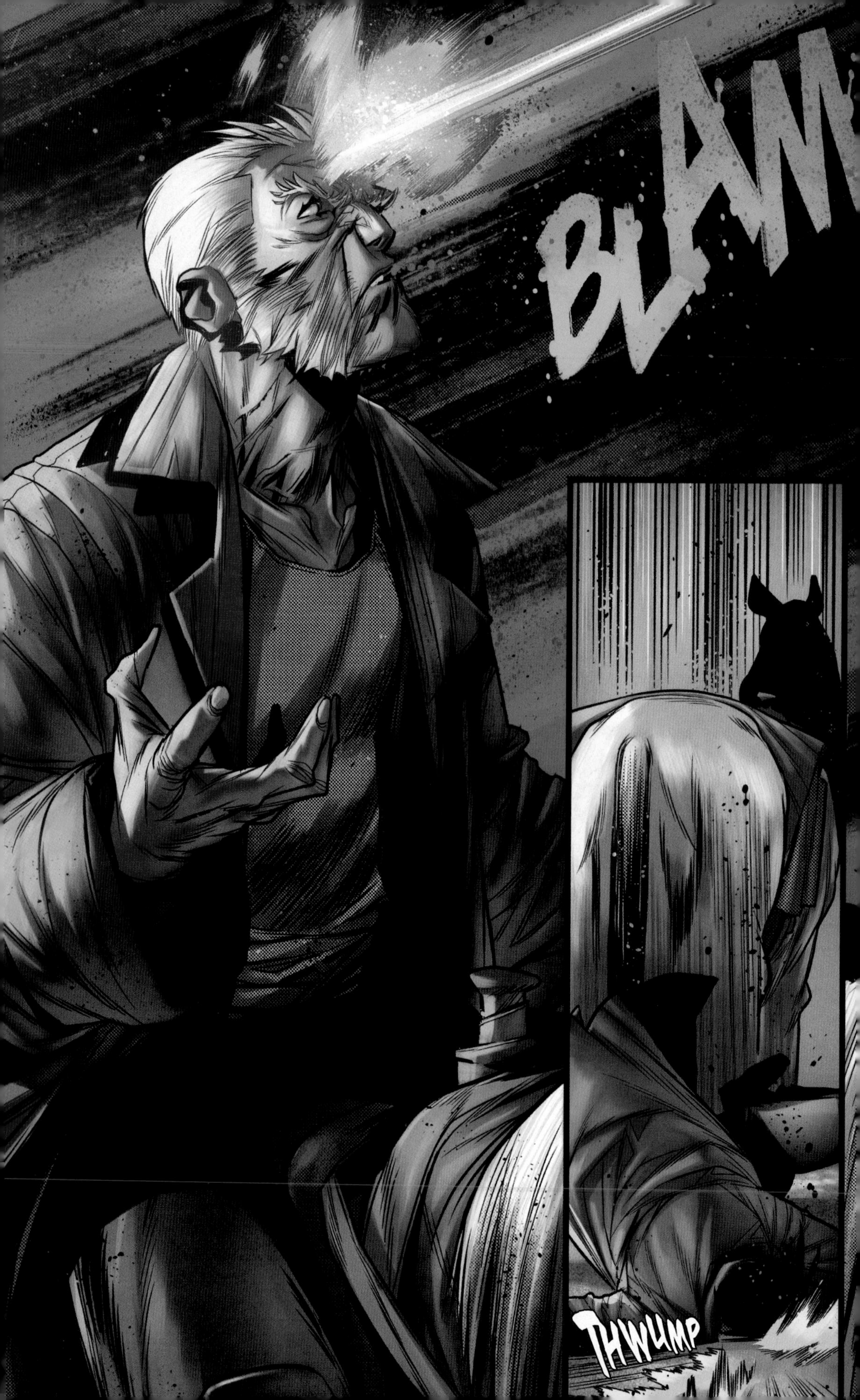
BLAM
THWUMP

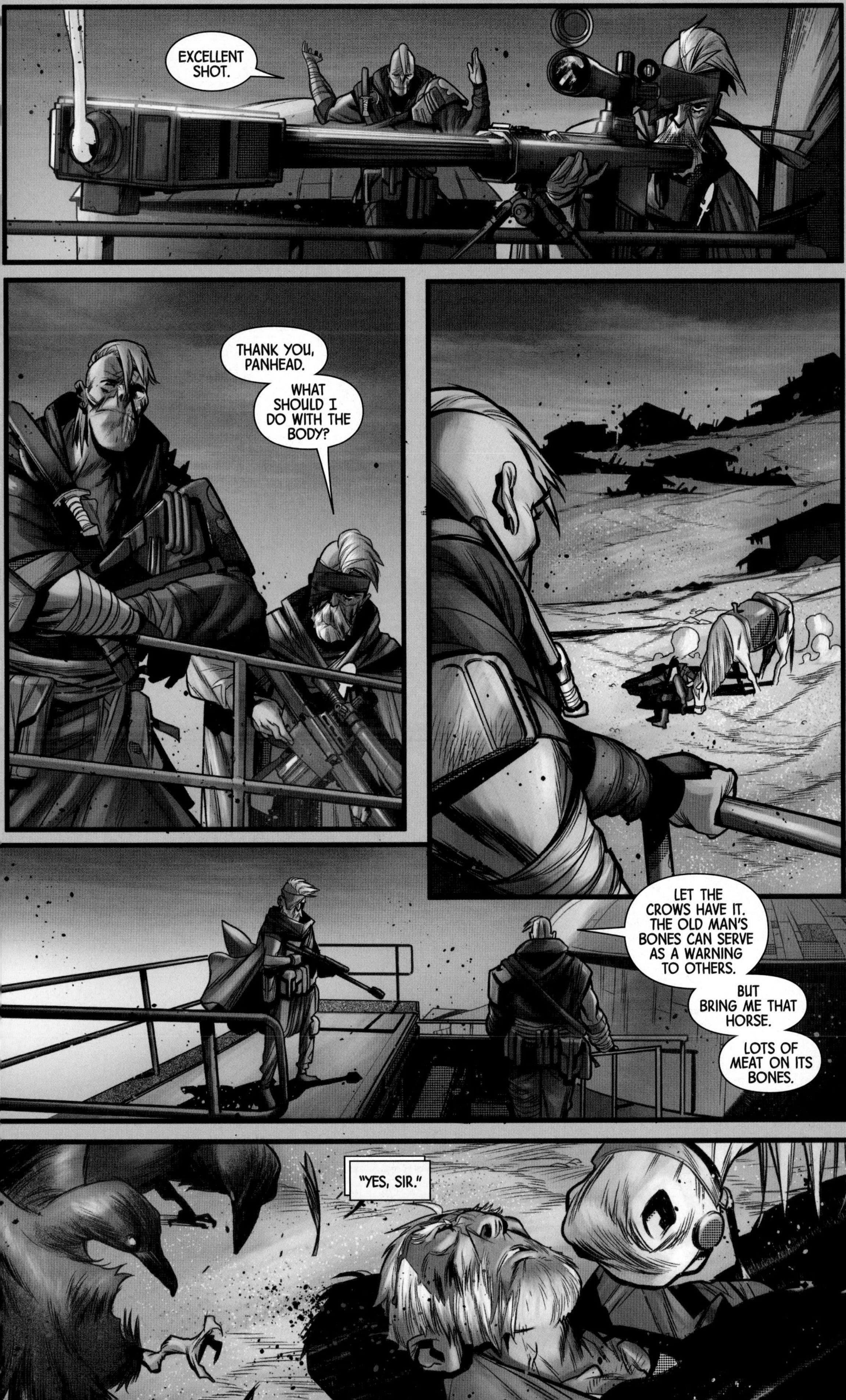
EXCELLENT SHOT.
THANK YOU, PANHEAD.
WHAT SHOULD I DO WITH THE BODY?
LET THE CROWS HAVE IT. THE OLD MAN'S BONES CAN SERVE AS A WARNING TO OTHERS.
BUT BRING ME THAT HORSE.
LOTS OF MEAT ON ITS BONES.
"YES, SIR."

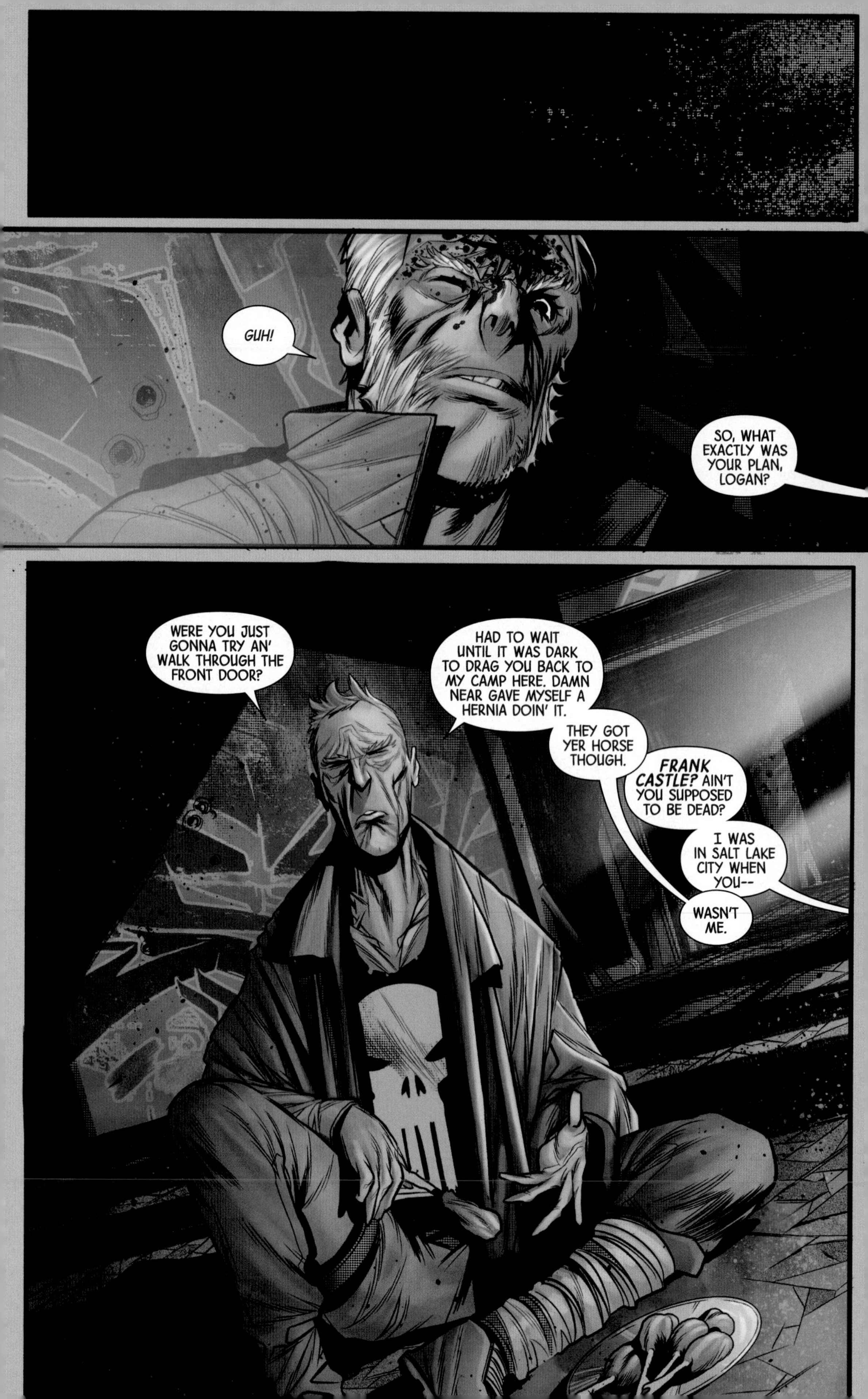
GUH!
SO, WHAT EXACTLY WAS YOUR PLAN, LOGAN?
WERE YOU JUST GONNA TRY AN' WALK THROUGH THE FRONT DOOR?
HAD TO WAIT UNTIL IT WAS DARK TO DRAG YOU BACK TO MY CAMP HERE. DAMN NEAR GAVE MYSELF A HERNIA DOIN' IT.
THEY GOT YER HORSE THOUGH.
FRANK CASTLE? AIN'T YOU SUPPOSED TO BE DEAD?
I WAS IN SALT LAKE CITY WHEN YOU--
WASN'T ME.

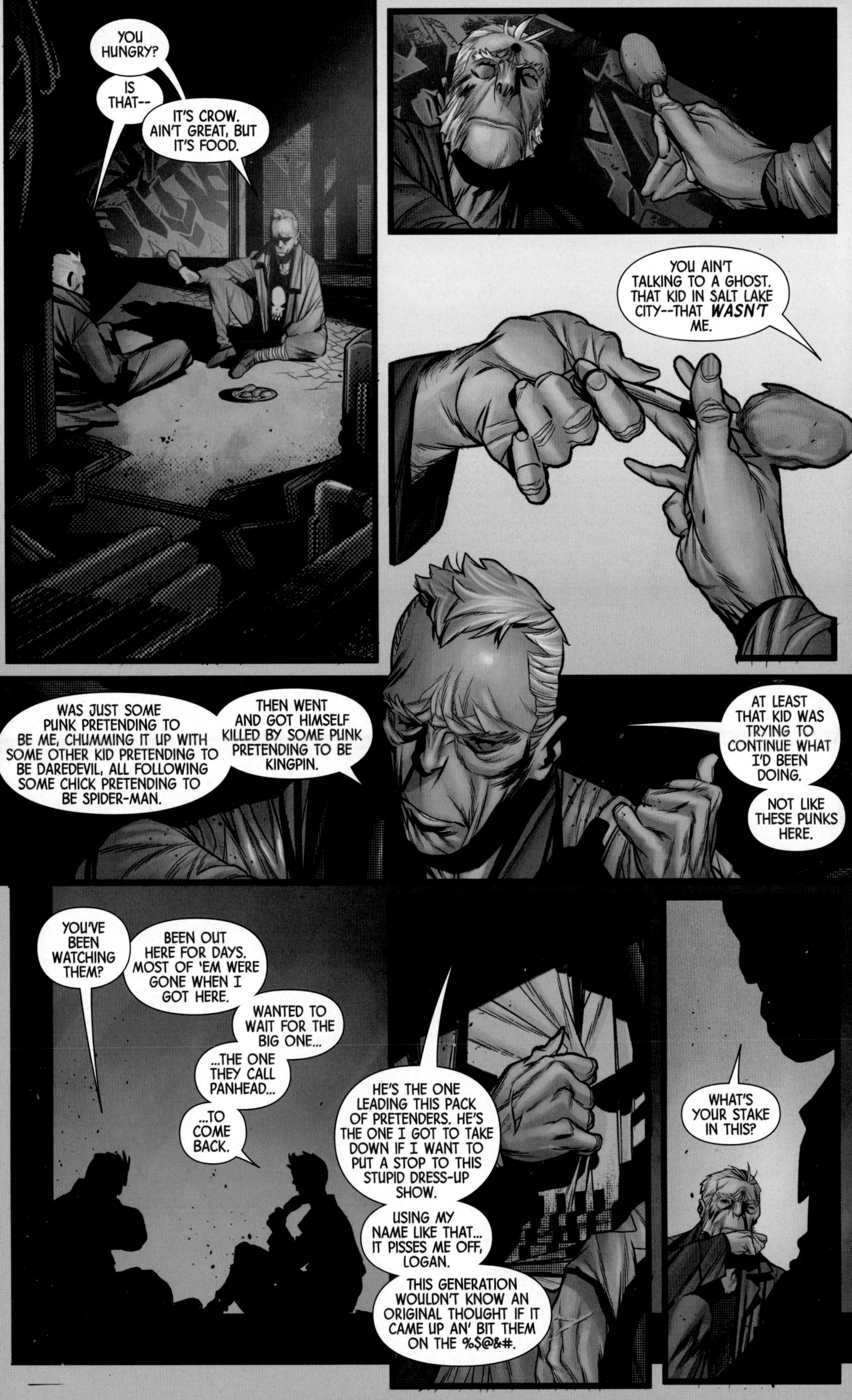
YOU HUNGRY?
IS THAT--
IT'S CROW. AIN'T GREAT, BUT IT'S FOOD.
YOU AIN'T TALKING TO A GHOST. THAT KID IN SALT LAKE CITY--THAT WASN'T ME.
WAS JUST SOME PUNK PRETENDING TO BE ME, CHUMMING IT UP WITH SOME OTHER KID PRETENDING TO BE DAREDEVIL, ALL FOLLOWING SOME CHICK PRETENDING TO BE SPIDER-MAN.
THEN WENT AND GOT HIMSELF KILLED BY SOME PUNK PRETENDING TO BE KINGPIN.
AT LEAST THAT KID WAS TRYING TO CONTINUE WHAT I'D BEEN DOING.
NOT LIKE THESE PUNKS HERE.
YOU'VE BEEN WATCHING THEM?
BEEN OUT HERE FOR DAYS. MOST OF 'EM WERE GONE WHEN I GOT HERE.
WANTED TO WAIT FOR THE BIG ONE...
...THE ONE THEY CALL PANHEAD...
...TO COME BACK.
HE'S THE ONE LEADING THIS PACK OF PRETENDERS. HE'S THE ONE I GOT TO TAKE DOWN IF I WANT TO PUT A STOP TO THIS STUPID DRESS-UP SHOW.
USING MY NAME LIKE THAT... IT PISSES ME OFF, LOGAN.
THIS GENERATION WOULDN'T KNOW AN ORIGINAL THOUGHT IF IT CAME UP AN' BIT THEM ON THE %$@&#.
WHAT'S YOUR STAKE IN THIS?

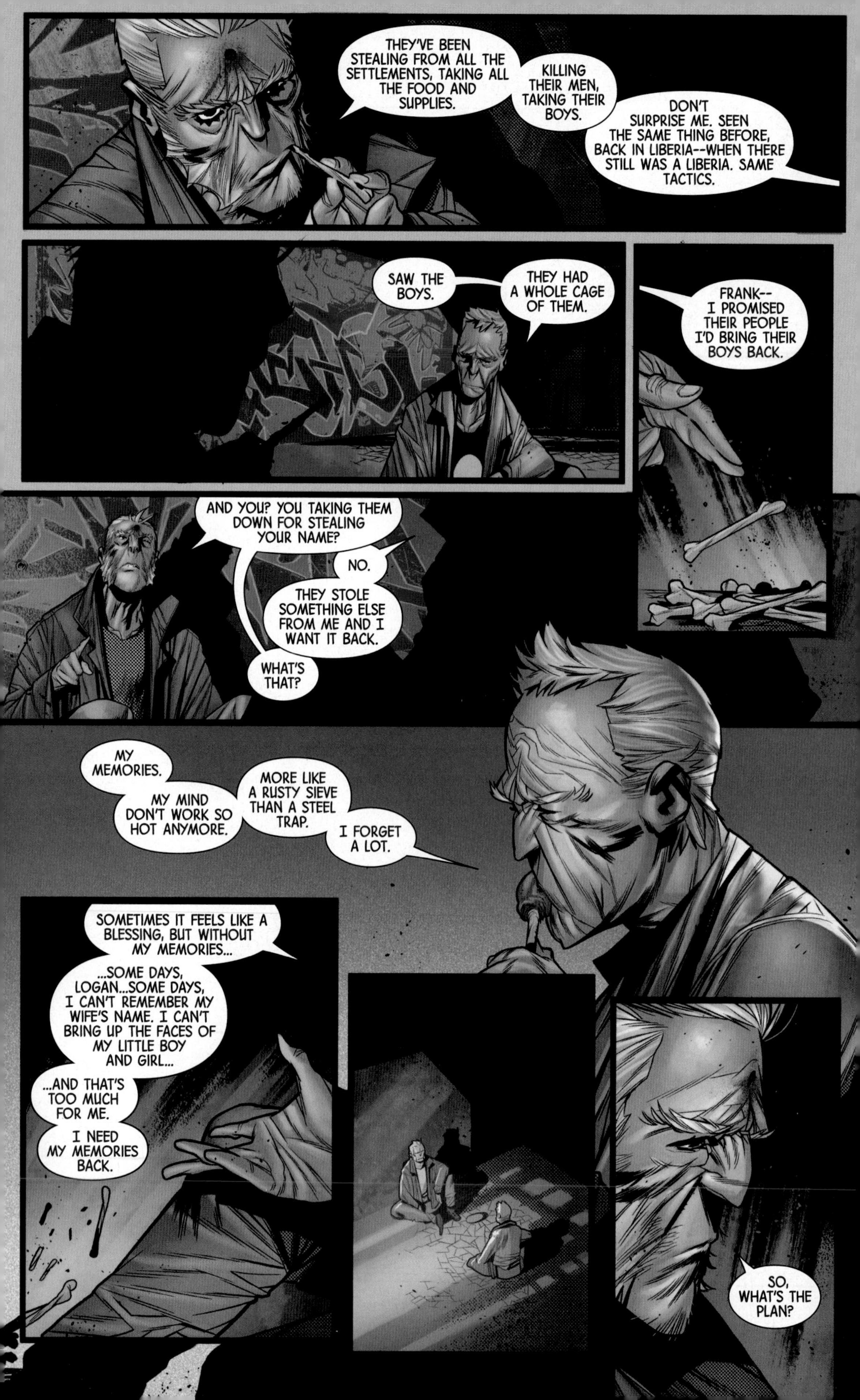
THEY'VE BEEN STEALING FROM ALL THE SETTLEMENTS, TAKING ALL THE FOOD AND SUPPLIES.
KILLING THEIR MEN, TAKING THEIR BOYS.
DON'T SURPRISE ME. SEEN THE SAME THING BEFORE, BACK IN LIBERIA--WHEN THERE STILL WAS A LIBERIA. SAME TACTICS.
SAW THE BOYS.
THEY HAD A WHOLE CAGE OF THEM.
FRANK-- I PROMISED THEIR PEOPLE I'D BRING THEIR BOYS BACK.
AND YOU? YOU TAKING THEM DOWN FOR STEALING YOUR NAME?
NO.
THEY STOLE SOMETHING ELSE FROM ME AND I WANT IT BACK.
WHAT'S THAT?
MY MEMORIES.
MY MIND DON'T WORK SO HOT ANYMORE.
MORE LIKE A RUSTY SIEVE THAN A STEEL TRAP.
I FORGET A LOT.
SOMETIMES IT FEELS LIKE A BLESSING, BUT WITHOUT MY MEMORIES...
...SOME DAYS, LOGAN...SOME DAYS, I CAN'T REMEMBER MY WIFE'S NAME. I CAN'T BRING UP THE FACES OF MY LITTLE BOY AND GIRL...
...AND THAT'S TOO MUCH FOR ME.
I NEED MY MEMORIES BACK.
SO, WHAT'S THE PLAN?

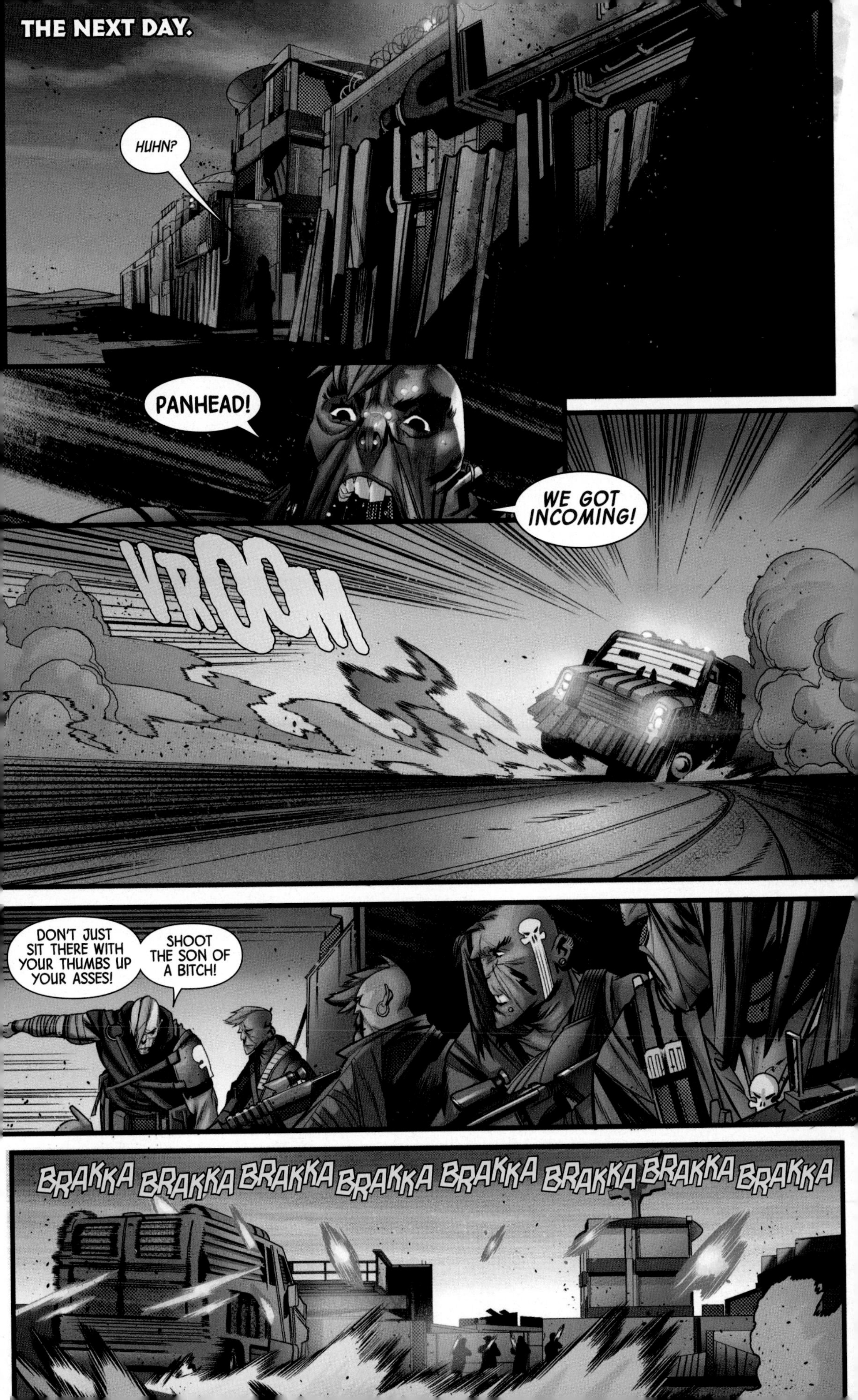
THE NEXT DAY.
HUHN?
PANHEAD!
WE GOT INCOMING!
VROOM
DON'T JUST SIT THERE WITH YOUR THUMBS UP YOUR ASSES!
SHOOT THE SON OF A BITCH!
BRAKKA BRAKKA BRAKKA BRAKKA BRAKKA BRAKKA BRAKKA BRAKKA

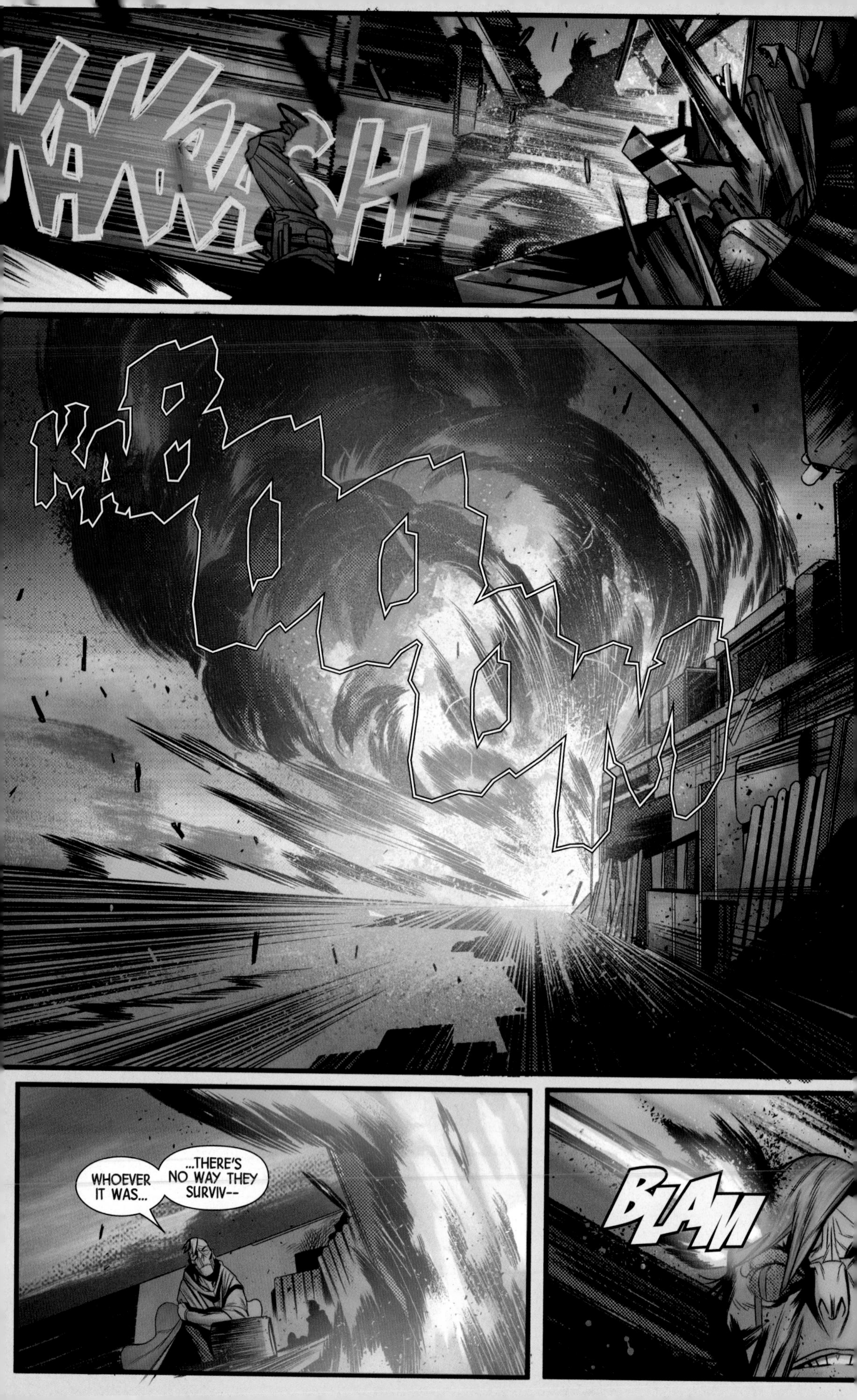
KRASH
KABOOOM
WHOEVER IT WAS...
...THERE'S NO WAY THEY SURVIV--
BLAM

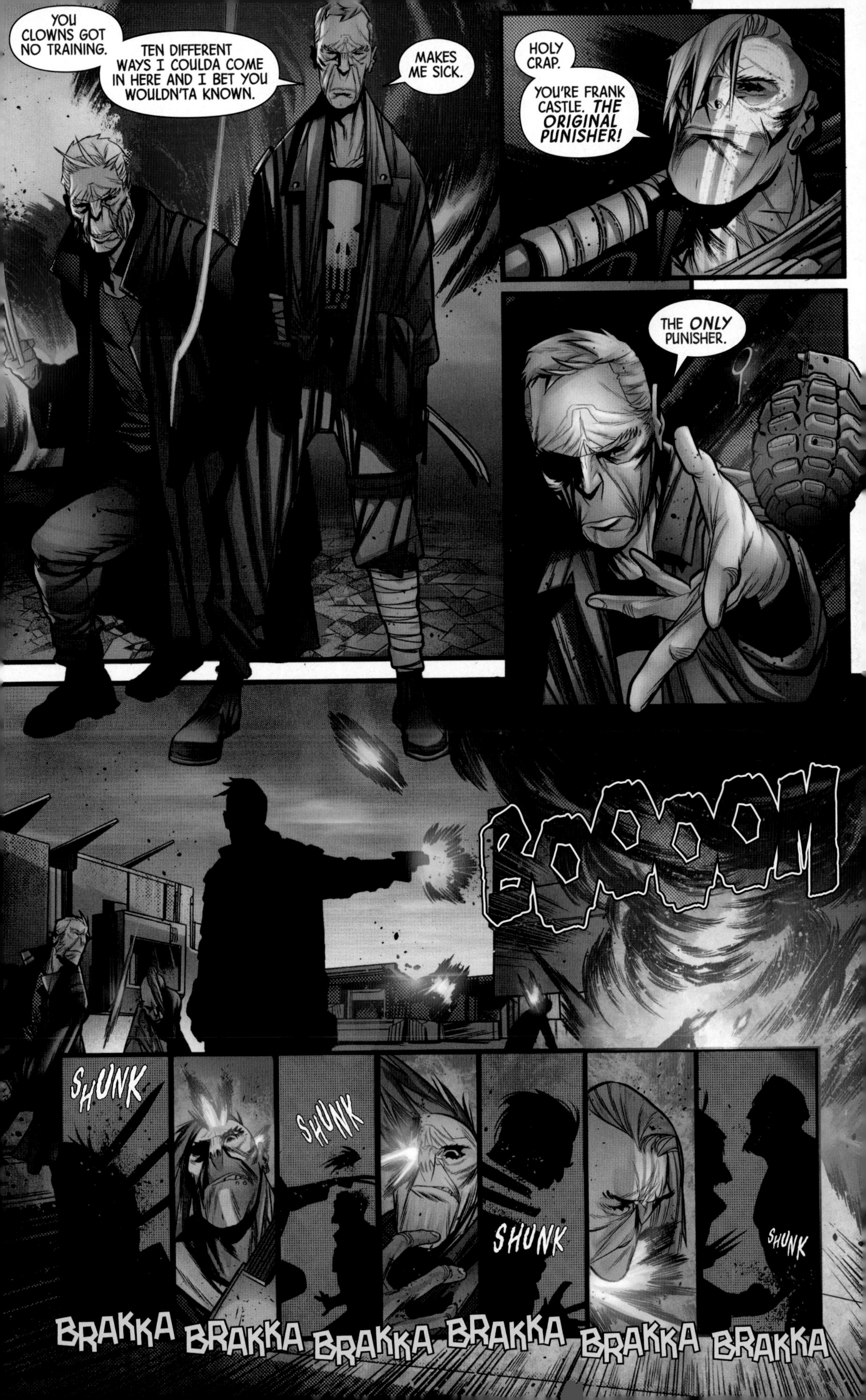
YOU CLOWNS GOT NO TRAINING.
TEN DIFFERENT WAYS I COULDA COME IN HERE AND I BET YOU WOULDN'TA KNOWN.
MAKES ME SICK.
HOLY CRAP.
YOU'RE FRANK CASTLE. THE ORIGINAL PUNISHER!
THE ONLY PUNISHER.
BOOOOM
SHUNK
SHUNK
SHUNK
SHUNK
BRAKKA BRAKKA BRAKKA BRAKKA BRAKKA BRAKKA

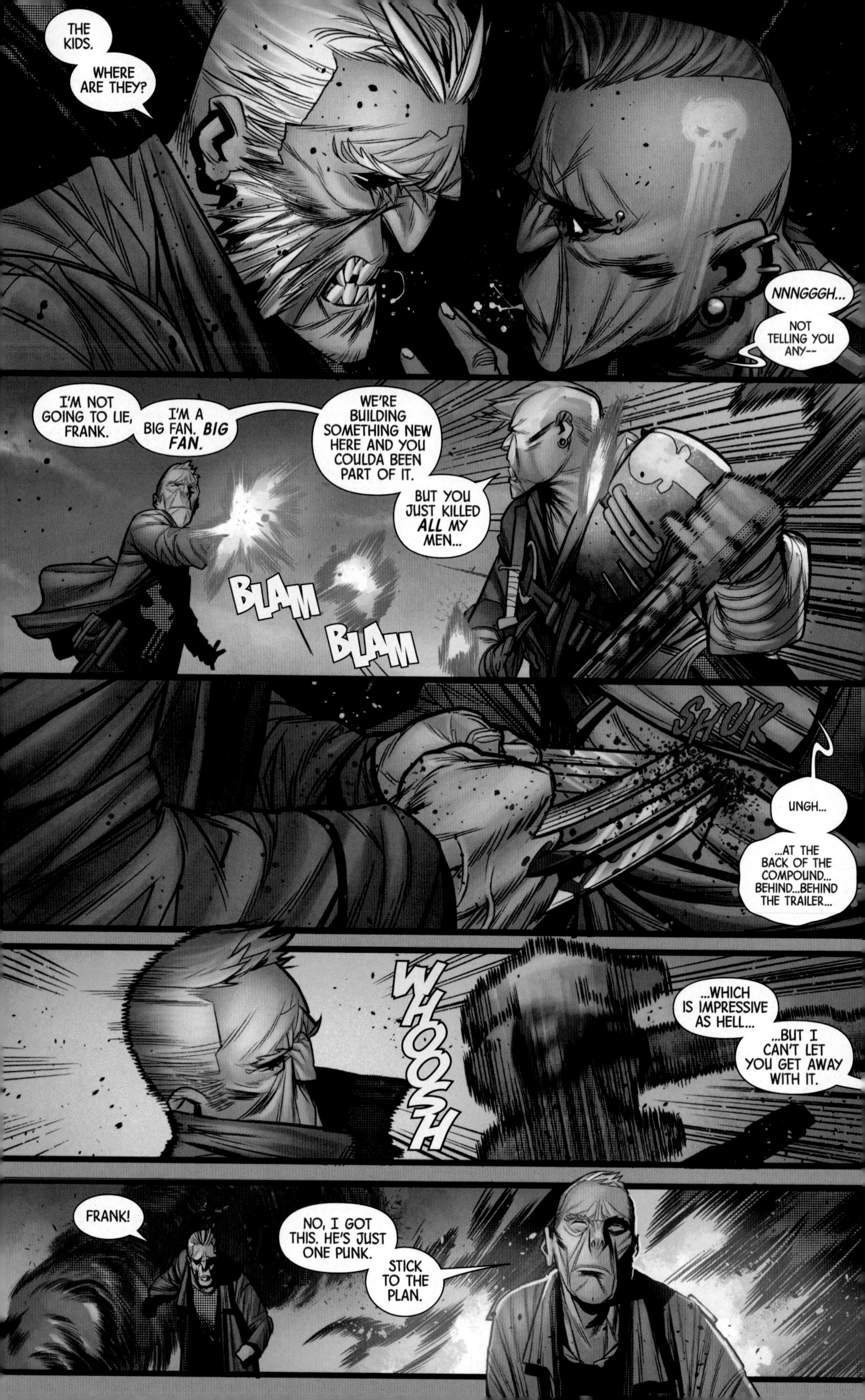
THE KIDS.
WHERE ARE THEY?
NNNGGGH...
NOT TELLING YOU ANY--
I'M NOT GOING TO LIE, FRANK.
I'M A BIG FAN. BIG FAN.
WE'RE BUILDING SOMETHING NEW HERE AND YOU COULDA BEEN PART OF IT.
BUT YOU JUST KILLED ALL MY MEN...
BLAM
BLAM
SHUK
UNGH...
...AT THE BACK OF THE COMPOUND... BEHIND...BEHIND THE TRAILER...
WHOOOSH
...WHICH IS IMPRESSIVE AS HELL...
...BUT I CAN'T LET YOU GET AWAY WITH IT.
FRANK!
NO, I GOT THIS. HE'S JUST ONE PUNK.
STICK TO THE PLAN.

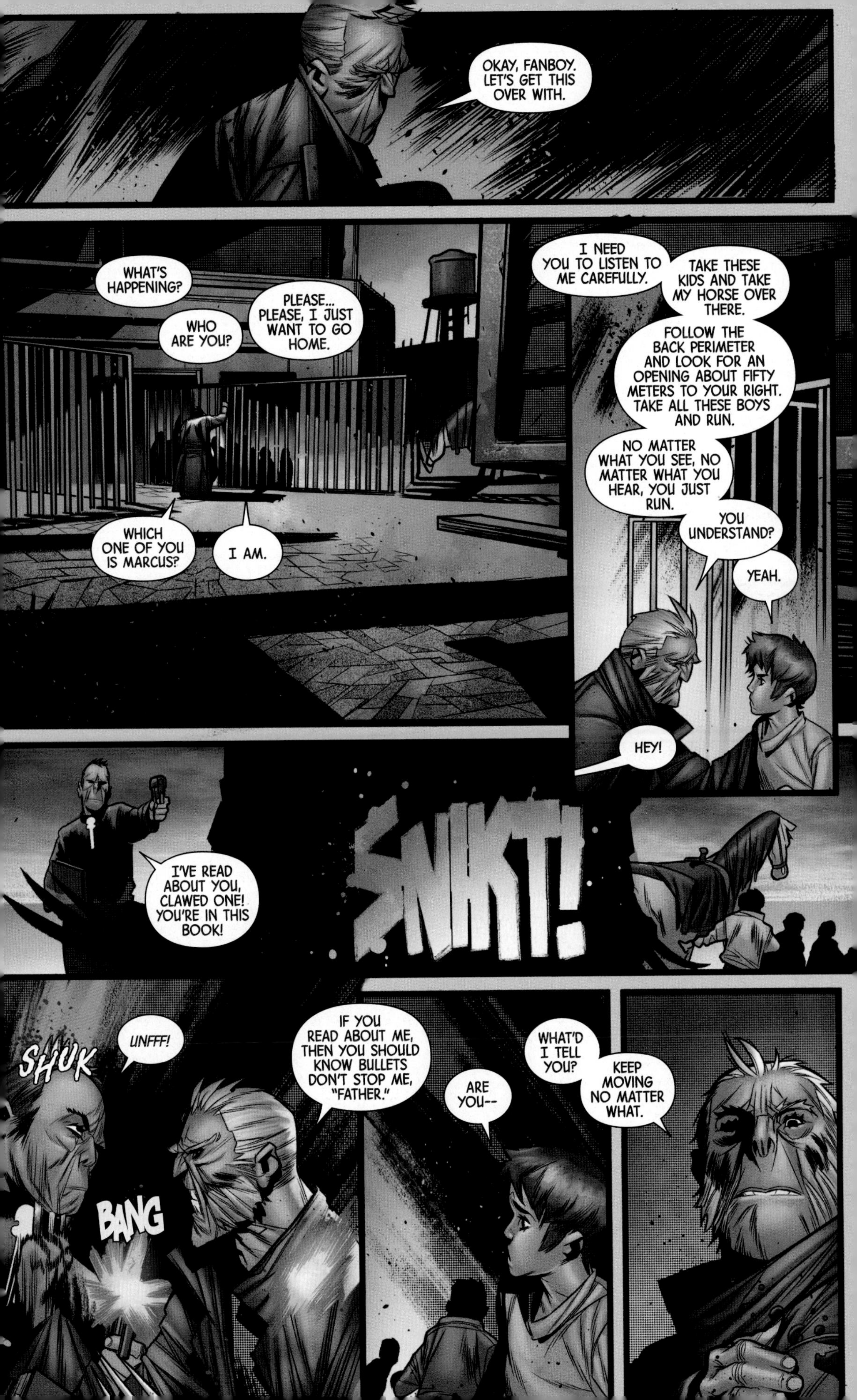
OKAY, FANBOY. LET'S GET THIS OVER WITH.
WHAT'S HAPPENING?
WHO ARE YOU?
PLEASE... PLEASE, I JUST WANT TO GO HOME.
WHICH ONE OF YOU IS MARCUS?
I AM.
I NEED YOU TO LISTEN TO ME CAREFULLY.
TAKE THESE KIDS AND TAKE MY HORSE OVER THERE.
FOLLOW THE BACK PERIMETER AND LOOK FOR AN OPENING ABOUT FIFTY METERS TO YOUR RIGHT. TAKE ALL THESE BOYS AND RUN.
NO MATTER WHAT YOU SEE, NO MATTER WHAT YOU HEAR, YOU JUST RUN.
YOU UNDERSTAND?
YEAH.
HEY!
I'VE READ ABOUT YOU, CLAWED ONE! YOU'RE IN THIS BOOK!
SNIKT!
SHUK
UNFFF!
BANG
IF YOU READ ABOUT ME, THEN YOU SHOULD KNOW BULLETS DON'T STOP ME, "FATHER."
ARE YOU--
WHAT'D I TELL YOU?
KEEP MOVING NO MATTER WHAT.

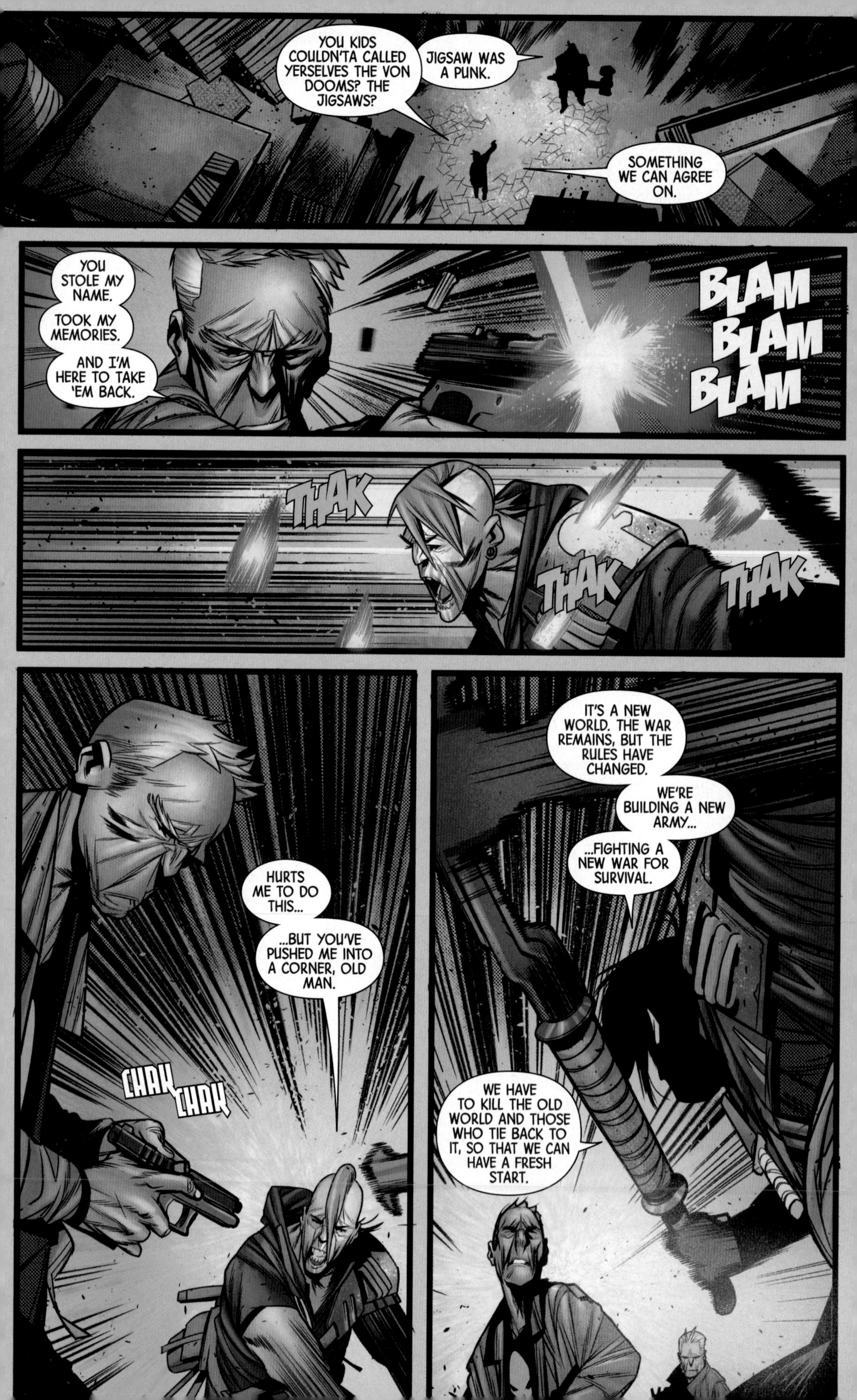
YOU KIDS COULDN'TA CALLED YERSELVES THE VON DOOMS? THE JIGSAWS?
JIGSAW WAS A PUNK.
SOMETHING WE CAN AGREE ON.
YOU STOLE MY NAME.
TOOK MY MEMORIES.
AND I'M HERE TO TAKE 'EM BACK.
BLAM BLAM BLAM
THAK
THAK
THAK
HURTS ME TO DO THIS...
...BUT YOU'VE PUSHED ME INTO A CORNER, OLD MAN.
CHAK CHAK
IT'S A NEW WORLD. THE WAR REMAINS, BUT THE RULES HAVE CHANGED.
WE'RE BUILDING A NEW ARMY...
...FIGHTING A NEW WAR FOR SURVIVAL.
WE HAVE TO KILL THE OLD WORLD AND THOSE WHO TIE BACK TO IT, SO THAT WE CAN HAVE A FRESH START.

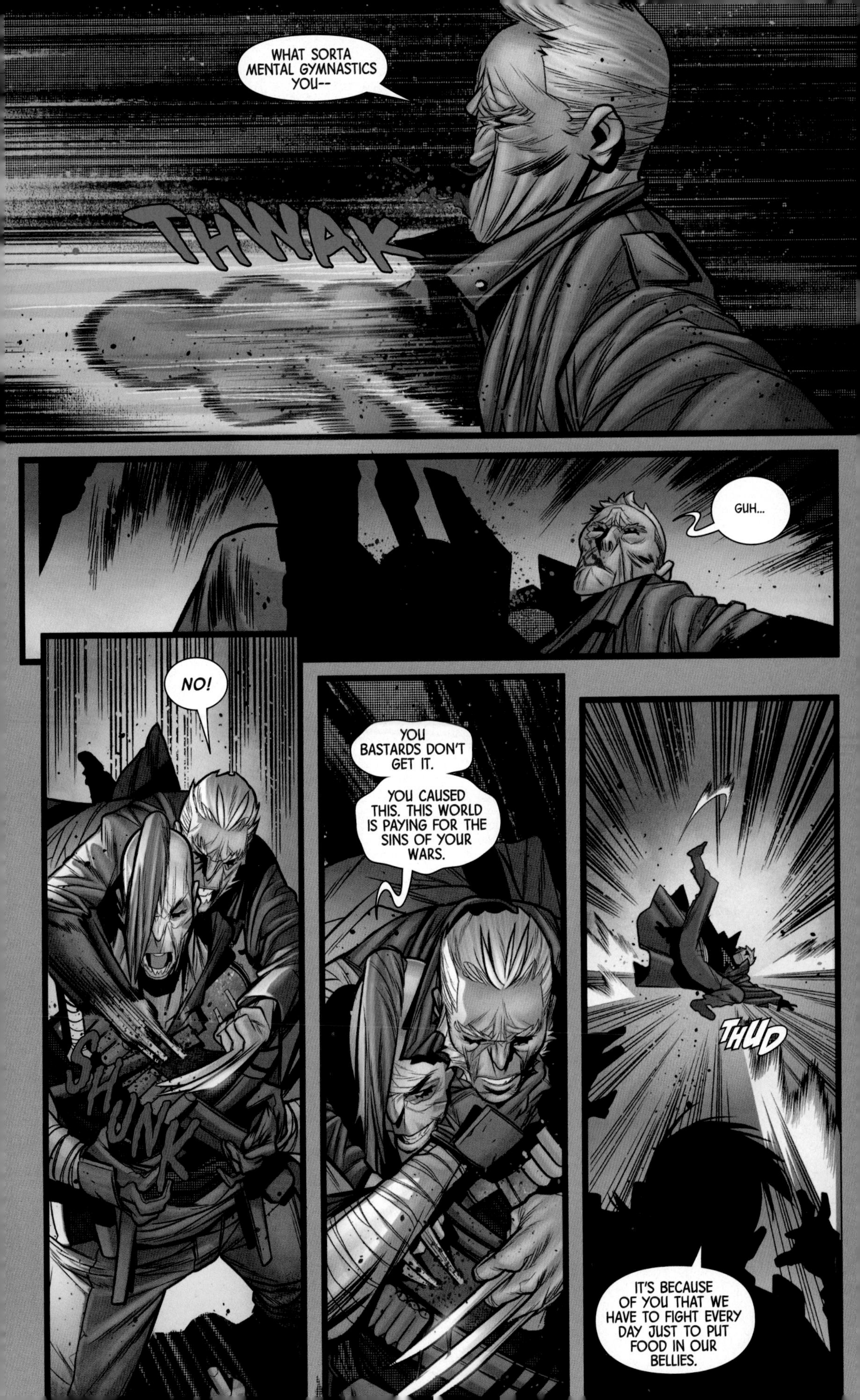

WHAT SORTA MENTAL GYMNASTICS YOU--
THWAK
GUH...
NO!
SHUNK
YOU BASTARDS DON'T GET IT.
YOU CAUSED THIS. THIS WORLD IS PAYING FOR THE SINS OF YOUR WARS.
THUD
IT'S BECAUSE OF YOU THAT WE HAVE TO FIGHT EVERY DAY JUST TO PUT FOOD IN OUR BELLIES.

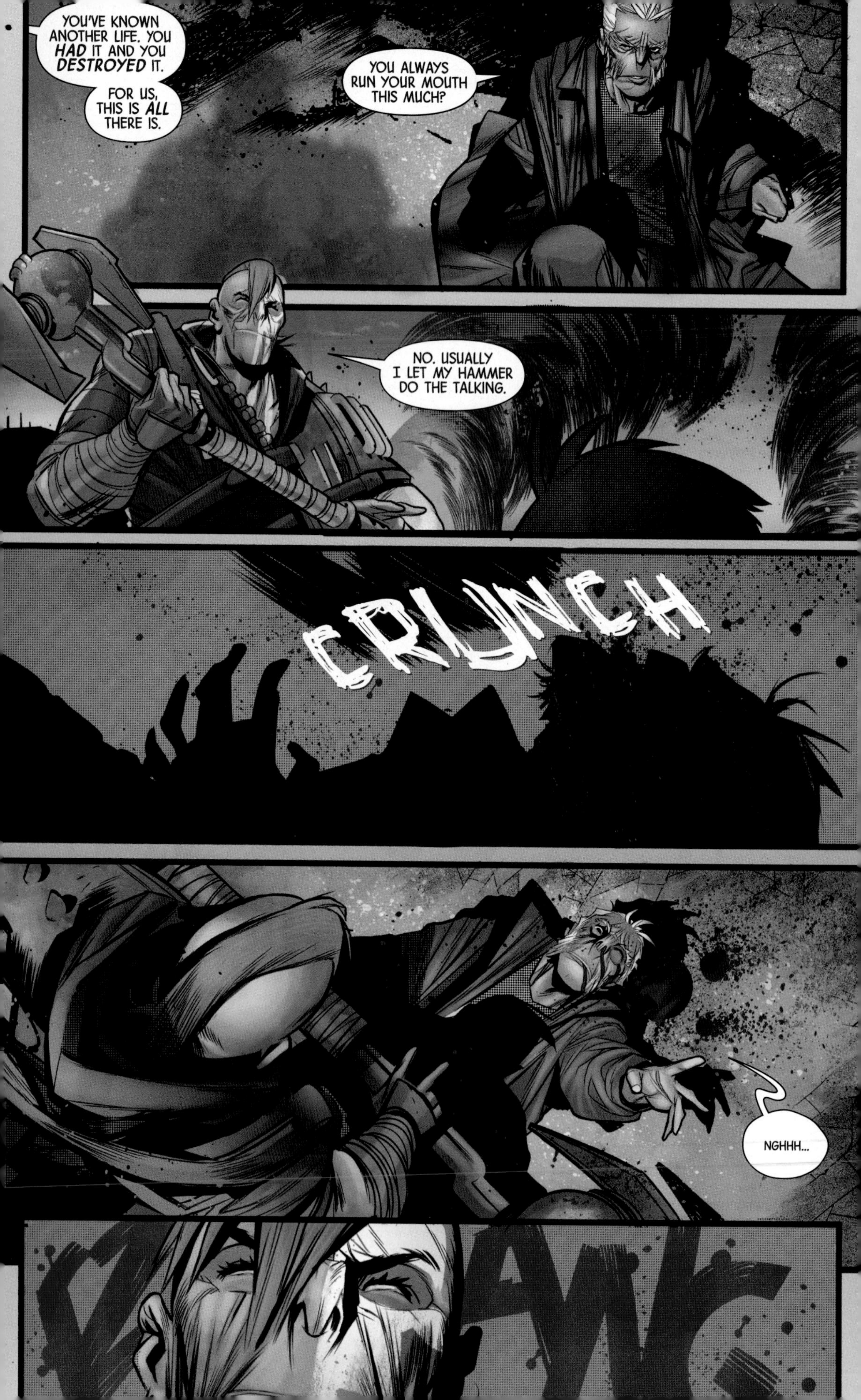

YOU'VE KNOWN ANOTHER LIFE. YOU *HAD* IT AND YOU *DESTROYED* IT.
FOR US, THIS IS *ALL* THERE IS.
YOU ALWAYS RUN YOUR MOUTH THIS MUCH?
NO. USUALLY I LET MY HAMMER DO THE TALKING.
CRUNCH
NGHHH...

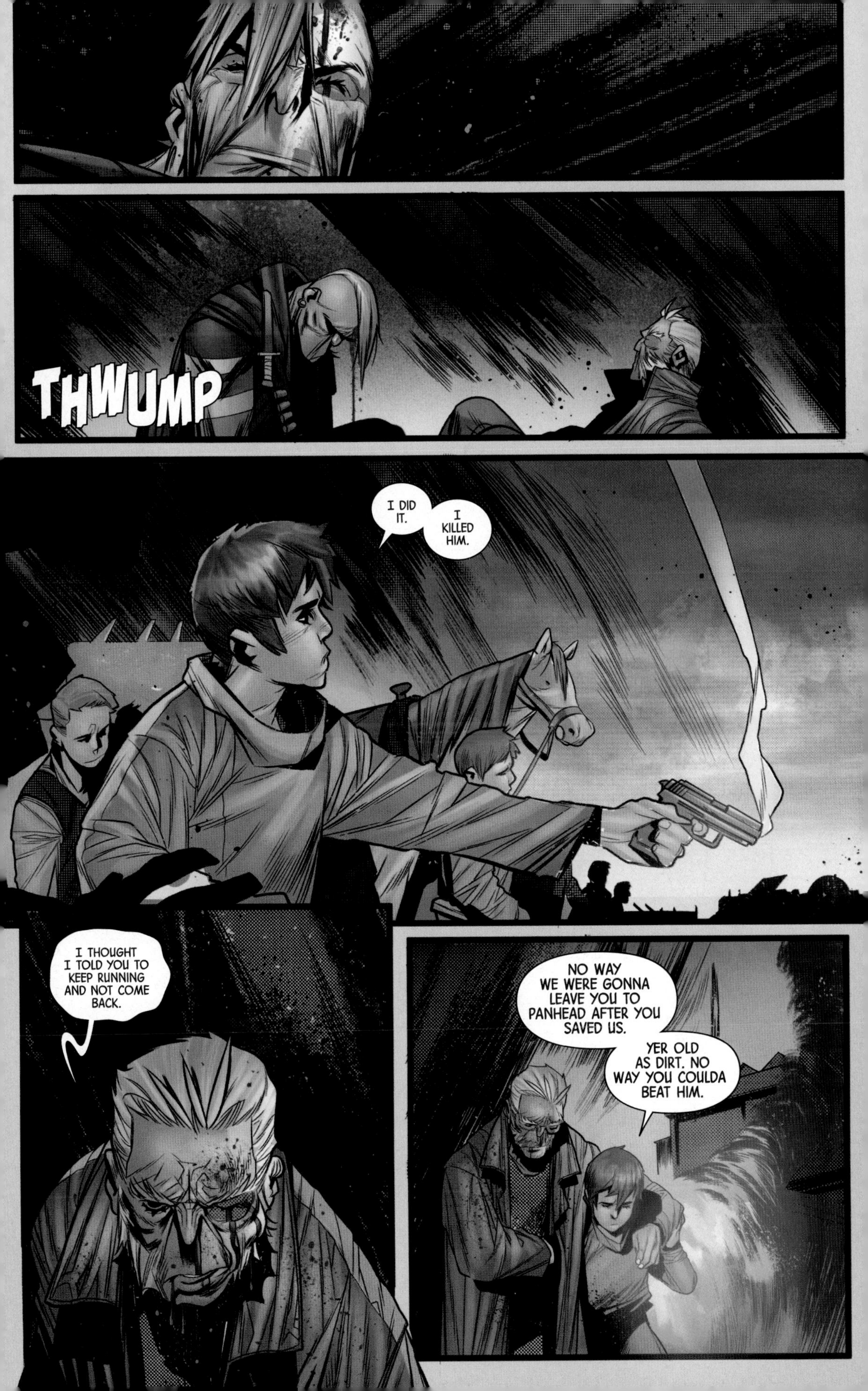
THWUMP
I DID IT.
I KILLED HIM.
I THOUGHT I TOLD YOU TO KEEP RUNNING AND NOT COME BACK.
NO WAY WE WERE GONNA LEAVE YOU TO PANHEAD AFTER YOU SAVED US.
YER OLD AS DIRT. NO WAY YOU COULDA BEAT HIM.

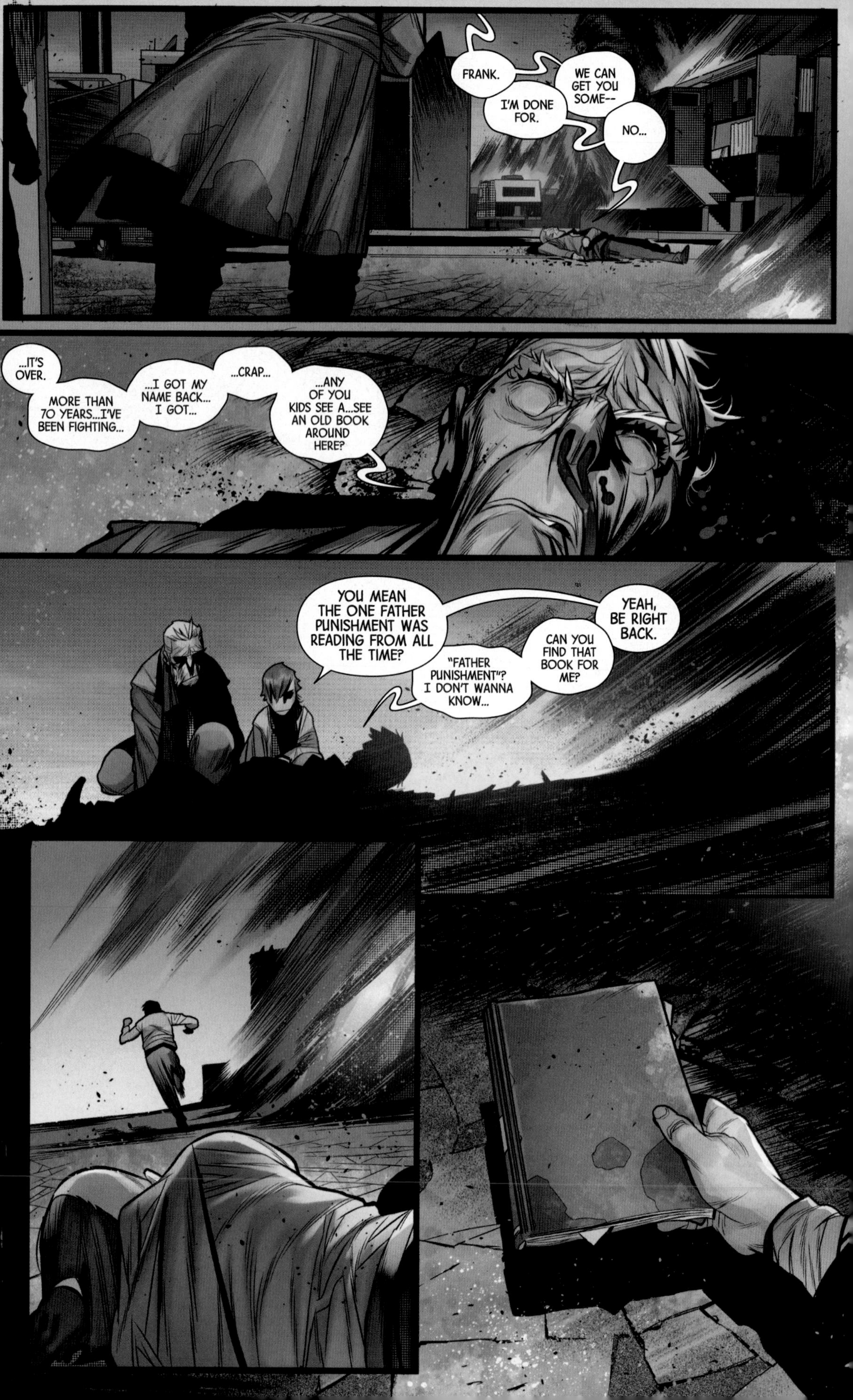
FRANK.
WE CAN GET YOU SOME--
I'M DONE FOR.
NO...
...IT'S OVER.
MORE THAN 70 YEARS...I'VE BEEN FIGHTING...
...I GOT MY NAME BACK... I GOT...
...CRAP...
...ANY OF YOU KIDS SEE A...SEE AN OLD BOOK AROUND HERE?
YOU MEAN THE ONE FATHER PUNISHMENT WAS READING FROM ALL THE TIME?
"FATHER PUNISHMENT"? I DON'T WANNA KNOW...
CAN YOU FIND THAT BOOK FOR ME?
YEAH, BE RIGHT BACK.

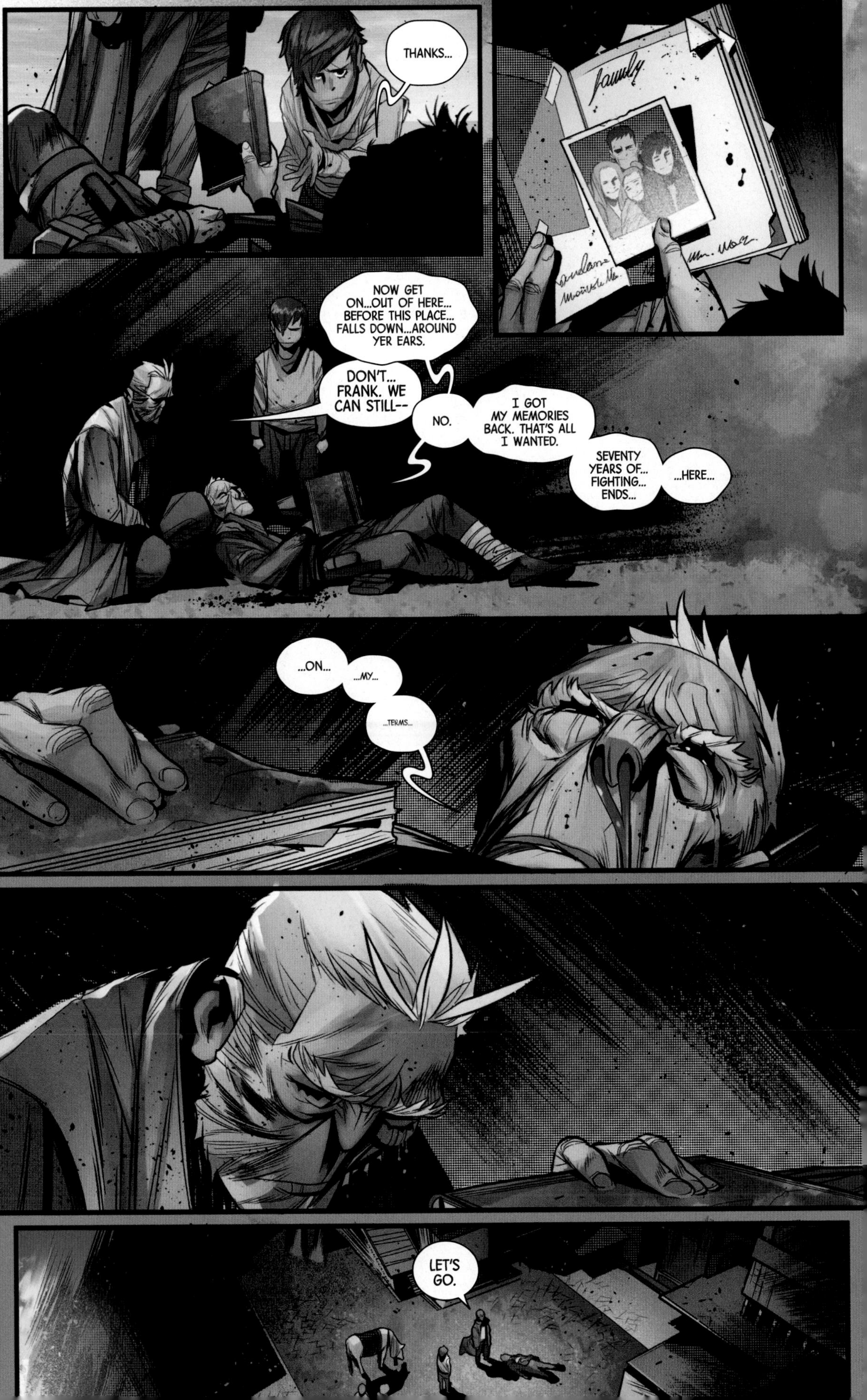
THANKS...
NOW GET ON...OUT OF HERE... BEFORE THIS PLACE... FALLS DOWN...AROUND YER EARS.
DON'T... FRANK. WE CAN STILL--
NO.
I GOT MY MEMORIES BACK. THAT'S ALL I WANTED.
SEVENTY YEARS OF... FIGHTING... ENDS...
...HERE...
...ON...
...MY...
...TERMS...
LET'S GO.

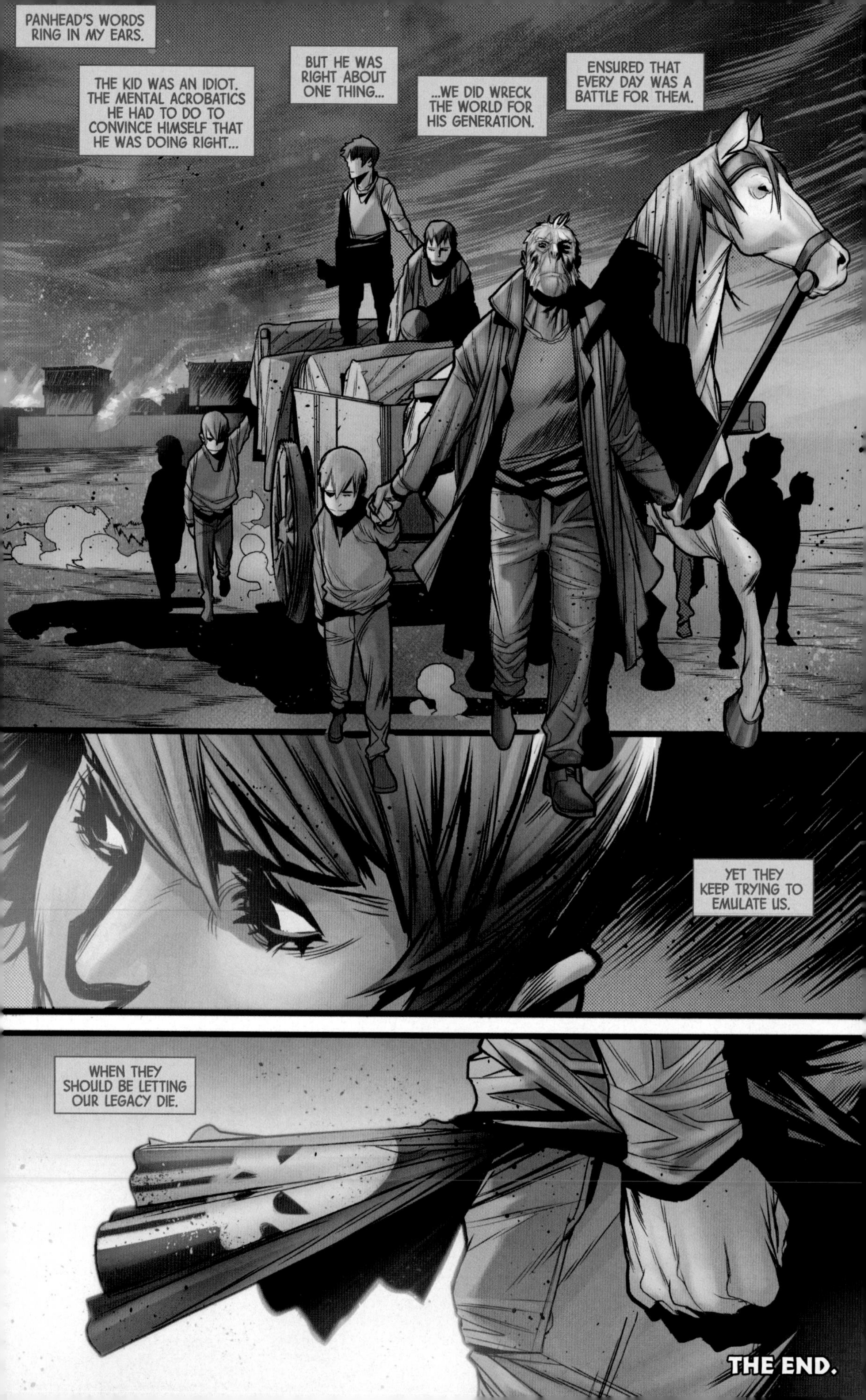
PANHEAD'S WORDS RING IN MY EARS.
THE KID WAS AN IDIOT. THE MENTAL ACROBATICS HE HAD TO DO TO CONVINCE HIMSELF THAT HE WAS DOING RIGHT...
BUT HE WAS RIGHT ABOUT ONE THING...
...WE DID WRECK THE WORLD FOR HIS GENERATION.
ENSURED THAT EVERY DAY WAS A BATTLE FOR THEM.
YET THEY KEEP TRYING TO EMULATE US.
WHEN THEY SHOULD BE LETTING OUR LEGACY DIE.
THE END.

CONGRATULATIONS, TRUE BELIEVER! YOU ARE HOLDING THE FIRST APPEARANCES OF OLD MAN PUNISHER IN YOUR VERY HANDS! A CHARACTER SO INTENSE, HE REQUIRED TWO CREATIVE TEAMS TO BRING HIM TO LIFE. MAKE SURE TO SPREAD YOUR THANKS AND ADULATION TO ED, SIMONE, RYAN AND HAYDEN EARLY AND OFTEN. HAS THIS EVER HAPPENED BEFORE? VISITING TWO DISTINCT PERIODS IN A CHARACTER'S LIFE IN THEIR FIRST APPEARANCE? PROBABLY! BUT NEVER WITH THIS MUCH STYLE, NATCH.

SUN'S OUT GUNS OUT

CROB

@chrisrobinson
8/10/18

BATTLE VAN AND WASTELANDS PUNISHER DESIGNS BY HAYDEN SHERMAN

OLD MAN FRANK DESIGN BY SIMONE Di MEO

FRANK CASTLE WAS A DECORATED MARINE, AN UPSTANDING CITIZEN AND A FAMILY MAN. WHEN HIS FAMILY WAS ACCIDENTALLY KILLED IN A BRUTAL MOB HIT, HE BECAME A FORCE OF COLD, CALCULATED RETRIBUTION KNOWN AS THE PUNISHER. EVEN AFTER THE WORLD DEVOLVED INTO A LAWLESS WASTELAND, HIS MISSION CONTINUES...

THE PUNISHER
wastelands journal

SONS OF THE PATRIOT

RYAN **CADY**	HAYDEN **SHERMAN**	DONO **SÁNCHEZ-ALMARA**	VC's CORY **PETIT**
WRITER	**ARTIST**	**COLOR ARTIST**	**LETTERER**

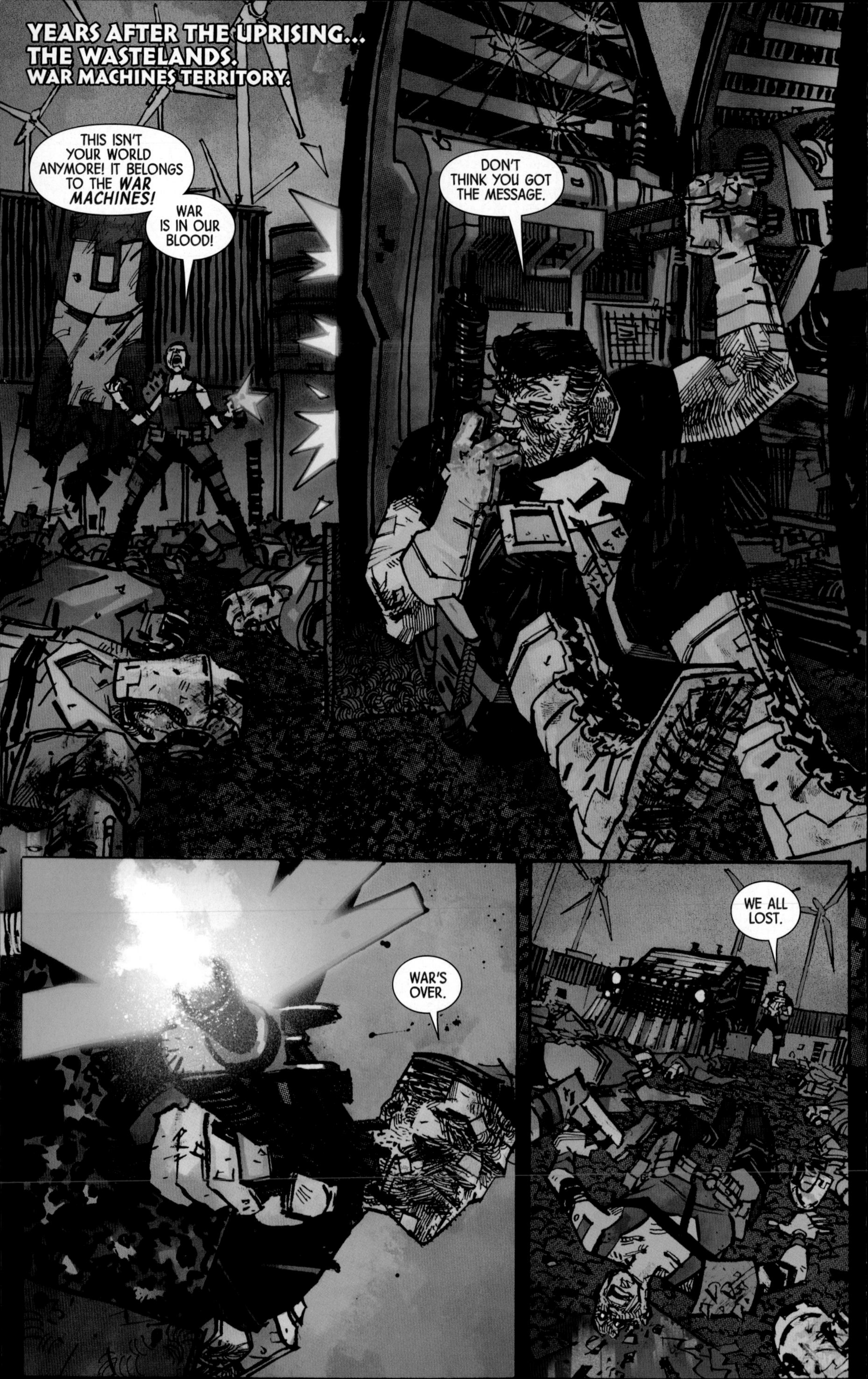
YEARS AFTER THE UPRISING... THE WASTELANDS.
WAR MACHINES TERRITORY.
THIS ISN'T YOUR WORLD ANYMORE! IT BELONGS TO THE WAR MACHINES!
WAR IS IN OUR BLOOD!
DON'T THINK YOU GOT THE MESSAGE.
WAR'S OVER.
WE ALL LOST.

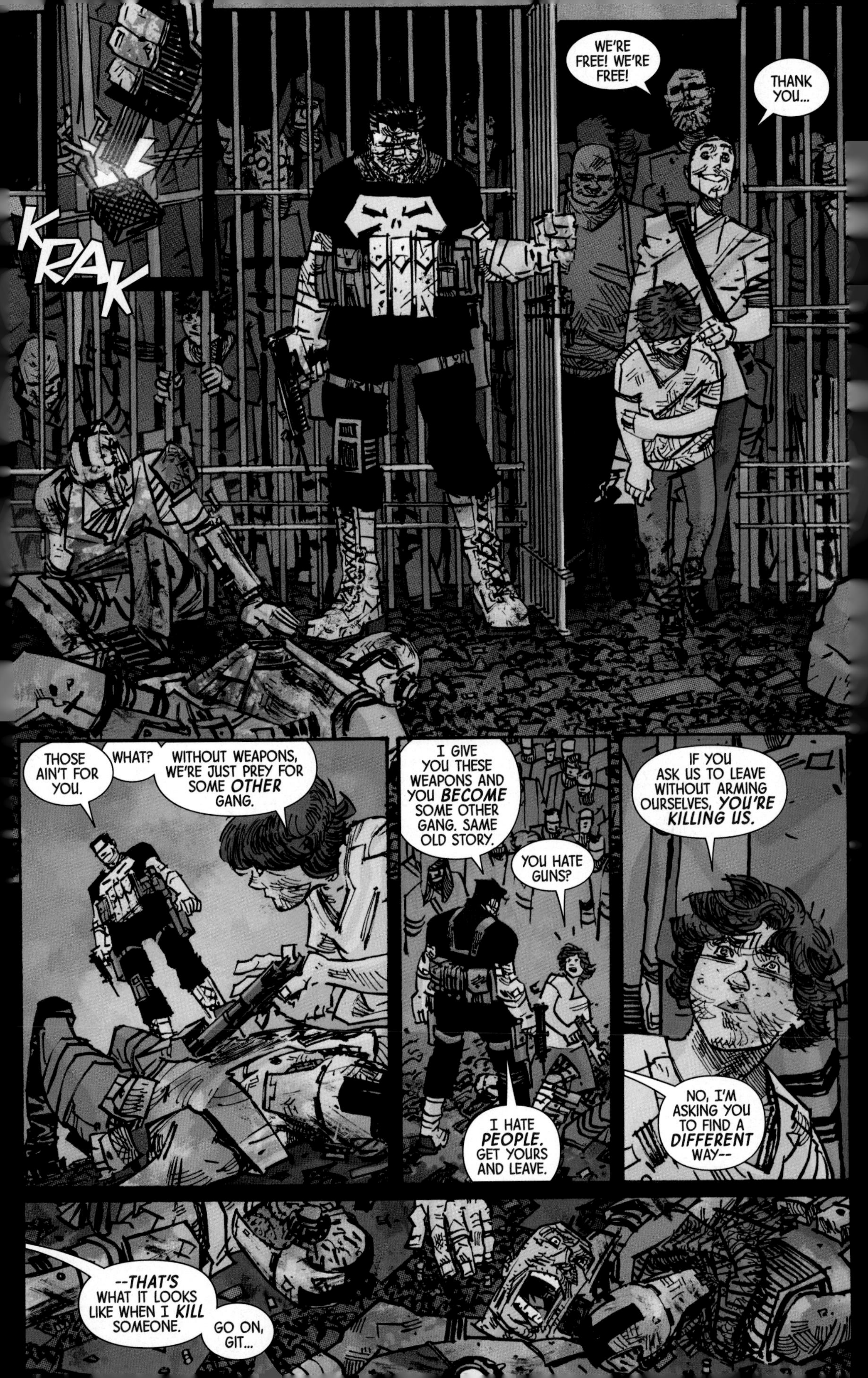
KRAK
WE'RE FREE! WE'RE FREE!
THANK YOU...
THOSE AIN'T FOR YOU.
WHAT?
WITHOUT WEAPONS, WE'RE JUST PREY FOR SOME OTHER GANG.
I GIVE YOU THESE WEAPONS AND YOU BECOME SOME OTHER GANG. SAME OLD STORY.
YOU HATE GUNS?
I HATE PEOPLE. GET YOURS AND LEAVE.
IF YOU ASK US TO LEAVE WITHOUT ARMING OURSELVES, YOU'RE KILLING US.
NO, I'M ASKING YOU TO FIND A DIFFERENT WAY--
--THAT'S WHAT IT LOOKS LIKE WHEN I KILL SOMEONE.
GO ON, GIT...

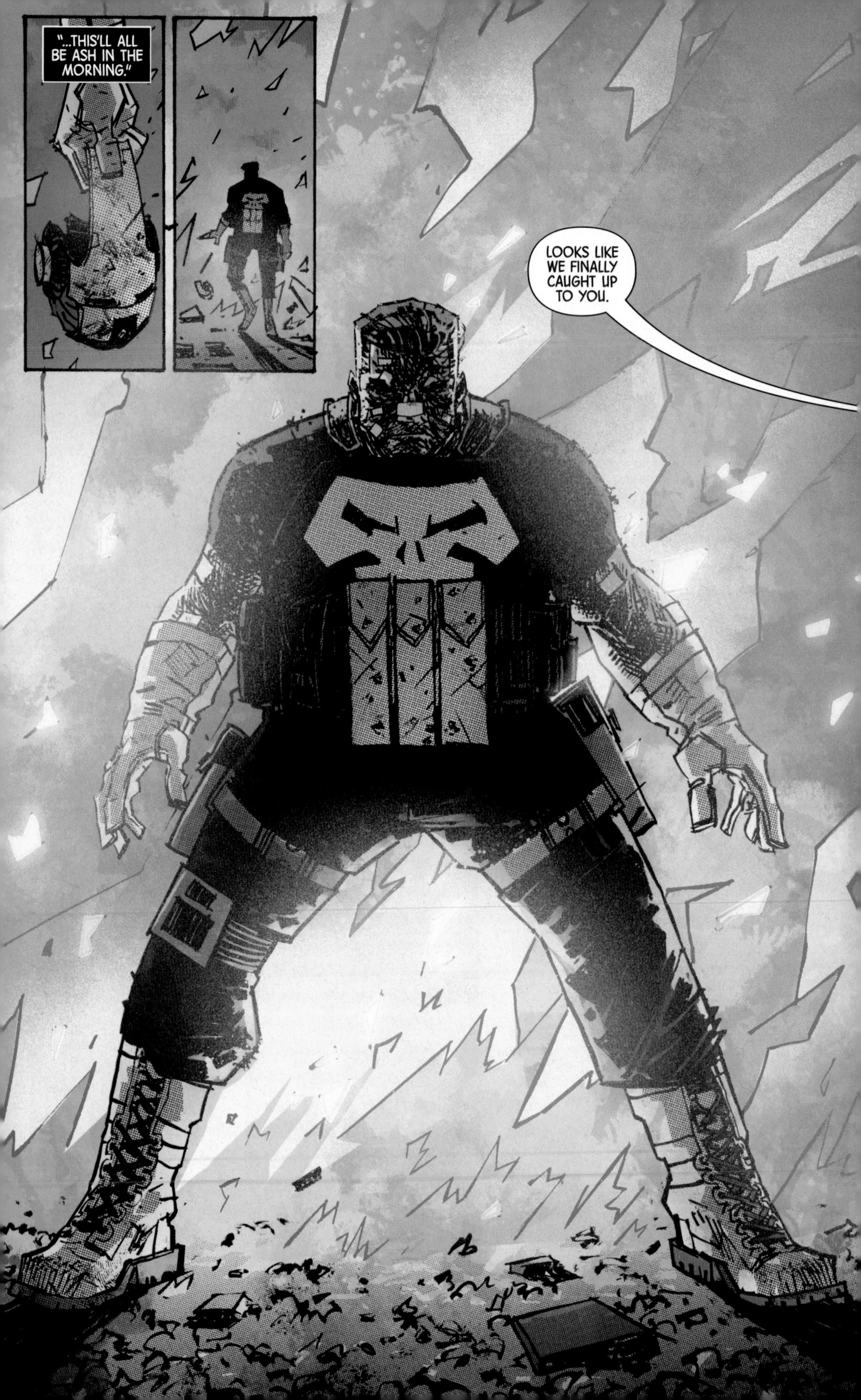
"...THIS'LL ALL BE ASH IN THE MORNING."
LOOKS LIKE WE FINALLY CAUGHT UP TO YOU.

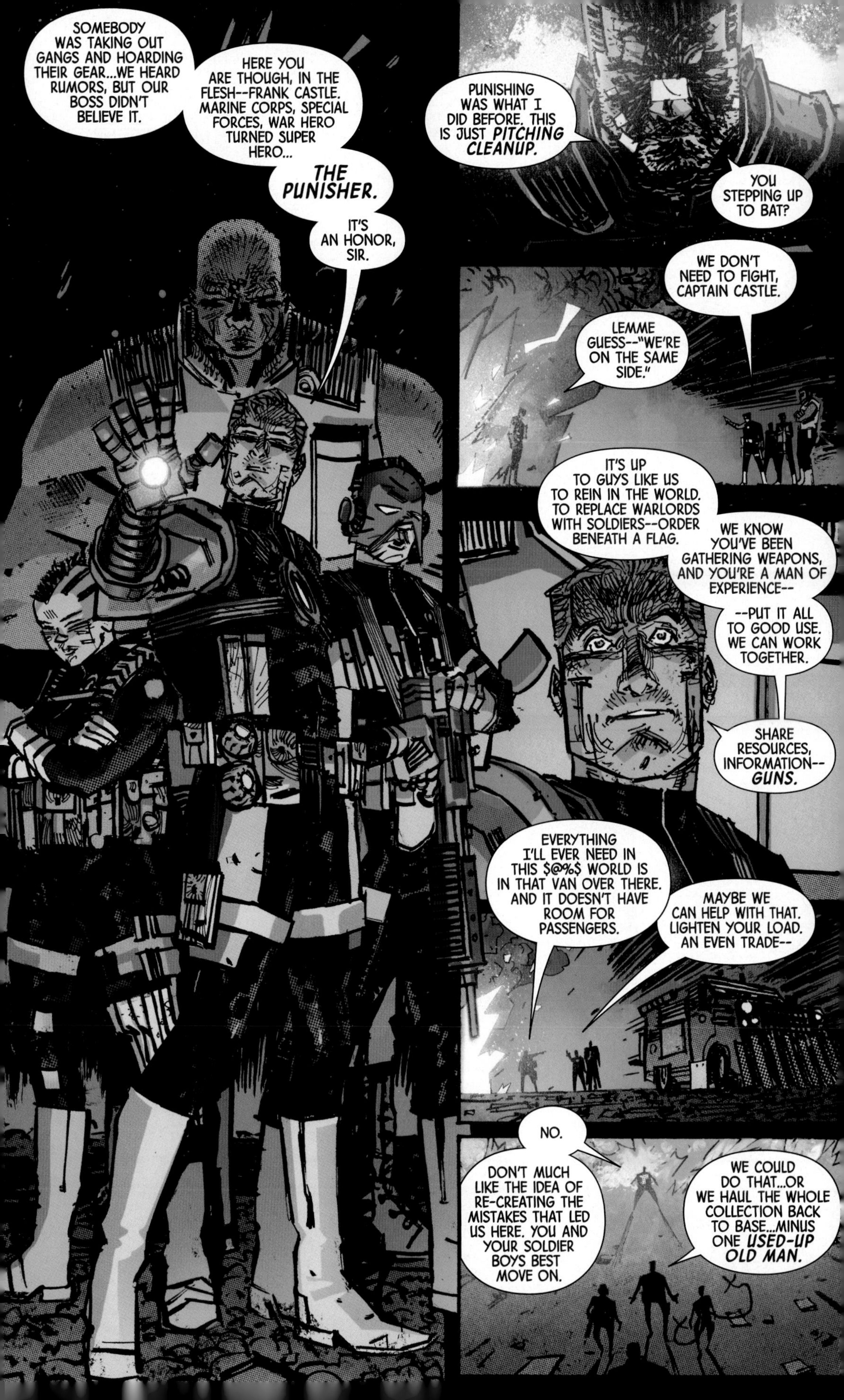
SOMEBODY WAS TAKING OUT GANGS AND HOARDING THEIR GEAR...WE HEARD RUMORS, BUT OUR BOSS DIDN'T BELIEVE IT.
HERE YOU ARE THOUGH, IN THE FLESH--FRANK CASTLE. MARINE CORPS, SPECIAL FORCES, WAR HERO TURNED SUPER HERO...
THE PUNISHER.
IT'S AN HONOR, SIR.
PUNISHING WAS WHAT I DID BEFORE. THIS IS JUST PITCHING CLEANUP.
YOU STEPPING UP TO BAT?
WE DON'T NEED TO FIGHT, CAPTAIN CASTLE.
LEMME GUESS--"WE'RE ON THE SAME SIDE."
IT'S UP TO GUYS LIKE US TO REIN IN THE WORLD. TO REPLACE WARLORDS WITH SOLDIERS--ORDER BENEATH A FLAG.
WE KNOW YOU'VE BEEN GATHERING WEAPONS, AND YOU'RE A MAN OF EXPERIENCE--
--PUT IT ALL TO GOOD USE. WE CAN WORK TOGETHER.
SHARE RESOURCES, INFORMATION--GUNS.
EVERYTHING I'LL EVER NEED IN THIS $@%$ WORLD IS IN THAT VAN OVER THERE. AND IT DOESN'T HAVE ROOM FOR PASSENGERS.
MAYBE WE CAN HELP WITH THAT. LIGHTEN YOUR LOAD. AN EVEN TRADE--
NO.
DON'T MUCH LIKE THE IDEA OF RE-CREATING THE MISTAKES THAT LED US HERE. YOU AND YOUR SOLDIER BOYS BEST MOVE ON.
WE COULD DO THAT...OR WE HAUL THE WHOLE COLLECTION BACK TO BASE...MINUS ONE USED-UP OLD MAN.

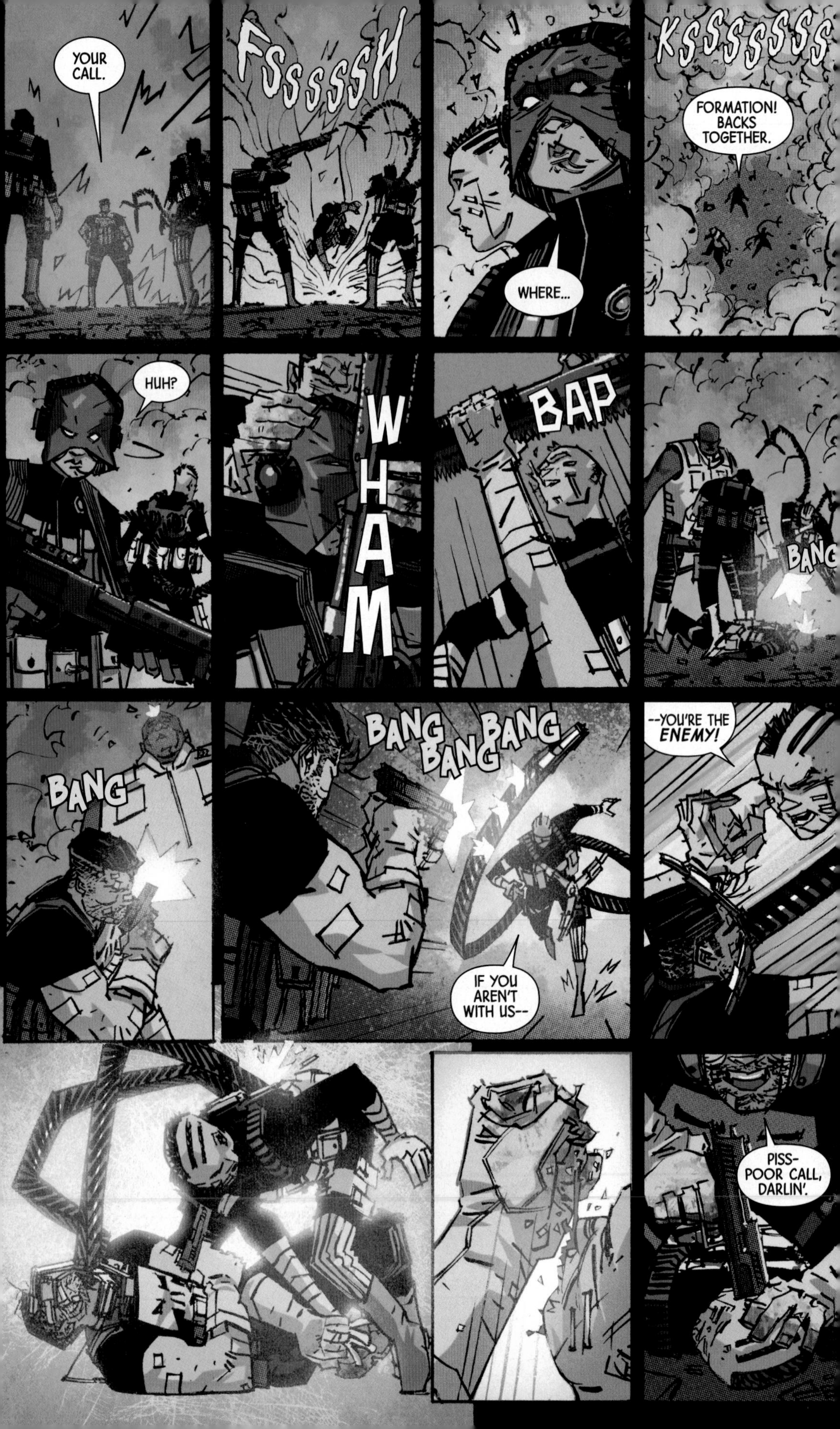

YOUR CALL.
FSSSSSH
WHERE...
KSSSSSSSS
FORMATION! BACKS TOGETHER.
HUH?
WHAM
BAP
BANG
BANG
BANG BANG BANG
IF YOU AREN'T WITH US--
--YOU'RE THE ENEMY!
PISS-POOR CALL, DARLIN'.

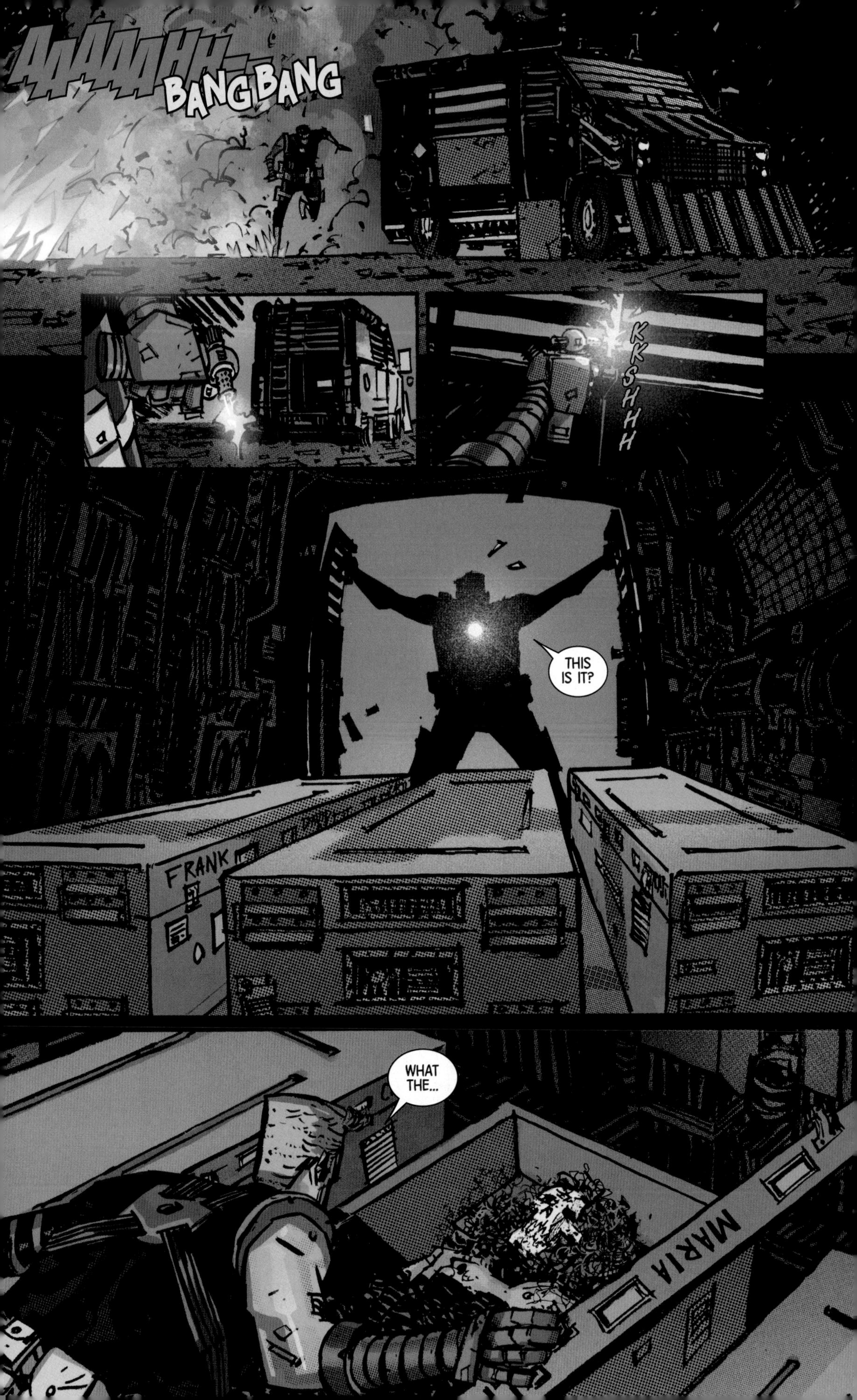
AAAAAHH—
BANG BANG
KKSHHHH
THIS IS IT?
FRANK
WHAT THE...
MARIA

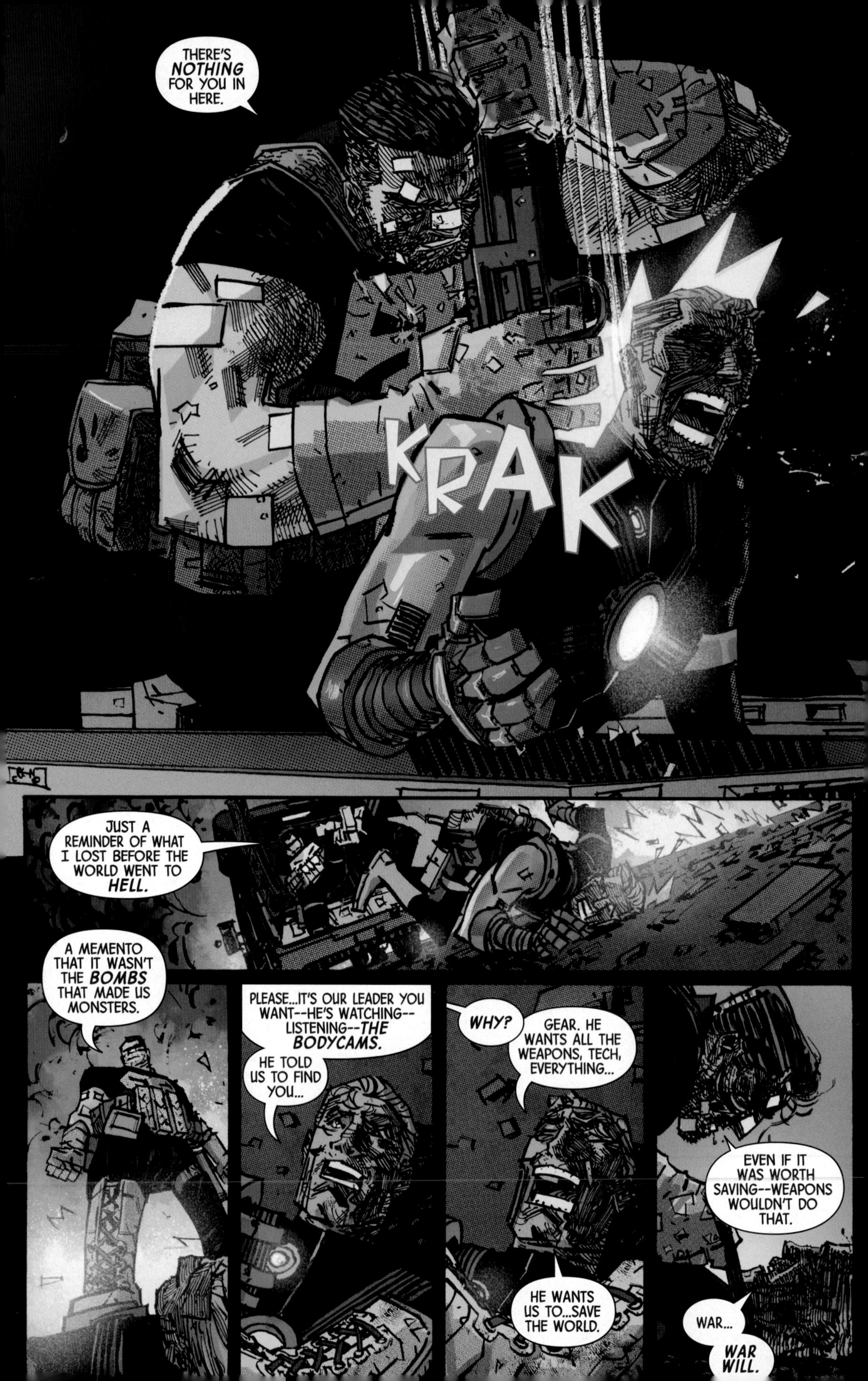
THERE'S NOTHING FOR YOU IN HERE.
KRAK
JUST A REMINDER OF WHAT I LOST BEFORE THE WORLD WENT TO HELL.
A MEMENTO THAT IT WASN'T THE BOMBS THAT MADE US MONSTERS.
PLEASE...IT'S OUR LEADER YOU WANT--HE'S WATCHING--LISTENING--THE BODYCAMS.
HE TOLD US TO FIND YOU...
WHY?
GEAR. HE WANTS ALL THE WEAPONS, TECH, EVERYTHING...
HE WANTS US TO...SAVE THE WORLD.
EVEN IF IT WAS WORTH SAVING--WEAPONS WOULDN'T DO THAT.
WAR...
WAR WILL.

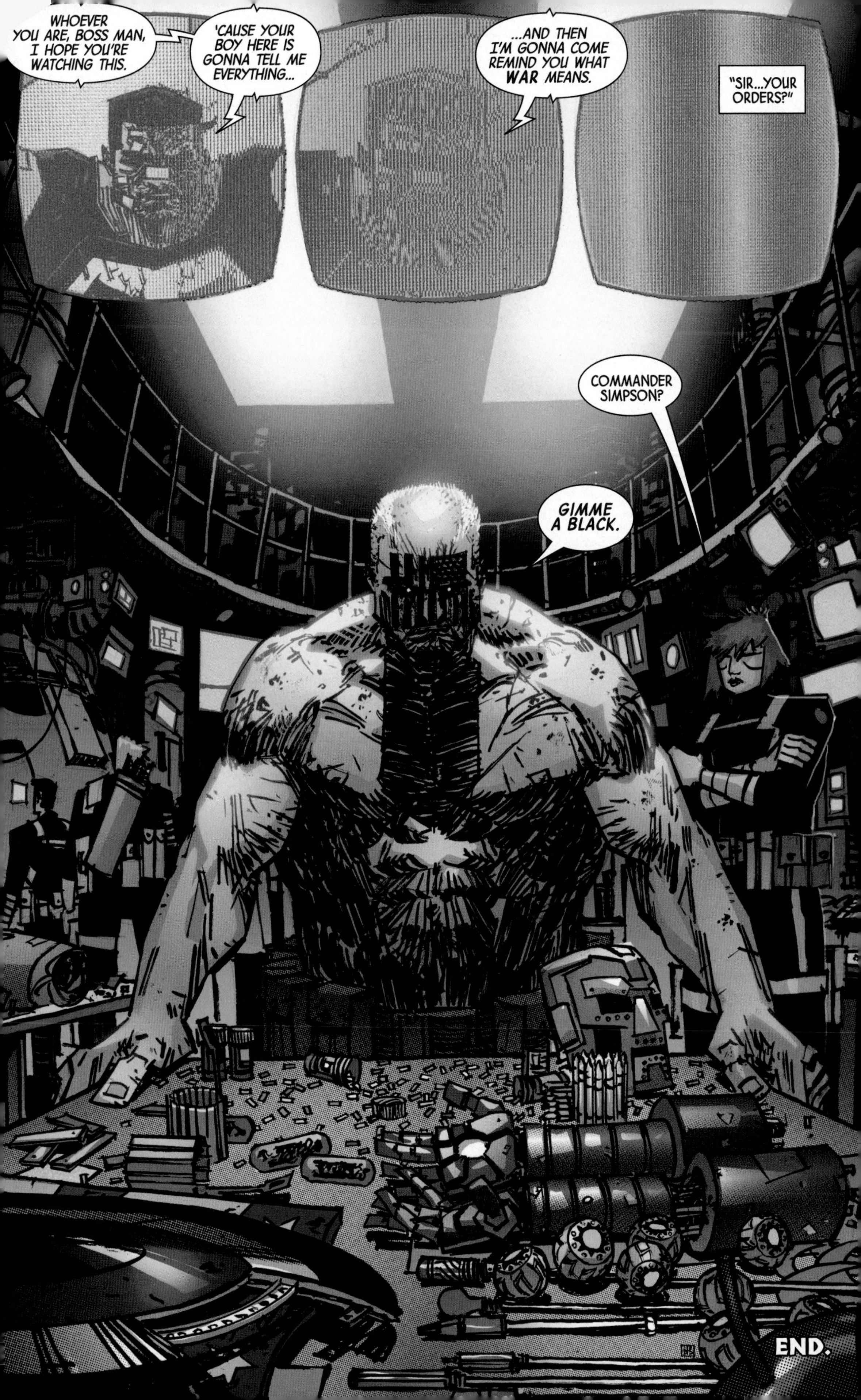
WHOEVER YOU ARE, BOSS MAN, I HOPE YOU'RE WATCHING THIS.
'CAUSE YOUR BOY HERE IS GONNA TELL ME EVERYTHING...
...AND THEN I'M GONNA COME REMIND YOU WHAT WAR MEANS.
"SIR...YOUR ORDERS?"
COMMANDER SIMPSON?
GIMME A BLACK.
END.

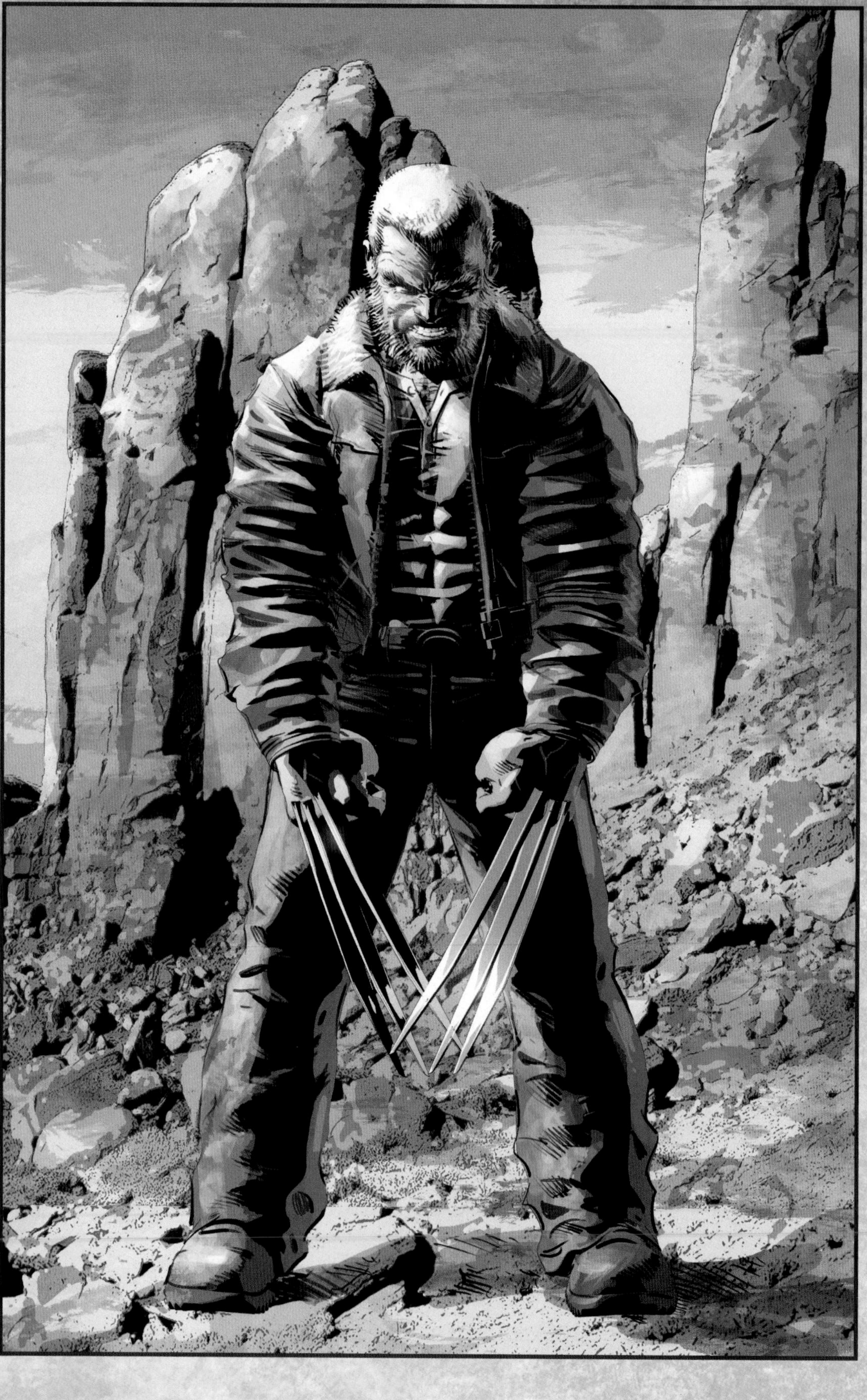

#50 VARIANT BY
MIKE DEODATO JR. & RAIN BEREDO

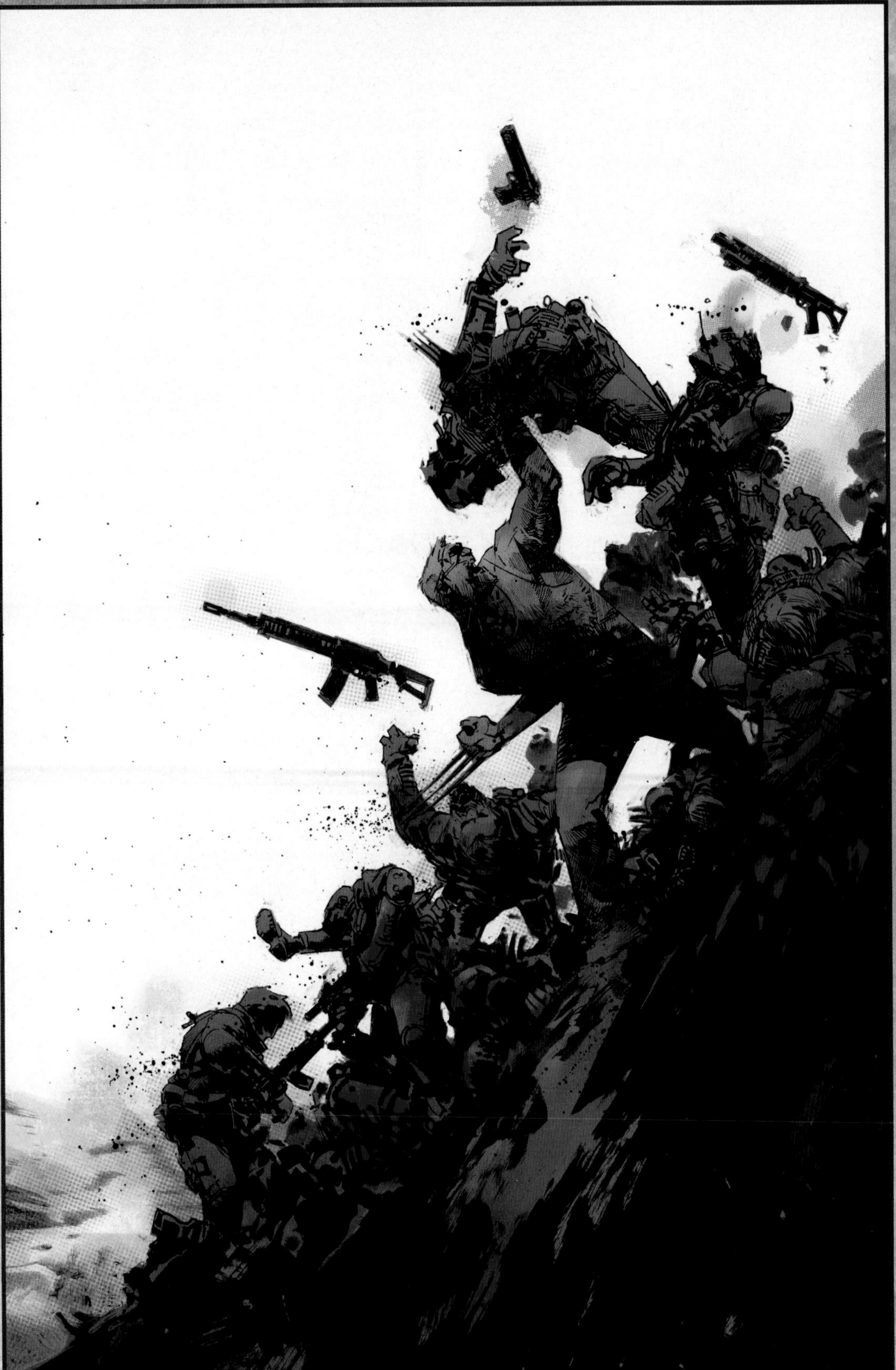

#50 VARIANT BY
GERARDO ZAFFINO

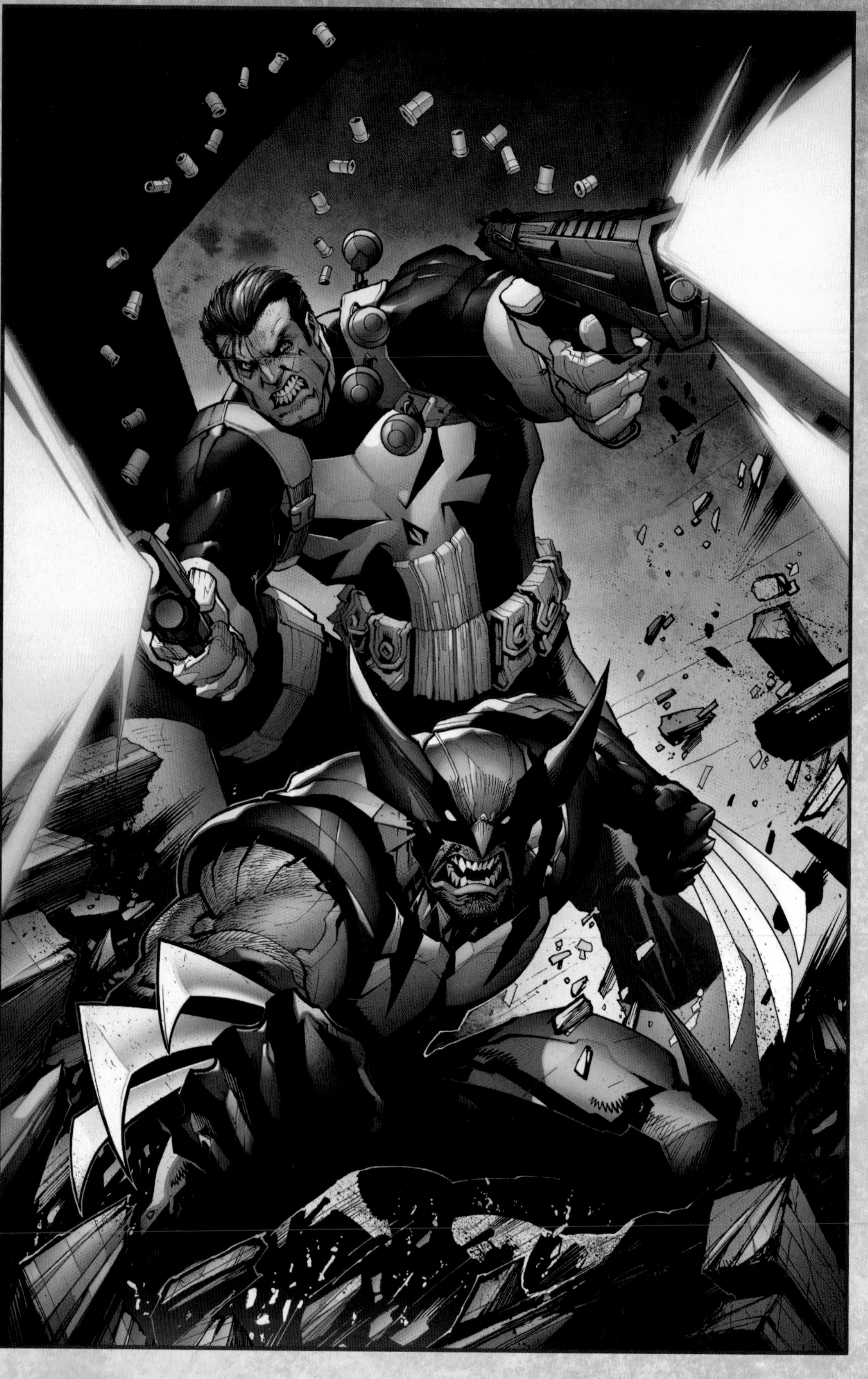

ANNUAL #1 VARIANT BY
GERARDO SANDOVAL & ERICK ARCINIEGA